The Gender of Piety

The Gender of Piety

Family, Faith, and Colonial Rule
in Matabeleland, Zimbabwe

WENDY URBAN-MEAD

Ohio University Press

Athens, Ohio

Ohio University Press, Athens, Ohio 45701
ohioswallow.com
© 2015 by Ohio University Press

To obtain permission to quote, reprint, or otherwise reproduce or distribute material
from Ohio University Press publications, please contact our rights and permissions
department at (740) 593-1154 or (740) 593-4536 (fax).

Printed in the United States of America
Ohio University Press books are printed on acid-free paper ∞

25 24 23 22 21 20 19 18 17 16 15   5 4 3 2 1

Library of Congress Cataloging-in-Publication Data
Urban-Mead, Wendy.
 The gender of piety : family, faith, and colonial rule in Matabeleland, Zimbabwe /
Wendy Urban-Mead.
    pages cm
Includes bibliographical references and index.
 ISBN 978-0-8214-2157-4 (hc : alk. paper) — ISBN 978-0-8214-2158-1 (pb : alk. paper)
— ISBN 978-0-8214-4527-3 (pdf)
 1. Brethren in Christ Church—Zimbabwe—Matabeleland—History—20th century—
Case studies. 2. Brethren in Christ Church—Zimbabwe—Matabeleland—Biography. 3.
Sex role—Religious aspects—Brethren in Christ Church. 4. Christianity and politics—
Zimbabwe—Matabeleland—History—20th century. 5. Matabeleland (Zimbabwe)—
Church history—20th century. I. Title.
 BX9675.A43M388 2015
 289.7'6891—dc23

                                    2015016213

Contents

Illustrations

Acknowledgments

First and deepest thanks belong to the people who shared their stories and hospitality, most of all in Zimbabwe, but also in the UK and in Pennsylvania. Special gratitude goes to Musa Chidziva for the love and assistance she so freely shared. To Musa and her mother, MaNsimango, and to the many others who have died since my research began: *Mina ngisalikhumbula sibili* (I will remember you, most certainly). There are several Bulawayo-based people whose constant support enabled this book's completion and to whom I am greatly indebted; they are Nellie Mlotshwa, Barbara Nkala, and Jacob and Nancy Shenk. Doris Dube, Danisa Ndlovu, and Bekithemba Dube have also provided much-appreciated assistance. I also thank Nondulo Vundhla for her research assistance in 1999, and Marieke Clarke, the Dlodlo family, the Gaitskells, the Ross family, the Siders, and the Stoner-Ebys for their hospitality.

My intellectual debt to my mentors is great, foremost among them Marcia Wright. In this category also belong Iris Berger, Deborah Valenze, Peter Krosby, and Mohamed Mbodj. A very particular thanks is due to the late Terence Ranger, who was steadfast in support of this research since it began. He awaited this book's publication impatiently, and I am sad his death occurred before he could hold it in his hands.

Many people have been unfailingly generous in helping me gain access to archival records. Foremost among them are Glen Pierce and E. Morris Sider at the archives and library of the Brethren in Christ Church in Pennsylvania, and Sihle Moyo and Jacob Shenk at the BICC office in Bulawayo. I also thank the Historical Reference Library in Bulawayo, the National Archives of Zimbabwe, the School of Oriental and African Studies in London, and Rhodes House in Oxford, for access to relevant records there. Thanks are due to the many who advised on cultural matters and orthography, shared various forms of expertise, and puzzled together with me to sort out ethical questions, most especially Musa Chidziva, Daryl Climenhaga, Mqhele Dlodlo, Katherine French, Deborah Gaitskell, Diana Jeater, George Hamandishe Karekwaivanane, Jill Kelly, Paul Landau, Devin Manzullo-Thomas, Ronald Lizwe Moyo, Isaac Mpofu, Enocent Msindo, Raphael Mthombeni, Pathisa Nyathi, Jessica L. Powers, Tim Scarnecchia, Eliakim Sibanda, and Lindani Hlengiwe Sibanda (MaMlotshwa). A variety of individuals offered technical assistance. I am indebted to Katherine Urban-Mead, who created the family tree. Brian Edward Balsley made the map. Nancy Jacobs also advised on the map, while Cecilia Maple provided technical assistance with the photos. Molly P. Feibel's assistance with the index was superb.

To the readers who gave feedback on drafts of individual chapters or the whole manuscript at various stages, it is hard to find the words to thank them for this gift of time and intellectual labor, but thank them I do: especially Cynthia Paces; also Jaime Alves, Myra Armstead, Andrea Arrington, Matt Bender, Jesse Bucher, Marieke Clarke, Julia Emig, Derek Furr, Natasha Gray, David Crawford Jones, Thai Jones, Priya Lal, Stephen Mucher, Derek Peterson, Sean Redding, John Shekitka, Alice Stroup, Katherine Urban-Mead, and the extremely assiduous and insightful anonymous reviewers.

Some of those who offered encouragement at crucial moments along the way are Misty Bastian, Kelly Gaddis, Petina Gappah, Natasha Gray, Nancy Kreider Hoke, Allelu Kurten, Eric Morier-Genoud, Jennifer Oldstone-Moore, Leslie Quick, Caroline Ramaley, Jan Bender Shetler, Lindani Hlengiwe Sibanda (MaMlotshwa), Yuka Suzuki, and Pat Townshend. I also thank the many colleagues who heard conference-paper versions of this work over the past years and offered helpful feedback. My history students in the Master of Arts in Teaching (MAT) program at Bard College have been a constant source of encouragement and valuable insights. The errors and disortions that remain are my own.

The research from which this book grew was funded in great measure by a research travel grant from Columbia University. I am thankful to Bard College for the support I have received since 2004 from the college's dean of graduate studies, the incomparably collegial MAT faculty, and many members of the Historical Studies Department at Bard College. I am very thankful to Gillian Berchowitz for her support of this project, and to Nancy Basmajian and Beth Pratt, and the editorial staff at Ohio University Press for many kinds of technical support.

My local friends and extended family helped keep me (somewhat) normal, and I treasure each of them. I cannot ever fathom what Charlie and Katherine, and most especially Russell, have given over the years we lived with this manuscript. This book is for Cynthia. There is no doubt that her endurance exceeded my own, and but for her midwifery, the book would never have been born.

Abbreviations

AMEC	African Methodist Episcopal Church
ANC	African National Congress
BICC	Brethren in Christ Church
BSAC	British South Africa Company
LMS	London Missionary Society
NC	Native Commissioner
NDP	National Democratic Party
PF-ZAPU	Patriotic Front–Zimbabwe African People's Union
SDA	Seventh-Day Adventist
SRANC	Southern Rhodesia African National Congress
UANC	United African National Council
UDI	Unilateral Declaration of Independence
ZANLA	Zimbabwe African National Liberation Army
ZANU	Zimbabwe African National Union
ZANU-PF	Zimbabwe African National Union–Patriotic Front
ZAPU	Zimbabwe African People's Union
ZIPRA	Zimbabwe People's Revolutionary Army
ZNA	Zimbabwe National Army

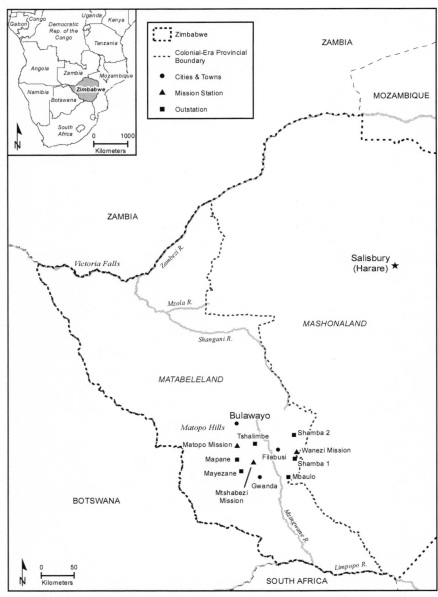

The Brethren in Christ in Matabeleland, Zimbabwe. *Created by Brian Edward Balsley, GISP*

Introduction

The Gender of Piety in Matabeleland

A GROUP OF BOYS GATHERED AROUND the sickbed and sang a hymn called "Woza moni odangele" (Come, weary sinner).[1] Among them was nine-year-old Huggins Msimanga; they were learning the hymn from Huggins's father, Zephania Msimanga, who lay dying.[2] It was 1955. This hymn speaks of the sinner who is depressed in spirit, who is broken or injured and announces that the Healer, the Savior, is here to provide comfort. Huggins recalled that his father, age thirty-seven, often sang this hymn in his "heavy times" and wanted to ensure the boys knew this hymn by heart before he passed on. "He knew how to prepare when he knew he was going."

This gathering of youthful boys and a dying man took place at the Msimanga family homestead in Southern Rhodesia (present-day Zimbabwe), in the Gwanda District of Matabeleland South. Typical for rural homesteads in this part of southern Africa, there were several structures: huts for sleeping, for cooking, and one to serve as a formal sitting room. All these were enclosed by a fence made of lashed-together boughs of small trees and large bushes gathered from around the homestead. It was dry and dusty there through much of the year, especially the cool and sunny winter months of June, July, and August. Following winter came the increasingly oppressive heat of September, October, and November. Each year the people of this region waited for the rain that might come as early as November, but often not until January. No matter

Figure I.1. A homestead in Matabeleland South, 1999. *Photo credit: Russell Urban-Mead*

what time of year, it was cool once the sun went down. There were cattle and goats out grazing during the day and safely penned into their kraal at night, and chickens scratched about. Outside the homestead fence was a garden of vegetables and grains: millet, maize, squashes, sweet potatoes, and beans.

The family consisted of Huggins's grandmother MaNdimande;[3] "the grandfathers" (the brothers of MaNdimande's deceased husband); the mostly absent "fathers" (sons of the grandfathers), away at migrant labor; "the mothers" (the wives to those men); and the children of all those mothers and fathers. Since the fathers were siblings, all their children were considered siblings to one another. The children of the Msimanga homestead attended primary school at Mtshabezi Mission run by the Brethren in Christ Church (BICC), just two miles away. Zephania Msimanga died at the Mtshabezi Mission hospital after his month of decline spent at home.[4]

Msimanga had briefly been a teacher for the BICC but left that work to become a dip tank operator. Cattle had to be dipped into a dug pit lined with rocks or concrete, containing pesticides that kept off ticks that carried deadly diseases and other pests. The Rhodesian government regulated dip tanks. Dip tank clerks, by the 1950s, were literate African men who had received their educations at mission schools.[5]

The grandmother of the family, MaNdimande—the mother of Zephania Msimanga and his siblings—was the energy behind Christian faith and practice at the Msimanga homestead. "In the evening it was cooking time, then sunset," when the women and children gathered around a fire in front of MaNdimande's dwelling. Before the children went to sleep, Granny, or "Gogo," would lead in evening prayers and hymn singing. Sometimes her daughters-in-law took a turn leading the devotions. The grandfathers and the fathers, if they were home, were sitting around another fire, doing "men things"—talking among themselves—perhaps speaking of an acquaintance's recent stint of work in Johannesburg or at a nearby mine, maybe wondering when the rains would come, or discussing politics. By the 1950s the anticolonial nationalist movement was gathering adherents all around, and was especially active in regional groups dedicated to protesting colonial land alienation and laws concerning land husbandry.[6] Occasionally the men would join the women and children in prayer and sing their favorite hymns. If the men were drunk, which sometimes they were, Huggins Msimanga recalled that Gogo would "speak against their habit of drinking all the time," yet he reflected that, nonetheless, "they looked really happy when they were drunk." Huggins's father was often away since his job took him to dip tanks around the region. On Sundays, Gogo, the mothers, the children, and sometimes Huggins's father attended church at the mission station.

This book is about Ndebele-speaking Africans who became Christians, and their gendered interactions with the teachings of the BICC, a North American Protestant mission church that sent its first overseas missionaries to Southern Rhodesia in 1898. These scenes from the life of Msimanga family illustrate aspects of how some Ndebele speakers have made sense of Christianity for themselves in the context of their families during the colonial period and after. The Christian devotion expressed by the men of the Msimanga family at the bookends of their lives, and the long stretch of steady devotion anchored by the womenfolk in that family points importantly to the themes of this book. It is about gendered and religious dynamics within families: between spouses, between parents and children, between grandparents and grandchildren, among siblings.

Women found it easier to negotiate an enduring relationship with the BICC over the course of their lives because the church did not directly interfere with their primary responsibilities as wives and mothers. Some women may have had a relatively brief interruption in their status as church members in good standing in their youth—if they had an interruption at all. Men, on the other hand, had more difficulty negotiating a steady relationship to the church throughout their lifespan. As youths and old men it was easier to live within the church's teachings, but in their middle years, being of good standing in the church meant they had to give up tremendous power and commonly practiced forms of masculine community by being unable to drink beer. They also had to adhere to monogamy and eschew involvement in anticolonial political groups, because the church forbade involvement in "worldly" political associations.

One of the original questions behind the research for this book started with: how did a church such as the BICC fare in colonial southern Africa—among the Ndebele speakers of Matabeleland Province, to be precise? My decision to focus only on members of one mission society, the Brethren in Christ Church, was intentional, and not for "missiological" reasons. I was curious to find out if the church would maintain its unique identity over time in the white-dominated settler society of colonial Zimbabwe (Rhodesia), if African members adopted all or some of the distinctive teachings and, if so, how. Visits to Zimbabwe in 1997 and 1999 demonstrated that something indeed had taken hold, that the Africans there had made the church their own: the BICC had a vibrant, growing, African membership. With over thirty-six thousand members in more than three hundred churches as of 2013, it remains a growing and regionally important group to this day.[7] I will argue that piety in the BICC-Zimbabwe follows a particular, gendered pattern.

The title of this book is *The Gender of Piety*. The term *piety* in this study has three meanings. The first comes from the BICC's historical connection to the pietistic strain of Christianity—which emphasizes a "warm," or heartfelt, relationship with Christ. The second meaning of piety refers to a more generally accepted understanding of moral goodness and sin as seen in most Christian mission groups—along with the BICC's more distinctive teachings against all forms of worldliness. The third sense of piety is my own conception of gendered piety. This third sense of the term is where Ndebele people's process of making this church their own comes into sharpest relief.

The word *piety* has important historical roots within the BICC. *Piety* is a term directly linked to a religious movement in Protestant Christianity known as Pietism, of which the BICC claims itself a part. Pietism is a religious movement originating in Germany in the seventeenth century that rejected overly intellectualized and overly formal religion, urging a more emotionally engaged spiritual experience.[8] Pietists value the so-called crisis conversion experience, which begins with acknowledgment of one's sinful nature, extreme despair over that fact, and an experience of blissful relief from this burden by acknowledging the saving power of Jesus Christ. Since its origins, the Brethren in Christ have valued a warm faith—a heartfelt sense of connection to God. The BICC were not only Pietists, however; the BICC were also from a Mennonite, or Anabaptist heritage, which emphasizes the rejection of worldliness and favors pacifist teachings and communitarian values. The Pietists' attempt to live free from worldliness included wearing plain clothing. The BICC emerged as a distinct group when a group of Lancaster County Mennonites responded in the late eighteenth century to the revival preaching of pietistic German preachers hoping to incite a great spiritual awakening across German-speaking Pennsylvania.[9]

BICC historian Carlton Wittlinger titled his history of the church *Quest for Piety and Obedience*. He characterized the

BICC as embodying a unique tension of commitment, first, to the views of Mennonites and second—but equally—to the revivalist, heartfelt, warm faith of the Pietists. Thus Wittlinger's choice of the word *piety* was intentional. It was a specific reference to the yearning for that warm relationship with the divine that characterizes all Pietist Christians. Pietists are found in some streams of Lutheranism, in the Moravian Church, and can be traced into the revival movements of North America's late-eighteenth-century Great Awakening and later nineteenth-century revival movements that affected many American denominations, including the Methodists. It was the Pietism in the Brethren in Christ that led them to go their own way, separate from the other Mennonites of Pennsylvania.

A number of ordinances (symbolic practices) were distinctive for the BICC. They practiced a trine-immersion baptism[10] and foot-washing ceremonies in conjunction with the commemoration of the Lord's Supper, or Love Feast, and greeted fellow Brethren in Christ adherents with a Holy Kiss. The BICC remained a very insular, nonworldly, rural and German-speaking subset of the North American Anabaptist world until their nineteenth-century migrations across North America. Over the course of the nineteenth century, Brethren in Christ members spread west and north from their Pennsylvania homes to Ohio, Kansas, Ontario, Manitoba, and California. Part of what continued to make the BICC distinct, however, was its rejection of all types of amusements and "levity," such as dancing, card playing, fashionable clothing, and even birthday parties.[11] Added to this was the church's aloofness from "worldly" politics, and skepticism at best on the merits of higher education, since that too suggested excessive worldly ambition.[12]

The BICC's Anabaptist and Pietist strains had, up to the end of the nineteenth century, existed in a balance favoring Anabaptist conformity and obedience.[13] During the later decades of the nineteenth century, however, the BICC became increasingly open to outside influences from other Christian groups. The late-nineteenth-century cross-denominational revival movements then reached the

Brethren in Christ churches, especially in Kansas.[14] The American holiness movement, also known as Wesleyan perfectionism, taught that the Christian could "stand on higher ground." To achieve this higher moral plane one needed a second work of grace beyond the initial conversion experience, known as sanctification, in which the Holy Spirit would lead the person to a lasting victory over continued sin.[15] Accompanying the holiness movement was increasing acknowledgment of the legitimacy of a "personal, inner 'call' to some special form of Christian service, especially missions."[16] Such ideas from the holiness movement contributed largely to the BICC's decision in 1896 to send missionaries overseas for the first time.

Over time, the BICC gradually became more like other Protestant groups, especially Methodists, and even took on the Methodists' antialcohol temperance teaching in the 1880s and 1890s. Thus, the BICC missionaries' objections against African beer, or *utshwala,* upon their arrival in Rhodesia, in the late 1890s, were based on a position only very recently taken by the church. Along with the increased enthusiasm for foreign missions and support for the temperance movement, the BICC started a denominational newspaper, the *Evangelical Visitor,* instituted Sunday schools, and began singing gospel songs, all reflecting the new openness to outside Protestant influences. These changes were adopted not without debate and dissension from the more conservative wing of the church. The midwestern wing of the church was known for being much more receptive to these changes than the home-base area in Pennsylvania, where the churches tended to be wealthier, more numerous, and less likely to support innovations feared for their potentially worldly impact.[17]

The communitarian authority that guided Brethren in Christ churches was patriarchal. Throughout the nineteenth century and well into the twentieth, men dominated all major seats of church power. As a 1901 BICC publication makes clear, "a woman professing godliness shall not appear in public . . . without having a plain and modest head-covering. This is worn not simply as a headdress but in reverence to man as a token of subjection and sign of authority."[18] Certain elements of church polity and theology, however, suggested that there was a kind of spiritual equality among all believers regardless of sex. For example, although women could not preach, they were permitted to vote in the church's decision-making processes, and—vitally for purposes of this book—the church taught that the confessed Christian was "no respecter of persons."

The idea of an individual, personal calling from God, although by all means a familiar strain in the history of Christianity, became significant in a new way for the BICC because it offered an opportunity to challenge the church's communitarian authority on an irrefutable basis: the called individual was responding to a direct communication of divine authority. If one accepts the validity of an individual call, then to interfere with such a calling would be to defy the will of God.[19] Individual callings in the context of sanctification made new room for women in the church.[20] The type of spirituality and openness to individual callings brought into the church by the Wesleyan holiness movement represented forces disruptive to the previous system of leadership and later represented fertile avenues for leadership initiatives on the part of both American and African members of this church.

The second meaning of *piety* used in this book refers to a more general connotation of righteousness and moral goodness as defined by the church, which emphasized chastity before marriage and monogamy—as did all other Christian mission groups— along with the BICC's more distinctive teachings against all forms of worldliness (fashion, politics, higher education, among others). *Piety* in this sense refers to a complex of spiritual attributes: the perceived quality of his or her relationship with Jesus, and his or her own holiness. Church leaders of the BICC have not tended to use the term *piety* so much as other terms and phrases like "gave his heart to God,"[21] the "Light of Jesus shining in her heart,"[22] or "finding victory" (over sin).[23] The use of the term *heart* in two of these phrases is important and indicates the link to the historic theological concept of pietism, in which the heart is warmed by one's relationship to God and saved through faith in Jesus. The worst that can happen is for one's heart to "grow cold" in the faith.[24] References in the BICC to the place of the heart warmed by God remain consistent throughout the twentieth century; even in the special series on the "heart" and faith written by missionary doctor Devee Boyd in the 1980s.[25] Piety, then, becomes a marriage of faith and practice—it is the interface between the two. The BICC vision of righteousness was demanding: one had to be correct in one's behavior, all the time, while maintaining and constantly refreshing an affectively warm relationship with the divine.

The third sense of *piety* comes from my own conception of the gender of piety and is the major contribution of this project: the particular ways in which men and women learned to express and model their religious belief, right practice, and warmth of devotion in tandem with or opposition to other gendered expectations in their culture. My understanding of piety as gendered enables me to offer new approaches to the study of Christianity in Africa and its relationship to colonial and nationalist politics. Most important, I interrogate the disparate patterns for women and men in the church: namely that there generally have been many more women than men in good standing and active as church members. While most women remained tied to the church throughout their lives, men displayed a pattern of repenting and returning to the church—and reclaiming their piety—in their old age.

The BICC missionaries came to their African field of evangelization in the 1890s and throughout the twentieth century with a fairly static view of piety. The Christian in good standing with the church was expected to abjure fashionable clothing, practice abstinence from sex until entering a monogamous marriage, abstain from alcohol, remain aloof from worldly political associations, practice daily devotions of prayer, Bible reading and hymn singing in the home, and have regular attendance at church. When this attitude toward piety encountered Ndebele society in colonial Rhodesia, later Zimbabwe, the very concept of piety became something new. As the BICC encountered a particularly gendered society undergoing tremendous stress successively over time from the imposition, enactment, and ending of colonial rule, Ndebele members of the church creatively refashioned their own quite gendered understandings of what it meant to be a Christian of the BICC. African members of the church, given their embeddedness in family webs and a wider culture featuring many values and practices that the missionaries deemed sinful, were expected to sever their relationship with all such sinful associations and practices, especially those regarding sexual promiscuity and spiritual access to the regional high-god Mwali, or attempts at communication with the ancestral spirits.

This book argues that men and women of the BICC in Zimbabwe experienced and sequenced their piety in different ways. Women usually remained tied to the church through their lifespan, while men experienced a tense push-pull with the church, which was not always flexible enough for men to perform expected gender roles, participate in political and economic institutions, or participate in important male communal traditions. Whereas women often found the church liberating, through its emphasis on education and monogamy, men often experienced the church's expectations to be intolerably confining during the middle years of their lives. These tensions for men could be reconciled only in one's elder years, when political and social participation among men was less central to their lives. Christian piety became an important indicator of a person's or a family's respectability, and one's right to claim membership in the associational aspects of a church whose influence reached—and reaches—across all of Matabeleland and its institutions. However, men often experienced difficulty reconciling their religious beliefs and their relationship to respectability with other social, economic, and political obligations.

This study, an intimate history of the BICC in Zimbabwe, works with six individual life histories that, taken together, indicate how the mission church became a multifaced institution, simultaneously reinforcing Ndebele ethnicity, while also becoming ever more institutionally rooted in Rhodesia's white-settler colonial world, leading to a devastating impact on the church during the 1970s war of liberation and a fraught transition into the postcolonial Zimbabwean state ruled by the Zimbabwe African National Union–Patriotic Front (ZANU-PF) political party. The church's membership, over the course of the colonial period, came to compose a segment of the aspirant African elite in Matabeleland. By profiling three men and three women church members over the span of a century, this study explores the highly gendered ways African BICC members rejected, adopted, and adapted the church's distinctive teachings. The BICC were enough like other, better-known mission churches, such as the Methodists, that the trends identified here have broader applicability. This denomination's simultaneous typicality and distinctiveness have thus provided an effective lens for conducting a close-grained study of gendered piety in an African colonial setting.

Scholarship on Christianity in southern Africa has demonstrated how the rural Christian mission station—during the colonial period—was an outpost of the colonizing metropole: a site of exchange between European religious ideas, commodities, and cultural idioms and indigenous African societies.[26] The hegemonic and violent elements of this encounter, from land dispossession to more commodity-based and discursive forms of coercion, are understood as givens. It is also well established that Africans met this encounter by creatively appropriating and refashioning various iterations of Christian teachings represented by the multitude of mission societies for their own purposes. Africans embraced according to their own cultural and political needs the rest of the mission package, from the reading of Bunyan's *Pilgrim's Progress* to tea drinking and the wearing of Western clothing.[27]

While resonating with other histories, from other periods and places, of the relationship between gender and power in religious organizations, this study offers a new set of understandings for the history of religion in southern Africa, and Zimbabwe in particular.[28] These understandings come vividly through the medium of the contextualized life histories that follow. Repeating patterns of men who found the church's expectations for piety to be at odds with the work of manhood—and of women for whom the monogamy teachings, educational opportunities, and spiritual leadership openings proved empowering—come to life in this format. I have worked with life histories so as to parse out gendered patterns in the African encounter with missions—gendered patterns that equally focus on men and women, and on the masculine and feminine elements of each sex's engagement with Christianity. It is an exercise in microhistory. John Lonsdale described the merits of how "thick description and studies of local processes can contain clues to larger causation." His assertion that "the small communities that most of us inhabit have wide connections" applies to *The Gender of Piety*.[29] Shula Marks's *Not Either an Experimental Doll* includes the correspondence of Lily Moya with Mabel Palmer. The emotional vividness that came to life in those letters suggested that histories could be written that forefront the affective world of Africans.[30] Addressing the theme of gendered piety in a southern African church through life histories thus makes for a more intimate engagement for the reader.

Historians have been less likely than religious and anthropological scholars to discuss the spiritual benefits and motivations of members of African churches, preferring to trace connections between church affiliation and material prosperity or worldly power. As an important exception, David Maxwell's historical study of Pentecostalism in southern Africa, Zimbabwe, and the wider world, *African Gifts of the Spirit,* paid attention to religious as well as instrumental motivations.[31] It is harder to ignore spiritual and religious motivations when encountering an individual's life story. The ways that actions taken according to faith might in some instances serve against aspirations of power or wealth come into sharper relief. Piecing together the stories of the six individuals in their colonial and postcolonial contexts elucidates how Africans in Matabeleland grappled with alien Christian teachings and cultural assumptions and how in turn these teachings affected family relationships and gender roles.

The BICC established its first mission in 1898 in the Matopo Hills of Matabeleland, in western Zimbabwe. The rugged terrain of the Matopos, strewn with massive granite boulders and towering rock formations, is a unique and important landscape. Some of the most impressive hills are enormous domes of pure granite. The hills are marked with caves and are interrupted frequently by small, fertile valleys watered by springs. The presence of springs in the Matopos landscape is particularly valuable for a region that is generally arid. The BICC arrived in the Matopo Hills just two years after the Ndebele Kingdom's defeat in a colonial war of conquest.

Surrounding the Matopos and Bulawayo are lands suitable for grazing, making the region attractive to the cattle-rich Ndebele Kingdom, which migrated into this region in the 1830s. The Ndebele Kingdom, led by a ruling class of Nguni speakers originating from present-day KwaZulu-Natal, had crossed the Limpopo River from South Africa and found there several peoples that they incorporated into the Ndebele polity and society. The structure of the whole kingdom was essentially organized to protect the cattle and their grazing areas.[32] To the west of Bulawayo the land grows ever drier and more prone to frequent droughts as one crosses into present-day Botswana and nears the Kalahari Desert. Farther to the north and west, the elevation drops, tsetse flies are endemic, and the vegetation thickens, becoming progressively less desirable for grazing as one nears the Zambezi River.[33] Though the Ndebele in-migrants did not settle in this northwestern region, preferring the higher-elevation savannas, or velds, near the Matopos, the Ndebele king Mzilikazi himself reached the Zambezi in one journey to the north and established a tributary relationship with the people living along the river.[34] As one moves east toward the central section of present-day southern Zimbabwe, in the Gutu and Masvingo areas, rainfall becomes more plentiful. South of the hills, the elevation gradually lowers and the climate becomes hotter and drier as one nears the Limpopo River and crosses into present-day South Africa.

Ndebele state building involved incorporation of conquered or captured people and voluntary refugees in such a manner that these non-Nguni newcomers also became "Ndebele." Rather than allowing the minority ruling class to be swamped by a majority of non-Nguni subordinates, by means of strict enforcement of marital endogamy and imposition of Ndebele, the Nguni elite, *abezansi,* retained power and linguistic control. Scholarship on the nineteenth-century Ndebele polity emphasizes its multipeopled character: three defined strands of people with different languages hierarchically arranged, but all loyal to the central figure, Mzilikazi Khumalo, and later, his son Lobengula. In the nineteenth century, the Ndebele formation was a polity not strictly defined by ethnic unity. Historian Paul Landau shows how there was a distinct pattern of polity formation across precolonial southern Africa centered on the gathering of people around a powerful individual who would be fashioned a chief. Thus understood, a chiefship on the southern African highveld "was an incorporative institution, and its success lay in bridging differences among varied constituencies."[35] Mzilikazi Khumalo came to the highveld in the 1820s with a band of warriors who then gathered a varied following around themselves based on their successes in war against other chiefdoms, which brought to Mzilikazi's followers captive women, children, and cattle. The core traits of Ndebeleness in the nineteenth century were political loyalty to the Ndebele royal family and king, the speaking of Ndebele, adopting Ndebele dress, and slitting the ears.[36] The Ndebele under the Khumalos thus were a political entity, a kingdom that began in the 1820s in present-day South Africa, eventually finding a permanent home in what are today the Matabeleland provinces of Zimbabwe.

The Ndebele ruling class's religious world was largely focused on relating to the male ancestors, for which the king's male agnatic ancestors were considered the national protective spirits. The king was both political ruler (and therefore war leader and provider of security) and chief priest. He appealed to his ancestors to provide rain, blessed the seed for planting, and authorized the enjoyment of the first fruits of the harvest at the annual *inxwala* ceremonies, at which the king was the centerpiece.

In contrast, the indigenous people in Zimbabwe who came to be ruled by the Ndebele, while also venerating their ancestors, looked to a powerful deity known as Mwali, or Mwari, for rain, successful crops, and the health of the land. Shrines dedicated to Mwali have been seated in the caves of the Matopos for nearly two hundred years, if not longer.[37] The Matopos shrines dedicated to Mwali served as focal points for priests, messengers, and itinerant adepts who traveled widely, singing the messages and praises to Mwali. This deity was characterized with powerful male and female imagery, and both women and men were incorporated in the operation of the shrine system.[38]

The early years of the BICC in Rhodesia coincided with the first years of British South Africa Company (BSAC) rule in Matabeleland. Under the direction of Cecil John Rhodes (1889–1902), the BSAC was a concessionary company whose army won two wars of conquest, in 1893 and 1896. The last Ndebele king, Lobengula Khumalo, had disappeared during the 1893 war and was never seen again. The 1896 war brought to an end the Ndebele Kingdom. Over the course of the 1890s a flood of white settlers entered the newly conquered territory. The BSAC administration welcomed mission societies as "better than policemen and cheaper" at helping manage the indigenous population, offering them generous terms in leasing large tracts of land.[39] Accelerating considerably after the end of the 1896 war of conquest, Christian mission societies came to Rhodesia in ever-larger numbers, to augment the preexisting missions of the London Missionary Society (LMS) and the Jesuits.[40] The Salvation Army, Seventh-Day Adventist, Dutch Reformed, Wesleyan Methodist, Anglican, Swedish Lutheran, and BICC missions were all among the noteworthy newcomers to Matabeleland at that time.

Mission societies followed a pattern of settlement by which each society would be granted a sizable portion of land, ranging from three thousand to twenty thousand acres each, from which to base their operations.[41] It was understood that each mission group was to work within the designated territory and take care not to infringe on the work of other mission societies. Eventually this pattern was regularized under the "three-mile rule"— no mission society was to actively recruit converts within three miles of another society's station.[42] Between 1898 and 1978 the BICC in Southern Rhodesia eventually established four enduring rural mission stations, two hospitals, and an enormous network of mission-run schools. In recent decades they have had a strong urban presence in the regional capital, Bulawayo. Unless a particular homestead straddled the boundaries of two different mission estates, most Africans who chose to associate with missionaries simply went to the mission station closest to their home. This is important, since otherwise one might survey the varied list of Christian groups operating in the region and falsely assume there was much choice involved when an African decided to go to a particular mission station.

The fluidity of institutional life in the early years after conquest gave the BICC, for example, space to craft its own concept of a Christian education. In the first years of the twentieth century the missionaries prioritized the conversion of young men, hoping that they would become the pastors and evangelists who would build an African church. Colonial institutions, including mission schools, were yet fluid. Before 1920, Africans had by no means felt the full impact of what was to become Rhodesian land dispossession and racist segregation policies.

As a relatively parochial sect in its American setting, the BICC was slow to interact with and absorb the segregationist ways of other, better-established mission societies. Other mission societies, such as the London Missionary Society at nearby Hope Fountain, regarded the BICC missionaries as "very sincere hard-working missionaries whose methods of work are very commendable." They misread the missionary women's dress, with bonnets and capes, as being exemplary of a "quaint Puritan custom of New England."[43] For their part, the BICC pioneer missionaries, while grateful for the hospitality and basic assistance given to them by the LMS and the Seventh-Day Adventist missionaries they encountered upon arrival, nonetheless held themselves aloof and attempted to forge their own way forward in crafting a style of ministry to the Africans. For example, they did not use conventional school primers for their students in the first BICC school in Matabeleland. Rather, they used a South African–imported Zulu translation of chapter 1 of the Gospel of John.

By the mid 1910s, in addition to a primary school at Matopo Mission, the BICC opened a special school for the training of (male) African preachers, pastors, and evangelists, together with training in the industrial arts. African men took advantage of mission schooling in the first decades of the twentieth century, not only to learn about (and in many cases embrace) a new set of spiritual teachings but also to become literate and learn crafts such as carpentry and plow-based market agriculture. As the first generation of youthful male converts came of age, in the 1920s, they expected to reap the rewards of their studies. Instead, they encountered the hardening of the colonial state as the BSAC handed over governance to the white settlers in 1923 and the paternalism of the mission church became more thoroughgoing and professionalized.

The title of *pastor* in the Rhodesian context referred to leaders of the local worshipping congregation. The BICC and other mission societies envisioned that these pastors would also serve as heads of the local village's church-run primary schools, serving in a dual pastor-teacher's role. Such an arrangement would ensure that the church-run schools would rightly convey Christian teachings amid the rest of the instructional program. The (male) pastor-teacher would earn his livelihood from the government subsidies paid to the mission churches for teachers' salaries. The pastoral function was not a paid position in the BICC in America, nor was it in Zimbabwe.[44] The only paid church positions for Africans in the Rhodesian church, in the pastoral mode, were those of the ordained ministers, or *abaFundisi*, and of the short-term itinerant evangelists, paid an extremely modest allowance for their seasonal work leading week-long evangelistic meetings. One exception to this was the BICC's paid female evangelist or so-called Bible Woman, Sitshokupi Sibanda, who, during the 1940s and early 1950s earned a very small amount from the mission church for her itinerant work preaching among the villages in Matabeleland South.[45] By the late 1960s and early 1970s a few other women earned small salaries for their itinerant preaching under the title *evangelist* (not *Bible Woman*).

The term *minister*, by the time the church was well established in Rhodesia in the mid-twentieth century, was reserved for the very few elite African men who had proven leadership skills and impeccable moral stature, and had been chosen to lead entire districts as overseers. The first African men were ordained as ministers in the BICC in 1944, almost fifty years after the mission's arrival. Once ordained, a man bore the title *uMfundisi,* a title usually reserved only for white male missionaries. By the mid-1950s, there were only three African abaFundisi: Manhlenhle Khumalo, Nyamazana Dube and Ndabenduku Dlodlo.

The rising African church leadership exhibited many signs of commitment to the Ndebele as a people, through the work of the church, evident in the church's development, printing and sale of Ndebele-language materials, and in the targeted evangelism aimed at following displaced Ndebele speakers sent to live in Matabeleland North, and eventually to Ndebele speakers living in the predominantly Shona-speaking city of Salisbury. In the postindependence era, BICC churches were established by and for Ndebele-speaking Zimbabweans living in Botswana, London, and South Africa.

Potent paradoxes emerged between the church as envisioned by the North American missionaries and as lived by the African Christians in Rhodesia. In possession of large tracts of land, and with its co-option into the Rhodesian educational system well in place by the 1920s, the BICC became a colonial mission church that helped produce, by the 1950s, a new class of aspirant, middle class Christian modernizers. The paradox is that the BICC's

North American members, as of the 1890s, avoided association with the centers of power in American society, shunned civil responsibilities such as voting and military service, wore plain clothes, and were rural people with rudimentary educations. By the 1950s the BICC membership increasingly found itself in the American economic and religious mainstream, embracing higher education and professionalization, and gradually abandoning the wearing of plain clothing. Their discomfort with their own modernization is perhaps evident in the mission church's attempts to stem such trends within the African membership of the church.

The BICC in Rhodesia made an explicit ruling in 1925 that "native" (i.e., African) members were forbidden to join political organizations.[46] All the other major mission societies, subject to government regulations, also required that their mission-trained, African teachers could not belong in African nationalist political groups.[47] The BICC's special emphasis on remaining aloof from worldly politics, including participation in war, became increasingly problematic and untenable in the colonial setting. As one African member of the church matter-of-factly stated, "Colonialism and missions went hand in hand."[48] The fact that the missionaries were white and enjoyed all the privileges of being white led many African members of the church to see the official church's silence on any number of colonial policies, from forced removals of peasants out of Matabeleland South during the 1950s to the perilous imperatives of the liberation war itself, as acquiescence to and even support of the Rhodesian government.

The members of the Brethren in Christ Church in Zimbabwe, up until independence, in 1980, were almost entirely drawn from the Ndebele people, a minority group that has been disadvantaged in the postindependence period. In the 1980s the newly independent government, led by the ZANU-PF party under Robert Mugabe, launched a sweeping campaign of torture, murder, and intimidation throughout Matabeleland in an effort to establish primacy over the rival political party, the Zimbabwe African People's Union (ZAPU).[49] Although ZAPU supporters could be found all over Zimbabwe, many of its followers were Ndebele-speaking people from Matabeleland. Ndebele ethnicity today has a de facto political resonance, given this situation. Although the study is not directed chiefly at ethnicity or nationalism both of these factor into the analysis.

Life Histories and Oral History

The life history continues to yield important insights into themes in African social history. Unlike studies that focus on multiple examples of a single type of dramatic episode of rupture in a brief window of years, studies based on life histories allow the reader to see those moments of conflict in a longer time frame. There are compelling stories of conversion in the early years of African colonial rule, which often resulted in painful incidents of generational and gendered conflict within families. Or, decades later, there were many shared experiences of another round of generational divisions during the liberation struggle, when youth castigated their elders for failing to embrace the full, radical agenda of the movement. Tracking individuals across the arc of their whole lives, seeing how they pass through their own childhood, youth, adulthood, and elder years, renders these dramatic moments of rupture or conflict less vulnerable to simplistic interpretation. Gendered imperatives differ across the life cycles and as one lived through different historical moments. Conflicts, which in the moment seemed to indicate permanent rupture of relationships—with one's parents, one's child, or with the church itself—in many instances did not last. In this book there is, among others, a daughter disowned after she refused her father's choice of husband for her, who later returned to her family home; a "backslidden" minister who made peace with the church when he was in his old age; and a rebellious, hard-living young man who later became a bishop. The intimate scale of this study precludes making sweeping statements about a broad cross section of Zimbabwean or southern African society. The aim instead was to look at a few people and draw out as much as one could from close range. My extensive reading of BICC documents across the decades and the secondary literature on colonial Zimbabwe and southern African church history provides a broader underpinning to the stories of these six lives. The trends we see in the lives highlighted in this book are echoed in the less deeply fleshed out but discernable material in the church's records.

The Gender of Piety offers six life histories of Ndebele-speaking people of the Brethren in Christ Church; they span the course of a long twentieth century. All the action takes place in Matabeleland, the western province of what is today Zimbabwe, formerly known as Rhodesia and Southern Rhodesia. The book's major themes run through each of the lives around which the chapters are built. Life history becomes the way I show how the themes of gendered piety, families, and the distinctiveness of the BICC in the colonial and postcolonial Zimbabwean setting interact and build on one another. Oral history interviews provide crucial evidence for the building of each of the life stories in this book. Three of the six individuals were no longer alive at the time of research and could not be interviewed. However, for piecing together the life history of each of the six, I conducted interviews with close relatives, African associates, and missionaries who knew each of the people, as well as consulted church documents at the Zimbabwe headquarters in Bulawayo and at the North American archive in Grantham, Pennsylvania, and materials at the National Archives of Zimbabwe in Bulawayo and Harare, and at Rhodes House in Oxford, UK.

Each person whose life forms the focus of a chapter was chosen because there was a rich cluster of people connected to that person's life and work who were available for interviewing, as well as enough documents to support many of the orally made assertions. They were selected to span the twentieth century. Each had watershed moments, decisions, or events that invited in-depth analysis that could yield broader insights to trends I had identified were running throughout the group.

Because the interview subjects were often variously aged members of the same families, *The Gender of Piety* gives insight into

African Christian family dynamics across at least three generations.[50] Oral history fieldwork has been the bread and butter of the historian of twentieth-century Africa since the 1960s and thus this work is not unique because it uses oral data. However, what is distinctive is, first, my attention to the arc of individual life histories and, second, their intersection with those of their family members and their linkage to the various epochs of colonial rule. Such an approach reveals subtleties and complexities that are otherwise invisible or opaque to the outsider. The unofficial nature of the oral sources (unofficial in the sense that they were orally transmitted, not written, and thus more suspect in the eyes of conventional historians) gives us access to the spontaneous side of this mission church and its African membership, whose official history is stilted considerably by its formal policy of separation from the world and its consistent erasure of the leadership of women.[51] The inclusion of the oral material makes it clear—official versions to the contrary—that this church was led by spiritually powerful women, that maleness and piety were often incompatible, and that it was a part of the colonial experience of its African membership and *not* separate from worldly African aspirations, fashion sensibilities, and political action.

Studies in the life history genre of Africanist scholarship reach back to the 1980s and 1990s, many of which were focused on women and based on oral historical work.[52] Some of the life history works were simply collections of oral narrations by African women, without much if any context or interpretation offered by the collector of the stories, and with little sifting of the oral material together with archival sources, such as Irene Staunton's *Mothers of the Revolution* or Jean Davison's *Voices from Mutira*. Reviewers have noted that such collections, left uninterpreted, not contextualized, can leave the reader needing more guidance and therefore work best when read in tandem with other monographs of the same time and place. *Women of Phokeng* by Belinda Bozzoli (with Mmantho Nkotsoe) is a collection of the stories of twenty-two women, all of the same age cohort. Nkotsoe forged the relationships that made the interviews possible; Bozzoli, a sociologist, offers a social-history-type synthesis of the patterns discernable across these twenty-two lives, in order to complicate, by virtue of her reading of these women's experiences, making overarching generalizations about black South African women's experiences under apartheid.[53] The thematic focus in *Women of Phokeng* demonstrated the complexity of the women's consciousness; the mention of church affiliations here is frequent within the testimonies but is not of primary analytical interest to Bozzoli. Her book came out of the impetus to create a people's history of South Africa, as was, for Zimbabwe, a collection of oral testimonies presented by Terri Barnes and Everjoice Win: *To Live a Better Life*.[54] Barnes's subsequent social history of urban gender relations, *"We Women Worked So Hard,"* drew on her growing, rich collection of oral testimonies from women, allowing her to analyze how the women of urban Harare, Zimbabwe, underwent a series of changes over the colonial period.[55] Barnes's discussion of respectability and "righteousness"—and women's pursuit thereof as they struggled to educate their children and cope with the need to move back and forth from their country homes to city residences—offered important insights into what she saw as many women's fervor to survive and to do so while adhering to shifting definitions of "good" behavior. While not an oral history, Deborah Gaitskell's study of South African Anglican and Methodist women's uniformed prayer associations highlighted intergenerational dynamics and captured some of the emotional meaning that African women attached to their Christian affiliation.[56]

This book, based on life histories, differs from many of the earlier generation of life histories. When *The Gender of Piety* began, in the late 1990s, I intended to work in the life history mode more typified by the generation of women's oral historians of Africa, such as Bozzoli, Barnes, the early work of Luise White, and Susan Geiger. And even though Marcia Wright's *Strategies of Slaves and Women*, about women slaves of central Africa at the turn of the twentieth century, did not use oral sources, that volume became a particular model. Wright's *Strategies* enticed my interest due to the arc of the *whole life* offered in the several life histories collected by Moravian missionary Elise Kootz-Kretschmer, and then given Wright's meticulously contextualized analysis of those lives as situated in the changing central African social, political, and economic context.[57]

Understandings of oral history work have transitioned, as have understandings about women's history and gender history. Scholars recognize that the subjectivity of orally gathered life narratives makes them valuable, particularly for work on piety—a human modality that is one of the most subjective one can imagine.[58] Further, studies investigating masculinity have shed new light into gender relations, especially Stephan Miescher's *Making Men in Ghana*.[59] But few studies really keep both men and women, and both masculine and feminine, in the analytical gaze throughout the book.[60] Actual men and the more metaphorically "male" elements in the lives of my female informants were crucial parts of the story. I came to bring questions to my informants and my previously recorded interviews that engaged more deeply the notions of gendered dynamics between masculine and feminine modes of spirituality, not only within a single person's life trajectory but in that person's life within its family web of relationships. Thus the major contribution of this work is that it is a gendered analysis that is interested in both masculinity and femininity, in both women and men.

I noticed early into my fieldwork in Zimbabwe that people understood themselves in terms of the web of people—chiefly their families—in which they lived their lives. People were quick to point out how they were related to others I knew, and they rejoiced when I noticed a point of familial connection. Over time, I discerned that piety was also set in a context of family networks. I concluded that piety is gendered, in a particularly family-based manner. Gender roles—at least in Zimbabwe and southern Africa more broadly—are largely shaped by understandings of kinship. Investigating dynamics and cycles of piety in terms of gender therefore led me to families. This is why I came particularly to seek out interviews with multiple members of the same family, of both sexes, and from different generations. The life histories presented here are about a single life, embedded therefore not only in the broader themes of Zimbabwe's colonial and postcolonial history but also in the network of relationships of that person's family. The salvation history of a single individual becomes more meaningful when set in the context of both her or his family and broader societal dynamics. A recent special issue of the *Journal of Southern African Studies,* devoted to religious biography, emphasizes the value of biographical studies' ability to show how "personal lives have spanned politico-spatial boundaries of all kinds . . . and in addressing the transcending of divisions between social, cultural and religious spheres as well as historical periods."[61]

The logic of the life history approach embedded in the family context allows us to see that a family devastated by forced removal from its home in Matabeleland South during the early 1950s, dumped into the distant and arid Gwaai region of Matabeleland North, could produce both a legendary woman pastor credited with mediating multiple miracles *and* a man—her son—who joined the armed wing of the nationalist political party, ZAPU, and fought in the liberation war. For cash-generating employment, men had to rely on migrant labor more than ever. Women of forcibly removed families—the ones who stayed put to care for the family and learn how to grow food in an alien environment—also became leaders of new church communities that during the 1950s began as small gatherings under trees. Men joined the nascent and growing nationalist protest movements, and in a trend well established before forced removals, increasingly conflated the "white man's church" with the colonial government.

Life histories offered in historical and familial context allow the reader to see that ostensibly mutually exclusive ideological stances of the liberation struggle and the colonial evangelical mission church could coexist within a family, and certainly within an individual. Gendered and generational patterns emerging from the careful work of life history–oriented oral fieldwork has rendered these trends visible and more comprehensible. The reader can begin to enter the worldview of people for whom their piety was central to their identity and has served as a bulwark against the call from rival deities. These African-generated tales of Christian exemplary living help us understand what it is that makes certain lives exemplary and others "fallen," how those dynamics of "fallen" and "exemplary" are gendered, and how these conditions of piety wax and wane within an individual life.

Oral historians know there is the very real possibility that the people they interview may craft stories about themselves to suit their understanding of the researcher's wishes. It seems likely that some of this happened in my interviews. That is part of the territory. And yet, the Zimbabwean members of the BICC were already composing their stories before I got there. The people I talked to were not merely telling me what I wanted to know. Such a conclusion assumes they weren't already thinking about their life stories, weren't already putting together narratives about themselves and their family members. I am in fact far from the first to have interviewed many of the people whose stories figure in this book.

African autobiography is another recent theme that has interested scholars of African history. For example, Derek Peterson highlights the prominent place of autobiography in the literary efforts of Kenyans, especially the Presbyterians of Tumutumu Mission.[62] Testimonies of faith were a carefully practiced literary form, encouraged by missionary schoolteachers, and embraced by African converts. Peterson's analysis brings out important observations about the resonance between the church recordkeepers and Gikuyu politics. Unlike the meticulous writers and record-keepers of these Presbyterians of Kenya, the BICC of Zimbabwe did not preserve as many documents, and hagiographic narration was more likely to occur orally, eventually recorded by an elite few who took it upon themselves in the 1980s and 1990s to begin to conduct oral histories in the effort to create a written record of the Zimbabwean church's legacy of exemplary lives. Fewer BICC

Christians were that engaged in actually writing their own auto-biographies. Nonetheless, the people of the BICC have long told and retold their own history; their purposes were and are pietistic, confessional, and conversion oriented. When I arrived for my first research visit to Bulawayo, in 1997, the church was preparing to celebrate its centennial anniversary. The church's literature committee, intent on producing a centennial volume celebrating the church's one hundred years in Matabeleland, were busily gathering stories—oral testimonies—from official leaders, long-serving missionaries, and elderly lay people with long memories.[63]

One of the long-serving, key members of the literature committee was Doris Dube. A member of the BICC-Zimbabwe since her birth, in the late 1940s, Dube has been a passionate collector—and reporter—of stories of the lives of the people in the BICC-Zimbabwe since her earliest contributions to the church newspaper, *Good Words/Amazwi Amahle,* from the 1970s. She published a volume of exemplary lives of BICC women in 1992 called *Silent Labourers.* Her aim in this book was to highlight the piety and resilience of the women of the church. The style was closer to hagiography than to biography. Eclipsing specificity of time and space allowed the almost-archetypal nature of the stories to predominate. The admirable Christian woman of the BICC—the righteous and respectable woman, based on the stories crafted by Dube and her informants—is a wife and mother, a matron, a "mother in Israel." Industrious, strong, productive, devout, generous to those in need, and devoted to her family, she is like the wife found in Proverbs 31:

> 10 A good wife who can find? She is far more precious
> than jewels. 11 The heart of her husband trusts in her, and
> he will have no lack of gain. . . . 17 She girds her loins
> with strength and makes her arms strong. . . . 19 She puts
> her hands to the distaff, and her hands hold the spindle.
> 20 She opens her hand to the poor, and reaches out her
> hands to the needy. . . . 27 She looks well to the ways of

her household, and does not eat the bread of idleness. 30
Charm is deceitful, and beauty is vain, but a woman who
fears the LORD is to be praised.[64]

I have come to view the oral material, and my role in generating
it, differently from when the interviews began, in 1997. My own
purposes for doing interviews with church members were different from Dube's; I aimed neither to find nor to present accounts
of exemplary lives. However, African members of the church were
accustomed to offering versions of their lives both to missionaries
and to African church leaders that conformed to these hagiographic
purposes. Because I wanted the broader political and social context to be integrated with these stories, there was a certain tension,
and at times even frustration, in the interviews with people who
either could not or would not ground their narratives in specific
times and spaces.

Luise White's perspective that the pursuit of authentic African
voices was overly earnest—along with the valorization of the non-
famous African informant as the only way to access "true" insights about African social history—helped make available more
open-ended and creative ways of prosecuting an oral history–
based research.[65] If informants avoided answering questions about
certain topics, or "talked back," these were important clues about
what was important to them. Oral informants are pushing back
by their silences, by the topics to which they repeatedly return and
to which they refuse to go. It was significant that certain people
determinedly avoided discussion of nationalist politics and that
their seemingly detail-free narratives were actually communicat-
ing important things.

The people I talked to, especially women, tended to strip their
stories of time and place. Men were far more likely than women
to reference their stories with larger political-context clues. This
trend is not solely explained by suggesting that more of the men
had more Western-style education and had been, as a group, more
integrated into the formal economic sectors of Rhodesia and

Zimbabwe, or were more likely to have been active members of a variety of political groups. Many of the women were also very highly educated, and some had had formal careers in education or nursing. However, the way people talked about themselves had a gendered pattern: men were more ready to admit to their engagement in worldly politics, and it is both women and men who attributed to women soft-hearted piety. This is articulated by a male pastor, who summarized it this way: "You act like a woman if you fall for this . . . teaching. Maybe men, when they see they don't want to easily follow, they'll be afraid to follow and be seen as weak. The gospel is so powerful, but you have to be following."[66] This does not mean that women were indifferent to nationalist politics or party politics after 1980. Nor does it mean that men were as distanced from their faith as they at times seemed. But it does point to a gendered convention of self-narration, and it indicates different modalities and sequencing of piety for men and women.

Names of Places and People

In researching her book about the experience of rural women of Chiweshe District during the 1970s Zimbabwean liberation war, Eleanor O'Gorman assured her informants that they would be anonymous. O'Gorman believed this would allow for greater openness and willingness to be interviewed on the part of the women.[67] Even so, she still found many of the classic evasion strategies by informants, such as issuing claims of having forgotten the war, or professing ignorance due to lack of education, or speaking of others rather than oneself, seeking advice from others before allowing an interview, or even simply refusing to be interviewed.[68] I found most of the same evasions in my attempts to find, meet, and talk with informants. I chose not to anonymize, and it was never a promise I made when conducting the interviews. This choice was largely motivated by my desire to write a history such that if any of the people depicted in the story, or their family members, came to read the book, they would be able to identify the people, in the spirit of offering a history that was precisely not anonymized or generalized, a choice I have come to believe is especially meaningful for people in Matabeleland, whose experiences and contributions to the history of the country have been de-emphasized in the years since 1980.

In this book I use the names of the people in all the multiplicity that I learned them. People are known by their family praise-names, or *izibongo* (sing., *isibongo*). They are known cross-generationally, either by their father's name ("child of Ngwenya") or by their first-born child's name ("mother of Charles," "father of Thandi"). They are known by the Western conventions of "Mr." and "Mrs." They are almost never referred to by the name given to them by their parents, what Westerners call the first name or given name. I provide many or all the available names for a person on first mention. To keep confusion at a minimum for Western readers, after the first mention, I refer to him or her consistently by a single name, usually the *isibongo*. In some cases, if a woman was most often referred to as "mother of," I use that name instead for successive mentions.

I do this because the people I interviewed will want to see their names. The decision to use names, and to name people according to the conventions by which they are known in their community, goes against the social-scientific convention that entails anonymizing all informants, giving them pseudonyms or numbers. This practice has validity for some situations, and some approaches, but is ultimately not what I decided was needed for this study.[69] This work acknowledges from the ground up that there is no single "African" point of view. That there are multiple African points of view, shaped by class, gender, generation, and ethnicity, is a given. One compelling way to disrupt the erasing and de-humanizing tendency to talk about "Africa," "Africans," and the problematic if not also nonexistent "African point of view" is to use the specific names of the people concerned. Not all Africans are alike, not even those belonging to the same church, the same language group, the same generation, or the same sex.

The ideal Christian matron depicted in the Bible's book of Proverbs overlapped in many respects with preexisting expectations for Ndebele women: the senior female of any Ndebele homestead was expected to work hard, overseeing and participating in the production of food crops; to bear children into her husband's family; to be a generous hostess to visitors at the homestead. The righteous woman—or wife—valorized in the book of Proverbs shared all these traits. This was an important convergence between the church's and the host culture's core expectations for married women. The church also offered women opportunities for influence and vital forms of mobility during the colonial period: the church provided access to education and support for escaping arranged and plural marriages, and—by the 1950s and after—women might become pastors.

Ndebele-speaking women of the BICC did not become church members without some important aspects of sacrifice, however. Choosing to remain a churchwoman in good standing—maintaining her reputation of *piety*—meant a potential sacrifice of familial harmony (particularly earlier in the twentieth century), alternate sources of spiritual power, and options for income that the non-Christian women around them had. Women were the brewers of their families. The teetotaling BICC urged its members not to prepare or drink alcoholic beverages, which not only led to female church adherents' potential conflicts within families but also denied Christian women the opportunity to make money by selling beer: an option that urbanizing African women found viable in the early and middle decades of the twentieth century. African women throughout southern Africa opted to work at the mines as providers of "home comforts" to the mineworkers;[70] this also was an unacceptable path for churchwomen. As Christian women, they had no access to the spiritual power of the local high-god, Mwali, that blessed the seeds and sent rain.

The Christian woman of the BICC also had to live within a world that focused on the female body as a site of "sin." Many women fell afoul of church teachings regarding chastity in their young adulthood. The process of finding a mate and bearing children frequently led to the out-of-wedlock conceiving of children. BICC women in such circumstances were considered to be "fallen," in a state of sin, and would have to be "out of fellowship" for a year. Many such women, however, chose to make a public confession of repentance, be re-received into fellowship, and, if they had in the meanwhile managed a Christian wedding ceremony, continue their lives as respectable Christian matrons.

Three of the six chapters of this book foreground the lives of African female pastors and evangelists. Although there is a growing secondary literature on the experience of African women in African Christian history, African women remain generally underrepresented in the primary documents, in published histories of the church in Africa, and in histories of mission churches in Zimbabwe in particular. One of Ranger's more compelling phrases about African Christianity is his description of African evangelists and church planters as "black St. Pauls."[71] St. Paul was a first-century CE convert to Christianity who did much to spread Christian teaching and establish new Christian congregations throughout the eastern Mediterranean region, thus Paul's name is synonymous with evangelism. Terence Ranger, Norman Etherington, and Rick Elphick have all emphasized the need to explore the role of African evangelists in the history of African Christianity. Louise Pirouet's study of the pioneer black evangelists of Uganda, based on research she conducted in the late 1950s, is another important and early example of the recognition of the role of Africans in bringing about the spread of the church.[72] However, relatively little has been said of women evangelists, or "female, black St. Pauls."[73]

As with many other African churches, a significant core of women evangelists and "church planters"—founders of congregations— have been active at the grass roots of the BICC in Zimbabwe ever since its inception, even while men have held virtually all the official titles of leadership. This book offers a history of the BICC that foregrounds Ndebele churchwomen's creative agency as un-official leaders. The analysis does not stop at "women's history," however. While some works on African Christianity have paid attention to women's experiences, few have closely attended to gender as a category of analysis within these settings. One significant exception is Barbara Cooper's *Evangelical Christians in the Muslim Sahel*.[74] Cooper's study is chiefly about the interaction among Protestant missions, Islam, and the people living along the Niger-Nigeria border; it is the work of a historian who incorporates gender into the analysis quite seamlessly. Her attention to women and gender leads her to indicate a similar phenomenon to that which I have observed in the BICC-Zimbabwe: that is, "the ongoing labor of unnamed women" is what "sustains the Christian community," and that for the church to recognize openly the importance of women would "undermine some of the central patriarchal tendencies of evangelical Christianity."[75]

The Gender of Piety demonstrates how Ndebele women of the BICC drew upon their favorite Bible stories and characters to inspire life choices that drew them into uncharted territory—both literally into new places on the map as well into new behaviors as women in their families. Most important, they passed down stories of women in their own families or circle of acquaintances whom they regarded as exemplary for their spiritual power or endurance as Christians against a variety of hardships generated by Ndebele and colonial patriarchal structures. *The Gender of Piety* also shows how women were able to build on the BICC's valorization of evangelism to win a place (albeit lowly) in the church's official leadership ranks, due to their work as evangelists, pastors, and church planters. Since much of this was not recorded in the official records of the church, speaking with the membership of the church, on site in Zimbabwe, became a crucial means of discovering and then setting out these trends. It proved most fruitful to structure this around individual life histories. This is a format that builds on hagiographic storytelling and remembering among the people, which then folds in added layers that spiral out from

the core narratives, drawing on the richness of secondary literature on Zimbabwe's social, religious, and political history.

Dorothy Hodgson's several published works on the interaction
between the Maasai of Tanzania and the Catholic Church emphasize how, in that people's interactions with the "cultural processes
and material structures of modernity," women lost economic rights
and Maasai came to be a largely male construct, limited to those
men who retained some claim to a "traditional" concept of maleness defined by being a warrior and a pastoralist. Hodgson importantly notes that masculinities are "multiple, historical, relational,
and contradictory."[76] This book is greatly indebted to Hodgson's
work and investigates the masculinities associated with the men
of the BICC of colonial Zimbabwe. An important insight that this
book offers and develops throughout is the contradictory nature
of masculinity in the men of the BICC as demonstrated in the
ways that some men resolved the tension between the church's
mandated forms of piety and those of Ndebele culture. Some men
who held prominent, official leadership roles could combine maleness with piety. Others left the church for good, while many other
men found their life paths revealing a *sequenced pattern* that un-
coupled masculinity from piety, reserving different stages of life
for different functions.

In fact, lending strength to Hodgson's insistence that masculinity is relational, we see that these other, more familial identities
prove to be key to understanding many aspects of men's more
public roles, an insight that builds on Carol Summers's point that
African male clergy had much less trouble in their interactions
with white (male) mission authorities if they had successful marriages to pious, child-bearing, matrons. It serves as an example of
the fruitfulness of considering masculinity in the history of missions in Africa.[77]

Ndebele male identity under the precolonial kingdom at the
official level was seamlessly connected between political and religious power, expressed in the unitary nature of the Ndebele king's
military, political, and religious authority. Under colonial rule and

mission Christianity these strands became unlinked. Beer had had a crucial place in men's oblations to their deceased ancestors and in their interactions with each other, and multiple wives had been the marker of high-status male prosperity and power. Ndebele male socialization since the nineteenth century centered on the evening gatherings around a fire, men together drinking the beer that the women had brewed. Into the twentieth century and as urbanization occurred, male socialization lubricated by beer shifted to she-beens operated by town women, or colonial-government-sponsored beer gardens. To refuse to drink beer separated a man from his age-mates, and isolated him from associational benefits connected with those gatherings.

The BICC's insistence on monogamy, and on abstinence from alcohol and "worldly" politics, virtually guaranteed that most African men would run afoul of the church during the course of their adult lives. Men therefore found the way to church membership in good standing exceedingly narrow, and few men achieved a lifetime of uninterrupted church attendance. It was not uncommon for male church members instead to find themselves cast as backsliders in need of repentance. Notably, many of these "back-slidden men" eventually chose to repent and be received back into church fellowship.

Nearly all mission churches were firm in their promotion of monogamy and the BICC were no exception. This proved to be more of a stumbling block for men than for women. A woman in a plural marriage might still join the church as long as she had been married before she came into contact with the church's teachings. A male polygynist who sought baptism and church membership was expected to "put away," or divorce, all wives but his first. Few men with multiple wives were willing to do this, for many reasons, not least the spiritual and economic bonding that occurred between families with the exchange of bridewealth and the birth of children. The BICC missionaries—informed by Anabaptist pacifism and Pietist tendencies toward political quietism—viewed political action as a sin. However, the mission church's compromised circumstances, in which the church received land on which to build its sizable mission station farms from the colonizing settler state, and substantial per-capita subsidies for underwriting the mission educational institutions, rendered the teachings against political action particularly bitter for the colonized African men in its membership. For all these reasons, men found that church membership in the BICC and political activism were incompatible: a conflict that became excruciatingly irresolvable, especially during the liberation war years of the 1970s, and took on complicated implications in the postcolonial years after 1980.

As the phases of colonial rule and African political mobilization changed over the course of the twentieth century, there were corresponding shifts in the relationship between African men and the colonial mission church. By midcentury African men affiliated with the church developed a pattern whereby they *sequenced* their manhood and their piety. Thus emerged the sequenced pattern in which boys grew up in the church and the church schools, left active church membership—or were thrown out—during the prime of their lives, to return to church fellowship and renewed claims of piety in their old age.

Demonstrating that Ndebele men's piety had to be sequenced with their actions *as men* within a single lifespan—a conclusion enabled by the life-history approach—is an important extension of the prior understandings of African men, politics, and mission churches. Historian Terence Ranger's work has demonstrated that many African men moved from Christian affiliations to political or nationalistic action.[78] The life histories in this book show that many men affiliated with the colonial mission church in their young adulthood, in the 1930s and 1940s, who left the church while taking on the activist political work of African nationalism in their middle years, during the 1950s, 1960s, and 1970s, then returned to the church and reclaimed their piety later in life.

The story of Huggins Msimanga's family brings into sharp relief the gender of piety that defined the BICC of Zimbabwe. Huggins Msimanga's father, Zephania Msimanga, died at age thirty-seven, of a cancer perhaps caused by the chemicals he encountered in his work as a dip tank operator. In his adult life he had strayed from strict observance of the BICC's teachings and was considered a backslidden man at the time he became ill. During those years of his adult life when he was not in good standing at church (compromised in part by his drinking), his wife, sister-in-law, children, and mother maintained a vibrant connection to the local BICC congregation. Before he died, Zephania gathered young Huggins and his brothers around him, and taught them to sing "Woza moni odangele." He could not rest until he knew his sons knew this hymn by heart, the one that had comforted him in his "heavy times." The weary sinner had come home. Circling back to piety after the work of manhood was interrupted by illness, Huggins Msimanga's father asked for a pastor to come and hear his confession at the end of his life and was thereby restored to full church membership before he died.

ONE || Matshuba Ndlovu
Masculinity and Faith in Matabeleland,
_1898–1930_

Turn, backsliding children, saith the LORD.

—_Jeremiah 3:14_

I PRAISE THE LORD BECAUSE HE
knows my heart. For a while I was greatly persecuted. I was
hunted like an animal, but Jesus was with me all the time.
He says in his word in reference to his sheep: "He gives
them eternal life and they shall never perish and no one is
able to pluck them out of my hand." I found these words in
John x. 21–29. I don't want to tell you all lest I should not
be able to finish, but I do beseech you to pray for me. May
the Lord bless you always. Praise the Lord O my soul! Praise
him. I am happy. My love to you and to all the brethren.[1]

Nineteen-year-old Matshuba Ndlovu wrote this letter in 1904. It
was addressed to missionary Frances Davidson, his teacher and
spiritual mentor, who was on furlough in North America. While
Davidson was on her yearlong tour of the congregations of the
Brethren in Christ Church (BICC) in the United States and Canada, Matshuba was in charge of the school that Davidson and her
colleague Alice Heise had started in 1898.

In the early years of the BICC's mission to Rhodesia, the colonial state was in its infancy, while the very unworldly BICC
missionaries were engaged in their first overseas venture and feeling their way about the work. This environment left many open
spaces for the missionaries and Africans who joined them at
Matopo Mission to enact new ways of living out the teaching that
"God is no respecter of persons." It meant that the official head
of the group, Jesse Engle—a married senior male—felt free to rely
heavily on a woman, Davidson, for much of the de facto leadership thanks to her energy, relative youth, and administrative and
linguistic ability. Davidson, an unmarried woman missionary in
her midthirties at empire's periphery, was a figure with a complex
gendered identity who herself acknowledged that her skills suited
more the role of a man than a woman, thus her self-dubbing as
an "unwomanly" woman.[2] It also allowed for a period of time—
albeit short lived—when the pioneering missionaries expected the
new African converts to become full partners, true brothers and
sisters in Christ. The African male youths who came to school at
the mission looked to Davidson to serve as their teacher and mentor, while within Ndebele culture, young boys might take guidance
from their grandmothers or aunts, past the age of maturity they
would mostly look to senior men—mostly within the family—for
the leadership they needed. Although many aspects of this early
phase's freedom and reach for spiritual equality were eventually
undermined by the increasingly unavoidable imperatives of the
maturing racist settler state, the dynamic of older female missionary teachers maintaining a close connection to their African male
students remained in place throughout the colonial period.

In the excerpt above, Matshuba related his spiritual struggle.
We do not know what exactly was persecuting him or hunting
him like an animal. But he indicated clearly that he found some
solace from these terrors by seeing himself as a sheep of Jesus'
own fold. The vagueness with which he treated his afflictions,
the use of a specific Bible verse, the flinging of one's well-being
into the hands of Jesus are conventions of pietist spirituality in

the BICC. Matshuba had within a few years already mastered the genre of pietistic prayer. By asking Davidson to pray for him, he acknowledges her fellowship in Christ and her role as his mentor. Additionally, he indicates his love for her "and to all the brethren." He is claiming a spiritual kinship not only with Davidson, whom he knows well, but also with the other Christians in North America, whom he will never meet in person. His world had been greatly enlarged by this kinship imaginary.[3]

Born around 1885, in the Matopo Hills of what is now the Matabeleland South province of Zimbabwe, Matshuba Ndlovu was the son of a "medicine man" (*isangoma*) who served Lobengula, the last king of the Ndebele. The 1890s were cataclysmic for him both personally and for his people. As firstborn son he played the role required of him at the rituals attendant upon the death of his father. He survived two wars of conquest and the resulting famine, as well as the widespread death of cattle in the rinderpest epizootic of 1896–97. In 1898 a group of white people—missionaries from Kansas—settled near his father's homestead, and Matshuba was first among the young people who came to interact with these strange newcomers. He became a Christian, baptized at about age thirteen, in 1899.

Davidson prioritized the conversion of young men—seeing them as the future pastors, evangelists, and lay leaders of the African church—and devoted much energy to instructing them at school and mentoring their spiritual growth. She deemed Matshuba "a philosopher and keen thinker,"[4] and he proved to be an able student and linguist. His angst-ridden confessions suggested a heartfelt desire for a deep conversion.[5] As Davidson hoped, he became a teacher, evangelist, church planter, and pastor. (A church planter is a person who, by his or her initiative at going from home to home to encourage participation in the creation of a new worshipping community, becomes the founder of a new church.) By the 1920s, as a grown man and head of household, in full possession of his gifts and leadership, Matshuba was part of a new generation of modernizing, Christian African men who were most well placed to rise to the (African) top of the colonial social order. And yet, deep frustration with barriers, condescension, and the limits of a segregationist colonial system that had begun to close in around them proved devastating. Ultimately, Matshuba left his work for the church; from the church's point of view, he became a "backslider." A backslider is someone who has been baptized and lived as a member of the church in good standing and then takes on behavior deemed sinful, such as drunkenness, extramarital sex, or "worldly" pursuits such as anticolonial protest politics. By virtue of having been baptized and of having been instructed in and accepted the church's teachings, the backsliding person ostensibly knows that the sinful behavior is wrong. He or she is thus seen to be slipping back—moving backward instead of forward toward greater depth of faith and closer to true union with God. Matshuba carried so many hopes from the missionaries and later, his converted mother and wife, to be a leader of the church. His turning away from the church's work was seen as proof that he had grown spiritually cold and was indeed backsliding. This chapter, a reconstruction of elements of Matshuba's life, helps illustrate that the work of manhood in colonial Matabeleland was incompatible with the BICC mission's understanding of Christian piety. African men in their boyhood and elder phases of life were required to engage in the male pursuits that the church deemed sinful and were more free to embrace the imperatives of BICC-style piety and less likely to be considered backslidden.

Matshuba's life is far enough away in time and removed from living memory that to piece together an account of his life from recent memory is elusive. And yet a variety of people have composed narratives of his life, and it is these on which I must rely to construct an accounting of his transitions into and out of piety. This reconstruction of Matshuba Ndlovu's life relies in part on remembered details handed down by oral transmission within his family and the community of people that he served and on the written records generated by missionaries who knew him. Unlike doing an oral history interview, in which a person can offer a narrative about themselves directly, which the interviewer can question and maybe even argue against[6]—there is little available in written or spoken words that comes to us directly from Matshuba. The letter cited at the head of this chapter is one of the rare surviving documents containing his own words, although even these words, recorded by Davidson, have been altered (or not) in ways we cannot now know. For example, it is not clear whether these letters were written in Matshuba's novice English or in his newly learned school Zulu and then translated by Davidson, and we do not know how much she may have edited or added words for the purposes of her audience, which was to share a success story of conversion with the North American membership of the church.

Indeed, we know Matshuba Ndlovu largely through the public and private writings of missionaries. More than any other chapter in this book, treatment of Matshuba's life requires reading the evidence "against the grain." Fortunately for the historian, Davidson was a copious chronicler of her early years as a missionary (1898–1904). She recorded many of her conversations with Matshuba and other young pupils under her charge. There are also accounts of Matshuba's behavior in the writings of the other missionaries who worked with him—or disciplined him. Documented references to Matshuba become rare after 1913, with the exception of a brief period in the 1920s. In a few instances, his name is not given but referred to by implication. This pattern calls to mind the vagueness of Matshuba's reference to the persecutions of his heart in the 1904 letter cited above. Matshuba's decision to leave his post as pastor of the Mayezane church in about 1928 was painful for his devout mother and wife, and for the missionaries, who had expected him to serve the church all his life, given his promising beginnings as one of Davidson's "first fruits" of the harvest of souls at Matopo Mission. The fact that he is not named in many of these later accounts suggests the depth of isolation meted out to backsliders.

This account of Matshuba Ndlovu's life pays particular attention to the interacting categories of gender and generation—and the dynamic of those two things with the very elusive quality called piety. It is not intended to be either a hagiography or a report on the disappointing ways of a backslider, as most of the missionary-generated documents about him are. Hagiography seeks to render the life of a saint in narrative form for the edification and moral uplift of the faithful and tends to float free of all but the most minimal specifics of social and political context. Filtering the missionary-generated material through the categories of gender and generation unflattens the missionaries' hagiographic tendency to focus on piety (or lack thereof) alone, as opposed to piety in its social, generational, gendered, and political context. With respect to gender, Matshuba's gendered condition is not taken for granted but rather considered purposefully, particularly with respect to the changing modalities of masculinity attendant on different stages of life. As Stephan Miescher aptly notes, "Most gender historians have concentrated on women. . . . In order to understand more fully the complex dialectic between gender and historical transformations, scholars need to expand their focus: they must unpack the multiple constructions of masculinity, look at the diversity among men, and recognize men as gendered social actors too."[7] Masculinity depends on factors including life stage, culture, and historical moment. Its defining features change over the course of a life cycle. Gendered identity in this community emerges from understandings of kinship. The attention to life stages and family networks leads to the corollary consideration of generation. An elder has different demands on his masculinity than does a youth. Matshuba's place as the firstborn son of a prominent man; as a youth who endured colonial conquest; as a modernizing, African Christian leader in colonial Rhodesia—each of these is relevant. Indeed, it is evident that *colonized* masculinity is something distinct. Tending to these categories of gender and generation renders a reconstruction of Matshuba's spiritual biography—his life trajectory as a Christian—more complex and contextualized than a hagiographical account. Why he became what the missionaries and African Christians called a backslider is not altogether knowable. And yet consideration of his case in light of gender, generation, and colonial periodization makes visible the sequenced pattern in the piety of Matshuba—and many men of his cohort.

Colonial Rule

Imposition of colonial rule in what is now Zimbabwe's Matabeleland brought a variety of cultural, psychic, and material disasters for the people living there. When an Ndebele king died, it was understood as the falling of a mountain.[8] The king's power was unitary: his religious and political powers were not separable. He was commander of the army, and his male ancestors protected the nation. His good relations with the shrine keepers who served the powerful local rain deity, Mwali, are what ensured life-giving rain.[9]

Powerful enemies, culminating with the British South Africa Company's occupation of Mashonaland, in 1890, had gradually encircled the Ndebele kingdom.[10] In both 1893 and 1896 the Ndebele state fought against the BSAC. Mqhele Dlodlo, born and raised in the BICC of Matabeleland, descended from the Ndebele royal family, and grandson of a BICC ordained minister, offered his insights into the wars of the 1890s:

> The Ndebele people . . . did not experience the end
> of the war as defeat in 1893. To them the end of the
> war was inconclusive. What irked them into battle
> in 1896 was the assumption by Cecil John Rhodes
> and his people that they had won the [1893] war and
> their subsequent brazen occupation of the land of
> uMthwakazi [Matabeleland]. . . . The war we lost was
> in 1896. The Ndebele nation had been systematically
> disarmed economically by the time they decided it was
> time to resume the inconclusive war of 1893.[11]

The impact of the loss of their king, their state and their livestock, on top of privations of famine and disease caused by stock confiscation and the rinderpest epizootic of 1896–97, cannot be overestimated.

The king's praise poetry hauntingly expresses the idea that the last Ndebele monarch, Lobengula, saw that his people were destined for servitude to the new invaders:

> You will miss and crave me,
> Though you don't know me;
> You thought you were betraying me, the son of a king,
> Behold, you betray yourselves,
> My fellow Zulu people,
> You will pull the wagons
> Of these people with transparent ears.[12]

The impact of colonial rule and mission societies co-opted into settler status by large land grants from the British South Africa Company was great. Ndebele religion and political power continued to be intertwined and to run along gendered patterns, retaining some elements of continuity from the nineteenth century. However, these patterns changed due to mission Christian teaching and the colonial condition of land hunger. Some of the most prominent Ndebele chiefs had made their peace with the BSAC, agreeing to become salaried arms of the colonial state in exchange for the right to continue to accumulate cattle. Two of these men, both chiefs of the highest social stratum, the so-called abezansi, became hosts to the Brethren in Christ missionaries who came in 1898 to settle in the Matopos.[13]

One of Lobengula's advisers, expert in mediating messages to the king from the ancestors, was Mjobhiza Ndlovu. He died around the time of conquest. On his deathbed Ndlovu allegedly urged his firstborn son, Matshuba, to learn what he could from the white people who were beginning to settle all around them.[14] Zimbabwean historians have argued that the chiefs and other leading men of the now-defeated Ndebele state saw themselves as too invested in the "old ways" to change their religious beliefs, while their children could go and learn about the white people's language and god. Historian Ngwabi Bhebe states that Ndebele elder males had realized that coming to terms with the European invaders was a necessity, and that their sons needed to know how to speak English, and thus encouraged their sons to be taught by missionaries.[15]

Matshuba Comes to the Mission:
Bonds of Christian Kinship and a Quest for Piety

Just eighteen months after the end of the 1896 war, four BICC American missionaries from Kansas arrived in the Matopo hills to set up a mission station. The BICC occupied a three-thousand-acre tract of land about thirty miles south of Bulawayo that Cecil Rhodes awarded to them, by right of the BSAC's conquest. While sixty-year-old Jesse Engle headed the missionary group, the most energetic of the four missionaries was a thirty-five-year-old single woman named H. Frances Davidson. She left her post as an instructor of Latin and German at a college in Kansas to join this first overseas mission effort of the BICC.[16] Davidson established and was head teacher of the first BICC school in Rhodesia. The longer she stayed in Rhodesia, Davidson's confidence grew, and she became increasingly comfortable in wielding influence over Africans; this dynamic was paralleled by the experience of many other women of ability who turned to the imperial setting as an arena in which to exercise their talents.[17]

Matshuba Ndlovu came to Matopo Mission not long after the missionaries pitched their first tents. According to Davidson's

Figure 1.1. First converts. *Far left,* Mnofa Nsimango; *second from left,* Mlobeki Moyo; *fourth from left,* Matshuba Ndlovu, 1899. *Photo credit: Clifford Cress*

rendering of a conversation she had with him, Matshuba had been aware of the existence of a new religion and wanted to know about it, and he found the missionaries' arrival near his home as an act of God in answer to his desire: "I heard His [the Christian god, Jesus'] Name once, and I wanted my mother to go where there was a missionary; then the Lord sent you."[18] He became the first pupil at the new school at Matopo.

The school day then consisted of three and a half hours of instruction with a primer based on a Zulu translation of the Gospel of John, with the balance of the day devoted to industrial labor on the mission farm or on the mission's building projects. The school came increasingly under the authority of the BSAC government. Starting in 1907, Matopo School received visits from the government schools inspector. Generally, the government inspector's reports praised the mission for the order, discipline, and industrial labor evident at the school. The 1907 inspector remarked, "I consider the moral influence is much more pronounced than the mental." The inspectors wanted to see the mission school reach a higher academic plane, using graded readers in the vernacular—not only the Zulu testament—as primers, and to teach English to more than just the handful who were receiving English instruction as of 1909.[19]

Davidson mentored Matshuba and another youth, Ndhlalambi Moyo, closely, hoping—and fully intending—to turn them into colleagues.[20] Admiring of the intellectual and spiritual potential that she discerned in them, she urged both boys to train for mission work. Her regard for Matshuba's skill is evident: "I have heard him deliver most excellent sermons and bring far more out of a Sunday-school lesson than the ordinary teacher. One day in reading the book of Isaiah, he came to the eighteenth chapter. He knows nothing about Ethiopia, but after he had finished reading, I inquired what people the prophet referred to. He thought for a moment and then exclaimed, 'I believe he means us, the black people.'"[21] When Davidson went on furlough to the United States from 1904 to 1905, Matshuba became the first African entrusted with the running of Matopo Mission School.

Matshuba was in the first group of Africans to be baptized as members of the BICC in 1899.[22] While the nearly all-white BICC membership was not free of racism, the church's doctrine emphasizing that God "is no respecter of persons" led the missionaries in the early years at Matopo to practice the holy kiss with the newly baptized. The kiss of Christian fellowship was performed at all baptisms and communion services, including with the first African "brothers and sisters" when they were baptized, in 1899, and thereby received into fellowship. Missionary Sara Cress wrote to the *Evangelical Visitor*, acknowledging that some folks at home might find this shocking, to think of [white] missionaries kissing black converts: "One by one the candidates entered the water and were baptized by Elder Engle, the service being nearly all in the Zulu language. We suppose those poor people in the church at home who think it would be a dreadful thing to mix with these natives would have been shocked beyond measure had they seen us greet our new brethren and sister with the holy kiss. Of course we observed that command the same as at home."[23] Cress is clearly self-conscious of the transgressive nature of this kiss when she indicates that folks at home would be "shocked beyond measure." For a time, in this remote and as-yet-informal setting, the missionaries at Matopo related to their new African brothers and sisters in Christ *not* according to the internationally recognized color line.[24]

Baptism did not bring one's spiritual struggles to an end. The Brethren in Christ form of spirituality assumed that one's maintenance of piety entailed ever seeking for fresh infusions of a conscious sense of God's presence and constant vigilance against sin. A group of youths, including Matshuba Ndlovu, came to Davidson on Christmas Eve in 1901 to confess their sins and ask that the other missionaries be summoned to hear their testimony. According to Davidson, the boys said, "we desire to confess everything and have all wiped away, and we do not want to repeat our wrongdoings, for we want to be ready when Jesus comes." At the end of this session, the missionaries and the boys kneeled together and "besought the Lord that they might be set completely free from their past life."[25] Davidson expressed her desire that they be done "forever with their heathen past."[26]

Davidson's band of young scholars, including Matshuba, reached for the type of spirituality modeled by the missionaries. Davidson was so keen to see her charges become aware of their sin, and therefore their need for God's salvation, that she meticulously recorded any indicators in that direction. She felt an intimate commitment to oversee Matshuba's spiritual growth. She reflected on her early encounters with him in her 1915 book: "Matshuba had many hard battles to fight, and often have we heard him out among the rocks praying for help and victory."[27] This is the Brethren in Christ's language of repentance, returning to the Lord, and having "gotten victory." Victory in these instances seems to mean that the person had a sense of God's grace, or freely offered forgiveness, infilling their consciousness after a "season" (hours or days) of prayer. It is not explicit here what battles exactly Matshuba was fighting. However, based on Davidson's recording of other conversations with Matshuba, we know he was learning to distance himself from the practices of his family that the church deemed sinful.

To become of aware of sinfulness would require that her pupils gain a different—and negative—view of their own families' ways of doing things. In a diary entry from 28 June 1899, Davidson recorded the following conversation between herself and Matshuba, who at this time was about fourteen years old. In this conversation, we see that Matshuba—at least in Davidson's understanding—was acquiring an understanding of the temperance teachings against alcohol and tobacco, and the church's stance on chastity:

> "Before you came the people used to drink so much beer. The chief induna and all the people (mentioning a number we knew) and they would get drunk[,] act so ugly. I drank it too and liked it, and I used snuff sometimes and smoked a pipe once when the queen gave me some tobacco. I told stories and did dirty things[,] licentious ones, but I don't

like them now[;] they are not nice, they hurt the body" and the look on his face indicated that he had such a loathsome feeling toward his former life.[28]

This understanding, newly developing in Matshuba, indicates that he had to a certain degree ingested the missionaries' view that separation from the culture and practices of his family was imperative. They were expected not only to separate from those things but also to acquire a view of them as wrong. How can one experience a sense of one's sinfulness, and need for salvation, if no wrongdoing is perceived? Davidson noted how the schoolroom fell into an astonished hush on the first day that Matshuba offered his own audible prayer, showing that "one of their number had learned to pray like the missionaries."[29]

Davidson regarded these "dear ones"—the boys whom she first taught at Matopo Mission as her "spiritual children," as seen in this passage from her 1915 book: "The true missionary bears much the same relation to his people as the parent does to the child; for they are his spiritual children."[30] The fictive-kin spiritual bonds served as some balm for the separation from one's blood kin required of new Christians. Davidson's protégés in turn regarded her as something of a mother figure. With Davidson at age forty-two and the boys teenagers (the youngest was ten, the eldest was twenty), this was not solely an adoption of colonial-style de-masculinization of African men by calling them "boys." There was also the indigenous pattern of naming, whereby fictive-kin relationships were and are often adopted; age-mates are siblings, elders are mothers or fathers, people in the generation younger are "my younger sister or brother" or "my child." The fact that there was also a long-held Christian pattern of kinship expressions among believers made a bridge between Davidson's and their worlds that was not bound by colonial hierarchies of race and class. According to former missionary bishop H. H. Brubaker, Matshuba thought much of the man who replaced Jesse Engle, H. P. Steigerwald. Given the naming patterns used in the church, he likely thought of Steigerwald as a father figure. The first missionary bishop was referred to by both missionaries and African converts as "Father Engle." Even today, African members of the BICC call their bishop "my father."

Along with his spiritual kinship with Davidson and Steigerwald and his newly converted fellow Christians, Matshuba's blood kin gradually joined the Christian fold. Matshuba's sister, Ntombi-yaphansi, was in the second group baptized, in 1902. Called Six-pence by the missionaries, Matshuba's sister went on to marry another early convert, Mnofa Nsimango; their daughter Sithem-bile's life is featured in chapter 5. Matshuba's mother converted to the BICC in 1906[31] and was remembered by her granddaughter as a woman of strong faith, who taught the grandchildren under her charge in the early 1920s to memorize Bible verses.[32]

African Evangelists: Dynamic Interactions of the Gospel and Land Alienation

A small number of youths committed themselves to the church in a way that exceeded what would be necessary merely for ac-quiring literacy or familiarity with the ways of Europeans. They were the new Christians—the first Africans to become leaders in the Brethren in Christ Church and the first Africans to undertake evangelistic initiatives supplying the first waves of African-fueled itinerant preaching in the church. Matshuba expressed longing to go out to preach the gospel to his own people, especially to those who had never heard the gospel before at all. Missionary Emma Long Doner, who in 1902 with her husband, Levi, started a new mission station some thirty miles south of Matopo, noted Mat-shuba's evangelistic zeal: "Last Sunday I went with Matchuba to visit his home. He told me that he does love to preach to his own people, but would like to go to those who have never yet heard of Christ. The boys all seem to be anxious to go with us to Amapani [Mapane], but we will not get off for a long time yet. Have just sent in an application for the lease of a large farm."[33]

The Mapane region became a destination for many Matopo African families, once they faced the impact of conquest and land alienation. In an attempt to smooth over one of the grievances that had led Ndebele leaders to fight in both 1893 and 1896, Rhodes personally assured leading *izinduna* (chiefs) that they could occupy the land they had held before 1893 for a period of two years, from 1896 to 1898.[34] After the end of the two-year grace period, Africans could be asked to pay rent in the form of cash or labor, or be evicted from the land, which was largely by this time pegged out and claimed by white settlers, concessionary companies and mission societies. In order to coax many of the leaders of the 1896 rising to come out of their hiding places in the Matopo Hills, Rhodes assured them they would be given ample and secure land, if nowhere else, then on the flat land south of the Matopos, known as the Mapane veld.[35] This promise was made by the ultimate male colonizer—Cecil Rhodes—to the leading men— the most powerful chiefs—of the defeated Ndebele people, and it was offered in the spirit of male honor: Rhodes gave them his personal assurance that the chiefs would receive land in the new dispensation. In fact, Matopo-area Ndebele chiefs began moving themselves and their followers out of the Matopos and onto the Mapane veld beginning around 1900. Some of these people were new Christians who had spent time with the BICC missionaries. Thus the impetus behind the first substantive attempt, in 1902, at opening a second mission station was partially fueled by these transplanted Christians, many of them sons of those same chiefs, wishing to continue with schooling and Christian worship in their new setting.[36]

The young men at Matopo included several whose families had originated in the Matopos and then were removed to the Mapane area. One of these in the same group baptized with Matshuba in 1899 was Masigwa Mlotshwa. When Mlotshwa first came to the missionaries in 1898, his family's home was near the mission. Mlotshwa's and Matshuba's mothers were close friends and in fact counted each other as "sisters."[37] By 1913 the Mlotshwa family had moved to the Mapane veld. Eventually, Matshuba's family also moved south to the Mapane region and Matshuba became the teacher at nearby Mayezane School. Mlotshwa's daughter speculated as to the reason these families moved: "I don't know but I think many people left when the missionaries got the farm because it wouldn't be good for the people to stay in the farm when the missionaries are working there because they build houses and—but I don't think that is the reason; I don't know."[38] This woman's delicate phrasing about the impact of land loss is a commonly occurring pattern in interviews with high-ranking churchwomen aware that politics was a taboo subject for church leaders. Matshuba's niece recalled that Matshuba's father's homestead in the Matopos had been located where later a primary school for the BICC was built, suggesting that indeed, as the mission expanded, Africans had to move to make way. The new Mapane Mission drew many from around the Mapane veld, both Ndebele and Kalanga speakers. The first thirteen local Africans baptized at Mapane in 1907 by Levi Doner included a brother and a sister of the Ndebele royal family who were drawn in to the church partly due to their connection with Matshuba. Although the former were of Ndebele royal abezansi descent, and Matshuba was not, they enjoyed a very close friendship that had an element of kinship to it, as a descendant remembers the two as being "cousins."[39] This web of blood-kin and fictive-kin bonds were a crucial conduit through which individuals found their way to church membership.

Gender and the Costs of Conversion

For men and women, conversion to Christianity, particularly the variety taught by the Brethren in Christ, required a level of change that touched on every aspect of life. Ngwabi Bhebe described this first generation of converts associated with any of the mission societies of the early twentieth century as belonging to a "quarantine" phase.[40] Davidson herself was aware, at least superficially, of the extreme demands conversion placed on individuals. She wrote, in a 1900 letter to the *Evangelical Visitor,* "only those who are willing to forsake friends and home can stand, and very few are willing to do this. We rejoice that a few are willing to take the Lord's way and we ask for your prayers for these as well for the rest."[41]

Indigenous ritual practice was woven into the major and the everyday elements of life: everything from encountering a snake within the homestead, to sowing seed, to giving birth. The seed used by people under the influence of Mwali had to be treated ritualistically before it could be sown, and in the mid-nineteenth century the king distributed the blessed seed. Christian converts were expected to use undoctored seed.[42] Similarly, converts were not to obtain or use the charms normally worn by people to ward off the negative influences of witchcraft or angry *amadlozi,* or ancestral spirits. Families applied special medicine to the fontanelles of babies, as these soft spots were seen as vulnerable to entry by evil spirits; this practice, too, was to be abandoned.[43] One young boy summoned home when his father died in 1913 faced conflict with his relatives when he refused to eat from the ox killed in propitiation of the amadlozi, and to "drink certain medicated water, lest he should have a great cough."[44]

The missionaries themselves saw their own work as "soldiers" in all-out spiritual "warfare" against "the enemy of souls," and the struggle of Africans to make the leap to Christianity as a struggle against the process of conversion as a challenge to shake off the practices and beliefs in which they were raised: "the bog and filth of the bottomless pit."[45] Given such a framing on the part of missionaries like Davidson, what did it mean for Ndebele men to become Christian in these early years after the arrival of the BICC, between 1898 and 1920? Their fathers urged them to go to mission stations and learn English; indeed, young men went to Matopo Mission. Many also fell away from church membership under the combined pressures to balance the need to earn money for bride-wealth and to live up to Ndebele ideals of manhood, which were at odds with a strict, alien Christian moral code.[46]

For some converts, opportunities for status provide an instrumental explanation for a decision to align with missionaries. Men such as Matshuba's classmate Ndhlalambi Moyo, as Christians, did enjoy certain markers of status unavailable to them in previous times.[47] Moyo's case illustrates also, however, how social isolation and dangers could also follow upon conversion and renders a strictly instrumental motivation inadequate to explain some African men's motivations for remaining in the church.

When Davidson and Adda Engle in September of 1905 went to visit and check on the work at Mapane under Ndhlalambi Moyo, it turned out that many people in the area were preparing for a major celebration of the wedding anniversary of the local chief. They visited, among others, Ndhlalambi Moyo's relatives, who lived in the area. As a young, unmarried man of a lower social stratum, the *abantu bakaMambo,* Moyo was of low status.[48] Furthermore, unmarried youths were referred to as *amajaha* and were not considered fully adult until they had married. His position as a Christian evangelist isolated Moyo from the mainstream of Ndebele manhood because it entailed giving up the drinking of beer. Yet the people in the Mapane area listened to him "with great respect" and addressed him as "Baba" (father), a title reserved for married men of some standing.[49] As an evangelist, Moyo thus acquired stature, which, for a lower-stratum, unmarried young man, would have been difficult to obtain otherwise.[50] Matshuba, for his part, came from a prominent family; but he, too, as a young unmarried youth, or *ijaha,* would have been of lower rank than when he became the one selected to head the school at Matopo, in 1904–5, and to interpret for the missionaries.

Even with some of these dramatic forms of rupture between the early Christians and their families and the larger African community, young male converts also found many ways to restate and maintain key aspects of their former identities, although at times recast to conform to Christian teaching. Davidson visited the Mapane Mission community in 1913 and provided an account of Matshuba in his developing role as first among the African converts: a leader.

> Let us visit some of the houses and see what changes have taken place. Here first is the home of Matshuba. As he was first in the fold, he is worthy of first notice. He lives

in a small, neatly-built brick house, with a well-swept yard inclosed by a fence. Inside the house are homemade bedsteads, chairs and tables, and here is Matshuba the same as of yore. . . . He is Elder Steigerwald's right-hand man and is capable of turning his hand to almost any kind of work. He can take the blacksmith tools and mend the large three-disc plow; he can make use of the small engine and grind the meal for the native food, or do any other kind of work about the place. Best of all, he can go out and tell the people about Jesus. He had hoped that the elder's many-sided ability might be his, and he seems to have had his wish. He could secure much larger pay as an engineer in the mines, but he feels that his place is in the Lord's work. May he have our prayers that he may always find God's grace sufficient.[51]

Davidson's photo of Matshuba's homestead speaks to us of Matshuba's transformed generational and gendered status. At this juncture he is a grown-up, although still a young man according to his own culture: married and a father and head of a homestead, albeit a new kind. Western clothing, Christian identity, a square house built of brick—were blended in continuity with other core elements of Ndebele patterns. His mother lived with them at the homestead, in the custom of Ndebele families. Hospitality and generosity were important. Along with a steady flow of visiting missionaries, Matshuba's family also hosted his sister's children at his home. His niece Sithembile Nkala remembered spending time with her grandmother NakaMatshuba at Matshuba's homestead in Mayezane.[52] He had become a person of status—not only a grown man by Ndebele definitions (being head of a homestead, married, and a father, able to extend hospitality) but also learned in reading and writing, fluent in English, holding a "position of prominence in the Native church."[53] A man in his midtwenties might not normally have been considered more than a youth. His book knowledge, handwork learned at the mission school that gave him

Figure 1.2. Matshuba Ndlovu's home, Matshuba Ndlovu and his family, ca. 1913. *Photo Credit: H. Frances Davidson*

the skills to build with brick and form chairs and tables from wood, his ability to read the Bible and preach "like the missionaries"—all seem to have allowed him to accelerate the timeline of acquisition of adult status.

The BICC as a mission society in colonial Rhodesia gradually compromised on its early moves toward living their ideals of spiritual equality. The neighboring mission societies, with whom the BICC missionaries frequently consulted, increasingly practiced segregation in their relations with converts. By 1916 the mission's deepening intermeshing with Rhodesian colonial values and power structure was evident when the missionaries in Africa petitioned the Foreign Mission Board at home for permission to discontinue the interracial holy kiss—not explicitly on grounds of race but hygiene (due to the many "loathsome" diseases that the "native convert" was prone to carry).[54] An important transition in the government then occurred in 1923. The British South Africa Company turned over control of the colony to the white settlers: a transition to "Responsible Government." Segregation between the races and continued alienation of land away from the indigenous blacks in favor of white settlers, similar to the systems developing in South Africa, were to be hallmarks of Southern Rhodesian rule.[55]

In 1922, Matshuba found himself part of a group of dissenters against the missionaries' authority. Matshuba now lived at Mayezane along with a cadre of the BICC's most well-educated and modernized African men who had moved south from Matopo over the prior fifteen years. Among them was fellow "first-fruits" convert and closest of friends, Masigwa Mlotshwa and his large family. With Sunday services drawing up to one thousand people at Mayezane by the mid-1920s, this thriving "out-station" church and school was part of the BICC's Mtshabezi District.[56] Mtshabezi Mission was the successor to the nearby, short-lived Mapane Mission. Matshuba and Masigwa Mlotshwa had both served as Mayezane's pastor and taught in its school. Matshuba and the other prominent Christian men at Mayezane vocally objected to the missionaries' refusal to allow their school to add higher grades. They also wanted their school to offer instruction in English. The missionary in charge, H. J. Frey, offered the teaching services of a fellow convert who had a standard 3 (US grade 5) level of English competency, but the men at Mayezane rejected the offer. They wanted a teacher proficient in English from South Africa. The mission refused to honor this request and temporarily shut down the BICC's Mayezane School.[57] Matshuba left his work for the church and took a job working for a white farmer. Masigwa Mlotshwa and his second-born son, Jonah, both decided to leave the BICC at this time, in favor of membership in the African Methodist Episcopal Church (AMEC), which tolerated beer drinking and smoking, and, as recalled by Jonah's daughter, was "a nationalistic" kind of church. Matshuba's mother and sister remained firmly attached to the BICC, a church that he, after over twenty years' service, left behind. Masigwa Mlotshwa's wife and his firstborn son, Samuel, also remained attached to the BICC.[58]

The dissenting men of Mayezane in the 1920s were reflective of the times. A whole generation of young African men had grown up under colonial rule and lived through the First World War.

American president Woodrow Wilson's promises to "make the world safe for democracy" through the war were not lost on this generation of men. Many of this generation of African Christian men participated more or less actively in a Zeitgeist of assertiveness from the larger black world, as seen for example in the politically tinged efforts of the AMEC black missionaries to Africa[59] and the impact of Marcus Garvey's pan-African vision of black agency and transatlantic mutual help. Historian Michael O. West has characterized the atmosphere of mobilization against the impacts of colonial rule that prevailed in southern African settler colonies during the 1920s. He notes that the emergence of several groups inspired by Garveyite rhetoric and organizational tactics "was evidence of a revolution in consciousness and mobilization that swept over southern Africa in the aftermath of the Great War. There, as elsewhere in the black world, the rising tide was much influenced by Garveyism."[60] Historian Terence Ranger refers to efforts of Christian, modernizing African men to advocate for themselves using newspapers, political associations, and petitions in southern Africa as being part of "the [African] Christian solution" to conquest.[61]

These movements were felt in Southern Rhodesia. The AMEC acquired a site outside Bulawayo in 1904 and its presence was well established, including in the BICC's Mtshabezi District, by the 1920s.[62] Simultaneously, the efforts of the heir of the last Ndebele king to organize among the chiefs and other Ndebele leaders to petition the Rhodesian government for a separate, desirable tract of land to serve as an Ndebele homeland reached its peak in 1920.[63] Eight years later, another son of the former king, Nguboyenja Khumalo, returned to Rhodesia after having been forced to live in South Africa since his youth. Nguboyenja's return to Rhodesia was enabled in part by the organizing of the African Universal Benefit Society, a Garveyite group in Southern Rhodesia numerically dominated by Ndebele.[64]

How might we understand Matshuba's role in the dissension and the defections of this group of BICC men at Mayezane, around

1922, in terms of masculinity and generation? In 1922, Matshuba was in his midthirties. He and his fellows in Mayezane had been spiritually mentored and educated by Frances Davidson, Bishop Steigerwald, and the other BICC missionaries at Matopo when they first came to the mission, in 1898. When they were boys and unmarried youths, it was appropriate to defer to, and be guided by, the adults in their families, including their fictive-kin Christian "parents in the Lord." They were now adult men, married and fathers of young children, and very well educated by the standards of that time. They were part of the new African elite: modernizing, plow-using, Christian, African men.[65] Their close relatives included the salaried chiefs (izinduna) of colonized Matabeleland, and migrant laborers who worked in the regional capital of Bulawayo and South Africa and had been exposed to African political movements there.[66] They had been entrusted with leadership in the African church; they were confident in their ability to know the Christian way, which to them also often meant the modernizing way.

The families of Mayezane aspired to more agency and leadership for themselves and certainly for their children. No village school in the BICC network reached beyond standard 2 (grade 4), and all instruction took place in the vernacular. The accepted practice was that a small minority from the village schools would proceed to higher standards, or grades, at the central mission station's boarding schools. Girls would go on to the girls' boarding school at Mtshabezi, while boys would go to the Matopo boarding school. Pupils of both boarding schools could be educated up to standard 6, or grade 8. Yet the families of Mayezane wanted their village primary school to give their children the best and highest-reaching education it could. This meant they wanted it to extend beyond standard 2 (grade 4) and to include English-language instruction.

Reflective of the various political and religious initiatives by black organizers of this decade, the men of Mayezane put their request to the BICC mission leaders, that Mayezane add grades.

The answer was no. The missionaries read this as an "Ethiopian" threat, and sent H. H. Brubaker, a young, unmarried, newly arrived missionary, in 1923 to pastor the Mayezane church as part of an effort to quiet down the radical, overly self-assertive stirrings there.[67] Reflecting on that conflict thirteen years later, Brubaker— by that time the bishop of the BICC in Africa—emphasized that the pressing for higher grades was due to a problem with the men's *piety:* they had grown "cold in the soul": "[Mayezane] was one of our strongest places in terms of church membership. It will be remembered by some as the place which gave the Missionaries a very anxious time about fourteen years ago. A number of the men church members who became *cold in their souls* pressed for very advanced education at the school. It was impossible to satisfy their demands many of which were unreasonable. The result of the condition was that most of the older members either went back into gross sin or went elsewhere."[68] Missionary Sadie Book wrote about the preponderance of men whose piety was in question at this time: "Just so the Lord still yearns over his backslidden children in Africa . . . there are a number of backsliders (especially men) who need our prayers."[69]

Masigwa Mlotshwa's son Samuel, born in 1913, would have been one of the children to benefit from an extended reach of Mayezane School's grades. I asked him what he thought of another man's assertion that involvement in politics is what drew men away from church. He replied, "Yes. I think politics is one of the things that hinders men from going to church." Mlotshwa first reflected on the 1970s liberation war years, but then offered this assessment of the years when he was a young schoolboy at Mayezane:

> Well, during our time the [1896] rebellion was over, people
> were no longer fighting, during my time when I went
> to school. But there was something of course that was
> worrying me. You know, the white men, they had, they
> always looked down upon a black man. You know that.
> You know, that color thing. Ja. That is one of the things

that make the politicians and how an African was treated during that time, they didn't like. That is politics. Yes. We cannot say some of these things that were done by the white man was good. *No.* There was a color bar; I couldn't talk and sit and chat with you, as we are chatting today.[70]

These utterances from Mlotshwa are crucial. He is articulating that the dislike of racist policies turned African men into politicians: "That is politics." As the church professionalized and became more integrated into the colonial regime, by the 1920s, the underpinnings for institutionalized racial segregation were well in place.[71] "How an African was treated during that time, they didn't like. That is politics." The pursuit of education, which had motivated the young men to come to the mission-run schools born of their desire to understand the white people's ways, became the same element that later drove them away. This is why I argue that the work of manhood was, in its peak phase, incompatible with the BICC's colonial-era understanding of Christian piety. Men in their boyhood and elder phases of life were not similarly bound and were less likely to be considered backslidden.

Matshuba left the church in the early 1920s; he returned for a short time after repenting and making a "return to the Lord."[72] Then he left again by the end of the 1920s. The most complete account of Matshuba's spiritual condition, from the point of view of the missionaries, came from H. H. Brubaker. Brubaker gave his own explanation for why he troubled himself to write such a detailed account of Matshuba: due to his having been so influential as an African leader, his actions would affect many in the church and thus required attention. In 1928 one of Matshuba's crucial father figures in the faith died: H. P. Steigerwald, the head of the BICC mission in Southern Rhodesia since 1902. "He thought a great deal of Bro. Steigerwald." By 1929, Matshuba had definitively left the church. In a 1929 letter to the Foreign Mission Board, Brubaker, now the newly appointed missionary bishop for the BICC in Rhodesia, reported his dismay at the growing influence of the "Ethiopian movement" in Rhodesia more broadly, and at Mayezane more specifically, a place he deemed "the most fertile soil for such movements." Brubaker blamed the influence of the Ethiopian ideas on the fact that "backslidden" members had lately joined the AMEC there. Among the most influential of those backslidden BICC members was Matshuba Ndlovu:

> I regret to say that Matshuba is again entangled in the coils of Satan. There have been rumors for some time now that he has fallen into sin. There was no real proof that such was the case. Bro. Winger [missionary superintendent of Mtshabezi District], in whose district Matshuba lives, undertook to take the matter up and enquire into it. He asked Matshuba to come to Mtshabezi for consideration of the matter. Matshuba refused to come and I believe wrote a rather nasty letter. This showed on his part anything but an humble spirit and also goes a long way toward proving his guilt. The matter is still unsettled at this time.[73]

Both Brubaker and Winger were clearly concerned about how much damage to the piety of those still in the church Matshuba might cause. Brubaker's letter went on to indicate that Matshuba's history of repenting, backsliding, and repenting had been caused (in his view) by never having properly and fully confessed his sins the first time. There had been an earlier cycle of "backsliding," separation from the church and his teaching work, repentance, and return, in 1911.[74] Matshuba's problems in 1929 were, to Brubaker, obviously due to a lack of repentant spirit. Brubaker concluded that he yet hoped Matshuba would "come humbly before God" and return to work for the church.[75] Humility is a cardinal Christian virtue that was especially emphasized by missionaries dealing with energetic and talented African male church workers. Missionary H. J. Frey used the same language in a 1911 letter rationalizing why he could not condone a pay raise for another African convert and mission employee, lest he lose his "humility" and therefore his "usefulness."[76] In Brubaker's view, the causal factors to Matshuba's disaffection with the church rested chiefly with an incomplete confession and the insufficient quality of his piety. Consideration of the indignities of rule under a racist colonial state on which this mission church relied for its own land and cash grants for running their schools did not enter their discourse or, it would seem, their minds.

Matshuba's son in 1935 married a girl who had attended the Mtshabezi Girls' Primary Boarding School. The attendance record for the girl, Musa Sibanda, indicated that Matshuba's son was "Ethiopian."[77] This suggests that the son, at least, was affiliated with the Mayezane-area AMEC. We know that Matshuba's mother remained in the BICC. Tracing Matshuba's later years proved elusive. In 1939 the missionary bishop indicated that Matshuba was working at a mine.[78] A 1950 history of the BICC missions in Africa and India indicates that Matshuba had broken his mother's heart due to his "waywardness."[79] One source indicates he repented near the end of his life: "He fell into sin in later years but in a letter last year said he had returned to God. Pray for Matshuba." This later source, the recorded memories of Abbie Bert Winger's time in Rhodesia as a missionary, is undated. Composed as a summary of her life, it must have been written before her death, in 1959.[80] Matshuba had joined the AMEC and apparently remained with that affiliation for the rest of this life.[81] Other men of Matshuba's generation repented and returned to church fellowship before they died. Masigwa Mlotshwa returned to BICC fellowship in the final years of his life, in the mid-1960s. Jonah Mlotshwa stayed in the AMEC for the rest of the more than ninety years of his life but made peace with the church of his upbringing and arranged to have a BICC minister preach at his funeral. Another Mayezane dissenter, Sima Maduma, did not return to fellowship—an option greatly hindered due to having taken a second wife—but he did maintain daily Christian devotions, prayers, and Bible readings in his home throughout his life.[82] The pattern discernable among these men, as a group, is that once their adult work as men—including affiliation with a variety of political associations—some but not all had concluded that they could afford to return to the church in which they had been reared, return to the comfort of grace and repentance that they had come to recognize as a kind of solace, and make peace with the blood and spiritual kin who longed for their return. Even those who remained outside the BICC, such as Sima Maduma and Matshuba Ndlovu, retained important elements of their BICC upbringing either by home observance (Bible reading and prayers) or continued church affiliation elsewhere.

<hr/>

Ndebele men found that Christian piety as strictly defined by the Brethren in Christ missionaries was incompatible with the work of manhood, especially that of a colonized African people. As Miescher has explained, "Approaching gender from a generational perspective moves age as a social category to the foreground. Because generational masculinities (and femininities) matter, personhood and subjectivity are determined by the social position derived from a specific age."[83] In order to make the cash required for paying the taxes levied by the colonial state, most young men had to leave their rural homes to find work in urban Bulawayo or Johannesburg, or to work in the mines that dotted southern Matabeleland or South Africa. This took them away from the daily devotions of the Christian homestead and village mission church. The male associational patterns involving the protonationalist organizations, the drinking of beer, the finding of comforts from women who may not have been their wives when living far from home, and the wearing of the latest fashions, such as double-breasted suits and fedoras or flashy neckties: all these were sure signs of Ndebele men having found that Christian piety, as strictly defined by the Brethren in Christ missionaries, was incompatible with the embattled manhood of a colonized African people.

Matshuba Ndlovu passed through three distinct life cycles that have proven traceable by consideration of the documentary and oral evidence. Each of these life cycles are informed by ideas of masculinity in play in the defeated Ndebele Kingdom of the first years of the twentieth century as well as those brought to Rhodesia at that time by the Brethren in Christ missionaries. First were his years as a boy, a new convert at Matopo Mission. His emergence as a promising Christian leader and young adult man followed. Finally there was maturation into a more established adult male status. Matshuba Ndlovu's boyhood and young adulthood coincided with the first decades both of British colonial rule and of presence of the BICC in what became known as Rhodesia. He was twelve at the time of conquest, thirteen when he first came to the mission, and fourteen when baptized. As both Matshuba and the mission matured, along with the firmer institutionalization of the colonial government's impact, we see distinct stages. The freshness of his life paralleled that of the newness of this very unworldly band of missionaries' first encounter with a foreign place and people.

Male converts such as Matshuba Ndlovu came to *sequence* piety with the work of manhood. Young boys were mentored and taught by missionaries in the mission school. Missionaries were one or two generations older than their African pupils. Deference to elders was consonant with the Ndebele culture. Bonds of love and mutual appreciation were possible in the context of the child-pupil and adult-teacher relationship established in mission schools. Youths expected to be guided by their elders.

Difficulties came when these boys grew up and needed, and were expected, to take on the work of adult men in their families and in their wider communities. Some of these duties clashed with BICC teaching. If the rest of the family was not Christian, expectations about appeasing ancestors, especially at times of death, including libations of beer or in some cases dancing to the ancestor-summoning drums, were incompatible with BICC teachings on temperance and vilification of dancing. Firstborn males were expected to participate in these rituals, lest the entire family be endangered by the actions of angry spirits. To survive economically, and to pay the taxes extracted by the colonial state, men often were driven to migrant labor at mines both in

Rhodesia or further afield in South Africa. Migrant labor took a young man far from his mother or wife or both, far from the home church (though there was a certain amount of Christian evangelism at the mines), and near to a plentiful supply of alcohol and women.[84]

The BICC also taught that worldliness—whether expressed in the wearing of fashionable clothes or participation in political activism—was a sin. The wider colonial culture found African men embracing the newest fashions in suits, hats, and ties as markers of a man's modernity, of his embrace of "civilization" and respectability. Bulawayo in the late 1920s was a colonial African city filling with new residents hailing from multiple regions of different cultural and linguistic origins. The African location in Bulawayo was replete with newly emerged understandings of ethnic identity marked by specific fashion trends, as well as differential adherence to a variety of associations and in types of labor preferred depending on one's sex or region of origin. For example, women were the landlords and brewers, while men worked as "houseboys" or on the railroads.[85] For the BICC, moving to town, the wearing of flashy neckties and membership in the Matabele Home Society or a Garveyite group such as the African Universal Benefit Society were all signs of backsliding.

The early years of the twentieth century in Rhodesia were a zone of openness and experimentation with what it meant to be a colony, and, for the BICC, what it meant to be involved with conversion of Africans. Similar to the frontier dynamic, in which there were openings for women to take on a man's position, it was also feasible and imaginable that a young "native" man would be welcomed as a brother and a coworker by a mission group whose core teaching was, "God is no respecter of persons." In this atmosphere, early African Christians might be open to violating the Ndebele culture's gender and elderhood expectations. As the colonial government became more formal, and masculinized, having ignored the Ndebele gender system, which though male dominated had space for women as leaders, so did the mission. The professionalization of the missionary staff by the 1920s and the standardization of the schooling imposed on the mission schools by the Rhodesian government both served to close off avenues for African men who had joined the church as youths in an era full of hope for Christian fellowship that operated "beyond race." The formalization and professionalization also firmed up and enforced racism. This happened at the same time that these young men, former youths and new converts, were by the 1920s growing up into Big Men in their communities and expecting to have more agency and more autonomy, not less.

Almost unfailingly when a woman "sinned" it meant she had out-of-wedlock sex (see chapter 3). But when a man was in "gross sin" it had broader meaning that could include fornication, alcohol consumption, or failure to attend worship on the Sabbath. As political tensions rose, sin might even encompass involvement with one of the several Africanist political groups active in the region in the 1920s pressing for relief from a variety of Rhodesian colonial impositions. The code words of pietism were used to denote divergent trends and choices. Matshuba's 1911 sins consisted of intimacy with two other female converts.[86] It was not clearly indicated what "sin" Matshuba engaged in to leave the church and go work at a mine and thereby earn the status of backslider in the 1920s, but we do know that the strict rules of BICC piety were incompatible with the needs and responsibilities of this adult, male Ndebele leader. No definite evidence exists to suggest that near the end of his life, like so many of his male age-mates and fellow "first fruits" of the mission, he made overtures at reconciliation with the church at last.

TWO || Maria Tshuma
Chastity and Female Piety, 1920–70

NTALI TSHUMA FACED A CRISIS.[1] HIS homestead in the Filabusi area of Matabeleland had fifteen wives and fifty-two children, and the crisis concerned his third wife's second daughter. Her parents had named her Masalantombi, but lately she was known as Maria at the local BICC village school. She set the homestead into an uproar. On this day in 1931 she was refusing to be married. As a young woman of perhaps seventeen years whose menstrual flow had begun, it was time for Maria to be married—she was an *intombi*. The use of the passive voice is intentional: a girl did not marry—she *was married*. Her father chose her husband for her. In Maria's case, the man her father chose was named Mayebe Mguni. Ntali Tshuma had intended Maria for him since she was very small. And in fact, she had already spent considerable time at Mguni's homestead, since her older sister, Sifile, was married to him. Maria often visited for extended stays to help her sister with the work around the homestead and to care for the children.

As Maria matured, it became clear that Mguni expected to have intimate relations with her.[2] One day Sifile helped Mguni drag Maria to his sleeping hut. Maria fought, escaped, and returned the several miles to her father's homestead. After this incident, she would go back and forth: help her sister for a while and then leave before Mguni could approach her. Finally her father said,

"You can't go back and forth anymore." It was time for Maria to stay there permanently, as the man's second wife. Maria firmly refused. She recalled, "I just didn't like it to be a second wife." Ntali Tshuma was surprised, and enraged. She had always been an obedient girl. While in his rage he blamed Maria's mother for encouraging her, Maria later insisted her mother had had nothing to do with it. Tshuma drove Maria away from the homestead, stating that she was no longer his child.

The arc of Maria Tshuma's whole life story is paradoxical and, in some important respects, exceptional. African girls who ran away from arranged marriages and found refuge at mission boarding schools have been an important theme in the history of colonial-era Africa, and in this regard the story of Maria's—MaTshuma's[3]—refusal to marry the man her father chose for her and her dramatic expulsion from the family home is a classic one.[4] The missionaries spent a significant percentage of their energy and spilled a similarly large proportion of ink in the cause of promoting Christian monogamy among African converts. The mission boarding school MaTshuma attended, Mtshabezi, was known for turning out young women perfectly suited for marriage to the educated, Christian men of the BICC. The intent was that such couples could establish Christian homes in which to raise their children and from which to inspire others to do the same: "Pray for them that they may be a blessing and an example of true manhood and womanhood among their own people. These and other young people who are being married by Christian rites need your prayers, as so much depends on them."[5] And yet, Maria Tshuma never married. She did, however, have children, and at a relatively advanced age: her forties. Maria Tshuma was in many ways *not* the exemplar of domestic Christian monogamy as envisioned by missionaries and that they and the African leaders of the church so actively promoted. After she left the mission school and became a village schoolteacher, MaTshuma and her father reconciled. He never mentioned Mguni to her again. MaTshuma recalled, "My father received me back with great love."[6] She enjoyed her family's support, sharing in the family resources of labor and materials, staying at or near her father's homestead for many years of her adult life.

MaTshuma's later years took her into a long period of service to the church in a role that was not defined by gender. In spite of being an unmarried mother of two, the African members of the BICC as well as the many missionaries with whom she worked revered MaTshuma. The official church's memory emphasizes two key points of her life: her youthful resistance to the arranged union into a polygynous marriage, valorized as a girl's courageous Christian stance against pagan ways, and her later-in-life saintly and self-sacrificing contributions to extending the church's reach. Her exceptional achievements as an itinerant evangelist and church planter in her postmenopausal years superseded the problematically unmarried maternity that marked her middle years. Ultimately, it was MaTshuma's dedication to evangelism in her old age that serves as the key to her reputation of piety. "I worked for the Lord for a long time for no pay. I gave myself to the work of the Lord because I loved it."[7]

Piecing Together Maria Tshuma's Story

The means by which I have pieced together Maria Tshuma's story illustrate the methodological challenges involved in my attempt to acquire the most basic sense of what happened over the course of her life, to find out how she understood and narrated her own life, and to then come to my own conclusions about her gendered piety. MaTshuma was interviewed four times for this project. The first time was in 1997, in the middle of a busy conference at Wanezi Mission; I posed the questions, which Musa Chidziva then translated. Chidziva was a junior married woman not closely related to MaTshuma. MaTshuma's answers were delivered in Ndebele, in the first person, then summarized by Chidziva in English, in the third person. Chidziva's summaries included her own interpretations of what she believed was MaTshuma's meaning and added observations of her own. Chidziva and I worked together to transcribe and translate the tape. This was the first interview. The second one occurred in 1999, at MaTshuma's rural home in Mbaulo. This time, she was ill with a bad cough and was unable to speak above a hoarse whisper, so the interview was recorded by means of pen-and-paper summaries of the words spoken. The second interview included a blend of Ndebele and English by myself and MaTshuma, as well as translation and interpretation by Nellie Mlotshwa, a senior woman very close to MaTshuma. The second interview elicited much more detail and frankness, attributable presumably to the more private and quiet setting, the fact that I was a repeat visitor, MaTshuma's closer connection to the interpreter, Nellie Mlotshwa, and my much greater knowledge of Ndebele, and the context both of MaTshuma's life and of the history of the church and the region. The third and fourth interviews were conducted in 2002 and 2003 by Nellie Mlotshwa alone and sent to me by post, as handwritten notes in Ndebele and English, summaries of her conversations with MaTshuma. Some of the most sensitive material of all—related to her short-lived stay in the 1920s at Mguni's homestead, and her family members' nationalist party affiliations and the impacts of Rhodesian government land policy on her family—was revealed in these last two interviews, presumably because I, a stranger and a white foreign visitor, was absent. The summary of events given above is a blended narrative drawn from all four interviews.

Beyond orally communicated material, I also consulted government and church generated documents, from attendance rolls at the Mtshabezi School and missionary diaries, to the terms of the Land Apportionment Act of 1930. In addition, missionaries who had worked with MaTshuma and African church members whom she mentored or who had known her in various capacities, as well as Maria Tshuma's daughter, were interviewed. MaTshuma herself was not terribly interested in discussing questions related to nationalist party affiliations or government land policy; nor was she interested in specific dates. She was born "before the German war," and she was incorrect by ten years when she gave the dates of her children's births. Her chief focus was on her experience of having been called to preach; she was most animated when discussing the health of the congregations she helped found. Not all the people interviewed were as sharply focused as she was on questions of faith. Others were notable for their intense focus on African politics, or their bitterness over disappointments experienced due to unfaithful husbands or poverty, or by their pride in their own and their families' achievements. As part of the effort to make ethical use of another person's testimony, it has been my aim to allow the interviewees' core interests and perceptions to have a role in shaping my own interpretations, while continuing to contextualize, historicize, and step back from the oral evidence.[8]

The Tshuma Family Context

Maria Tshuma came from a large family. She was daughter to a man considered wealthy according to the precolonial definition of wealth: rich in people and cattle. With his many wives and children and extensive cattle herds, Ntali Tshuma was a Big Man.[9] He was also a subchief under the local chief, Maduna Mafu. His younger brother had fought in the wars of resistance against the British South Africa Company. Ntali Tshuma never became a Christian, nor did his sons; his daughter Maria was the unusual one in her family of origin in this regard, although MaTshuma seems not to have been the only one with a special spiritual calling.

One of MaTshuma's sisters participated in ritual observances at a small shrine dedicated to Mwali, the rain deity and highgod of the region whose main shrine is at Njelele, further to the west. MaTshuma described this sister's involvement at the shrine as *being chosen*. Serving Mwali at the shrine became her life work, and she also never married: "Njelele had chosen her for the job."[10] When asked what MaTshuma would like the students in America to know about her if she had to pick one thing, she said it would have to be about her Christian faith, emphasizing her belief that she was *chosen*: "because she feels she did not choose to be a Christian, but God chose her."[11]

Ntali Tshuma had to move his sprawling homestead to make room when the BICC mission was established at Wanezi in 1924, but at first he did not move far—less than a mile, to a site near the village school. The mission required that any family remaining on land now claimed by the mission send their children to the mission school. Maria therefore attended Shamba School when she was at her father's home, and the village school at Malole when she stayed at Mguni's homestead.

As Diana Jeater has pointed out, the presence of mission stations offering a site of refuge from arranged marriage had the potential to undercut the authority of African male family heads to determine marriage paths for their daughters.[12] The father's role as marriage broker was important to men whose ability to make marriage alliances for their children was key to their capacity to acquire wealth in people.

It was the exchange of lobola cattle that made her union with a man legitimate in the eyes of the community and her family. Bride-wealth exchange was a bride's assurance that she could appeal to her father and his relatives, and expect their support, in the event her new husband abused her beyond socially acceptable norms. A father could prevent a disobedient daughter from marrying within locally accepted bounds of legitimacy. From the father's point of view, to drive a daughter from his home was an extreme act. On an economic level alone, it was against his own interests. He expected to acquire a number of lobola cattle or other livestock as part of her marriage arrangement. Sending her away in disgrace, unmarried, would also cost him the use of her labor at the homestead. In Maria's case, her father's authority was utterly undermined, which was exemplified by ceding his parental role to the missionaries. After Maria refused to marry Mguni and ended up in the care of the missionary couple, Harvey and Mabel Frey, the Freys spoke with Ntali Tshuma. He told them to "do what you see fit for her." She thereafter became known as *umntwana kaFrey*—child of Frey.

Ntali Tshuma resented other ways the arrival of both the colonial government and the mission station affected him and his extended family. Having moved once already, around 1924 to make way for the building of Wanezi Mission, he moved twice more over the course of his life, each time to cope with the changing terms of access to the land: once due to the mission's imposition of rents, and the second time due to the colonial government's delayed enforcement of the 1930 Land Apportionment Act. Tshuma disagreed with the taxes in livestock imposed on him by the mission as "rent" in exchange for the right to graze his cattle on land he had occupied before the missionaries had arrived. A new requirement stated that he had to pay one beast per year. "He felt the missionaries were stealing his cattle."[13] So he moved to Lufuse, a short distance south of the mission farm property.[14]

Maria Tshuma's family was one of the many affected by the enforcement of the 1930 land act. As part of this enforcement, the Rhodesian government designated the land Ntali Tshuma occupied at Lufuse as "purchase area." To stay, he would have to buy the land. If he did not purchase the land, he would be forcibly removed to Matabeleland North. MaTshuma recalled that her father said, "We do not buy land." Due to his close connection with the Mafu chieftaincy, Tshuma was able to relocate to Mbaulo, in the Filabusi area, rather than face the move north. MaTshuma later established her own homestead at Mbaulo, near the rest of her family. This was made possible because her brothers, the headman at Mbaulo, and the local agricultural demonstrator all agreed to it.[15] The Tshuma family's upheavals were not as severe as others, yet many of the people who lived near her father's homestead at Shamba and later in Gwatemba were those who were forced to move to Matabeleland North. It was their plight that tugged at MaTshuma and many others who went north to preach between the 1950s and the 1970s.[16]

The Role of "Aunties"

"That very day when I was driven out, I went out to the bush and prayed."[17] As she prayed in the bush, MaTshuma discerned that she should go to the African evangelist and teacher, Manhlenhle

Khumalo, for guidance. Manhlenhle Khumalo had come to the Filabusi area in the early 1920s as an evangelist, a forerunner to the arrival of the BICC missionaries in that region. He had been a child at Matopo Mission since its inception, one of Frances Davidson's "dear ones," or favored boy protégés. He was also a close relative of the last Ndebele king, Lobengula. As a member of the royal family, Khumalo enjoyed high status, as the precolonial social strata continued to be relevant in the early decades of the twentieth century.[18] Also educated by the white missionaries, Khumalo's status was now enhanced by being among the first to master the literacy skills needed for advancement in the new, colonial dispensation. In 1923 he came to the area near Ntali Tshuma's homestead, preached, and established Shamba School.[19] The BICC missionaries established an eight-thousand-acre farm, Wanezi Mission, on the land where the Tshuma family lived. She stated that she was too young to remember the day the missionaries arrived, but MaTshuma's older family members told her that everyone nearby turned out to see what a white man looked like. MaTshuma attended Shamba School soon after it opened, in 1923, as well as Malole School, near Mguni's homestead, taking the subprimary courses called sub-A and sub-B. She would have been about eleven years old when she started school. The African teacher who succeeded Khumalo as schoolmaster gave her the name Maria, deeming Masalantombi to be too long.

MaTshuma's memories of her Christian formation are inextricably linked to her relationship with Khumalo's wife MaNzima. Each time she was interviewed, MaTshuma mentioned the importance of the African evangelist's wife in her own development as a Christian. Maria confided in MaNzima "more than in her own mother." The interpreter in the interview was quick to explain to me that this was "culturally a normal practice not to confide in one's own mother."[20] A senior female relative of one's mother's generation was usually the person to whom a young woman would turn as she matured and became ready for marriage. It was such "aunties" who gave a bride advice on how to be a married woman on the eve of her marriage, during the marriage procession, or *umthimba*.[21] Precolonial Shona and Ndebele societies reserved an important place for the role of paternal aunts and grandmothers in the lives of their nieces and granddaughters.[22]

MaTshuma also attended worship services at the Shamba BICC. Simply attending worship, however, did not make one a church member or give one the right to call oneself a Christian; that required baptism. The Brethren in Christ emphasized that the true Christian needed to have a keen sense of her own sinfulness and then to experience repentance. As we saw in the case of Matshuba Ndlovu and his cohort at Matopo Mission, the aspiring Christian first confesses sin and expresses a desire to turn his or her life over to Christ. Revival services, complete with altar calls for people to come forward to confess sins publicly, were a regular occurrence both at the central mission and at the remoter outstations. The procedure for baptism included a rigorous attempt to discern who had had a genuine repentance experience and sense of being saved. Would-be members went through two-year classes in basic BICC Christian doctrine and Bible instruction. Baptism occurred after the applicant passed a catechism exam administered by a missionary, and only if no others among the African Christians spoke out when the congregation was asked whether this person was ready for baptism. Aspiring church members then were baptized in the distinctive BICC triple-immersion style.

When MaTshuma asked for baptism at the Shamba church, MaNzima spoke against it. Apparently the fact that she had been given to Mguni and spent time at his homestead cast too much uncertainty on the question of whether she was indeed a virgin. An unmarried girl who was known to have been with a man would be considered to be in a state of sin, and in need of repentance. MaTshuma apparently did not view herself as compromised. She applied for baptism three times at Shamba, and each time MaNzima spoke against her. It was not until later, when Maria came to Mtshabezi Mission, sponsored by Harvey Frey's wife, Mabel, that mission superintendent Walter O. Winger finally baptized her.

While MaTshuma emphasized the bond of love she felt with MaNzima in her interviews, it is clear that MaNzima's readiness to block Maria's bid for baptism speaks of a disciplining, stern love.[23] MaTshuma's experience with MaNzima points to the continued and crucial role of aunties in the lives of Christian African women. There was continuity of role between that of the traditional senior female relatives preparing girls for marriage and MaNzima's role in blocking Maria's baptism. In both instances, the senior woman exercises authority in matters relative to the young woman's sexual condition. MaNzima's concerns about MaTshuma's fitness for baptism, centered on the possibility that her connection to Mguni might have compromised her sexual purity, shows the extent to which sexual purity as a key ingredient of Christian piety was enforced by senior African churchwomen.[24]

Girls of the Gate: The Mtshabezi Girls' Primary Boarding School

Maria Tshuma enrolled at Mtshabezi Mission's girls' primary boarding school in August 1931.[25] The attendance rolls indicate that she entered standard 2 (grade 4). She stayed until December 1937, having reached standard 5 (grade 7).[26] The girls at Mtshabezi were known as *intombi egedini,* or the "girls of the gate."[27] BICC chronicler Doris Dube explained that the girls of the gate were a discrete generation of girls recognized by missionaries and African church members for their purity and piety. An actual gate marked off the living quarters for the girls of the gate who attended the Mtshabezi Girls' Primary Boarding School in the 1920s and 1930s. Dube mentioned the double meaning of the gate in the popular memory: "Visiting with any of these girls had to be under great supervision. These girls were known to stand for no nonsense from possible suitors. Jokes were told of how some young men referred to a group of these girls as 'a gate,' even when they were away from their enclosure."[28] The still-repeated stories of Mtshabezi Mission's girls of the gate emphasize that the mission school was a haven for girls escaping arranged marriages, and that it sought to prepare these same girls for life as Christian matrons. The girls of the gate story remained an orally communicated phenomenon until it first appeared in print in Doris Dube's book. Dube's own mother, Melina Tshuma, was one of the girls who, like Maria Tshuma, caused a crisis in her family by refusing to go into an arranged polygynous marriage, and became one of the intombi egedini.[29]

Not all girls who came to Mtshabezi, however, were running away from their "irate fathers." Mtshabezi boarding school pupils found that they had to balance tremendously complex and often conflicting imperatives from both within (the missionaries and African mission matrons) and without (their families at home) the famous gate. Marrying according to a non-Christian father's plan, referred to as "going by native custom" in the mission record, would constitute "falling into sin" and signal the end of a girl's school career. On the other hand, refusing to marry according to a father's plan could result in a girl being expelled from her home and losing access to her family. The fact that the mission frequently equated sexual purity with piety meant that both sexuality and marriage, for mission-educated girls, was a terrain fraught with high, frequently conflicting stakes.

Interviews with former girls of the gate suggest that fathers often were the chief influence behind a girl's decision to attend the mission school, whether it was because the father was arranging an unwanted marriage and thus the daughter was running away or because, as a Christian, he wanted his daughter to have a mission education. Some women credited fathers who nurtured their daughters' faiths and brought them to the school with expectations that the mission would inculcate Christian-cum-European cultural knowledge and Christian faith as well as keep their daughters sexually pure until making Christian marriages. Other women insisted that sexual purity before marriage was a value held by Ndebele "tradition" before the arrival of the missionaries and that their fathers would have expected them to stay virgins until married whether they went to a mission school or not.[30] In either case, fathers' roles in the lives of Mtshabezi girls were substantial; in this regard, Maria Tshuma's case fits the girls-of-the-gate legend. Ntali

Tshuma's arranged marriage, for her, precipitated the crisis that brought her to Mtshabezi as well.

The BICC opened its second enduring mission station at Mtshabezi in 1906 on land purchased from a white settler.[31] The circumstances of Mtshabezi's founding illustrate the conflicted relationship mission societies had with the colonial government: missions received per-head grants from the government for schools and established mission farms on land purchased from white settlers who acquired the land after the 1896 war with the indigenous people. Many mission societies from the first decades of the twentieth century were concerned about arranged marriage for African young women and acted on their sense of urgency by offering places of refuge for young women seeking to escape undesired marriage arrangements.[32] Yet the mission societies disagreed with the BSAC government on some matters. The colonial administration sided with African chiefs and headmen against mission societies in the debate over whether polygyny should be legal (it was and has remained so). Missionaries, thus, had few allies from the colonial administration, white settlers, or African family heads in their zeal to stamp out polygyny, which was a prime motivator behind establishing Mtshabezi as a rescue home for African girls.

Mtshabezi Mission is located about sixty miles southeast of Bulawayo, just south of the Matopo Hills. The Mtshabezi River flows through the mission farm and school campus. The river, nearly always dry in recent years, was, in the early decades of the century, dry only during the winter season. The Mtshabezi River had water during the wet summer season and was the site where many of the girls of the gate were baptized. The six-thousand-acre mission farm grew crops intended to feed the growing school population. The number of boarding school girls staying at the mission grew from sixteen pupils in 1909 to 140 in 1924.[33] Boarding girls would have attended the subprimary grades at their village schools, going on to complete standards 3 through 6 at the mission.[34] In the 1920s and 1930s the main mission campus had thatched roofs and brick buildings, including the church, academic block, and clinic, and a tidy cluster of mud-and-thatch huts serving as the girls' hostel—an area indeed separated off by a fence and the famous gate.[35]

Boarding school girls at Mtshabezi had a very closely programmed day beginning at 6:00 A.M. with prayers, continuing on with mornings of academic work and afternoons of "industrial" training, followed by chores. Industrial training, designed to prepare the girls for their envisioned role as Christian homemakers, emphasized skills such as sewing, knitting, mat making, laundering, dairying, and gardening.[36] Late-afternoon chores of manual labor included killing locusts, tree clearing, plastering newly built residence huts, cutting grass, harvesting peanuts, and even carrying female missionaries over the river during times of peak flow.[37] The day closed with an evening meal, prayers, an hour of study, and bed. In the 1920s and 1930s, the girls slept on mats on the floor in simple huts.[38] The girls dressed in plain garments they sewed for themselves as part of their industrial training and wore a white or black *iqhiye*: a very tightly wrapped headscarf, as a sign of their biblical "subjection." This head wrap for African women had its counterpart among the missionary women, who also wore a head garment, which in their case was a small bonnet. Plainness of dress was part of the church's emphasis on remaining separate from the world—"worldliness" being in some respects a stand-in for modernity, including "modern" fashions.

Male family members, even fathers and brothers, visiting at Mtshabezi who wished to see girls enrolled at the school were not permitted near the girls' hostels. Girls could see their male family members only from the porch of a building in full view of missionary supervisors. Suitors were not permitted near the girls under any circumstances. Girls were required to report to the missionary nurse when their monthly periods arrived to supply proof of their continued sexual abstinence.[39] Failure to do so resulted in punishment, most commonly expulsion. Girls and young women could even get into severe trouble if their suitors attempted to contact them secretly with letters slipped into books that could be passed into, and out of, the famous gate.[40]

For male suitors less focused on piety, girls of the gate were sought after as brides due to their elite education, marking them as modern and thus desirable as status enhancers for African men who had embraced various elements of Western culture. It is deeply ironic that the Mtshabezi girls came to be viewed as desirably modern and Westernized, since the BICC missionaries were intent on living a faith that kept them "separate from the world," themselves dressing plainly or unfashionably. The colonial setting led to some distortions in this message. In early-twentieth-century southern Africa, anyone wearing Western-cut woven cotton and woolen fabrics was seen as Western and "more civilized." It did not particularly matter to modernity-seeking Africans that the girls' dresses and head wraps were not regarded as fashion's cutting edge in Western urban settings.[41]

A marker of aspirant African modernity was the so-called white wedding, or Christian wedding ceremony, complete with the bride's white wedding dress and the groom's smartly cut suit and tie.[42] Mtshabezi girls expected to have a Christian wedding ceremony. Thus, "the [white] wedding needs to be looked at from the viewpoint of a modernizing institution. It was a practice that carried with it prestige and glitter and glamour. It was a practice of the civilized, the conqueror, whose ways were viewed as superior to those of the vanquished."[43] Not all men who married mission-educated women embraced the Christian teachings on monogamy. While a man's first wife might be a mission school graduate, a second wife might join the household whether she was mission educated or not.

Part of the need to display visible forms of piety at the mission included pressure to make a public repentance. Some women remembered their confessions at school as trivial in hindsight, noting that their altar-call confessions at school were instances of mimicry of those around them, or a desperate grasp to name some transgression that could be termed a sin. There was every attempt, however, on the part of the elder female mentors and hostel matrons to ferret out "false confessions." One woman recalled, "Pretense was not tolerated."[44] Indeed, one girl with a fake, and likely frivolous, confession was refused when her name came up for approval for baptism. She discovered later that her aunt, who was one of the elder female matrons at the school, decided her niece was immature and unready for baptism.[45] These auntie figures at the school were vitally important as teachers, models, and monitors of Christian piety among the girls at the mission. This dynamic at school had its village-based version, as occurred when MaNzima spoke out against Maria's baptism at Shamba.

As one might expect, not all girls of the gate were as pure, chaste and pious as the legend states. Many girls were expelled due to their sexual infractions. The following are sample entries from the school attendance register's "remarks" column, each associated with an individual student:[46]

> Fell into sin during the August holidays. Expelled.
> Falls and goes to live at the [mining] Compound.
> Goes [gets married] by Native Custom in 1937
> Expelled[:] married by native custom.
> Fell into sin expelled first year, awful sins
> Fell into sin Baby first of 1934

Many Mtshabezi pupils left school to marry by "native custom" in the 1930s and were bemoaned in the mission record as having "blighted their lives."[47] These types of circumstances, in which a girl was expelled because she had "fallen," were particularly true for the girls who entered school between 1927 and 1933, in which some 23 percent (64 of 280) of entering girls were expelled or suspended due to "moral lapses."[48] This is a high rate of sexually related expulsions for a school living on in current memory as a place of purity. However, of the girls entering between 1933 and 1940, only 9 percent were noted as having "fallen." This shift points to a trend that became much more prominent in the 1940s and after. The mission education became increasingly viewed as a stepping-stone to professional training in nursing or teaching. Also, girls began to enter school at younger ages as the 1930s progressed. During the 1920s most girls who came were in their late teens or early twenties, whereas by 1940 most girls entering at standard 4 were closer to age twelve and not yet sexually mature. Maria Tshuma was in that earlier cohort of girls who entered the school as sexually mature young women, thus her continued "purity" while in school is all the more noteworthy.

While Maria Tshuma was a student at Mtshabezi in the 1930s, one episode in particular illustrated the depth of trouble that a young woman's pregnancy could bring, as well as the intimate connection the mission school had with the bodies of African girls. There is a distinction between material that the interviewer asks for and whole stories that are offered, unasked. MaTshuma offered this story unbidden. She recalled that she and a friend went to pray along the dry riverbank of the Mtshabezi River. Their feet stumbled upon the body of what they realized was a fetus. They reported the dreadful find to the African matron, who in turn notified the missionary nurse, Martha Kauffman. A search immediately ensued to discover who was responsible. Every girl in the school had her breasts squeezed, to find out who was producing colostrum.[49] Martha Kauffman does not indicate exactly how the girl was found, only that "all the girls were examined." Lessie Moyo (MaSibanda) was Nurse Kauffman's assistant in the clinic. MaSibanda also volunteered her story of this incident, unaware that MaTshuma had also mentioned it in her interview. The girl determined to be the mother was Sofi Sibanda: she then stood trial for murder in the court at Gwanda, was found guilty, and given a six-month prison term.[50] It was a traumatic memory for all involved. This story of the girl whose baby was in the riverbed, and the search for her, was volunteered testimony from two different women: MaTshuma and MaSibanda. The episode also took up many entries in Kauffman's diary, who agonized over the entire process and found it profoundly disturbing.

Piety, Purity, and Repentance: The Wider Church

The commitment to attaining and maintaining piety took up the attention of the missionaries and the efforts of the African members of the church. An African preacher, speaking at a 1929 baptism ceremony, exhorted the faithful that no one can receive baptism unless she has experienced a "new birth" in her heart. At this particular baptism, missionary Walter O. Winger baptized four girls after he spoke of their sins and how they experienced forgiveness. The account of this baptism appeared in the BICC's North American paper, the *Evangelical Visitor*. The author of this account did not provide the name of the African preacher, nor that of the girls who gave testimonies, only that of the missionary. The researcher looking for African names often looks in vain. The account is still useful, however, for the reminder of the importance that both African converts and BICC missionaries placed on a warm faith: that is, an experiential faith that touches the heart. It also points to the routine nature of hearing of baptized Africans who had "backslidden" or "fallen into sin," repented publicly, and then were "taken back into church fellowship." "It was a peaceful scene by the riverside just as the sun had disappeared below the horizon. God's own stillness seemed to breathe upon the evening air. The Sunday services were opened by a short session of Sunday School. Before preaching service a young girl was taken back into church fellowship. She had fallen into sin some time ago but again repented."[51] As noted in chapter 1 and described in this missionary's 1929 letter, special gatherings to celebrate admittance of new members through baptism and readmittance of repentant backsliders, occurred in each village area once per year. In terms of the gender of piety, the work of womanhood—that is, maternity—was imperative enough that women of the BICC found a way to negotiate both becoming mothers and retaining their piety. Women's reasons for backsliding made it easier for them to repent and return within a one-year cycle than it was for men, whose political affiliations or other entanglements with the ways of the world were more ongoing than a single episode of pregnancy and childbirth.

The trend that emerges from examining many life stories together with that of MaTshuma demonstrates that, while the school environment itself was narrowly controlling of a wide range of behaviors, especially those related to maintaining sexual purity, the church as a wider institution offered much more room to maneuver. A "fallen" girl at school would have to be expelled, while "fallen" women in the broader church setting, though they might go through a period of having their membership suspended, could and frequently did take advantage of the church's teachings on repentance, confession, and reinstatement to reclaim their piety and their Christian identity. The possibility that backsliders or those who returned to ways deemed sinful, could repent again and be re-received into church fellowship is crucial to understanding the waxing and waning of perceived states of piety over the course of women's lives, including that of Maria Tshuma.

After safely navigating her years at the boarding school with a blameless record, MaTshuma went on to become a teacher at the subprimary level for approximately twenty years. She became pregnant in her forties, likely in the early 1950s. The church would have understood this pregnancy to be an indication that she had "fallen into sin," and therefore she would have been barred from church fellowship for a year. It meant she could not participate in the annual Love Feast—or communion and foot-washing ceremonies. Although the church's archives in Bulawayo contain the minutes of district council meetings, and proceedings of the all-Rhodesia or all-Zimbabwe annual general conferences, there do not seem to be lists of names of people barred from fellowship and then re-received after making their public repentance. One can only assume that this is the process that MaTshuma would have followed: most likely standing before her local church community and making a public statement of repentance, and then after a year being readmitted into fellowship. Doris Dube wrote a sketch of MaTshuma's life. In that account MaTshuma said she was saved from sin as a girl at Mtshabezi Mission School in the 1930s, shortly before her baptism. She knew she was experiencing the grace and forgiveness of God at that time because "flakes of light came from heaven and fell on my head and shoulders," and her heart was full of joy for weeks afterward. Dube's account indicates that MaTshuma fell into a "sinful" condition again later in life, at which point "God again cleansed me by letting me experience the falling flakes and the accompanying peace and joy."[52]

She continued teaching school throughout the 1950s and then became pregnant again around 1960. MaTshuma had only been educated up to standard 5 and had had no formal teacher training. That was enough education to qualify for a lower-primary teaching position in the late 1930s. However, by 1960 the Rhodesian government allowed untrained teachers such as MaTshuma to keep their positions only if their service remained uninterrupted. She had to lose her teaching job due to interruption of service caused by the pregnancy.[53]

Relieved of her teaching position at Ntunte around 1960, MaTshuma was left without a formal source of income. Once MaTshuma embarked on this phase of her life, with no formal income, she said that for sustenance "the Lord just provided." What this meant day to day is that she relied on the hospitality provided by the people to whom she paid evangelistic visits on behalf of the overseer's wife, and later, when she became a traveling evangelist in distant regions. Likely she also had support from the beasts and crops at her homestead. It was extremely unusual that MaTshuma was head of her own homestead, since almost all women living in rural areas stayed at homesteads headed by their fathers, husbands, or sons.

The wife of the African overseer for Wanezi District, Mrs. Hannah Sibanda (MaNsimango), was the women's leader for the whole district. She asked Maria Tshuma to assist her with women's work as an unpaid subleader coordinating church outreach to women in a subset of churches in Wanezi District. The fact that so soon after her dismissal from teaching Hannah Sibanda selected MaTshuma for service as a subleader suggests that Sibanda had great confidence in her as a model of Christian piety. Either her repentance and readmission to good standing was perceived as being thorough and sincere and her piety was thereby restored, or perhaps there is more to the story of this pregnancy than people felt comfortable discussing. A missionary who served as the schools superintendent for the Wanezi District schools at the time of her second pregnancy indicated that "the pregnancy was not her fault."[54] How she came to be a mother was a subject MaTshuma preferred to leave unmentioned and was not a part of her public identity.

The paradoxical Maria Tshuma thus was an unmarried mother of two, and yet she carried the status of a "good woman." As Teresa Barnes pointed out in her discussion of respectability and women in mid twentieth-century Salisbury, "Good women were ideologically separated from bad primarily according to their marital status." The importance of being married is also obvious in the standards for membership in the BICC's mother's union, the Omama Bosizo (Women who help).[55] In spite of her ambiguous situation, Hannah Sibanda chose MaTshuma to lead and instruct Christian matrons of rural Filabusi District in the ways of Christian womanhood, with the classic mission-church blending of prayer, Bible study, and Western domestic arts. Sibanda's husband, Rev. Mangisi Sibanda, later chose MaTshuma for evangelistic work both in Matabeleland North and in Salisbury. MaTshuma was also accepted as a member of the Omama Bosizo.

One day, probably in the mid-1960s,[56] MaTshuma experienced a compelling and overwhelming feeling that she must heed, a feeling she later referred to as a calling from God to preach the gospel to the people who had been forced to move away from her home region and resettle in Matabeleland North. The Tshuma family's home was in the Filabusi area, which in the 1950s saw large numbers of people being forcibly removed from their homes to resettle in the remote corners of Matabeleland North, a region called *eMaguswini*, or "in the place of forests"—an event discussed further in chapter 4. MaTshuma's relatives were among the removed. On the day she experienced a powerful urge to go out and preach in far places, the feeling took the form of a song about preaching the gospel that entered her consciousness and wouldn't go away. It was followed some days later by a summons from the church leadership based at Wanezi Mission: she was wanted to be an evangelist eMaguswini.

> One day people from the village were chatting near a dam being built, both Christians and non-Christians. There was discussion of the fact that there were some people doing ministry eMaguswini. I was lying on the sand and I said, no, that's not for me. Later, the next day, I don't know why, I got a song in my heart all day. "*Alihambe ivangeli*"—let the gospel go. I kept singing it. I would go in to prayer. I was wondering what was happening. That same day a boy was sent from [the mission station at] Wanezi to say, "If you think you can do it, please go to Emaguswini." Then my father said, "No, people are dying of malaria. You are now going there to die." I left that same week on a Sunday. "If I die, it doesn't matter," I said to my father. Gokwe was my first destination. We were following some who had been removed from Shamba, who had been church people in Filabusi but they were not worshipping.[57]

Her father did not want her to go so far from home where the conditions were understood to be dangerous and unhealthy. Yet again, MaTshuma, now a mature woman of middle age, said no to her father. If she indeed did have a child in 1960, it suggests that at the time of her response to the call to go out preaching in distant Matabeleland North, she had a school-age child attending the BICC village school at Mbaulo. Given the size of the Tshuma family (MaTshuma had fifty-one siblings, some of which can be assumed to have lived nearby), it seems she trusted the daily care of her daughter to the extended family.

Her acceptance of the call marked the beginning of MaTshuma's extensive career as an evangelist and church planter for the BICC in Matabeleland North. MaTshuma and another woman, a BICC pastor named NakaGininda, paired up in 1969 to make an evangelistic tour of the Gwaai region of Matabeleland North.[58] Doris

Dube's profile of Maria Tshuma's work for the church, based on her own interviews with MaTshuma and others who knew her, highlights an instance in which she miraculously channeled God's protective power. MaTshuma and NakaGininda were walking through remote footpaths in the Gwaai region one day, singing hymns as they walked, when MaTshuma found herself involuntarily stopped. She remained strangely rooted for some minutes. NakaGininda fussed, was concerned, and asked if she needed to rest. "Suddenly, as if freed from captivity, MaTshuma could move her feet and continue walking." The women later encountered a herd boy who said he had seen that a pride of lions had passed very near the women and seemed not to be able to see them. Dube's account of MaTshuma also mentioned her power over demons and evil spirits.[59] Rather than highlight the ways that MaTshuma's life choices did not reflect the monogamously married mother-at-home model of womanhood promoted by the mission church, Doris Dube framed MaTshuma's path as a sacrificial one: "She is the woman who has forsaken marriage and the comforts of a stable home life to track through life telling other people about God and the way of salvation."[60] My own interviews with MaTshuma did not hint at any time when she had the opportunity for marriage and a settled life, except when she refused to become a plural wife of Mguni, when she was a young girl. The important, exemplary aspect about Maria Tshuma that brought her so much approbation from the missionaries who knew her and the African members of the church was not the details of her domestic life but rather the exceptional quality of her piety.

MaTshuma's method of evangelism combined her ability to work with her own widely disbursed and sizable kinship network together with her tenacity in wanting to awaken a vibrant faith in others. She looked for kinship connections in areas she entered, intent on starting a new church. She counted on their hospitality.[61] One missionary characterized MaTshuma's method: "And she would go and stay with this person and that person, and culturally, they had to take care of her. And she would just stir up these people, men and women, to their lackadaisical spiritual standing and they would listen to her."[62] The respect accorded her superseded gender. She may have been an impoverished single woman, but she was also a grandmother, and she was rich in family and rich in family support.

A missionary who worked with Maria Tshuma to build the BICC congregation in Hwange in the early 1980s characterized her style of leadership in the young congregations she had nurtured into being: "She was leading. And then she would get the others involved. She knew, I think she knew when to step back and let the local men do it."[63] MaTshuma provided the organizing energy and the door-to-door visits to find former BICC-affiliated people living in the area, to summon them to worship, while moving quickly to put a man in the front of the church officially to lead the services, providing feedback privately after the service. This is similar to the style of leadership exercised by another woman, Majerimane Khumalo (MaSithole). MaSithole pastored a BICC congregation at the Sitezi church for several decades beginning in the 1950s. When asked how she, as a woman, was able to win and maintain the support of the men in the congregation, she attributed her success to her ascribed position as the daughter of a chief, as well as to the spiritual power she was known to exercise with her effective prayers. "Furthermore, I have always continued to give men their leadership roles as heads even though I am their leader."[64]

MaTshuma went on to plant churches in areas previously untouched by BICC outreach, in Salisbury (now Harare), Gwanda town, Hwange (formerly Wankie), and Binga, along the Zambezi. By the end of her decades as an evangelist for the BICC (1960s–1990s), she was credited with establishing at least nineteen different congregations throughout Rhodesia (later Zimbabwe).

MaTshuma's evangelistic work in the 1970s was marked by the dangers and population shifts engendered by the liberation war. As the rural guerrilla war heightened, people came to live in Bulawayo in large numbers, including people from the BICC areas of Filabusi, Gwaai, Lupane, and Gwanda. As they arrived

Figure 2.1. Maria Tshuma, ca. 1975. Photo credit: George Bundy

in town, the church reached out to them with door-to-door visits offering prayer and affiliation with newly burgeoning urban-based congregations. Maria Tshuma was in the heart of these efforts and has been credited with being an essential cofounder of the BICC's largest congregation, in Lobengula Township. The BICC during the liberation war is discussed in greater depth in chapter 5. During the 1980s, the first postcolonial decade when Rhodesia had now become Zimbabwe, the violence of the ZANU-PF government's Fifth Brigade against the people of Matabeleland did not stop MaTshuma's work in the far north, along the Zambian border.

———————

In a history of life strategies taken by women slaves in central Africa at the turn of the twentieth century, Marcia Wright emphasized that "successive political environments shaped her options, as did changing socioeconomic conditions, but in interpreting her story we must take special care also to consider age-specific aspects of status within the female life cycle of preadolescence, fertility, and postfertility."[65] It is similarly valuable to analyze Maria Tshuma's life history—and cycles of piety—in terms both of the options available to her as determined by the wider conditions of the colonial and postcolonial state as well as those shaped by where she was in her own female life cycle.

Maria Tshuma was a girl who ran away from the man her father intended for her to marry in the early 1930s—a time when the colonial state was new but beginning to be well established, and at a time when the presence of Christian mission stations as sites of refuge for girls refusing plural, arranged marriages was beginning to be well known in the rural areas. She was intombi—a young woman who had reached sexual maturity but was yet unmarried. As such, she was junior to her father and her older (married) sister; refusing the union led to expulsion from her home. She was also junior to the local evangelist's wife, who judged that having been at the man's homestead at all, MaTshuma's purity was indeed compromised. Already her purity was in question from the point of view of African churchwomen: had she had sexual contact with the man? Based on that concern, MaNzima felt free to exercise significant influence over her by denying Maria's baptism bid. Maria went to the mission boarding school, where teachings about sexual purity saturated the air. She worked as a lower-primary teacher in her home region until her second pregnancy caused her to lose her teaching position. By the time she lost her teaching job, in 1960, the Rhodesian state had been supporting the creation of an African middle class and allowing for higher levels of credentialing for positions such as schoolteachers.[66] Maria Tshuma's standard 5 (grade 7) education was no longer considered sufficient preparation for the work of a primary school teacher. She became an unpaid subleader in the service of Hannah Sibanda. Hannah was a high-status woman; she used her position to help MaTshuma find a place after the birth of her second child caused her to lose her teaching job.

This back and forth with her own fertility, her lack of a husband, and her reclaimed piety did not dint Maria Tshuma's career as a traveling evangelist. Her first wave of itinerant preaching occurred before her second child was out of school. As she aged, and became postmenopausal, child-rearing duties over, she devoted herself full-time to itinerant evangelism from the 1970s through the 1980s.

Unlike Asante women of West Africa, who Ivor Wilks and Stephan Miescher have argued could achieve a kind of "female masculinity" in their postmenopausal years,[67] Maria Tshuma did not so much attain a status as "female masculine" so much as successfully negotiate her female status as postmenopausal "granny," or Gogo, within her kin networks as a means for carrying out her evangelistic calling. Miescher also writes about senior women in Akan society who exercised their senior status differently than men—Miescher's observations have parallels with MaTshuma's mode of leadership:

> Although both men and women may become elders in
> Akan societies, they are expected to act differently. . . . Her
> input should be less public than that of her male colleagues.
> She should use her influence behind the scenes, playing the
> *aberewa* (old woman) who is consulted. [Historian] Arhin
> Brempon (2000), writ[es] about the *ohemaa* (queen mother),
> the most senior female chief, who is . . . the "moral guardian
> of the females of the political community and a kind of

moral censor: she examined adolescent girls before the main puberty rites which ushered them into adulthood and licensed their marriage" (106).[68]

Maria Tshuma's relationship with Manhlenhle's wife, MaNzima, is like this *ohemaa* who is the guardian of the females—due to MaTshuma's uncertain marital and therefore sexual history, Manhlenhle's wife was her moral censor—barring her from baptism, advising her, showing her what path to take (go to the mission). We see this generational dynamic among the girls of the gate.

Maria Tshuma's leadership in her later years was that of an elder grandmother. By the time she was exercising that leadership, it was largely below the radar of official channels for such a role, both according to the mission church and the colonial structure. But the resilience of a cultural idiom of a certain female leader during her elderhood persisted nonetheless. And the mission church had a loophole—one that allowed such a thing to carry on in spite of the male headship's emphasis of the mission church. The loophole was evangelism. Anyone who could add to the church's numbers, who could plant a new church, who could make a church grow— that person was appreciated no matter their sociological category. A pietistic organization in which acquiring, developing, and spreading faith was the highest value, gave space for an unmarried grandmother to exercise the kind of faith-based leadership that she did. She was not going to earn official money or garner official titles—but she could go ahead and do the work and gain many expressions of praise for the same and, as seen in the work of Doris Dube and the oral testimony of many who knew her, earn an informal reputation as a saint. MaTshuma's exceptionally devoted work in the later decades of her life as a door-to-door evangelist and grassroots church planter was the essential element in her construction of an identity as a holy woman who lived somehow beyond normal categories of gender role and female respectability.

THREE || NakaSeyemephi Ngwenya
A Church Planter eMaguswini, 1950–73

I've always wanted to write a history but who
would care.

—*Mrs. Moyo, Bulawayo, 1999*

A HANDWRITTEN POSTSCRIPT TO A LENGTHY,
typed 1963 letter read, "My mother is still living. She is miles
away and is a leader of a little church group in the remote areas
of eMaguswini across the Shangani River."[1] The author of the letter was raised from her infancy at Mtshabezi Mission School, and
she was writing to her former mentor, retired missionary Walter O.
Winger. At the time of writing she lived in Salisbury (present-day
Harare) with her barrister husband and several children. Almost
four decades later in an interview with me, she was very keen to
tell all about her mother's work to build a church eMaguswini
(locative form meaning "in the place of forests"). Her mother was
NakaSeyemephi (Sinini) Ngwenya. Because I had never met her,
my introduction to NakaSeyemephi Ngwenya came through the
words of those who held her in high esteem. Due to the means by
which I uncovered this woman's story, this chapter is by necessity
as much about NakaSeyemephi's daughters and granddaughter as
it is about NakaSeyemephi herself. It was not until I interviewed

her granddaughter MaGwebu (Orlean Dlodlo), in 1999, that I first learned of her existence. MaGwebu was very proud to tell about her grandmother, who had been a woman pastor in Matabeleland North. By this time in my research, I realized that there were all kinds of stories of women pastors, pastors' wives, and female evangelists hidden in people's family histories. Here was another woman's leadership for the church held in memory outside of official church records. NakaSeyemephi died in the mid-1970s, long before I came to do research in Zimbabwe. Her story is that of a woman whose life is scarcely visible in the written records of the official church, who nonetheless founded a congregation and became a pastor.

NakaSeyemephi was one of a significant group of women who became the first generation of women anywhere in the global history of the BICC to serve as congregational pastors. It happened in response to a forced migration started in the late 1940s, instigated by the Rhodesian state. Africans who were living on ancestral lands in Matabeleland South, in that region's more favorable climate, enjoying access to markets in Bulawayo as well as a well-developed network of mission schools, were forcibly removed under the terms of the 1930 Land Apportionment Act, which had sat largely unenforced until that time. Due to the remoteness and undesirability of the new lands to which people were removed, in congregations far from the eyes of both white and black male church leaders, women were able to establish themselves as leaders of new BICC.

When looking back at the 1950s and 1960s, in an effort to explain why women became pastors in Matabeleland North, Rev. Raphael Mthombeni made an explicit link between the harshness of the forced removals and the dearth of men in church leadership up north. Mthombeni was acquainted with many of the long-time church leaders there, both men and women, and gave an assessment of how women became church leaders. As the former BICC overseer in Matabeleland North, he used Gwaai, the name of one northern district, as shorthand for the whole region:

> Yes, the first leadership of women was from the Gwaai.
> Simply because in the southern part of the country where

the church was planted, in Matopo, Mtshabezi, and Wanezi mainly the leadership were men. . . . They were forced to be moved by the white government, to be settled out there in the Gwaai, which was tsetse infested and there were animals and there were no roads and schools out there and they were just dumped out there. As a result, there was tension between men, who were regarded as the head of the family—between the head of the family and the white person.[2]

Mthombeni further explained that people conflated the white missionaries with the white government, so that when the BICC mission tried to encourage men to assume leadership of the nascent congregations forming in the north, "men didn't take up the leadership because the missionary was a white man who was following them up there—just mixed the missionary with the government. And as a result men didn't take up the leadership and women were then incorporated into the leadership."[3]

This chapter, using the story of NakaSeyemephi as the focal point, highlights the flowering of women-led congregations in Matabeleland North in the 1950s and after. Nascent BICC groups emerged in the Gwaai and Lupane areas of Matabeleland North. The Lupane area was in the northern half of the Shangani Reserve, near the Mzola River. Ndebele speakers knew it as eMaguswini—the place of forests, or *gusu* trees. In spite of, or perhaps because of, its remoteness and its notoriously poor soil, Lupane proved to be a rich ground for generating female pastors. Women pastored seven of the ten new BICC congregations in Lupane by the mid-1960s. NakaSeyemephi's story helps us see that the phenomenon of women-led congregations cannot be understood separately from the church's response to the forced removals, the dynamic of piety in the church, the colonial political economy, and the nature of the nationalist liberation movement as it took shape in Southern Rhodesia during the 1950s and 1960s.

Up to 1950 the church remained entirely within its original base of operations in Matabeleland South with influence radiating out from the three mission stations at Matopo, Mtshabezi, and Wanezi. The Rhodesian government oversaw large-scale evictions of Africans from Matabeleland South in the years following the Second World War and forced them to resettle in Matabeleland North. African-initiated evangelism and church planting among the new arrivals in Matabeleland North goaded the mission leaders into following their displaced members with institutional and financial support. The harshness of the removals exacerbated gendered patterns of church affiliation already at play in the south. Grassroots congregations in Matabeleland North were largely gathered and led by resettled BICC women. For their part, the men in these resettled families continued to claim a "Christian" and progressive identity but generally avoided involvement with church work, favoring instead to engage in nationalist politics.

Conversations with men and women about the church's experience of these forced moves followed a gendered pattern. Women tended to mention men's spiritual failings, defined in terms of their fondness for beer or penchant for taking second wives, while men more generally emphasized that men were drawn to the emergent nationalist political movements. Mthombeni's remarks at the beginning of the chapter resonate with those of the other male informants: he also explained that men's distancing from church leadership at that time was due to their anger at the colonial government. Both sexes suggested that essential differences between men and women explained why women were more likely to be faithful church members. As one male pastor or deacon from the Gwaai said in 1999, "Men do not understand as women do. They hardly understand. They hardly repent. Women usually trust, they put their trust wherever they want to put it. It is not easy for women to go back. A man can go to and fro."[4] Along the same lines, when asked why men were not in church as much as women, a woman pastor from the Gwaai in 1999 suggested that men just had not yet been "called" by God, that "maybe all these men and boys are worldly influenced; they like beer." Another woman stated, "Men are always a bit different from women. There are always more women than men [in church]. Men are difficult to convince; they are not like women anyway."[5] This thought is echoed by the aphorism that the *nyembezi zendoda* (the tears of men) must never show on the outside.[6] When asked about the responsiveness of men and women on her evangelistic tours of Matabeleland North in the late 1960s, Maria Tshuma observed that men would actually refuse to have prayers. Offered prayers, the men in a village responded with "no, we are finished with that. That's for women, it's not for us."[7]

The orally transmitted memories routinely associating men with their involvement in protests against the colonial government is borne out in the membership numbers of one protonationalist group that devoted energy to protesting the forced moves to the north. The African Workers' Voice Association, involved in organizing for a major strike in Bulawayo in 1948, turned its attention afterward to advocating for the grievances of rural people. In 1948 the African Voice Association had approximately three thousand members, mostly resident in Bulawayo, and by 1952 there were ten thousand *male* adult members, "nearly all of them resident in the rural areas."[8] Women protested, for their part, but it was a kind of protest not logged in membership records, newspapers, or government documents; rather, multiple interviews suggest their refusals, and forms of noncooperation were frequently directed within households and communities. The women pastors eMaguswini did not act in the nationalist political arena, but rather advocated for themselves vis-à-vis the men in their families, whether fathers, husbands, or other male relatives. A more inclusive sense of what constitutes protest—beyond the paradigm permitted by nationalist history—may give us a better sense of how women and men exercised agency in the political, cultural, and social arenas of the time. Although aware of colonial oppression, family-based limits were more present to women, and the church—sometimes in spite of itself—offered some women more scope to effect change in their lives than they could in nationalist political parties such as the National Democratic Party (NDP) and its later incarnation, the Zimbabwe African People's Union (ZAPU).

After the Second World War, white men who had served in the British armed forces received land in the colonies, including Southern Rhodesia, as a reward for their service to the British Empire. The land that in the 1930 Land Apportionment Act had been designated for white occupation was now, some *twenty years later,* to be distributed. White war veterans received rewards from the Rhodesian government from the so-called Crown Lands,[9] particularly in the Filabusi area, southeast of Bulawayo. The fact that many blacks of Southern Rhodesia had also served in the war was ignored.[10]

Removals began in earnest in the late 1940s and then were temporarily halted by protest actions by the African Voice Association. Yet, in 1952 the Southern Rhodesian government's crackdown on the African Voice Association and redrafting of the Land Apportionment Act opened the way for forced evacuations of Africans to begin again. Of 1,995 families (approximately ten thousand persons) removed from prime areas of central and southern Matabeleland in 1951, for example, 995 of the families were from the BICC areas of Matopo and Insiza (including Filabusi) Districts.[11] People were forced to leave their homes and remove to Matabeleland North, especially in Gwaai and Lupane Districts.

At first, the church leadership did not make any official response to the situation of their members now living in a remote place far from church, schools, and roads. Support for the status quo was central to the BICC's unworldly stance, a condition exacerbated by the church's institutional and financial binding to the colonial state. Over five decades of growth, between 1898 and the early 1950s, the BICC had settled into its rural domain in Matabeleland South. The three BICC mission stations with their attendant boarding schools and the hospital at Mtshabezi used the efforts of twenty-nine North American missionaries and 125 African teachers and evangelists. There were some twenty-one hundred baptized members and nearly the same number of aspirant members, known as Enquirers, thus totaling over four thousand Africans closely linked to the BICC.[12]

Memories shared by African church members indicate their belief that the mission church's leadership did nothing to protest the removals at the time.[13] The areas of Matabeleland North that received earliest institutional attention, in the form of paid evangelists and eventually the erection of dual-purpose school-church buildings, were those closest to Bulawayo, in Gwaai District. The northernmost area, Lupane, or eMaguswini, remained "untamed" or "undomesticated" the longest. Lupane congregations did not have built churches in which to worship until the 1970s. The "untamed" Lupane area is where women pastors emerged in the highest numbers. When interviewed by historian Eliakim Sibanda, former missionary bishop Arthur Climenhaga indicated, however, that he wrote directly to the government on behalf of African BICC members being uprooted from Wanezi and Matobo Districts.[14] In any case, the church did not engage in a high-profile course of protest on behalf of its membership.

Once the scale of the removals was understood, the mission leadership focused on understanding this evangelistically: as an opportunity to extend the reach of the Gospel into the "Regions Beyond." The 1954 General Conference theme for the African BICC, two years after the forced removals had begun in earnest, was "Malihambe iVangele emazweni onke" (May the Gospel go to all regions). This theme reflects the largely pietistic tenor of the church's response. The emphasis was on the Regions Beyond, with special reference to the Gwaai and Lupane areas northwest and west of Bulawayo, "where so many of our people have been moved in the last few years. A missionary spirit was manifest when several older men stood in consecration to whatever call God laid upon them and the church gave an offering of £28 for missionary purposes in the new areas, the largest on record for a conference."[15] Key phrases in this passage are "missionary spirit" and "missionary purposes." The missionary writer of this report was very happy to see the African membership taking on the work of going to the relocated people and preaching to them. In another report written a year later, in 1955, the missionary editor of the

Evangelical Visitor expressed the idea that relocating Africans by force into Matabeleland North was giving the African membership an opportunity to be missionaries themselves: "The shifting of people [by the Government] certainly has changed many communities. We hope that the Christian families will be lights for Christ. We can hope also that what was said of the early Christian Church at the time when they were persecuted in Jerusalem will be said of the African Church: 'they went everywhere preaching the Gospel.'"[16] The situation would give African Christians an opportunity to imitate their biblical heroes. Given Mthombeni's emphasis on the wildness of the area, and its isolation from the benefits of economic development enjoyed in the south, one might consider that these generous donations to the church's evangelistic campaign might also have been intended to help the building of schools and roads.

The missionaries who in the mid-1950s visited Gwaai, the closer of the two districts to which people had been forced to move, tried to put a positive cast to the change in their writings addressed to the North American membership. The *Evangelical Visitor* contained a steady stream of reports on the situation of the relocated members of the church. While acknowledging the disruptive impact of being forced to move, the accounts generally highlight not only the evangelistic opportunities afforded by the relocations, but also comment favorably on the rational, planned nature of the new settlements. The following report, written in 1954, is typical:

> The country is well developed in comparison to the older reserves. The roads are well laid out—not just where a cow path was; the village locations are well planned; and since there are no rivers close, there are wells, dug by government. The villages are grouped together in "lines" each line having its number. Then there are a number of "lines" located around each well. I understand no natives are allowed to move in of their own choice, but only those who have been forced by government to leave their old

homes. We were happy to find that the people were quite content and satisfied. There are Bushmen near, and we had the chance to visit them and preach to them. During the rains, elephant, lions and other wild animals come up from the river areas and are a nuisance. I brought home the jaw of an elephant which was shot last rainy season. It was of great interest to our more "civilized" people here.[17]

The writer of this account, ordained missionary and schools inspector Alvin Book, rejoiced in the straightness of the roads, in the foresight of the government in digging wells for the people's use, the placing of dwellings in "lines." In utter contrast to the testimonies of every forcibly relocated African interviewed for this study or cited in others such as *Violence and Memory*,[18] Book indicated that the people were "quite happy and satisfied." Book's perspective is colored by his upbringing in California, where streets were laid out on a grid and the idea of fresh, open space was appealing. Also, the Africans welcoming him, his wife, and the other missionary couple upon their arrival were not likely to share their grievances with the white visitors. Rules of hospitality alone would have required a joyful welcome; in addition, the African membership had thoroughly internalized the need for silence around political topics when in the company of missionaries. The mention of the wild beasts and curiosity of the "more civilized" African membership of the south reflects both how long it had been since wild beasts roamed freely in the more settled southern province and the tone of wildness that both Africans and missionaries associated with the north.

The growth of the BICC in the north depended on both the work of evangelists from the south and the new arrivals seeking to reestablish familiar Christian patterns in their new situation.[19] These two processes were simultaneous: campaigns of evangelism conducted by Africans from the south and church-planting activities led by the relocated people. Sandey Vundhla in particular was crucial to the opening of the first BICC schools in Matabeleland North. He was one of the better documented and celebrated of the (male) evangelists of the 1950s with homes still in the south who ventured into the north to preach. Much later, in the 1960s, two women, NakaGininda Ndlovu and Maria Tshuma, took up a portion of the evangelistic burden for BICC evangelism in Matabeleland North.[20] In the meantime, tiny new BICC congregations began to form not long after their arrival in the north, due to the initiative of displaced (mostly female) church members wishing to reestablish regular worship in their new situation.

As a man regarded by the white missionaries as the exemplary evangelist to Matabeleland North, and about whom much was written, it is worth detailing some of Sandey Vundhla's achievements and the manner in which they were depicted. He traveled from his home, near Matopo Mission, in Matabeleland South, to visit relocated BICC people living in the Gwaai District of Matabeleland North. The missionary in charge of overseeing the "Bulawayo outstations," which included the nascent congregations north of Bulawayo, wrote of Vundhla in 1954, "Others of our people have been moved to Gwaai District, which is about 140 miles west of Bulawayo. This seems to be a better area and more people have been moved there. Evangelist Sandi Vundhla has given a number of months there, holding meetings, meeting with the people, also working with them."[21] With skill as a builder, Vundhla worked on the construction of the first BICC School in Matabeleland North. The Khumbula School opened in the Gwaai in 1954, celebrated by a festive occasion attended by Vundhla and two white missionary couples, including Alvin Book and his wife. Book wrote,

> [We] took a trip up into the Gwaai Reserve, about
> 150 miles north of Bulawayo. We were happy to reach
> Kumbula, the first Brethren in Christ school to be
> completed in the Gwaai. And what a lovely school it is!
> Few outschools in our established circuits surpass it. The
> people were glad to see us and what a thrill it was for
> us to dedicate the first church-school and attend the first
> baptism-communion service in this new area to which a
> number of our people were moved from Matopo a year

ago. So we have a nucleus of members there. We have three schools completed or near completion which Brother Mann hopes to open with the new year. (Evangelist Vundla has been busy helping to build the schools. His wife Daisy faithfully and uncomplainingly carries on at home.)[22]

Vundhla's many long journeys north to preach to and visit with recently arrived BICC members went a long way toward bringing the mission authorities around to support of the church's institutional extension into the Gwaai. Vundhla's strong commitment to the area was staunchly supported by the confidence and financial and institutional follow-through of Bishop Arthur Climenhaga.[23]

The BICC opened a mission station in Matabeleland North in 1959, to the west of the Shangani Reserve in the Gwaai Reserve. The new mission station was to serve as the administrative center for a new church district serving all of Matabeleland North, located in Gwaai District. It included the Gwaai, Lupane, and Nkayi areas. The station was named Phumula ("rest").[24] School superintendents came to visit the newly dedicated schools as they were built, one by one, and missionary and African ordained ministers (overseers) also came to conduct the baptism of new members and officiate at the annual Lord's Supper, or communion service.

Both male and female African members of the church in many ways demonstrated initiative and commitment in reaching out to their "Brethren" in the north.[25] The mission reports had lamented, from the 1910s on, the lackluster levels of financial support given to the church by its African membership.[26] Thus it was quite noticeable to the missionary leadership when the 1954 General Conference (the annual all-church gathering) yielded a record offering from the African membership. This level of offering, in combination with the work of high-profile evangelist Vundhla and the many shorter-term efforts of others based in the south, conveyed a clear message to the missionary leadership that African church members of the south were committed to remaining in fellowship with their relatives and associates who had been removed to the north and northwest.

Men's increasing alienation from the church and women's simultaneous assumption of church leadership roles are both linked to the trauma of displacement into Matabeleland North's hostile environment. Simply stating that "men hardly repent" does not do justice to the interconnectedness of the two phenomena. Nor does assuming that women are more ready to trust than men adequately explain women's new church roles. The stresses incurred by being forced into the remote periphery of the colonial economic infrastructure led both men and women into new places, and in fact served to prefigure dynamics of change that accelerated and deepened in the liberation war of the 1970s and the immediate postcolonial decade.

Men's and women's responses were rational adaptations to their linked but different situations in Matabeleland North. Both men and women suffered from the evictions and knew to level their blame against the Rhodesian state. Men who hitherto had seen church affiliation and church-funded teaching positions as markers of their modernity, and a means to recouping lost precolonial status in the Rhodesian setting, bitterly discovered the limits of playing the "mission boy" game.

In contrast, rurally based, church-affiliated women's interactions with the sharpest edges of racist colonial rule were blunted in comparison to their lives in male-dominated rural homes far from colonial urban settings and mining compounds. I am referring here to a specific subset of women whose lives were centered on the church and "traditional" Ndebele homestead life. There were plenty of women in Matabeleland and Zimbabwe as a whole who, for various reasons, were not in this situation. Also, as mentioned in chapter 2, a good number of mission-schooled girls ended up working in town or next to the mines.[27] Women were generally denied access to real property ownership and status under both the colonial government and in the church and were not as likely as men to see the church as a worthy target for their dissatisfaction over the forced removals.

Far from the reach of their "home" mission stations in the south, resettled Christians of all denominations, including the

BICC, "largely had to rely upon themselves as Christian pioneers rather than on the patronage of a mission station . . . in most cases, the evictees had to bring their Christianity in with them."[28] Women became these Christian pioneers. Women who had been committed Christians in the south but denied the opportunity to exercise leadership now could do so far from the eyes of the official church and unhindered for the most part by men wishing to take the lead.[29] The first women to head congregations came from this subset of deeply committed churchwomen raised or schooled (or both) in the church in the south.

The women who started these remote BICC congregations were less mobile than the men in their families, since men had greater opportunities to leave the area in search of labor. As women throughout southern Africa had been doing for almost a century already, when the men in their families went away as migrant laborers, women took up a larger part of the work of social reproduction. The women pastors were also more tied to the area than the itinerant evangelists who passed through from the established areas of the south and eventually went home again. The same is true of those BICC teachers trained at the mission stations of the south who took "frontier" postings in Matabeleland North but could then leave for more promising positions in the south or in Bulawayo. People such as NakaSeyemephi Ngwenya lived, remained, and died in their new homes in Matabeleland North; they experienced its environment more deeply, harshly, and permanently than these other, more well-documented heroes from the southern church.

Sinini (NakaSeyemephi) Ngwenya: Piecing together the Story

NakaSeyemephi's granddaughter MaGwebu mentioned her church-planting grandmother in an interview, prompting me then to pursue MaGWebu's mother and aunt for more insights. NakaSeyemephi's firstborn daughter, NakaOrlean, lived in Gwakwe, a rural area south of Bulawayo. NakaSeyemephi's younger daughter, Mrs. Moyo, lived in a prosperous suburb of Bulawayo and was a highly educated, upper-middle-class woman.

What follows in this section, then, is a piecing together of the life of NakaSeyemephi as told to me by her daughters and granddaughter. Based on the cues they gave me, I found further scraps of documentary evidence in the archives at the church office in Bulawayo that supported aspects of what they had narrated. Other than seeing her name listed in the pastoral rolls for Gwaai District,[30] and mentioned in passing by a missionary who wrote an account of the life of her second daughter,[31] however, NakaSeyemephi was not visible anywhere else in the church documents.

The resulting narrative, a composite of archival research and the oral interviews, teaches us almost as much about her three female descendants as it does about NakaSeyemephi herself. It is a reiterative dialogue about the content of her biography. By *reiterative dialogue,* I mean that I carried points made to me by MaGwebu back to her aunt and her mother when I interviewed them, to see how Mrs. Moyo or NakaOrlean might extend, ignore, or contradict. This approach helped me understand, for example, how important it was to NakaSeyemephi that she have a proper church building when all three of her female descendants made much of the fact that this church never came to be built before NakaSeyemephi passed away. Her respective generation, gender, and the social and spatial realities shaped the testimony of each informant. For example, NakaOrlean (Seyemephi) had lived the longest in her mother's marital home in contrast to her younger sister; she knew more about that setting than either her sister or her daughter. Mrs. Moyo, the second daughter, had a strong relationship with the leadership elites of the church, and had more information and understanding of the ways the institutional church related to her mother's congregation than did her older sister, NakaOrlean. MaGwebu was generationally furthest removed from her grandmother in contrast to her own mother and aunt, and thus her testimony was much less detailed.

Mrs. Moyo, the younger daughter, was married to a prominent barrister, also a son of the BICC from the Gwatemba area. They had lived in the UK and made visits to the United States; her children had British educations. The home I visited in Bulawayo on the day I interviewed her was a large house on a beautiful property in the former "white suburbs." We sat in an elegantly furnished lounge (living room or parlor) and were served tea. Her husband came out and greeted me warmly before we began our interview. She did not want to have the tape recorder, so I took notes. We spoke in English; her use of English was fluent and confident. As I did with all informants, I sent her the transcript of my notes; unlike most others, she pored over it and edited carefully. She struck out parts that she did not want me to use and selected the option to have her material cited under a pseudonym. She was a sophisticated woman with an eye for the legalities of the process. Nonetheless, she seemed keen for the opportunity to tell her stories about her mother.

My interview with Mrs. Moyo's older sister, Seyemephi Gwebu, known as NakaOrlean, took place six weeks later under very different circumstances. It began first with a drive to Mtshabezi Mission, south of Bulawayo, where we added Mrs. Nellie Mlotshwa to our party. Mrs. Mlotshwa was teaching at the Ekuphileni Bible Institute at that time and lived in faculty housing provided by the mission. We drove from there to Gwakwe, the small village where NakaOrlean lived. NakaOrlean's homestead had a fence around the main cluster of dwellings, which included separate structures for cooking, sleeping, and hosting guests. There was a chicken house and a grain storage place. There were several people at the homestead that day, including various relatives. Mrs. Mlotshwa and I were taken to the structure containing the "lounge" furniture: sofas, chairs, and coffee table. NakaOrlean was very glad to see Mrs. Mlotshwa; they spent some time speaking together in Ndebele, with greetings and exchanging of news about their families. NakaOrlean had lost two sons and was herself unwell. They had been wishing to see each other for some time. Mrs. Mlotshwa counted it a blessing that I wanted to go to Gwakwe to see NakaOrlean; by accompanying me and helping with the interview, she was able to make this condolence visit.[32] After sharing their

Figure 3.1. Seyemephi Gwebu (NakaOrlean), 1999. *Photo credit: Russell Urban-Mead*

own news, they included me in this conversation, and NakaOrlean asked about my family and how long I had been in Bulawayo. She agreed to let us use the tape recorder. After the interview, Mrs. Mlotshwa listened to the tape and handwrote a transcript of the interview.[33] What follows is an account of the life of Sinini Ngwenya, later known as NakaSeyemephi.

Sinini (NakaSeyemephi) Ngwenya

Sinini Ngwenya was born in the hills near Esigodini, in Matabeleland South. When she was a girl, her family moved east, to a small place called Gwatemba. The people of Gwatemba were under the authority of Chief Mafu, whose family had ruled in this area since the 1830s.[34] People married strictly within their own social stratum. The ruling group, or abezansi, could trace their family heritage all the way to the kingdom's origins in KwaZulu, South Africa. When the Ndebele established their own kingdom further north, during the 1820s, they conquered and incorporated many local Sotho speakers.[35] The second social tier was known as the *abenhla*. Sinini's family name of Ngwenya placed her in the second of the three tiers of Ndebele society. As Mrs. Moyo, put it, "you were supposed to strictly stay within the abenhla clan. We knew our groups very well. It was part of daily talk."[36] Thus Sinini Ngwenya was married—as arranged by her father—to another member of the abenhla, Tshenke Mguni. Each of Mguni's three wives came from abenhla families.[37]

Unfortunately we do not have access to much information that lets us know how old Sinini was, how willing to be married she was, or what it was like specifically for Sinini to have been married to Mguni.[38] Mrs. Moyo said, "My mom was one of those honest girls who did not rebel against council and custom."[39] This comment, offered without prompting, implies she knew well the stories like Maria Tshuma's (highlighted in chapter 2), of girls who disrupted their families by refusing arranged marriages. As we shall see, Sinini did rebel against council and custom—later— but not at this point. She did not rebel against her father's decision that she marry Mguni. Sinini Ngwenya went to Mguni sometime around 1914. The British South Africa Company's final conquest of the Ndebele Kingdom had occurred just eighteen years before, probably around the time she was born.

To be a third wife was to occupy a lowly place within a family. The female elders at Sinini's own homestead would have sent her off to her husband's homestead with advice on how to behave, urging her not to speak too much, not to destroy her husband's family's home, to follow the ways at their homestead.[40] As practiced by Ndebele speakers in rural areas of Matabeleland in the early decades of the twentieth century, as third wife Sinini Ngwenya would enter her husband's homestead lower in status than each of her two cowives, and lower than her husband's mother and sisters. Sinini would be expected to defer to all of these higher-ranked females. There were specific modes of address and postures of humility she was expected to observe. She was forbidden to speak the name of her father-in-law, if he lived there, too. It was the job of a daughter-in-law to haul water and sweep the homestead, and to serve her mother-in-law in any way asked. Brides were warned to be careful of the mother-in-law, to be "careful of enemies."[41] If the mother-in-law were alive and active, a bride would cook with her mother-in-law, at her fireplace, until the mother-in-law decided the younger woman was ready to have her own fireplace.[42] Like any other wife, if Sinini failed to bear children she could be returned in shame to her father's family. Her husband's family could rightfully demand return of any of the lobola (bridewealth) they might have paid so far. Or, her family could send a younger sister to bear children on behalf of the barren older sister. Sinini's best hope, therefore, was to bear sons. Unless by some series of unlikely events the two wives ahead of her proved barren or bore only girls, no matter what she did she could not become the revered mother of her husband's firstborn son.

Sinini's first child, born in 1915, was a girl named Seyemephi, and from then on Sinini was called mother of Seyemephi or NakaSeyemephi.[43] Seyemephi means something like "what are we leaning against?" When I asked Seyemephi if her mother ever told her a story about how she got that name, the answer was no.[44] NakaSeyemephi bore three daughters; the first- and last-born lived. The surviving daughters were Seyemephi and Ntombiyelanga, "girl of the sun," who was born in the drought year of 1922.

Mguni's homestead in Gwatemba was near the site of a village church of the Brethren in Christ also called Gwatemba. According to NakaOrlean, who unlike her younger sister remembered the household in Gwatemba well, all the adults except her mother—the two older cowives and her father—"were drinking" (babenatha). To say that someone "was drinking" or "was from beer" was a way of saying that he or she was not a churchgoer, reflecting the church's ban on all forms of alcoholic beverages. NakaSeyemephi was the only one in Mguni's household who attended church. NakaSeyemephi went to church with her mother's younger sister and her daughter. But it was more than beer drinking that kept Mguni away from church. As a polygynist, he would have been expected to "put away" all but his first wife were he to seek baptism and church membership. In such an instance, second or third wives would have to be sent back to their father's home. There was a lot of discussion within the African membership in those years over what a polygynous man who wanted to convert should do with his wives. Could such a man convert at all? From the point of view of the missionaries, a man who retained multiple wives was an adulterer. From the point of view of the Ndebele sensibility, to ask a man to send away his wives was a shocking expectation; to do so would have violated spiritual, economic, and human contracts.[45] Few polygynous men agreed to convert; it was most common for older men with multiple wives, if they were interested in the church and its schools at all, to send their sons to the mission.[46]

There was also a village school at the Gwatemba church, but NakaSeyemephi could not attend school. Her daughter, Mrs. Moyo, told me that NakaSeyemephi had too many duties around the homestead to go to school. Mrs. Moyo was an infant when she left that homestead, however, and could not have her own memories of this; it is quite probably how her mother told it to her. Mrs. Moyo stated that her mother "used to get through her work in a hurry, get it done, so they could go to church without getting in trouble." Mrs. Moyo noted that NakaSeyemephi was in fact fortunate that her husband did not forbid her attendance at church.[47] NakaSeyemephi attended services at Gwatemba Brethren in Christ Church and was baptized by missionary H. P. Steigerwald in 1918.[48] Given the requisite two years of prebaptismal instruction, NakaSeyemephi had to have been in regular attendance at least since 1916.

Shortly after the birth of her second child, Ntombiyelanga, NakaSeyemephi's husband, Mguni, died. At the time of Mguni's death, NakaSeyemephi was a committed Christian and now adrift in her status as most junior widow. She did not know where to go. She would have been expected to stay in her husband's homestead and marry one of his close surviving male relatives. As the wedding advice stated, "your husband's brothers are your husbands."[49] Mrs. Moyo remembers that her mother wanted something different for her own daughters. Paraphrasing what she remembered her mother having said: "If my children go out in the country they'll end up in polygamous marriages." Thus, "She bid the people at Gwatemba farewell."[50] Her older daughter put it this way: "That was the time of my father's death when my mother moved back to her people." This indicates that when Mguni died, NakaSeyemephi refused to stay on as the wife of one of her husband's brothers and then went back to her father's homestead for a period of time before moving on to Mtshabezi with the infant Ntombiyelanga.[51]

Due to her exposure to the local BICC African pastor and the yearly visit of the white missionaries for the love feast—or Lord's Supper, the holy communion service—NakaSeyemephi knew there was a BICC girls' boarding school to the west, at Mtshabezi Mission, near Gwanda. She may have known some girls from Gwatemba who had gone off to the boarding school. Precisely what she had seen and heard is not clear, but it is known that NakaSeyemephi decided to relocate to Mtshabezi Mission.[52] Eight-year-old Seyemephi stayed in her father's homestead; she was transferred to the guardianship of her older brother, Magwaza, the son of one of NakaSeyemephi's older cowives.[53] Even though he was her brother, she called him *malume* (uncle). Seyemephi lived at her uncle's, herding cattle, until she was fifteen, in 1930. She was freed to go join her mother and sister at the mission station at this point because Magwaza's child, also a girl, was now old enough to mind the cattle. The testimony of Seyemephi (NakaOrlean) was punctuated here by frequent repeating of the fact that she had to mind the cattle and that she did not go to school much when at Magwaza's. This repetition indicated to me that she felt keenly the limits that cattle tending had placed upon her.

With her infant daughter, having left her elder daughter, Seyemephi, behind, NakaSeyemephi arrived at Mtshabezi Mission, probably around 1923. At that time, Mtshabezi Mission School for "girls" had many grown young women in its student body. Few had already had children, however, so NakaSeyemephi was something of an exception, though she did have age-mates among her fellow pupils. She learned to read. NakaSeyemephi renamed her second daughter (Mrs. Moyo) with a biblical name, one taken from the book of Exodus.[54] It is speculative but tempting to consider why the book of Exodus was NakaSeyemephi's point of inspiration. Did she regard Gwatemba as the land of Egypt—a place of slavery, to be left behind? Renamed before she turned five years old, Mrs. Moyo did not recall ever being called by her original, given name, Ntombiyelanga.[55] Renaming her daughter with a biblical name was a significant marker of NakaSeyemephi's new literacy as well as her embrace of a Christian identity for both herself and her daughters.

Wanting her girls to be educated and to avoid arranged marriage to polygynous men, NakaSeyemephi stayed at the mission after acquiring her own education. By the 1930s NakaSeyemephi served as matron and all-around helper to the girls who boarded at Mtshabezi. Mrs. Moyo began to attend classes at the girls' boarding school as a little girl, unlike so many of her classmates, who were full-grown. Even girls attending the mission's day school for grades sub-A and sub-B and standard 1 were often grown up.[56] As for the moral climate at the mission station, Mrs. Moyo put it this way: "Every day of your life was Sunday School. My mother was at it all the time—my mother was a prayer woman." Her tone when she said this conveyed pride in her mother's piety and satisfaction with her own upbringing at the mission.

Mrs. Moyo lived at the mission station longer than her older sister did, acquired a higher level of education, and knew everyone at the mission station well, including the missionaries. She had a strong relationship with the mission superintendent, Walter O. Winger, and maintained a strong bond with him and his family throughout her life. Winger's papers are punctuated with frequent reference to his sense of wonder over how far Mrs. Moyo had come from the tiny baby strapped on her mother's back to the diminutive girl teaching girls much bigger than herself at the mission school.

After serving as matron at the mission for some years, Naka-Seyemephi left Mtshabezi and went back to Gwatemba to live with Magwaza. One explanation for this move surfaced: that her husband's family called her back to Gwatemba. The primary education of the eldest daughter, NakaOrlean, started in 1930 and lasted through 1937. She said her mother went back to Gwatemba before her education was complete, which places NakaSeyemephi's departure from Mtshabezi at sometime in the mid-1930s.[57] By that time, Mrs. Moyo had already gone to the BICC teacher-training program at Matopo Mission. NakaSeyemephi's granddaughter had heard that "she left Mtshabezi Mission, went back to live with her brother, because her brother said that, no, if she continued living at the mission it would be like she was not happy and so on. Her brother called her to live with him."[58] It seems that Magwaza, by this time the male head of the family, felt he had a claim on NakaSeyemephi through their half-sibling connection. The family accepted the motivation that took her away from Gwatemba to live at the mission some fifteen years earlier—to educate and launch her daughters. Magwaza apparently could see no other reason to justify her continued absence from the family. MaGwebu's phrasing, "it would be like she was not happy," suggests Magwaza did not want to believe that NakaSeyemephi did not want to live with her family. She responded to this; she went back.

In 1952 the Mguni family, including NakaSeyemephi and Magwaza, learned that their land was to be given to whites. The Godhlwayo chieftainship was in Filabusi District. Filabusi commissioners from the Rhodesian government informed them that they were to remove to the Mzola area of Lupane, in the Shangani Reserve of Matabeleland North. If people refused to move, and the Mgunis were among those who refused, the government forcibly evicted them. Mrs. Moyo said, "They refused to move; [the government officials] came and told them, 'We are moving you. Now you'll see what we'll do.' Four in the morning, there were trucks."[59] Colonial government officials would arrive at a given homestead in the early hours of the morning, use bulldozers to demolish the buildings, load family members and their movable belongings onto trucks and transport them to be left, in most cases, near a government-drilled borehole. Mrs. Ethel Sibanda, a BICC deacon in the 1990s, recalled that in the early 1950s her parents and grandparents lived on a white-owned farm in Filabusi and were moved to Maguswini, at Nkayi in the Shangani Reserve. "The truck came. I could see my grandmother crying, sitting on top of all the luggage. She'd never been on a truck or [in a] car before. My mother took me there to say good-bye to them. I have that picture in my mind."[60] Boys in the family would remain with the family's cattle, accompanying them onto livestock trains headed to train termini in Matabeleland North and driving the stock on the hoof to the family's new location. Most oral recollections of the move north emphasize the forbidding nature of the new territory, with its thickets of trees and the abundance of wild animals. BICC members who recall forced removals from their homes in Matopo and Filabusi echo the informants quoted in Jocelyn Alexander's, JoAnn McGregor's, and Terence Ranger's works,[61] emphasizing the hardship of the arid, malarial climate and the poisonous plants that killed their cattle as well as their distance from stores, churches, and schools. Many families' beasts died due to attacks from lions and hyenas or from eating the *mkausaan* plant, which did not grow in the south.[62]

NakaOrlean described her mother's removal to Maguswini in a manner consistent with this way of understanding and naming the experience. She emphasized how the Rhodesian officials cut open the family's granaries and spread around the grain, wasting it. Given that NakaOrlean was married by the time her mother was forcibly removed, living far away from Gwatemba, her mother must have shared these details with her later. NakaOrlean's voice did not change tone while she narrated this story. Throughout the interview she spoke in a very quiet voice inflected with humility and sweetness. However, she responded immediately to my question, "I have heard from others that the time of removal to the north was very painful. Was this true for your mother?" NakaOrlean, unlike after other questions, did not leave a few moments of silence as she thought; instead, she rushed to agree, and used versions of the word for pain (*ubuhlungu*) repeatedly. Her family members were "carried to unknown places and just dumped in some bush"; she emphasized that in the forests of Matabeleland North the denseness of the trees was foreign and difficult to handle.[63] Most accounts mention the lorry (*ilory*), or truck. In the accounts quoted in Alexander, McGregor, and Ranger's book *Violence and Memory* as well as in the testimonies from NakaSeyemephi's family and other BICC members I interviewed, Africans describe what happened to them during these forced removals. The terms "hauled" (translated from the Ndebele *ukuthwala,* to carry) and "dumped" (from *ukuchitha,* to throw away), connote that the people were unwanted belongings, like "trash bins hauled some distance and then dumped over the edge of a truck."[64]

NakaSeyemephi and Magwaza, along with many others from their home area of Godhlwayo, now had to adjust to establishing a new homestead in this remote place not of their own choosing. Each family was allotted ten acres of land near government-installed wells. They were told to live at Mzola 3, or the third borehole (well) at Mzola. Even though the wild animals moved away after people moved in, the predators still visited, and, as MaGwebu put it, "perhaps come and get a goat or two at night."[65]

As indicated above, Filabusi Africans had been forceful in their resistance against the prospect of forced removal. The colonial officials administering the Filabusi people's incorporation into the land in Matabeleland North were wary of this group. Fearing a new round of political organizing and protest against the new terms of settlement, the government in 1952 implemented an accelerated pace of enforcement of the Land Husbandry Act. This act required practices such as controlled de-stocking of livestock, compulsory labor on government-mandated contour ridges, and strict limits on the size of fields that could be put into cultivation.[66] None of the testimonies with which I worked mentioned whether Magwaza or anyone close to the Mguni family was involved in the protests against the land husbandry regulations that were widespread in that region in the 1950s and early 1960s. All we know in terms of "worldly" protests is that "they refused" when the government told them to move to Matabeleland North. Given that most men interviewed for background understanding of the forced removals and their impact on the church were more likely to have specific references to politics—in this instance, protests against the removals—had it been possible to interview him, Magwaza's testimony, had it been available, might well have emphasized specifics about how exactly the family "refused" the order to move.

The trauma of removal to this harsh territory, and people's negative feelings toward the land were crucial to understanding why BICC women pastors emerged in this territory at this time. As Ranger and Alexander put it,

> Christianity was an essential part of the self-identification of the Ndebele- and Shona-speaking peoples evicted from the plateau in the late 1940s and 1950s. It defined their

"progressive" life-style; it shaped their protest against eviction; it gave them a sense of connection with the wider world once they were dumped in the sandy wastes of Nkayi and Lupane or in the "jungles" of Gokwe; and it intensified their convictions of superiority over the illiterate non-Christians already living in the North-West, whether these were the "indigenous" Tonga, Nyai and Shangwe, or earlier Ndebele-speaking settlers.[67]

The remoteness of the territory explains why these female-led congregations were able to establish themselves, initially invisible to the church's official white and black leaders.

While it is known that women were predominant among worshippers and that they were able to become pastors, the challenge is to try to understand why men were so starkly absent from the new churches built by the people who were forced to settle in Matabeleland North. Memories from the families of church members of the years following eviction emphasize that the men who lived through the trauma of forced removals from Filabusi, in spite of a vigorous protest movement, left the church because of their disaffection with its white leadership.

Missionary Jake Shenk, who served as a teacher at Matopo Secondary School in 1960 saw that by then, many young men were being drawn away into nationalist politics and purposely engaged them in discussions on the topic in the effort to dissuade them:

> When I came there was a fair amount of political unrest.
> . . . And it was the men. A lot of the women couldn't
> care less. They were more concerned about their lives,
> their families, their children, and so on. And so it was the
> women, then, who saw education and church, in a sense,
> as a way of helping them, and helping them improve their
> lives and so on. Whereas the men reacted because they
> felt that they wanted to go on this route of independence,
> trying to rise up against what they saw as their masters.
> And personally I feel we [the BICC church leadership] lost
> an opportunity there. Somehow we allowed that kind of

thing to happen, and the men to slip away, and I think personally it wasn't the right move.[68]

The exodus of BICC men from church by the late 1950s—prompted by their alienation from the church and all other white-run institutions, especially the government in the wake of eviction—in fact is an indicator of the more general trend of the nationalist movements, when in order to broaden their base to non-Christians, the Christian link was submerged and even derided by the time the NDP reached its zenith, around 1960. Shenk's account of the nature of political activity among the African pupils he taught at Matopo Secondary School in Matabeleland South is confirmed by the patterns in the north indicated in testimonies of MaTshuma, when she described how her arrival at a homestead in order to evangelize entailed the men waving her off to speak with the women with the dismissal "we are finished with that," and Mthombeni's comments about how men, angered by the forced removals from Matabeleland South, consequently felt alienated from the "white man's" church.

Missionary and African church leaders in the south in the 1950s and 1960s were so concerned about losing male teachers and church members that they launched a campaign in the mid-1960s, directly aimed at bringing men into the church, called Every Man Win Another.[69] Careful examination of the trends in the established church centers of the south suggest that whether it was because of beer, "moral" (i.e., sexual) failings, or involvement in nationalist politics, men were falling away everywhere, not only in Matabeleland North.[70]

At this point it is useful to put the BICC in a comparative perspective. Some of the most notable nationalist leaders during the early to mid-1950s in the Shangani region of Matabeleland North were the London Missionary Society–affiliated John Dakamela, the staunch Free Presbyterian Nathaniel Mpofu, and Lakatshona Samuel Ndebele, all active in the (anti-eviction) African Voice Association, or in the National Democratic Party (a forerunner of ZAPU). All retained their church affiliations. According to Alexander, McGregor, and Ranger,

In the Shangani, the pioneers of nationalism were Christian modernizers. But as confrontation with the state intensified, many teachers, preachers, and storekeepers became identified as at best "moderates" and at worst "sellouts." Furthermore, the need to develop a nationalism that embraced the (mainly non-Christian) "originals" as well as the evictees meant an appeal to multiple histories and to multiple religious legitimations. Local nationalism became less Christian and more "traditionalist" over time.[71]

The key here is that, for a time, many non-BICC men unproblematically combined their Christian affiliations with their nationalist work. Nathaniel Mpofu even joined the NDP and the Free Presbyterian Church in the same year, 1960. Some men of the BICC did retain both church and nationalist political affiliations simultaneously through the 1960s and 1970s, but they could not do so openly as far as the church was concerned. Mthombeni stated that a number of the male BICC pastors who served in Matabeleland North were ZAPU members, at least by the time of the war's outbreak in the 1970s.[72] This continues to be a difficult subject for informants to discuss openly, however, due both to suppression of ZAPU since 1980 under Mugabe's ZANU-PF government and to the church's political stance whereby, only until very recently, political—and thus "worldly"—involvements were denounced as sin.

Men of the BICC had to make an either-or choice between the church and politics, from the beginning, not just later, after the NDP, and later ZAPU, saw that the mission-church link had to be submerged in order to gain broad legitimacy. In this context, John Dube's testimony resonates. When asked about his relationship to the church, God, and politics in his own life, Dube equated politics ("war") with worldliness; he expressed gratitude that God had empowered him to run away from all worldly things, including "war, drink, and smoking."[73]

NakaSeyemephi's Church at Guga

Not long after her unhappy arrival eMaguswini, NakaSeyemephi became the pastor of a small BICC congregation. It was known as the church at Guga. Seyemephi said, "she opened churches in places where there were no churches."[74] NakaSeyemephi had already proved to be a woman who took initiative to preserve and nurture her Christian identity—often courageously and in conflict with her family's expectations of her as a woman. She had left her husband's family after her husband died. In her mind, as a churchgoer, it would have been adulterous and un-Christian to marry one of her husband's male relatives. She was determined not to rear her daughters in a traditional, rural homestead, where they might become subject to arranged marriages to polygynous men. She also left her father's family behind and made a life for herself and her daughters at Mtshabezi Mission for more than ten years. In the 1950s she found herself in a remote place, far from all her prior networks of church and school. She decided to start a worshipping community herself.

Mrs. Moyo provided a starting point for understanding many of the key factors involved in the emergence of her mother as a female pastor in this region in the 1950s and 1960s. As a long-time active member of the BICC's prosperous Bulawayo Central congregation, Mrs. Moyo was well acquainted with the church's leaders, including the missionary and African bishops who led the church over the preceding fifty years or more. Her testimony became animated when she described how her mother's church was established, and she offered crucial insight as to how the institutional church based in Bulawayo related to it:

> [My mother and my half brother] were moved by the white people [in the early 1950s] out to Maguswini. When they were removing people out of good lands, [they were] sent to Mzola. That's where she started the church. . . . But people lived there from nothing. . . . So they were punished I tell you, it was one of the worst areas. That's where my mother opened up a church, from a tree, with little boys and girls—because those people didn't want anything to do with Christianity. . . .
>
> It took them quite a while to settle. I found her later having started with those little children and slowly it grew. [Overseer P. M.] Khumalo came to visit eventually

and gave her permission. The audience came afterward. Mother liaised with one of her cousins, MaSithole, worked together to begin at her area in Mzola—they worked until it had become what it is. They have a school now. When you saw my mother there with her kids under a tree. Now they don't even know where [the school and church] came from. MaSithole's daughter-in-laws are still strong, out there in Mzola. I've always wanted to write a history but who would care? Oh, they were strong, oh my God. That's how the Brethren in Christ got to be there. They paved the way. Without them, forget it. Then the bishops drove in. P. M. [Khumalo] has to get some credit; he helped them.[75]

NakaSeyemephi's elder daughter, NakaOrlean, recalled that it was mostly women and children who attended her mother's worship services. They were people who also had been moved from Gwatemba. The Tonga people, who had been in the region already, were not living nearby and were not part of the congregation.[76] In Mrs. Moyo's account, one sees her struggling to balance her mother and MaSithole's sense of isolation from the support of the institutional church, and her personal friendship and connection with leaders such as Khumalo, wanting to acknowledge their support when it did finally arrive. She is keen to acknowledge P. M. Khumalo for helping the women gain approval for building the church. By her commenting in reference to the school that is now at Mzola 3, that "they don't even know where it came from," we sense Mrs. Moyo's desire that the efforts of women such as her mother not be forgotten. The prosperous overseer and the bishops' cars ("then the bishops drove in") are juxtaposed to her mother's church humbly sheltering under a tree. They "lived from nothing," started with children under a tree, and yet were "strong" and built a church community.

As seen above, the BICC's documented institutional response to the forced removal of so many of its members to the distant north focused on the work of male evangelists and celebrated the fact that the removals had given Africans an opportunity to work as missionaries to their own people. However, tracing the story of NakaSeyemephi's church makes it clear that when initially the missionaries began to notice and lend their support to this outreach, the place of women in the church in the north was ignored. There was also almost exclusive emphasis on the BICC churches being established in the Gwaai area, ignoring the nascent congregations further to the north and east, in the Shangani reserve's Lupane and Nkayi Districts.

Thus the churches being nurtured into existence by NakaSeyemephi and her neighbors remained invisible in the church documents generated during the mid-1950s. In a 1955 article in the BICC's North American newspaper, intended to encourage the home church to lend its financial support to work in the north, the author acknowledged the struggles of the recently evicted to run a church without much in the way of infrastructure even while erasing the fact that many of these church founders were women: "No outstations were available for them and their church life was in a near chaotic state. A few brave men were carrying on a semblance of church worship, gathering the people under trees or in villages for Sunday services."[77] There were indeed a "few brave men," such as Rev. Elliot Ziduli's father, Red Ziduli, in Nkayi, or John Dube in the Gwaai. Echoing the familiar theme of worship under a tree, Rev. Ziduli recalled his father's church but mentioned what the missionary author above did not: that the majority of the people under the tree were women and children, something emphasized also, above, in Mrs. Moyo's testimony. Ziduli said, "He [Ziduli's father, Red Ziduli] started a church there; it was under a tree. . . . A few women joined him. The men did not join."[78]

Mission record mentions of the congregations in Lupane, yet further away from Bulawayo than those such as Kumbula, in the Gwaai area, emphasize again the mission leadership's appreciation that these groups served as a bulwark against Roman Catholic influence in Lupane coming from Mariannhill Mission.

> Another highlight of the year was the visit to the Lupani
> area, 150 miles from Bulawayo, here a number of Brethren

in Christ families now live and are almost completely cut off from church contacts. They maintain their own services and worship together in the midst of a strong Roman Catholic area. Some of them had not enjoyed the privilege of a Communion Service for five years. The appreciation and interest expressed by this small group as evidenced in the Baptism and Communion Service was worth all the expense, and heat and flies.[79]

NakaSeyemephi's church at Guga would have been one of these groups "almost completely cut off from church contacts."

By noting that P. M. Khumalo's appearance on the scene occurred well after her mother's efforts to start a congregation, Mrs. Moyo points to the grassroots beginnings of the BICC in Matabeleland North as a whole. The BICC's institutional expansion into Matabeleland North reached congregations headed by women far behind those of men's. Generally, all new worship groups without a building met under trees. Women-led congregations remained meeting under trees long after most of the men-led groups had buildings that functioned as both church and school. The church-school building at Khumbula—the first BICC building in Matabeleland North—was built in 1954,[80] well before nearby female pastor NakaGininda's dual-purpose church-school building at Mpisini was built in 1971, and NakaSeyemephi's, which was not built until after she died, in the mid-1970s.

Like NakaSeyemephi, NakaGininda's church in the Gwaai area began under a tree. NakaGininda decided to take action on behalf of her congregation's desire for a church-school building at Mpisini. She found a woman builder and enlisted the women in her congregation to make the building a reality. NakaGininda's reputation as a woman of exceptional spiritual power, initiative, and leadership skill was reinforced in multiple interviews as well as in Doris Dube's sketch of her life. Dube describes how NakaGininda carried on her pastoral work with a husband whose support for her church involvement wavered between tolerant and obstructive.[81] NakaGininda is said to have overcome the witchcraft of her husband's second wife with the power of prayer, leading eventually to the second wife being driven from the home, restoring NakaGininda as the sole wife and opening the way for her husband's deathbed repentance and return to church fellowship.[82] NakaGininda was also known for the resplendent fertility of her fields in a very arid region, with crop yields exceeding those of her neighbors. When asked the secret of her harvest, she declared, "God is my manure."[83] The wife of a former missionary bishop, Thata Book, recounted an incident in which NakaGininda's eyesight was failing, and through prayers conducted in the feminine wilderness space "in the bush," it was restored, allowing her to continue to read the Bible and thereby lead her congregation.[84]

Unlike NakaGininda, NakaSeyemephi did not find a place in the church's written accounts of exemplary lives, and she did not live to see "her" worshipping community acquire a built church. NakaSeyemephi was the acknowledged pastor of her worship community at Guga for around twenty years. After meeting under a tree in the early 1950s, they later convened in the home of a member until the mid-1970s. Only the church building's foundations had been laid during the early 1970s. "People were about to say this is [NakaSeyemephi's] church, but her time had come"—and she died before it was complete.[85] NakaOrlean said, "but her time had come" several times, to emphasize the sense of loss that her grandmother never got to see the church building completed. The year of NakaSeyemephi's death is not available, though in 1973 she was still listed as pastor at her church in Guga, Lupane District.

Mrs. Moyo's description of how her mother's church acquired an official existence within the institutional church highlights the role of overseer, then bishop, P. M. Khumalo. "My mother was pastor of her own making, then Khumalo came and gave her a certificate. She'd send some young girls to conference to submit what little offering they had collected. She just came to conference as a regular person; she would never shout about it. She was just purely dedicated and felt it was her duty."[86] Mrs. Moyo finds it admirable that her mother came to the General Conference as a "regular person." She cited this as proof of her mother's humility about her leadership role and of the quality of her dedication. NakaSeyemephi had started her church by the mid-1950s. Khumalo served as overseer for Matopo District in the 1960s, with the Maguswini churches also under his jurisdiction.[87] In 1967, Khumalo arrived at NakaSeyemephi's church at Guga to officiate at its first baptism-communion service, noting that "spiritual hunger was evident as sinners and Christians assembled."[88] This visit marked the beginning of the Guga congregation's existence on an official level, while the oral testimony indicates that it had existed in embryo for at least twelve years.

Although her mother may have exhibited humility and "pure dedication" to the work of leading her church, Mrs. Moyo's lament echoed the words used by her niece: "People were about to say this is [NakaSeyemephi's] church, but her time had come." Her mother would have been proud indeed to see her congregation enjoy further enfoldment into the official church networks, and the benefits of a real church building, one of which would have been the ability to start a school. As a young woman, Naka-Seyemephi had exercised courage in leaving her husband's family in her motivation to get an education for herself and her daughters. Mrs. Moyo emphasized that "there is a school there now," implying her mother's hope that acquiring a proper church building at Guga would enable the creation of a school.

An important element in Mrs. Moyo's account of her mother's work with the church is the reference to NakaSeyemephi's relationship with her cousin MaSithole and then the mention of Ma-Sithole's daughters-in-law. Women in church leadership in the north universally mention the importance of other women who served as mentors, coworkers, or supporters in some form. Within this pattern, a noteworthy element is the frequency with which female pastors were aided, and then often succeeded, by their daughters-in-law. NakaGininda (Nkanyezi Ndlovu) started and pastored the BICC church at Mpisini starting in the 1950s; her daughter-in-law assisted her. As of 1999, NakaGininda's daughter-in-law was still the pastor at Mpisini. In her old age, NakaGininda often relied on her daughter-in-law to take over leadership of the worship services. NakaGininda said, "She is my assistant pastor and she is very good. God gave me a Timothy."[89] NakaSeyemephi did not have a daughter-in-law but she did enjoy mutual support for her work as pastor from her cousin MaSithole.

The fact that women take care to specifically mention the positive relationships they had with their daughters-in-law, or mothers-in-law, suggests that such relationships were unusual. As seen in the discussion of NakaSeyemephi's marriage to Mguni, extreme forms of deference marked the customary relationship between a mother-in-law (*mamazala*) and her daughter-in-law (*malokazana*). There was often also suspicion and distrust. If at all possible, a young wife would return to her parents' homestead to give birth to her first child, to be sure of safety from potential danger from the women in her husband's homestead. Whenever the mother-in-law and daughter-in-law might get along well, it was considered noteworthy.[90] Another mother-in-law–daughter-in-law relationship to consider is the one between NakaSeyemephi's daughter NakaOrlean Gwebu and her own mother-in-law. In that instance, the two Gwebu women were allied as Christians against their son and husband, Douglas Gwebu, whose "backslidden" ways caused grief to them both. Similarly, there are many other instances of this type of female alliance within families, notably MaNdimande (nakaSibonane) of Mtshabezi District, known to her children and grandchildren for her close relationship with her daughters-in-law, all of whom lived at her homestead during the 1950s and recognized her leadership at daily Christian devotions, and supported her in her unceasing campaign to reform her beer-drinking sons.[91] These stories point to an element of separation of spheres between men and women that overrode the in-law animosity, and they speak to a pattern of mentoring, and of succession in spiritual leadership between senior and junior women. Strong affective ties and cooperative church work between women and their sons' wives was one important but little-recognized way that Christianity shifted the alliances within families along gendered lines.

═══════════

It is significant that many of the "black St. Pauls" of the BICC in Zimbabwe over the course of the twentieth century were women.[92] Before the 1950s many of the congregations of Matabeleland South had had women as founding members, but not as pastors. In spite of a mission church that consciously favored the conversion and training of men to be pastors and leaders of congregations, already as of 1918 a large number of Sunday school teachers were women.[93] By midcentury, women married by Christian rites tended to be the backbone of the church and the leaders of family devotions in the many families in which the husband became a backslider. Thus, the fact that women would take the initiative when Christian families were forced to move north should not be surprising.

References to the area's wildness—images of animals, wild forests, virgin land—were the ones invariably employed by Zimbabweans when asked to describe Matabeleland North, and resonate with female symbols. NakaSeyemephi's granddaughter NakaOrlean said, "Thickets, forests, impenetrable forests. Rough land, almost virgin land, actually, and the animals made it their domain."[94] Former missionary bishop Arthur Climenhaga described the evangelistic work by Sandey Vundhla in the Gwaai: "This is virgin territory that is being plowed well." The arrival of school buildings, roads, bishops in their cars, ordained ministers, and mission stations, into this region call to mind the rational, "male" impact of colonialism and institutionalization. The wildest place of all, Lupane, in Maguswini, was left untended by such markers of institutionalization longest. The wistful, grief-inflected comment by NakaOrlean that her mother died, that her "time had come," before she could see her Lupane congregation's church building completed suggests that these women pastors, while appreciating the nonmaterial benefits of fellowship, and taking full advantage of their remote location to become church leaders still yearned for the buildings and institutional recognition that their male counterparts enjoyed more readily. The complementary stories of the much-celebrated school built by Sandey Vundhla at Kumbula, and NakaGininda's church's joy at completing the church building at Mpisini reinforces that.

Church builders in Matabeleland North in the 1950s, such as NakaSeyemephi of Lupane and NakaGininda of the Gwaai or evangelist and urban church planter Maria Tshuma,[95] certainly qualify as the kind of "spirited, articulate and determined women believers found in marginal religious groups"[96] noted by historian Susan Juster.[97] That women became *pastors* in the 1950s and 1960s in a church that up until then had never had an officially woman-led congregation is what is notable. It is partly due to the institutional vacuum resulting from the remoteness of the Gwaai and the even more remote Lupane area in Maguswini. BICC missionary Frances Davidson also had chosen a peripheral location to allow her scope for operation.[98] In the 1950s and 1960s women who did not have a choice of place became an especially notable force in the remotest, most inhospitable area, Lupane. Men, on the other hand, were ripe for political recruitment as well as for taking work far from home in an effort to make a living. Both these factors in the lives of men left openings for spiritually motivated and organizationally effective women to exercise leadership. The BICC placed such a high value on conversion, new birth, and church growth that the existence of female-led congregations was tolerated in the interest of church expansion.

Doris Dube's hagiographic accounts of NakaGininda or those of NakaSeyemephi by her female descendants, which emphasize these women's spiritual leadership—however compelling—overlooks some of the other aspects of these women's lives that point to the fact that they were often "unruly" or "unwomanly" according to notions of proper female behavior whether defined by the missionaries, African church leaders, or African male family heads. NakaSeyemephi showed her independence even as a lowly third wife of a prosperous Ndebele man when she opted to convert to Christianity, then in 1922 when she opted not to marry one of her husband's male relatives once widowed. Instead, she chose to build a life for herself and her daughters at Mtshabezi Mission. Her later career as a pioneering female pastor in remote Maguswini for the church at Guga does not strike one as surprising given this background.

FOUR || Sandey Vundhla
Being Fruitful for the Church, 1950–70

TWO MEN RODE THEIR BICYCLES ALL THE way from Matopo Mission to the city of Bulawayo on the rough, unpaved road that passed northward out of the Matopo Hills and into town. The one-way trip was about thirty miles. One, the senior pastor, was Sandey Vundhla, in his midforties; the other was a young man in his twenties from the United States named Donald Zook. Vundhla's rural home was just half a mile from the Matopo mission station, where Zook was teaching at the mission's secondary school. They bicycled to Bulawayo many weekends in the years 1956–57. Their aim was house-to-house visits, following up on the home visits started the year before by missionaries Mary Brechbill and Dorothy Martin. Visiting and praying with formerly active BICC members or former BICC mission school pupils now living in town filled their Saturdays; Sunday mornings they co-led Sunday school and then a worship service at three in the afternoon before cycling all the way back to Matopo.[1] Zook admired his companion: "Vundhla was a natural leader; power just flew his direction. . . . Vundhla was the better preacher by far . . . he had the heart of an evangelist."[2]

One witness recalled a sermon in which Vundhla grew near tears as he exhorted his listeners, "thatha ithuba, thatha ithuba": take the opportunity—take it—avail yourself of salvation.[3] Vundhla was known to be a man with a heart for sinners, with a passion for reaching men with the aim of converting them to the BICC church, a man of tremendous physical energy, capable not only of heroic-scale bicycle evangelism but of hands-on work to erect the structures in which the people responding to his preaching could worship. His work for the BICC took place just as the anticolonial nationalist movement was gaining maturity and intensity.

In the years after the Second World War, African nationalists took an increasingly stark view of the urgency of their struggle for independence. By the 1960s fellow Africans came to be viewed as either comrades or sellouts. And, as we have seen in previous chapters, the mission churches during the colonial years tended to dichotomize between the saved and the unsaved, the civilized and the uncivilized, the pious and the backslidden. These discourses were at odds with one another. The BICC held that anyone involved with politics was too worldly: a backslider. The nationalist liberation parties regarded the mission churches as large institutions composed of their extensive landholdings and injunctions against political action. They dismissed the church as a sellout entity, the institutional face of the "white man's" religion.[4] The implications for this dynamic in the lives of BICC-affiliated Africans in the rural parts of Matabeleland North were explored in chapter 3. In this chapter, we see the work of a male evangelist, Sandey Vundhla, who began itinerant preaching in rural Matabeleland South in the mid-1940s, then went to plant churches in Matabeleland North and moved into an increasingly politicized urban Bulawayo in the late 1950s and early 1960s.

In the eyes of the white BICC leadership, Vundhla fulfilled the church's vision of ideal Christian leadership. As a charismatic and successful male evangelist, church planter, and pastor, Vundhla's achievements were well documented both in the BICC's North American newspaper, the *Evangelical Visitor,* and in the mission church's administrative records in Zimbabwe. Vundhla's efforts to rewin former BICC members to join a new BICC church in Bulawayo—back from other churches or from being backslidden—were successful. While enjoying the favor and support of key missionaries, Vundhla won the trust and loyalty of a wide swath of Africans, both urban and rural, both church members and the unchurched. In recognition of Vundhla's evangelistic and church-planting successes in the rural areas, he became only the sixth African ordained as minister, or uMfundisi.

Vundhla exercised his initiative within the church; he was not openly affiliated with nationalist politics. And yet he operated in an ultrapoliticized milieu.[5] Bulawayo in the early 1960s, in particular, was bristling with anticolonial, African nationalist organizing and the rising tensions that ultimately led to the guerrilla war for liberation that broke out in full force in the 1970s. When longtime Bulawayo BICC lay leader Zama Ncube was asked to speculate why she thought her husband never became a church member, Mrs. Ncube said, "One thing I think really made him [keep out of church] . . . [is that] he became active in politics. . . . He was arrested about twice, detained, and so on. Ah, then politicians were always anti-Christ." Zama Ncube reflected further on the ways that it was very difficult for politically active men to be connected with the church:

> They said that they wanted to be free, they wanted freedom
> of [for] their country, so realizing that religion was brought
> by Europeans, and they were against them, so whatever
> they taught them, they were cheated, so they could not
> [be in church]. . Most of them did not really go to church,
> although they were [members] prior, they were church
> members. They went to their different churches, but when
> they got into politics, ai, they were against whites, then
> they were against religion.[6]

It is worth exploring reasons for Vundhla's relative success at recruiting men to attend church in that environment.

The church was a platform from which uMfundisi Vundhla could direct the expansion of the BICC in Bulawayo. Vundhla took on the challenge to bring the church to Bulawayo, where he established himself as an example of populist, African male Christian leadership. His populist bent is evident in his zeal for door-to-door preaching, even to the domestic servants living in the eastern (white) suburbs, his willingness to build the Mpopoma church next to a beer hall so that it might better minister to that group seen as sinners, his presence on the streets during the Bulawayo riots of 1960, and his allegedly political sermons. Vundhla's status was entirely self-made, coming from a non-Christian family, marrying a woman with minimal education from a nonelite family. He was the perfect man to pastor the urban male population, where earned status was more widely valued than in the rural population.

Vundhla's marital history is crucial for understanding the gendered face of his evangelistic successes and failures. Vundhla both reflected and subverted commonly held notions of masculinity among Ndebele speakers in the mid-twentieth century. That, together with the way this career undermines neat categories of "apolitical and pious" versus "politicized and antimission," indicates that Vundhla's story is worth a closer look.

The BICC Church in Town

Before entering the narrative of Vundhla's life and urban evangelistic work, we must understand the Bulawayo milieu that the Brethren in Christ encountered when it sent Vundhla to open a new church there in the late 1950s. The BICC was a rural-based church. In 1961 the BICC of Southern Rhodesia had fifty-one missionaries based at the three rural mission stations of Matabeleland South and the recently established Phumula Mission in Matabeleland North. The church employed 260 "native workers" who worked as teachers, paid evangelists, nurses and other hospital workers, and general staff at the mission stations. Membership was at a high point compared to the numbers that continued to fall through the course of the 1970s liberation war, with over ten thousand combined communicants and "inquirers" spread across the three southern mission districts and Phumula in the north.[7] The missionaries and African leadership, throughout its Rhodesian history up through the 1960s, strongly advised its membership not to go to "town"—the city of Bulawayo. In fact, Ndebele speakers were relative latecomers to that booming colonial city, where in the early decades of the twentieth century migrants from Mashona-land and Nyasaland and other areas constituted the majority of urban African wage earners.[8] The Brethren in Christ Church re-mained intentionally detached from Bulawayo and other cities, or "towns," throughout its first sixty years in colonial Zimbabwe, which is why the decision to open a church in "town" was a sig-nificant change. Unlike other denominations that had had some presence in Bulawayo for several decades, the BICC stayed out because Bulawayo was perceived to be a place of evil.[9] The BICC understood the colonial city of Bulawayo to be a vice-filled cen-ter of prostitution, drink, and other worldly pursuits, including nationalist politics and organized sports.[10] While other churches might view the city as an ideal location for finding sinners to re-deem, the BICC's official vision of itself as a separated community of Christian people, celibate or monogamously married, unambi-tious for worldly accomplishments such as higher education, per-sonal wealth, or political influence, found little to endorse in the African urban scene. "At one point the church assumed if you moved to town you'd give up your church affiliation," explained Vundhla's evangelistic partner Donald Zook.[11]

African BICC rural elites at this time were inclined to share the official view of any city as a center of immorality and vice. Alice Ndlovu (MaNkala), educated at the Mtshabezi Girls' Pri-mary Boarding School and the Matopo teacher-training program in the 1940s, quit her job at the Mtshabezi boarding school over disagreements with mission policy and sought another position.[12] She had definite ideas of where an appropriate posting might be. When she was offered a teaching position in Bulawayo, MaNkala said, "No, please give me a mission school, because they thought everyone that came to town was not really, not a good girl, would not really be someone who is good enough. Town was for . . . bad people."[13] Nonetheless, she took the job in Bulawayo and discov-ered that her Christian identity was not substantially endangered.[14]

One African elder, by 1999 a twenty-year resident of Bulawayo, echoed the antiurban bias of his upbringing: "I remember very well as a young boy my parents never liked city life. . . . They used to warn us against it, telling us, 'when you grow up, never think of going to live in town.'"[15]

Even after the Second World War, when the Native Affairs Department attempted to encourage "wholesome" recreation for the Africans living in Bulawayo and built more housing for married Africans, the BICC initially remained aloof. Bulawayo's Native Administration Department was established in 1949 with the aim of shaping and "taming" African initiative into channels more acceptable to the Rhodesian authorities than the protest organizations that emerged after the war, such as Benjamin Burombo's African Voice Association or the new labor-organizing drives that were centered in Bulawayo. Preben Kaarsholm explained: "Rather than creating a township cultural life from scratch, the contribution of the municipality was one of providing support for selected existing activities," such as boxing, which had been popular in Bulawayo since the 1920s. The city council sponsored a boxing ring at Stanley Square in Makokoba, formerly known as the Old Location. The government encouraged membership in all sorts of organizations, except nationalist political organizations.[16] In 1959 the range of social-welfare activities in the African location included women's clubs, a day nursery and crèche, an African choral society, domestic-science classes, boys' clubs, a library, a Bantu brass band, football, boxing, swimming, cycle racing, cricket, tennis, weightlifting, and parks and playgrounds.[17] The city council built additional municipal beer gardens, both to get ahead of the illicit brewers and to garner additional revenue for the city council.[18] Certainly municipal beer gardens, but also boxing, musical instruments, dancing, and Girl Guides and Boy Scouts were considered too worldly for members of the BICC.[19]

The numbers and clout of BICC members in Bulawayo after the Second World War helped convince the church hierarchy to reverse the previously long held assumption that the church would not expand into town. As early as 1920 the African members of the BICC at the annual African Conference asked for approval to obtain a site in Bulawayo since there were many BIC members working in the city "without spiritual oversight."[20] Their request was denied. It was not until another wave of African initiative after the war that the official church would rethink its policy on urban ministry. More Africans found work in Bulawayo during the 1940s than ever before, and during the 1950s Africans continued to move to town. Residents of colonial Zimbabwe's cities, Bulawayo included, were far more likely to have had formal education.[21] BICC members came to Bulawayo in the 1940s, 1950s, and 1960s in order to go to school, to work as factory laborers, bricklayers, trained builders, and teachers, and some women came because of their husbands' jobs.[22] By the 1960s an increasing number of BICC church-wed African professional couples began to make the city their home, and more women were available to join the newly forming urban congregations.[23]

After some of the female missionary teachers from Matopo Secondary decided to visit their former students living in town during the mid-1950s, Bishop Arthur Climenhaga became increasingly open to allowing evangelism and church planting in the city. The Brethren in Christ Church went through many significant changes during the years that it was moving to town, between 1957 and 1978. The missionaries, as was the case in most other mission societies, handed over leadership of the church to the African members,[24] its symbolic culmination occurring when the first African bishop of the BICC, Philemon M. Khumalo, took office, in 1970. Churchwomen who lived in town, unlike their rural counterparts, had a great deal of exposure to other denominations, which led to changes in the way BICC women organized themselves and influenced the creation of a new churchwomen's organization, modeled after the Methodist manyano: the Omama Bosizo (Women who help). The Rhodesian government's policy of consciously fostering the creation of an African middle class, indicated in the expansion of government-sponsored secondary education for Africans, was also reflected in the church's decision to establish a secondary school at Matopo Mission.[25]

At the same time, the church adhered to the Rhodesian policy of racial segregation in the matter of housing, especially in the cities. Thus the residence of the white bishop, when moved to town, was in the white suburb of Hillside, and the missionary children attended white schools in Bulawayo. The church's move to town was directed solely at Africans living there, not at the substantial white population. The BICC was not one of the all-Rhodesia churches, such as the Anglican Church or the Baptists, Methodists, or Catholics, all of which had ministered to both whites and blacks since their arrival in Zimbabwe. The BICC's move to town did not change its singular attention to Ndebele-speaking Africans, and the new church was built in a newly laid out middle-class African suburb called Mpopoma.

The BICC has had a place in Ndebele ethnic-linguistic development, and it was during the urbanizing decades of the 1960s and 1970s that the official language of the church changed from Zulu to Ndebele. Up to that time, the church almost exclusively used Zulu-language hymnals, Bible translations, religious tracts, and school primers. Many of these were imported from South Africa. As of 1967, the BICC's Matopo Book Centre, based in Bulawayo, sold a major portion of all Ndebele and Zulu scripture purchased in Southern Rhodesia.[26] Isaac N. Mpofu, an Ndebele linguist and leading member of the BICC, created a collection of Ndebele proverbs that were used "specifically in Christian circles."[27] In 1973, at the time of the seventy-fifth anniversary of the church's 1898 arrival in Southern Rhodesia, Mpofu and Rev. Jake Shenk wrote a history of the church that was published in isiNdebele under the title *Izithelo* (Fruits).[28] The first Ndebele-language radio broadcasts in Rhodesia happened at the BICC radio station in 1975. *Ibhayibhili elingcwele*, the first complete Bible in Ndebele (rather than Zulu) was published in 1978.[29] The publication of these books points to a shifting ethnic identity for the church—from its rural bias in which the rural elite abezansi, whose language was closest in grammar and vocabulary to Zulu, to the newer, more urbanized pan-Ndebele identity.

The larger Ndebele identity that developed in the later 1950s has been noted by Terence Ranger, who describes the emergence of a newly evolving Ndebele identity that partly grew out of the urban experience and was envisioned also by the emerging group of nationalist leaders such as Joshua Nkomo. Ranger argues that Nkomo's self-understanding came in layers: "[Nkomo's] identity at home was Kalanga; in Bulawayo it was Ndebele; in Rhodesia as a whole it was nationalist."[30] As BICC members moved to town, they, too, broadened their ethnic identification beyond the social strata that remained important signifiers in the rural areas; social categories of the absezansi, abenhla, and abantu bakaMambo had led to, most significantly, fairly persistent patterns of intramarriage. During the 1960s and 1970s in particular, patterns of intramarriage among BICC faithful broke down, not completely, but to a large degree, and particularly among the educated town dwellers.[31]

Sandey Vundhla

This account of the life of Sandey Vundhla is constructed from church documents held in Bulawayo and Pennsylvania, other written accounts of his life, and many oral interviews with people who knew him. I never met him myself. Some parts of his life are richly documented and vividly remembered; others are shadowy or unknown altogether. One of the most important interviews supporting this narrative was with his widow, MaMoyo. Another important source for my understanding of Vundhla's work and the milieu of the BICC in Bulawayo in the 1960s comes from the transcripts of interviews conducted by Daryl Climenhaga, which occurred about eight years earlier than mine and reached people who had already died before I came to Zimbabwe. Eliakim Sibanda's dissertation and his exceptional generosity as an informant in multiple interviews and email exchanges provide invaluable insights, given his position as both a BICC insider and a professional historian.[32] Finally, Doris Dube's profile of Vundhla's work for the church in BICC-Zimbabwe's centennial volume, *Celebrating the Vision,* offers a fascinating take on Vundhla's career. The inclusion of Vundhla in that volume's collection of exemplary African leaders in the church is significant, indicating the degree to which the contemporary African membership of the church is willing and wishing to accord him their appreciation for the church-building work he did at the height of his career, in spite of the abrupt end of his work for the church, in 1971. Doris Dube interviewed Vundhla in the 1990s before he died, in 1994, and interviewed many others who had known him when he was actively leading the Bulawayo churches—all of which underpins her account of his life as it appears in *Celebrating the Vision* and in turn influences this analysis as well.[33]

Sandey Vundhla's life enters the documentary record in the 1940s, at the point when his affiliation with the Brethren in Christ Church mission at Matopo became official. Dube's account of Vundhla's life states that he "repented" and began to attend church at Matopo Mission in 1939, and that Rev. Walter O. Winger baptized him in 1941.[34] He and Dazzie Moyo were married at Matopo Mission later that year. According to the marriage certificate, "Sande Vundhla" was thirty-four years of age in 1941, putting his birth at about 1907.[35]

Vundhla's birth was thus approximately eleven years after the 1896 final defeat of the Ndebele people by the forces of the British South Africa Company. It is safe to assume that he grew up surrounded by his elders' vivid memories of life under the kingdom and of the traumatic events of conquest and its aftermath. He was from rural Matabeleland South, from a family based in the Matopo Hills. Vundhla was of the Ndebele subgroup known as the abantu bakaMambo. As seen in the discussion of NakaSeyemephi's life in chapter 3, the precolonial social strata continued to be relevant social markers, constituting one of the innermost layers of identity in Matabeleland well into the twentieth century. The absezansi elites of the precolonial kingdom in many instances became the Rhodesian government-stipended chiefs in the twentieth century. For those of the abantu bakaMambo, the colonial era offered them ways to achieve status—through acquiring literacy and therefore access to better jobs in the colonial labor force—while the ascribed status of the precolonial society continued to affect social interactions in the rural areas.

Vundhla's family was fortunate in the sense that they were not forced to leave the Matopos. In the early years of the twentieth century, many Africans were evicted from the Matopos' well-watered environs and sent to the dry Mapane veld, in Gwanda District just to the south, once white settlers claimed their land in the aftermath of colonial conquest. However, a certain number of Africans remained in the Matopo Hills if their families resided on the mission-leased property or in the few remaining nearby "communal lands." The mission required—in exchange for permission to remain on mission-controlled land—that homestead heads send their children to the mission school. Yet Vundhla did not attend much, if any, school, as a child; his family lived on communal land.[36] As "people of beer"—and thus also venerators of the local deity, Mwali—the Vundhlas, living on communal land, might well have not wanted to send their son to the school run by alcohol-abstaining, mission-educated Africans. By being part of a non-Christian family and from the abantu bakaMambo, Vundhla was not an elite according to either precolonial or colonial definitions.

What young Vundhla did for the years between his birth and his pursuit of an education as a young man in his late twenties is not known. As an unmarried man, even one nearly thirty years old by the later 1930s, he would have been considered a youth. He is likely to have spent some time in the migrant labor force—he could have worked in one of the mines in nearby Gwanda District, or further south, in Johannesburg, "eGoli"; he could have gotten a job at the mission doing menial labor requiring no book learning; he could have gone to Bulawayo and worked there—on the railroad or in one of the new manufacturing ventures. What we do know is that during the later 1930s he decided to acquire an education. He arranged to study with Timothy Ndlovu, a BICC teacher ten years his junior.[37] Under Ndlovu's tutelage, Vundhla learned to read and write up to about a standard 2 (grade 4) level.[38]

During the years that he learned to read and write with Ndlovu, Vundhla courted a young Christian woman, Dazzie Moyo. Her memory of their interaction emphasized that he was not a churchgoing man but that he followed her into church. As MaMoyo put it, at the time of their marriage, "No, he was not in the faith; he followed me when he saw my worshipping. His people, where he was from, they were people of beer."[39] He would have had to be baptized in order that they have a church, or "white," wedding, which both the photograph hanging at their rural homestead and the church wedding certificate indicates they did. Did he decide to be educated and baptized in order to win Dazzie? Or did his experiences in the harsh colonial economy lead him to conclude, as it had for so many others, that an education would serve him well?

It was not unusual for young men of minimal Christian affiliation to court churchgoing women. The male suitor then had to demonstrate an active commitment to the church in order to win the approval of the young woman in question, of her father, if he was a church member, or her village pastor, who sometimes played the role of the father in arranging Christian marriages, or of each of them.[40] By repenting in 1939 and commencing regular church attendance between then and his marriage to Dazzie Moyo, in 1941, Vundhla's path is consistent with that pattern of other young African male suitors' attempts to win a young Christian woman. Not long after he and Dazzie Moyo were married, Vundhla's began his career as a church leader. He became the (unpaid) pastor of the village church near Matopo Mission. His subsequent career as a pastor, evangelist, and church planter suggests his conversion was more than a courtship strategy.

An interview with MaMoyo in 1999 at the Vundhla homestead proved to vividly evoke access points of an understanding of Vundhla's life as a rural aspirant, pastor, and evangelist. At that point I already knew the outlines of Sandey Vundhla's story. Doris Dube had provided me with the introduction to MaMoyo. My companion and translator that day was Nondulo Vundhla (MaKhumalo), whose grandparents had lived near Matopo. Driving south from Bulawayo that day, using directions supplied by Doris and augmented by Nondulo's memories of the area, we came to the fence surrounding the Vundhla homestead, just half a mile from Matopo Mission. Someone there told us that MaMoyo was in her fields. So we walked beyond the homestead to look for her. There was high vegetation; it was very green. We were in the well-watered, rocky Matopos. We found her in her field—small, thin, barefoot, in a simple cotton work dress. She welcomed us, and brought us back to the homestead, which was enclosed by a fence, stockade style, with fairly uniform tall sticks lashed tightly together. There were massive, dwelling-size rounds of granite inside the homestead fencing. The surface of the ground inside the fence was sandy and swept very smooth. There were dwellings for sleeping, cooking, and one with a corrugated metal roof that contained a space for receiving guests.

We sat for some time in this last building. Inside were a wooden table topped by a lace-trimmed tablecloth, four chairs, an area mat made of linoleum, and two rag rugs.[41] The spare walls were painted in blue on the lower half and in white on the upper half. Many framed photos and certificates hung neatly from a strip of wood that surrounded the room high on the walls. The photos included one of Vundhla and MaMoyo's wedding, one of Vundhla and MaMoyo on the day he was ordained as uMfundisi, a photo of Billy Graham, and one of a gathering of missionaries and African evangelists. There were also certificates: from Wanezi Bible School; from the Emmaus Bible School (Durban), and from the Franson Memorial Bible School correspondence course in Zulu.[42]

MaMoyo had gone off to kill and prepare a chicken for our food. After the meal, we talked with MaMoyo for some time. Nondulo translated. For some reason, we briefly entered MaMoyo's sleeping hut, where there was very little open floor space—almost

Figure 4.1. Dazzie Vundhla (MaMoyo), 1999. *Photo credit: Wendy Urban-Mead*

none. There was a bed, some stools, and in the corner a wooden trunk or barrel—very large, about four or five feet tall and as wide. On it was written in bold letters "Arthur A. Climenhaga, Matopo Mission." This useful storage piece must have carried belongings from the United States to Matopo for Climenhaga. It had been forty years since Climenhaga had served in Rhodesia, and Vundhla's now very aged widow still had the piece in her sleeping hut, likely still serving as storage.

The framed photographs and certificates on the wall of the Vundhlas' home tell of an aspirant, striving to take advantage of all forms of modernizing self-improvement available to someone not born into one of the elite families whose children had been sent to the mission boarding schools. Vundhla farmed his land according to Rhodesian government standards and earned his master farmer certificate in 1954.[43] Vundhla must have proven a solid leader to the village church near Matopo Mission, to the extent that the mission leaders supported his desire for further theological training. He was the first and only pupil at the BICC's Wanezi Bible School when it opened, in 1948.[44] After completion of the course at Wanezi Bible School he became a (paid) evangelist for the Matopo circuit in 1950.[45] According to the BICC-Zimbabwe's centennial volume, "His work was so appreciated that the church sent him for advanced studies at Sweetwaters in South Africa in 1952."[46]

When the Rhodesian government forcibly removed people from their land in the Matopos once again, this time in the early 1950s, and relocated them to Matabeleland North, Vundhla extended his evangelistic efforts to that region. Doris Dube's account indicates while he was home for vacation in 1952 after his first year at Union Bible Institute near Pietermaritzburg in present-day KwaZulu-Natal, South Africa, Vundhla was approached by Sitshokupi Sibanda. MaSibanda, an older woman, had just visited the traumatized people who had arrived in Matabeleland North three years earlier and determined that they needed intensive evangelistic and pastoral attention. She came to Vundhla—a younger and more energetic person, a man, and a Bible school–trained evangelist—and challenged him to respond to this need.[47] He did respond and helped plant the BICC church in Gwaai.[48] This account, written by the bishop of the Rhodesian BICC in 1955, indicates the extent of the mission leadership's admiration for Vundhla's work as an evangelist in Matabeleland North:

> Last year, one of our more enterprising evangelists, Sandi Vundla, was sent up to this area for a preliminary tour. Although Vundla completed only Standard Three or so in academic education, he has had considerable experience with Europeans, has taken our two-year evangelist's course at Wanezi Bible School, and has picked up a fair knowledge of building.
>
> He found the people most receptive . . . and made important contacts. Later on, our superintendent for this area, the Rev'd R. H. Mann, made a trip there. Vundla stayed on, helping and supervising in the building of three

church units, which can also be utilized for school, and one district school building. Mr. And Mrs. Mann tell me that these buildings are a credit to our outstation program and are better built than most . . . in the older circuit areas. . . . We have three more sites applied for. We plan to send Evangelist Vundla back there again this year for further consolidation. While there, he carries on a full program of preaching and village visitation evangelism.[49]

Having thus proven himself a tenacious and effective rural evangelist by the mid-1950s both in the Matopo circuit and in Matabeleland North, Vundhla was tapped by the missionary leadership for a new assignment—to extend the reach of the church into the regional capital, Bulawayo—the second-largest city in the colony of Southern Rhodesia. Vundhla's career in the Brethren in Christ Church shows a man who did not enjoy ascribed status but rather exerted himself to earn it. In this regard, he was the ideal man to lead the church's move into urban Bulawayo, the provincial capital, to which flocked large numbers of African laborers in the years after the Second World War seeking wage labor and personal betterment.

While many people had a hand in bringing the BICC to town, the official mission publications and documentary records highlight the work of Sandey Vundhla. His role was certainly crucial.[50] He was chosen to be the first pastor at the Mpopoma church. The fact that Bishop Arthur Climenhaga ordained Vundhla as uMfundisi was indicative of high expectations that the new venture would be a prominent project in the church's work. Vundhla and Zook were ordained on June 1, 1957, together with two other African men slated immediately to become overseers for the church's rural districts.[51] Vundhla's ordination was extraordinary not only because he was only the sixth African to be ordained by the BICC but because he was the first ordained African who was not directly intended for service as an overseer. District overseers, who presided over entire districts with as many as forty or more congregations, were the only Africans until this time who had attained the BICC title of uMfundisi. The wives of the candidates for ordination stood up with them during the ceremony. Wives of abaFundisi were accorded high respect and expected to be leaders of the women in their husband's flocks. They did not receive pay for their services, but were seen, in a sense, as sharing both the privilege and responsibility of the office of the ordained man.[52]

MaMoyo was Vundhla's helpmate in the work of the church in Bulawayo. When the Mpopoma church building opened, late in 1957, Vundhla and his wife, MaMoyo, found someone to look after their farm in the Matopos and they moved to town.[53] He oversaw the building of the church structure and pastored a rapidly growing congregation, which in turn spawned "preaching points" that grew into yet more congregations.[54] The Mpopoma church was built in an aspirant, middle-class section of the western (African) suburbs. The church served as a haven for its founding members, recently urbanized Christian matrons, who could claim monogamous Christian status. In 1958, after only one year in the new Mpopoma building, services were drawing 150 worshippers each Sunday.[55]

Carol Summers has written persuasively about the importance of a successful monogamous marriage for African male church leaders.[56] Summers notes that the male African leaders serving through the American Board Mission at Mount Silinda (in eastern Zimbabwe) who were most successful at walking the tightrope between the missionaries and their people had formed an enduring marital partnership with a "respectable" Christian matron. This was a dynamic that holds true for the African male leaders of the BICC, Vundhla included. The success of Vundhla's church career is precisely linked to his and MaMoyo's period of intact monogamous marriage.

Like her husband, MaMoyo was also not from an elite family by either precolonial or colonial definitions. Unlike rural overseers' wives Hannah Sibanda and Joyce Khumalo, Dazzie Vundhla did not attend the Mtshabezi girls' boarding school and did not come from an established Christian family. Born sometime in the

1910s, she came from a polygamist household. Her mother died during the 1918 influenza pandemic, leaving behind Dazzie and her younger brother, who was only crawling at the time of their mother's death, to be cared for by their father. There were other children born to her father by another wife, but they were already grown. Her father was not a churchgoer. Evangelists from nearby Matopo Mission came through, preaching, encouraging children to go to school. "We were called to the mission." She attended school only rarely, however, since she had to care for the cattle: "If we went to school, when we came home, Father would say, 'with whom did you leave the property' [the cattle]? We were supposed to let the cattle out, herd them, and bring them back in the evening. Oh, it was difficult."[57]

Nonetheless, Dazzie went to school as much as she could and attended church services. She became a Christian earlier in life than did Vundhla, and by her reckoning her faith helped draw him to the faith. Both from lower-stratum abantu bakaMambo families, and initially both minimally educated, their earned status made them both well suited to church in urban Bulawayo at this time, and MaMoyo found her new environment stimulating. With married women as the majority in early urban congregations, one could see the BICC as a refuge of support for the monogamously married women. The BICC was not alone in this, of course; other mission churches such as the Methodists served this function as well. However, it is helpful to keep in mind that the mission churches in the rural areas had specific areas of operation, and if one moved from a BICC area such as Godhlwayo or Mayezane, a person newly arrived in town would be most likely to try to find a church home at a BICC congregation.

When MaMoyo discussed her life in town as the wife of uMfundisi Sandey Vundhla, the first thing she mentioned was the vibrant world of cross-denominational women's church work. This was surely one of the first times a BICC African minister's wife had had so much interaction with other denominations. Church groups with whom she mixed were the mainstream

Protestant mission societies active in Bulawayo at that time: the Church of Christ, the Methodists, the Baptists, the Seventh-Day Adventists, the Salvation Army, and the Anglicans.[58] The BICC interacted with neither the Roman Catholic Church[59] nor with the Independent churches, such as the Apostolics (or *Vapostori*). MaMoyo said of her work among women in town, "There were many kinds of churches in town. Our church came later. We were working. Women would visit houses, distributing tracts. That was our job there. We are the ones who were holding women's meetings. Hey, in town there is faith. Even if you think they don't believe, they believe. This really revived some of them."[60] MaMoyo's remark, "even if you think they don't believe, they believe," may be a response to the commonly held belief at the time she moved to Bulawayo that people in town were backsliders, people who had fallen away from or rejected their Christian faith. Her interdenominational work in Bulawayo is an important part of the history of women's work but it does not have a prominent place in the official church histories. The urban BICC established weekly women's meetings under MaMoyo's leadership.[61] One of the few mentions of her work with women in the documentary record was as an aside to an account of the labors of her husband, when they started the church at Mpopoma: "His wife, a rather retiring person, has done remarkably well as leader of the women's work and as his helper in visitation."[62] Brethren in Christ Church missionary women and African leaders' wives had been working with African women, sponsoring "women's meetings" in the rural areas since the beginning of the century.[63] It was not, however, until the church moved to town that women's uniforms were introduced in the BICC. It is not a coincidence that a BICC official organization, the Omama Bosizo—a Rhodesia-wide,[64] uniformed version of women's meeting—therefore emerged in 1969, ten years after the urban churches opened. All aspects of the women's work conducted by wives of rural district overseers and by Dazzie Vundhla (MaMoyo) in town were incorporated into the Omama Bosizo when it was founded, in 1969.

The women of a BICC congregation expected the pastor's wife to be their local model of Christian womanhood. In the colonial Zimbabwe setting, that meant piety, purity, and "modern" (i.e., North American) housekeeping. As demonstrated in chapter 2, sexual purity and deep personal piety were expected of BICC women. Women were expected to become wives of Christian men and keep homes according to the standards set at the mission stations. Other denominations also had this pattern whereby the wife of the uMfundisi led the women under his jurisdiction.[65]

Another antecedent to the Omama Bosizo is the broader phenomenon, touching all major Protestant denominations in southern Africa during the twentieth century, known as the manyano (mother's union). These women's church organizations featured the uniforms worn by members, the vibrancy of their prayer and singing, and the influence they wielded in some of the denominations where they were active.[66] This latter point is particularly applicable to the Methodist women's groups. In colonial Zimbabwe the first women's uniformed prayer association was the Methodist manyano, locally called the Ruwadzano, which began in 1921. The group's aim was to enhance women members' Christian spiritual life as well as to teach "Christian" homemaking skills. Their largest bases being on the Wesleyan Methodist Missionary Society's rural mission stations, the Ruwadzano gained a reputation for enhancing its members' fertility, and on a practical level often functioned as a mutual-aid society.[67]

Blending piety, propriety, and the teaching of homemaking skills, the BICC's Omama Bosizo branches were modeled not only after the "women's meetings" of the BICC, and the uniformed women's manyanos of the Methodists and other denominations, but also on the secular women's clubs. Secular women's clubs, devoted to teaching homecraft, performing philanthropy, or serving as women's auxiliaries to the trade unions or nationalist political parties, had been in colonial Zimbabwe for at least as long as the Rhodesian Bantu Voters' Association, which helped establish a Bantu Women's League in the 1920s in Bulawayo.[68] After the Second World War, "homecraft clubs for African women flourished" all over colonial Africa. The Rhodesian government supported the creation of women's clubs. The most notable effort along these lines was the Federation of African Women's Clubs, organized by European women, the wives of civil servants. These clubs focused exclusively on rural African women. Their aim was to promote homecraft skills, self-help, and limited democratization for rural Africans, as part of the government's answer to African nationalism.[69]

After her husband's departure from church leadership, in 1969, MaMoyo retired to Vundhla's rural home near Matopo Mission after 1969 and was no longer active in BICC-wide women's leadership. Perhaps one answer to why her work went relatively unnoticed is found in the fact that, unlike other wives of the ordained ministers, Dazzie Vundhla was not a girl of the gate. During her childhood in a non-Christian family living near Matopo Mission, with daily obligations to care for the family's cattle (an unusual but not uncommon duty for a girl), it had been very difficult for her to attend school in spite of her proximity to the mission. She never reached standard 1. (That means she attained something equivalent to a first- or second-grade education.) After her husband resigned and she retired to Vundhla's rural home near Matopo Mission, in 1969, MaMoyo's scope of influence shrank considerably. After 1969 until the time of her death, in 2009, she instead confined her sphere of leadership to those women at the Matopo church and its environs.[70] The significance of her inter-denominational work in town during the 1950s and 1960s, then, is best understood in light of how new it was that there was a BICC minister's wife in town at all and that she was working in cooperation with other denominations' church groups.[71]

Spiritual Power in the Politicized City

By the mid-1960s, the church's presence in Bulawayo had expanded considerably beyond its origins at the Mpopoma church. This was in spite of an overall drop in church membership in the 1960s, attributed to the pressures exerted by the influence of mass nationalist organizing. Enough growth had occurred in Bulawayo that several new congregations had opened.

By all accounts Vundhla was a man of spiritual power. One missionary with whom he worked remembered that he "was passionate for the Lord; he was compassionate."[72] He was an effective evangelist, known for his tenacity and tirelessness in reaching out to individuals in their homes. He cycled all over urban Bulawayo in order to speak to people. His preaching was highly regarded. One missionary's account from 1959 offered fulsome praise: "Into the Bulawayo Church program this year has gone [Vundhla's] untiring energy, impassioned praying, unceasing seeking and shepherding, and hard manual labour—yes, one could well say, his 'blood, sweat, and tears.'"[73] In a 1964 report uMfundisi Vundhla was said to be "still working overtime."[74] African members of the

Figure 4.2. Bible men, early 1960s. *Left to right,* Bafanya Mlilo, Mangisi Sibanda, Davidson Mushala, Sandey Vundhla, Philip Mudenda, Nasoni Moyo. *Photographer unknown*

urban church also praised his emphasis on house-to-house visitation, adding also that he was popular with all the urban churches.[75]

Many have attested that Vundhla was particularly interested in reaching out to the most marginalized of people. His widow, MaMoyo, suggested that the mission church leadership elevated Vundhla to the position of uMfundisi as a result of his work in Matabeleland North: "He went to *Maguswini* [Matabeleland North] and started evangelism there, up until his time for him to be chosen [as uMfundisi]. They [abaFundisi] were chosen from among the evangelists. They then chose him, thinking he is a better person to handle God's work, even going [to distant] places, he's such an understanding person. And he was sympathetic and merciful to people out in remote places, you see."[76] Vundhla could relate to marginalized groups; he was "a man who served and was identified sometimes with sinners."[77] Although Vundhla's political beliefs were kept discreetly from the mission establishment, the very fact that his ministry drew him to the most vulnerable groups, whether it was those forcibly removed to Matabeleland North or the domestic workers, jail inmates, the hospitalized, and beer hall regulars of urban Bulawayo, suggests that he was keenly aware of the human costs among the African population of Rhodesian colonial policies.[78]

One reason Vundhla's work for the church was so highly prized by the leadership is that he was so effective at reaching out to men. As we have seen, the migrant labor system and Rhodesian priority of keeping most African women and children in the rural areas meant that most Africans living in town were men.[79] It is also true that, included in the 82,617 Africans registered to live in Bulawayo in 1957 were 9,264 families.[80] Membership statistics for these years are not broken down by sex, making it difficult to determine whether men or women predominated in church membership in the early years of the urban church. An African deacon in the urban church from the 1950s recalled that six women were among the ten or so founding members of the Mpopoma church and concluded that "there were many men in Bulawayo, but they were not in the church."[81] One instance of Vundhla's ability to move men was featured in the *Evangelical Visitor.* In 1965 one of the General Conference themes was "Every Man Win Another Now." "Some of the spirit of the meeting could be seen when Rev. Vundhla, conducting a short praise service, called for ten men to stand and approximately thirty men stood simultaneously."[82]

Vundhla was also known for mixing with and reaching out to unchurched African men. One example can be seen in the relationship he established with the husband of Zama Ncube, mentioned at the beginning of this chapter. Mrs. Ncube is a steady, long-serving member of the Mpopoma congregation. Vundhla reached out to her husband. She said, "[My husband]'s not a churchgoer. . . . Although he's a good man, he has not decided. Reverend Vundhla was very interested in him, would come and visit him, talk to him."[83] Mr. Ncube's involvement in politics precluded, for him, joining the church, in spite of Vundhla's efforts to build a relationship with him and thereby lead him to join the church. The Mpopoma BICC church's foundational years—from 1958 to 1965—were coincident with major, rapid changes in the African political nationalist movement, from the black elites' hopes for "partnership" under the Federation of Rhodesia and Nyasaland (1953–63), in the 1950s, to attempts to assert for a negotiated transition to black political leadership with the successive nationalist parties, starting with the Southern Rhodesian African National Congress (SRANC), which became the National Democratic Party in 1959, in turn leading to ZAPU's creation out of the banned NDP, in 1961. The splitting off of ZANU from ZAPU, in 1963, led to serious factional conflict in Bulawayo and Salisbury in 1964. In 1965 the Rhodesian government issued its Unilateral Declaration of Independence, effectively shutting down all chance of conversation and negotiation between white government and black political activists—a shift that led ultimately to the guerrilla war of the 1970s.

The formation of the ANC, and its banning and subsequent rebirth as the NDP, was happening in the midst of Vundhla's work to build up the church at Mpopoma and in Bulawayo more broadly. A 1959 report by the native commissioner (NC) for Bulawayo emphasized that in Mpopoma "hooliganism" was rife and that there were "cases of molestation of women in this township" supposedly (according to the NC) attributable to the presence of single male lodgers lacking family or "tribal" connection.[84] In spite of the city government's efforts to distract the African population with the dizzying array of "wholesome" entertainments mentioned above, demeaning treatment from the city authorities against Mpopoma residents for being delinquent in their mortgage payments was one of several factors that led to Mpopoma becoming "an important nationalist stronghold by the late 1950s."[85]

As indicated in chapter 3, the forced removals of hundreds of BICC families into Matabeleland North led to the politicization of many BICC members, in particular men. Other elements that played a part in the growth of an explicit anticolonialism included education and exposure to wider ideas that were available in town, especially trade unionism and contact with people who had worked in Zambia or South Africa, where the antiapartheid movement was sophisticated and well advanced.[86] Many young men educated in the rural mission schools, especially the Matopo Secondary School during the 1950s and 1960s, went on to work for different mission societies, where politics was not as taboo as it was for the BICC, or they took positions in government schools in town. The church's history cannot be divorced from either the rural or urban nationalisms that flourished during these years.[87] Rural and urban are in any case hard to separate, since the migrant labor system meant that most urban workers continued to identify strongly with their rural homes, in spite of the church's bias that nationalist worldliness was to be blamed on the urban influence.

The mission church itself stressed a clear line: on one side was worldliness and sin, including politics, and on the other was piety, righteousness, and detachment from the "the world." As indicated already, the mission establishment prized Vundhla for his spiritual gifts. A 1962 urban church report demonstrates a dichotomized view of the place of politics and piety: it states that "attention to political happenings has distracted a few of our men [while] Rev. Vundla faithfully migrates between Nguboyenja and Mpopoma."[88] The men "distracted by politics" are placed in negative contrast to the "faithful" work of Vundhla.

Yet Vundhla's focused outreach to disadvantaged groups challenges the mission's dichotomized view of spiritual versus worldly concerns. Some of Daryl Climenhaga's transcripts of interviews with leading male churchmen indicate that there was "political content" in Vundhla's sermons.[89] ZAPU historian Eliakim Sibanda made this explicit when he stated that when the National Democratic Party was banned, in 1960, Vundhla opened the Mpopoma church as a refuge to men fleeing arrest from the Rhodesian government during a series of clashes in July 1960 known as *zhii*.[90] Vundhla's friend and member of the Mpopoma church, Timothy Ndlovu, recalled in a 1996 interview with Eliakim Sibanda that when the police came to the church gate in order to pursue the fleeing men, Vundhla stood at the gate and refused entry, insisting that the church was a place of refuge.[91]

Given that a church member, let alone an ordained uMfundisi, was forbidden to be involved in African nationalist politics, it is perhaps not surprising that the extent of Vundhla's political affiliations, words, and actions remain outside the documentary record and mainly only hinted at in oral history interviews with those who knew him. It seems Vundhla was exceptionally skilled at walking the fine line between identification with the people's sufferings and grievances, and satisfying the mission church's insistence on nonworldliness in the matter of politics. His success at negotiating that tension was a crucial ingredient in his success at reaching out to men spawning a cluster of new and growing Bulawayo congregations.

By the later 1960s, Vundhla and MaMoyo's success at building the church in the city of Bulawayo was clear. As an uMfundisi who was soon pastoring a relatively large congregation of people who earned cash wages, Vundhla became the first congregational pastor in the African church to receive a living wage.[92] As additional urban churches opened, Vundhla's stature and charisma led him to become a de facto overseer, in a de facto urban district, appointing and mentoring the other, newer pastors in town.

However, thirteen years after the Mpopoma church was founded, Vundhla's career in the church came to a crashing halt. Vundhla's rise and fall has most often been told either from the pietist standpoint that he was nothing more than a man hungry to see men's souls brought home to Christ, or from the desire to understand the dynamics of church organization and leadership issues. Some believed that by 1968 Sandey Vundhla was considering breaking away and starting his own independent church. Others insist that rumors of his aspirations to break were only rumors and rather that Vundhla wanted nothing other than to stay as uMfundisi of the BICC congregation at Mpopoma.[93] In that year, an evangelistic revival was held at the Mpopoma and Nguboyenja churches in Bulawayo. The guest preacher was an Assemblies of God preacher from South Africa named Mr. Mkwananzi. Another visiting evangelist who preached at BIC outstation churches the same year was Shadreck Maloka of the Dorothea Mission (Apostolic Faith Church). According to interviews conducted by Daryl Climenhaga, Vundhla received encouragement from both these men, who were heading African independent churches, to follow their example and "establish his own church outside mission control."[94] Vundhla had a core of deeply loyal followers. Vundhla's supposed contemplation of a break-away apparently only stalled over the fact that the Mpopoma church building was owned by the BICC. The push from lay leaders of the urban churches to come out from under the authority of Matopo District, and form their own urban district, can be understood in a different way in light of the suggestion that Vundhla was considering breaking away altogether. P. M. Khumalo and the other mission authorities' hard stance on keeping the urban churches under their control may well have been driven by their concern that Vundhla might break away and their insistence that such thriving churches not be lost to the BICC. Whether he was a victim of the machinations of others keen to be free of the control of the rural mission establishment, or whether he indeed was making moves to break away and take Mpopoma with him, Vundhla's church career was stopped short. By 1970, Vundhla's ordained status was revoked, he was removed from the pastor's position at the Mpopoma church, and he eventually left church fellowship altogether.

Rural Elites and the Urban Church

The urban churches' placement under the jurisdiction of the largely rural Matopo District led to a power struggle that took years to work out, and it is an important element in explaining the end of Vundhla's church career.[95] Urbanized African church members wished to have more control over the policies governing their churches. Each of the church's four major districts (Matopo, Mtshabezi, Wanezi, and Phumula) had their headquarters at the rural mission stations and came under the authority of a district overseer. P. M. Khumalo was overseer for Matopo District and the Bulawayo churches from 1959 to 1969. He was ordained uMfundisi in 1960. The church sent him to study theology in the United States from 1961 to 1962; in 1969, when the BICC's first African bishop was elected, the choice was Khumalo.[96] He represented the interests of the missionaries and the rural African Christian elite, while Vundhla represented the interests of the urban church members. It has been observed, however, that Vundhla operated as a de facto overseer over the Urban Bulawayo churches.[97] Because the urban churches were under the authority of Matopo overseer Khumalo's, however, Vundhla technically was only a congregational pastor who happened also to have been ordained.

Unprecedented since district councils were established in the 1930s, the urban churches wished to have independent access to the church's highest authority, the Regional Conference, an annual meeting of the entire Southern Rhodesia church membership, without having their issues mediated by the African overseer for their district. "We did not believe that we could be supervised effectively by an overseer out in a rural area."[98] The Regional Conference's decisions were binding on the church as a whole. No issue was supposed to be brought to Regional Conference except those that had been processed through the individual district council meetings first. In 1968 delegates from the Bulawayo churches insisted that matters pertaining to their churches should be brought to the Regional Conference only by the minister in charge of these urban churches. It was highly irregular that the urban churches requested to bring their own issues directly "to conference" without having them first approved by the district overseer.

The Matopo district council decided, in response to this request from the urban churches, that all issues should be forwarded to the overseer without the signature of the pastor of the congregation, from which the matter would be sent to conference. The accompanying handwritten note in the margin of the minutes from this meeting added, "Khumalo at Bulawayo to tell people."[99] The handwritten note points to the fact that Overseer P. M. Khumalo felt it necessary to go to the urban churches in person to emphasize that he, not Vundhla, was the conduit through which their concerns would be addressed by the wider church. Significantly, after 1967 Vundhla's name disappeared from the yearly mission reports filed for publication in the *Yearbook of Missions*. Ever since the urban churches opened in 1957, "Bulawayo churches" had been a separate category in the mission reports. Starting in 1968, P. M. Khumalo filed a report as overseer of Matopo District, "including the Bulawayo Churches."[100]

The following year, 1969, the urban churches—undeterred in their quest for autonomy from the rural district's authority—came to the Matopo district council meeting requesting recognition of a separate district. In this instance the council recommended that this request be forwarded to the church executive committee for consideration.[101] Daryl Climenhaga analyzes this power struggle:

> The urban churches were not part of the top level of
> leadership. They sought to break into that level when
> they requested the right to be their own district with their

own overseer. The actions of Vundla in town, appointing pastors for the preaching points and caring for them more generally, suggest that he and those with him were the real strength in the urban churches. When the church executive committee asserted its control over Mpopoma in Bulawayo, they confirmed that the strength of that church had been outside their control . . . [Vundhla's] supporters were those most strongly committed to urban life. They included the better educated elite, who, while strongly traditional at their core, understood well how to live in contemporary [colonial] Zimbabwe.[102]

By 1971 the representatives of the urban churches at the Matopo district council meeting were asking why their request for a separate district did not come up at the Regional Conference. Told that the church executive had rejected the idea, the urban churches asked to have their request put to the church executive again.[103]

Matopo council minutes from 1970 indicate that the urban churches were making an issue as to whether they had been properly invited to the council meeting. This is also the year when Sandey Vundhla left the church, as his second marriage became public knowledge. Daryl Climenhaga argues that although it seems clear that P. M. Khumalo and Vundhla had disagreements, the fact that others agitated for more autonomy for the urban churches indicates that the issue of the urban church's identity went beyond the two men's power struggle and beyond Vundhla's personal transgressions against monogamy.[104] Vundhla's removal did not make the essential issue go away; this fact lends credence to the point of view that Vundhla himself was not seeking a bid for independence so much as his followers hoped he would. In the end, the urban churches were not allowed to form a separate district until after independence, in 1980.[105]

Monogamy, Masculinity, and the Church Leader

Climenhaga's work explaining this power struggle emphasizes the rural-urban dynamic and its interface with the structures of church polity. It is crucial, however, to mark that the years of this power struggle ended with Vundhla marrying a second wife. The ending of his monogamy was the end of his church career. His second wife was a woman who had previously been married in a ceremony at which Vundhla had been the officiant.[106] And it was a disastrous turn of events for his first wife, MaMoyo. After Vundhla left the church, MaMoyo, who had been his supporter, helpmate, and partner in the building of the Mpopoma church, returned to their rural homestead in the Matopos while he continued to live in town with the other wife. "He changed; he caused me a lot of pain."[107] When he died, in 1994, MaMoyo did not want Vundhla to lie in state at the rural homestead, but he did. Bitter over having been abandoned, MaMoyo refused to wear the mourning garb for widows. Vundhla's second wife wore the blanket over her head and her dress inside out, as a bereaved wife is expected to do for the one week following the burial, until she put on the mourning dress, to wear for one year. In his will, however, Vundhla left everything, except his house in town, to MaMoyo.[108]

Doris Dube's account of Vundhla's life views his decision to marry another woman as Vundhla's "fall." She offers a motivation that was at once personal, familial, colonialist and gendered, based on an insult to his masculinity generated by an insensitive white missionary. It is worth citing in some detail:

> What made Rev Vundhla fall? Possibly, very few people appreciate the curse that comes with being childless in our culture. Rev Vundhla and Mama MaMoyo had no child. Many people who talked to Vundhla about his fall were told the story that Vundhla had requested an allowance from the then Bishop, as he was doing a lot of mileage on his scooter to visit people in the hospitals, jails, schools, and various suburbs in Bulawayo. The Bishop seemingly laughed that off and said, "Uyayenzani imali? Awula mntwana." (What do you need money for, you have no child.) Vundhla questioned his manhood, and then decided to take another wife, with whom he had two children.

> He proved he could have children at the expense of his
> position in the church and his noble work for the Lord.[109]

According to the logic of this version of his story, Vundhla was hurt and shamed when his childlessness was used to deny him a pay increase. It served as an insult to his manhood too unendurable to resist the urge to take a second wife and finally acquire children. Why had Vundhla and MaMoyo's infertility not led him before 1969 to marry a second wife? This bears closer examination. He and MaMoyo had been childless throughout their marriage of, at the time of his ouster, some twenty-eight years.

Monogamy was a marital standard introduced with Christianity and the influence of missionaries. Mission societies seeking to win the conversion of Africans had to decide whether a man with multiple wives could become a Christian while being a polygamist. The mission churches of Rhodesia eventually set the policy that a polygamous man had to "put away" all his wives but his first one before he could be baptized. This policy did not change in the BICC until the 1980s, after independence. Polygyny, however, was an accepted strategy for African families to ensure sufficient progeny. If, for example, a woman proved not to be able to have children, the husband would then take her sister as a second wife. In this way the offspring of the younger sister would still accrue to the honor of the first, barren, wife. If the couple were Christian, this option was closed down. Also, multiple wives were a marker of wealth, since only a man (or a family) with many cattle could afford the bridewealth to bring more than one wife to the homestead and thereby be able to claim offspring for a man's own family line.

Michael O. West very helpfully discusses the challenge of monogamy for Christian, elite African men of the mid-twentieth century, referring to what he calls "monogamous recidivism." It was a common pattern among African men who married by Christian rites and who then due to infertility, migrant labor, and the consequent lengthy separations from their wives, came to marry or otherwise liaise with other women.[110] The second marriage could not be contracted in any other way than by "native custom," leaving such an African man no other choice but to be considered back-slidden and out of church fellowship. This is what happened with Sandey Vundhla when he "took" a second wife, in 1969.

The way Dube's account is structured gives enormous power to the missionary bishop—the power of his suggestion of inadequate manliness was enough to goad Vundhla into marrying a second wife. While it is not possible to know how much the bishop's remarks can be given as the direct cause of Vundhla's actions, it is illuminating to contrast this exchange with another encounter Vundhla had with a prior missionary bishop, thirteen years earlier, at the time of his ordination.

One observer who was present on the day of Vundhla's ordination, in 1957, recalled a special prayer offered for Vundhla and MaMoyo by then missionary bishop Arthur Climenhaga. Climenhaga, who was also childless, empathized with Vundhla's lack of children. His prayer for Vundhla and MaMoyo included mentioning that the Lord had withheld children from "some of us" in order that they might have spiritual children, and the prayer went on to ask that Vundhla and MaMoyo now go on to be fruitful for the church.[111] The sorrow of childlessness was shared by both Bishop Climenhaga and Vundhla: John L. Dube of South Africa, ordained minister of the Congregational Church in South Africa and cofounder of the African National Congress there, also struggled with barrenness. After many years of childlessness in his marriage to his first wife, Dube got into trouble when he impregnated a student at the school where he served as head; after his wife died, he remarried a much younger woman and through her became the father of six children.[112] Strivings for fertility could get men into deeper trouble with the church than it did women. Women who gave birth to children out of wedlock could repent and be returned to church fellowship. Since a woman did not need to marry a second spouse in order to have a child, unlike men, women's transgressive motherhood could be overcome eventually. For an ordained man, marrying a second wife in pursuit of fatherhood put him in a perpetual state of adultery from the point of view of the church. Unless he was to divorce the second wife, he could not easily be restored to fellowship. Thus Vundhla's transgressive fatherhood was more permanently damaging to his piety than was Maria Tshuma's unmarried childbearing.[113]

Juxtaposing Climenhaga's handling of Vundhla's childlessness in 1957 with that of the other church leader—whose remarks in the mid-1960s are considered, by Dube, to be largely to blame for Vundhla's decision to marry a second wife—complicates and enriches the potential answers as to why Vundhla took an action that he knew would lead to his demise as a church leader. In 1957, flush from his successes in church planting and evangelism in Matabeleland North, Vundhla became the first African man ordained who was not intended immediately to become a district overseer. Having been chosen to head the church's ministry in urban Bulawayo, it is conceivable that Vundhla read his ordination as a promise of a future position as overseer for a new urban district. In addition, there was apparently a strong bond of mutual respect and shared suffering between missionary bishop Climenhaga and Vundhla, both of whose marriages had proved childless.[114]

Vundhla's dismissal also illustrated the narrow line that all African men had to walk in order to retain their positions in church leadership, or even just in church membership. Men such as Vundhla, whose careers imploded because of "sins" such as taking a second wife, rarely returned to church in any significant way until their old age, or on their deathbeds.[115] Vundhla followed this pattern of male return to church fellowship after one's work of manhood was complete: in 1986 some church members went to visit him and urge him to come back to church. That same year, he appeared at worship in Bulawayo, made a public confession of sin, and expressed a desire to return to the Lord. He was received back into church fellowship and attended church sporadically from then until his death in 1994. Here we see the cycle of piety for Vundhla concluding as it did for so many other men: with an end-of-life repentance and return to good standing as a churchman.[116]

––––––––––

The official church was in a period of modernization, part of which included allowing a church to create a new congregation in urban Bulawayo. Bishop Climenhaga chose Vundhla to build that church: both literally and figuratively, Vundhla laid the stones and recruited the congregation. Vundhla was an evangelist who responded courageously, even extravagantly, to the pain experienced by their people due to the conditions of colonial rule. The celebration of Vundhla's work in town is so effusive precisely because he fulfilled an ideal of the official church—of an African man, monogamously wed, whose leadership capacity and commitment to church growth matched, even exceeded, that of the church hierarchy. Taking full advantage of the opportunities given by the church, Vundhla's energy, determination, and effectiveness as an evangelist led him first to success within the church's leadership structures and then to test the limits of leadership available to an African man. The reasons for the directions Vundhla's career took can be linked to the currents determining Ndebele masculinity and masculine piety and how these interacted in a colonial mission church.

Vundhla's frustrated aspirations for leadership played a part, in addition to the obvious problem of violating church doctrine on monogamy, in explaining the reasons for his departure from church leadership. Vundhla likely had aspirations of heading a separate urban district under his overseership. While polygyny was incontrovertibly against church teaching, his decision to marry a second wife was chronologically in tandem with his loss in the power struggle that ensued between the Bulawayo urban church and the Matopo District leadership under P. M. Khumalo. Even if the missionaries were fostering African initiative in the church in response to the church's version of nationalist pressure, they did so only up to a point. The church's rural power base at the mission stations retained its ascendancy. Vundhla's short-lived exploration of possibly heading an independent church led nowhere. His willingness to endure childlessness with MaMoyo had been fed by the promise of ever-greater opportunities to lead and be influential. When it became clear to Vundhla that he was likely to become neither an overseer of a new urban district nor the head of an independent church, he was no longer prepared to abide by the church rules regarding marriage.

Vundhla's career demonstrates that evangelism could be used as a form of African initiative that was welcomed by white missionaries and tolerated by the Rhodesian authorities. The unworldly, pietistic focus of the church worked to his advantage, since African leadership was only tolerable within very narrowly prescribed bounds. Sandey Vundhla attained a position of considerable influence as the sole ordained minister in urban Bulawayo while treading carefully amid the entrenched powers of the white missionary establishment, the African ordained leadership, the colonial Rhodesian government and nationalist pressures within the urban African population.

While the structural and institutional limits to Vundhla's ability to exercise power are important, juxtaposing Vundhla's career with the political history in which he lived and worked is also illuminating. Sandey Vundhla's relationship to the church, his meteoric rise and then fall, lopes along almost chronologically exactly parallel to the nationalist movement—from the black elites' hopes for "partnership" to attempts to assert for black leadership under the Federation of Rhodesia and Nyasaland during the 1950s, and when rebuffed, a move to radical rejection and exit from discussion (beginning with the formation of the NDP and ZAPU in the early 1960s and then, by the 1970s, guerrilla war). In Vundhla's case it was a bootstrap-style education after reaching adulthood, along with Christian marriage (1930s) and deliberate moves toward respectability, then missionary-anointed leadership of a new urban district (1955–57), an attempt to get that district declared its own administrative zone under his leadership (early 1960s), then an attempt to go for independence (Ethiopian style) (1967), and then finally, taking a second wife and leaving the church altogether (1970). Vundhla's path within the BICC as a leader tracks the political story, but in an ecclesiastical setting.

And yet Vundhla experienced a period of years when his leadership operated in spite of being in violation of African definitions of "ideal" gender identity, and the church gave him and MaMoyo a space to occupy in leadership that was essentially beyond gender. While he and MaMoyo never had children, for a time—especially during their work in Bulawayo—Climenhaga's prayer came true, and they had been extravagantly "fruitful for the Lord" instead. But by customary standards Vundhla's manhood was in jeopardy due to his lack of children. MaMoyo, too, endured a life of knowing that she had been, from the point of view of what an Ndebele woman should be, a failure as a woman for failing to have children. Although Vundha had been within his customary rights to send MaMoyo to her father's home in 1970, she refused to go, clinging to her claim, as a woman married by Christian rites, to be his wife and till his land, children or not. In the end, he honored that claim. Indeed, Bishop Climenhaga's prayer that he and MaMoyo might be "fruitful for the church," suggested an alternate type of fatherhood for him, a spiritual parenthood for both of them. In spite of the shame of her childlessness, MaMoyo continued to enjoy a position of respect as a leader of women in the Matopo church after 1970. And people whom Vundhla mentored in their growth as Christian leaders even today refer to him as their "father in the Lord."[117] That contemporary African church leaders who had been mentored by Vundhla voluntarily and spontaneously call him their "father in the Lord" makes a compelling contrast with the customary Ndebele view of fatherhood. It was Vundhla's prolific spiritual fatherhood, and MaMoyo's continued spiritual motherhood even in her waning years at Matopo, that earned them both a place in the church's hagiography.

FIVE || MaNsimango (Sithembile Nkala)
Sellouts, Comrades, and Christians in the Liberation War, 1969–78

> She manages to go through.
> —*Musa Chidziva, describing her mother*

IN A DUSTY CLASSROOM AT THE WANEZI mission station in August 1997, an old woman named MaNsimango[1] and her middle-aged daughter, Musa Chidziva, leaned over a microphone and sang in Ndebele a song that translates as "Father we have been blessed by your word; we have been given light because of your light." Musa later explained, as our interview drew to a close, that her mother chose this particular song to open the interview because "it has made her life better; even under difficulties, she manages to go through."[2] Some of the difficulties she passed through in her lifetime, and there were many, occurred during the liberation war years, in the late 1970s.

Why did Musa and MaNsimango start the interview in song, and with this particular song? MaNsimango was setting the tone. The original aim of the interview was to learn more about MaNsimango's education during the 1930s at the Mtshabezi Girls' Primary Boarding School. We were at the church's annual General Conference; I came recommended to them by church connections. For MaNsimango, the interview environment was a feminine

Figure 5.1. Musa Chidziva and Sithembile Nkala (MaNsimango), Nketa, Bulawayo, 2000. *Photo credit: Wendy Urban-Mead.*

space of Christian piety. It was a performance.[3] Thus, even though that interview in 1997 ended up becoming three interviews over three years, and spanning many more topics beyond MaNsimango's schooling, the tone of our interactions remained guided by MaNsimango and her daughter's focus on her Christian walk (see photo of MaNsimango and Musa Chidziva).[4]

This chapter's analysis of MaNsimango's experience with the guerrillas in her village during the war opens the way to demonstrate the complex interactions between understandings of two kinds of piety—Christian piety and nationalistic piety—and of gender at this time in Zimbabwe's history. After some broader historical context identifying the major elements involved with the 1970s war, the chapter features MaNsimango's own account of her experience of the war and then sets it into a variety of analytical contexts. First I discuss this mission church's stance on, and experience with, the liberation war, with attention to the gendered dynamics of piety in this era. A section then follows discussing other tales of faith and valor demonstrated by women of the BICC during the war. The final section sets MaNsimango's life into a multigenerational familial context that shows points of connection from MaNsimango to her sister Hannah, and back to her mother and her mother's brother, to the earliest years of the twentieth century.

Sellout Politics and an Apolitical Church:
The BICC during the Liberation War

In the 1970s the anticolonial nationalist leaders were already calling Rhodesia by a new name: Zimbabwe. They acted through two political parties that had, since the mid-1960s, been resolved to use force to bring about the end of the Rhodesian state. The parties were the Zimbabwe African People's Union, or ZAPU, led by Joshua Nkomo, and the Zimbabwe African National Union, or ZANU, led by Ndabaningi Sithole and later Robert Mugabe. Ian Smith headed the Rhodesian state. Smith's ruling party, the Rhodesian Front, made the unilateral decision to break away from the United Kingdom in 1965,[5] to retain control of the white-settler regime, free of the pressure from London to make accommodations for the nationalist movements and their aspirations. This struggle took place in the midst of the 1970s global cold war. The United States was still extracting itself from Vietnam. South Africa's apartheid system was under strain but still firmly in place. Europe was split in two by the Iron Curtain. The liberation parties of ZANU and ZAPU found philosophical, monetary, and material support from the communist powers of China and the Soviet Union, respectively, as well as from Sweden and Norway. Starting in the 1970s and peaking from 1977 to 1979, the armed forces of ZANU, called ZANLA (Zimbabwe African National Liberation Army), and of ZAPU, called ZIPRA (Zimbabwe People's Revolutionary Army), mounted attacks into the rural areas of Rhodesia. The war came to be known as the Second Chimurenga (1966–79), after the original Chimurenga (1896–97), the rising against the

British South Africa Company's attempts to create a new colony called Rhodesia.

Other studies demonstrate how some churches supported the liberation war, at least in some measure. Ian Linden and Janice McLaughlin address the relationship between the Catholic Church and the liberation struggle, and Ngwabi Bhebe treats the Swedish Lutheran missions in southwestern Zimbabwe.[6] The place of traditional religion in the Zimbabwean nationalist movement has been featured in important works such as those by David Lan, Terence Ranger, and Mark Ncube, who highlight its place in shoring up both ZANLA and ZIPRA guerrillas.[7]

There is a temptation to categorize the various Christian organizations in Rhodesia during the liberation war as either pro-liberation or pro-Smith. Several studies detail different denominations' struggles to respond to an increasingly pressured environment in which every person, and every institution, was expected to come out in clear support of one side or the other. These studies reveal that mission societies, and individual mission stations and their missionary and African personnel, each had to grapple with being in the middle of this conflict. The Catholic Church gained a reputation for being a virtual fifth column of anti-Smith activity. Overt activities included the journal *Moto*, Mambo Press, the Catholic Commission for Justice and Peace, and the outspoken antiracist pastoral letters of Bishop Donal Lamont. However, the Catholic hierarchy also had a pro-Smith element. According to Linden, some Catholic leaders concealed their support for the Smith regime within a "disingenuous clinging to the status quo under the banner of reconciliation and noninvolvement in politics."[8]

Ngwabi Bhebe's thorough treatment of the Evangelical Lutheran Church's interaction with combatants from both the ZIPRA and ZANLA guerrilla armies provides an invaluable point of comparison and contrast with the BICC. Bhebe makes fruitful use of Carl Hallencreutz's method of categorization of the various types of churches active in Rhodesia. Churches are divided among the "national churches," "regionally based mission-related churches," and "independent church movements or Spirit churches."[9] The national churches ministered to white and black, both Shona and Ndebele, and had nationwide reach. Such churches were the Roman Catholic, the Anglican, and the Methodist. The mission churches had a predominantly African membership and were based in a single region of the country. Bhebe summarizes that "with their predominant African affiliation most mission-related regional churches were sympathetic to the nationalist aspirations."[10] He also points out, crucially, that there was a trend whereby church leaders based in urban centers, such as Bulawayo, were more likely to support the moderate wing of the nationalist movement (Abel Muzorewa's UANC, or United African National Congress), while local pastors and parishioners from the rural areas tended to support radical liberation movements. Even the Swedish Lutheran church hierarchy, reaching back to the mission board in Sweden, in the end gave financial support to both ZAPU and ZANU during the 1970s. This move was in line with the World Council of Churches' policy of support for the struggle for majority rule in Rhodesia, issued in the 1970s.[11]

The Brethren in Christ Church, like the Evangelical (Swedish) Lutheran Church, was a regionally based mission church with a predominantly African membership. Both had their bishop's residences in urban Bulawayo, though the BICC's bishop's 1956 move to town occurred twenty years earlier than did the Lutheran bishop's.[12] Both Bhebe and Linden have pointed out how elder clergy in both the Catholic and Lutheran churches tended to be suspicious of the guerrillas and their methods, preferring less confrontational means of addressing the people's grievances. This holds true for the BICC as well. Both cases echo the findings of Norma Kriger's study of peasants during the liberation war, which demonstrates that the war brought out generational conflict between radicalized "youth" and conflict-averse "elders."[13] Yet there are some salient differences between the BICC and the Lutheran church in particular worth highlighting. The BICC's territorial reach was exclusively in Ndebele-speaking areas. The Lutheran church, by contrast, straddled both Shona- and Ndebele-speaking areas in the south of the country and included a large number of Sotho speakers in the extreme southwest. Another key difference is that the Lutheran church was a "magisterial" church. It was a state church with institutional affiliation with the government of Sweden, unlike the apolitical and separatist Anabaptist stance of the BICC in North America. Thus, although both the Lutherans and the BICC had pietistic strains that emphasized heartfelt devotion, their churches' polities had strongly diverging approaches to their relationship with earthly powers and governments.

This chapter continues from the setting out of the distinctly gendered character of political and church affiliation in chapter 4. In line with how the term was used and understood by the people I interviewed, *politics* refers to the formalized nationalist political parties dedicated to the end of colonial rule, and to the Rhodesian government and its political components. To be apolitical in this narrower sense meant choosing neither to formally join one of the parties nor to work for political or governmental changes. As we have seen in the prior chapters, especially chapters 3 and 4, men were more likely to become active members of the nationalist political parties and thereby compromise their standing in the church—a standing often kept within reach indirectly by their wives' or mothers' continued active church engagement. This dynamic was greatly exacerbated during the liberation war of the 1970s.

Were the combatants of ZANLA and ZIPRA terrorists—or freedom fighters and guerrillas? Was this violent struggle one of heroic nationalism? Was it a communist insurgency? The phrasing in these questions is stark and leaves little room for an answer that is anything less than extreme. The starkness reflects the times. The struggle to birth the nation of Zimbabwe was in fact dangerous. There were informers,[14] there were black men serving in the Rhodesian army and Rhodesian police forces, there were African moderates such as Abel Muzorewa envisioning a gradual integration of African elites into the Rhodesian structures, and there were white Rhodesians wanting to hang on to their world. Muzorewa's attempts to walk a path of compromise were ultimately unsuccessful.[15] It was his "seeming lack of bitterness and nationalist vigour that offend[ed] the leaders of the Frontline States and the militant leaders of the guerrillas."[16] All these interests in varying degrees ran counter to those in ZAPU and ZANU who sought to do away entirely with all that was Rhodesia and remake a new Zimbabwean nation.

Within the discursive spaces opened by nationalism, Zimbabwean nationalists' worldview thus was formed around determining who was a comrade and who was a sellout, while the Rhodesian Front was concerned to find out who among the black Africans was a "friendly" and who was a "terrorist." Word choices made all the difference. *Guerrilla* was a term used by those sympathetic to majority rule, to connote the combatants serving in the ZANLA and ZIPRA forces. The Rhodesian government referred to the same as "terrorists." References to "soldiers" specifically connoted armed men who served in the army of the Smith government. There was scant place for moderates or peace advocates in this time.

In a discussion of the formation of the nationalist parties during the 1960s, Tim Scarnecchia carefully distinguishes between the two kinds of violence present in the movement: violence against the settler state, and violence within the party factions due to the dynamics of what he calls "sellout politics."[17] *Sellout* in its most simple sense refers to someone understood to be working in support of the settler government. The aims of both ZAPU and then ZANU were to create a disciplined, loyal African support base. To achieve that, actual discipline—punishment—of perceived sellouts was seen as a necessity. For example, trade union leader Reuben Jamela opened himself in 1961 to sellout accusations from ZAPU leaders due to his independent access to foreign funds. Attacks on Jamela's credibility as an African on the side of liberation were fueled by an "escalating imperialist-versus-communist rhetoric."[18] In 1961, as ZAPU organized meetings in urban Harare, people who failed to attend were often beaten, their failure to attend being understood as tacit support for the Rhodesian regime and thus proof that the person was a sellout. They beat up people they deemed to be "running dogs of the imperialists."[19] ZAPU party power struggles for leadership during this time were also couched in the language of sellouts: Joshua Nkomo and Ndabaningi Sithole both were accused of selling out the struggle at various points. In this modality of nationalist party politics, sellout accusations that worked off of the cold-war-era fears and fields of tension were a core mode of establishing discipline among the rank and file as well as a mode of establishing dominance within the leadership.[20] Thus we see that sellout accusations within the formal nationalist parties have a history going back well before the war.

During the liberation war of the 1970s, the disciplining of sellouts escalated and expanded into the rural populations as guerrillas sought to attain sustained support for their efforts to topple the Rhodesian state. Sellout accusations took on a mode of enactment that worked within understandings of kinship. Richard Werbner notes that the liberation war used the discursive and conceptual framework of parents helping children. The "boys" (the guerrillas") depended on the "parents" and "grandparents" in the rural areas to support their work as guerrilla warriors. MaNsimango's brother-in-law, Rev. Mangisi Sibanda, when telling of his interactions with guerrillas, exemplifies this pattern: "those people, those young people, our boys who would fight for us, they told us that we should leave teaching."[21] As Werbner has insisted, we must "get right the very pervasiveness of the appeal to 'kinship,' and the forceful ambivalence it entailed, when the appeal came along with the ill-controlled threat and, all too often, the actuality of physical coercion."[22]

The almost closed binary of sellout versus comrade, or terrorist versus "good African" was paralleled by another almost closed discursive binary of piety versus sinfulness found in Rhodesia's mission churches, most sharply in the avowedly apolitical BICC. What we see by looking at people whose lives intersected both these worlds—that of the mission church and that of the nationalist struggle—is that the lived reality in the midst of two such separate yet similarly closed systems of understanding the world was both dangerous and complicated as well as gendered. Piety and sellout discourses hit against one another because the war was causing a moral dilemma. Anticolonial nationalism had a kind of piety—a nationalist piety with its own moral imperative. The nationalists' understanding was, and in many cases remains, if you didn't participate in the armed struggle, you were outside the struggle, and outside a claim to belonging. Members of the BICC were aware of the political landscape. Some joined the formal political parties, especially ZAPU and its armed wing, ZIPRA, and some did not, especially those at the top levels of leadership. Generational and other kinds of familial linkages allowed for some members of the same family to do the work of apolitical Christian piety while others attended to the work of political liberation. Few were individually able to do both. Thus, when these family networks are viewed as parts of the larger moral world, we see the erosion of the stark binaries between those cast as political and those cast as apolitical.

MaNsimango and the Guerrillas

In 1969 a small church in the village of Tshalimbe, near what is today Esigodini, had just lost its long-serving pastor, a man named Philemon Nkala. He and his wife, MaNsimango, had also been the teachers at the village's school since the 1940s. Both church and school operated under the auspices of the Brethren in Christ Church. Philemon Nkala's death occurred shortly before the beginning of the liberation war; soon after Nkala died, the church members asked his widow, MaNsimango, to take on the work of pastor. A few years later, ZANLA and ZIPRA guerrilla forces fought against the soldiers who supported Ian Smith's Rhodesian government. Combatants crisscrossed the region in the mid- and late 1970s, leading to a variety of dangers for the inhabitants and their pastor. During the war, as articulated in hindsight in a 1980 editorial in the church's newspaper, "some of the big classrooms which had been used as church houses of worship were destroyed also. Even where the churches were not destroyed, the Christians could not worship as they had done in the past. They were fearful."[23]

Thus, somewhat unusually, MaNsimango (Sithembile Nkala)'s congregation continued to meet and worship throughout the 1970s liberation war, and she managed to survive without beatings, in spite of the guerrilla war that reached near her home of Tshalimbe. There came a time in the late 1970s when both Rhodesian forces and ZANLA guerrillas were camped in the hills not far away from Tshalimbe. As occurred all over Zimbabwe during the war, the guerrillas demanded to know which people, among the local inhabitants, were sympathetic to the Rhodesians. In a 1999 interview, MaNsimango told me of her encounter with ZANLA guerrillas. I asked her, how did the time of guerrilla war affect her work as pastor of the village church at Tshalimbe? She began to answer in English.

> Ayi, I was not affected so much by the *impi* [war]. I was afraid yet I didn't have hard time with those. I talked to them as a Christian, trying to lead them out of what they were to what I saw was right for them to do. I was brave enough that time. I talked to them. People were beaten, ah—hard beating. [At this point she switches to Ndebele.] Then it came to pass that one day there were so many white soldiers on top of the mountain just near my home and we ran away to those beyond the river. We were there with them and I talked to them and said do you know what? You, you are holding guns, we are holding nothing. If someone comes and tells you lies saying so and so is like this, you believe them because you do not know. What I am asking from you is to be careful about people who come to you saying so and so is a sellout. Why? You do not know . . . [I then asked what language she was using.] Ah, there were some who understood Ndebele, then they talked to them in the Shona language, those that did not clearly understand what I was saying. Then they told

them that Gogo [Granny, meaning MaNsimango] is saying we beat people, torturing them because of other people who come and say so and so is a sellout, yet we do not know what type of life they live, not knowing the real life they live.

[Musa asks] But they accepted that?

[MaNsimango] They really accepted, they did not do it again . . . after that they announced that whoever will come to report someone, we will beat him instead of the one being reported.[24]

MaNsimango's account here highlights her courage and her faith. The dynamic between MaNsimango and me was at times a struggle between my efforts to establish specifics of time, place, and person, and her mode of narration, which was not so concerned with specificity and identifiability. I was interested to know if the guerrillas in question were ZIPRA or ZANLA. By indicating that most of them spoke Shona, MaNsimango allowed me to conclude that they were most likely ZANLA. She did not specifically say that they came to Tshalimbe. But I knew she lived at Tshalimbe during the war, so I know we were talking about movements of combatants in the area near Tshalimbe.

MaNsimango did not talk *about* sellout accusations as a political topic. Instead, the telling was a means of conveying her courage to act according to her faith. "I talked to them as a Christian, trying to lead them out of what they were to what I saw was right for them to do. I was brave enough that time." She did not specify by name or any other identifier who was facing a sellout accusation. MaNsimango had already been accused of being a sellout before the war due to her prominent role in the community as a teacher, pastor, and one who encouraged cooperation with community development projects; by the time the war came that accusation seems to have been old news. Her daughter's understanding was that "by then people knew her activities so well that she was protected."[25] Her brother-in-law, Rev. Mangisi Sibanda, was named as a sellout by the guerrillas during the war. His niece attributed the greater danger he faced from this to the fact that he did not live in Tshalimbe very often, because his church duties kept him away for months at a time.[26] If others in the village were accused—and it is likely there was more than one since she speaks of "people" being beaten, in the plural—we cannot learn from this interview who they might have been.

Shying away from specifics of group and individual names is prudent for reasons of safety, survival, and social harmony. In terms of social harmony, at the time of the interviews with both MaNsimango and Sibanda in 1999, Sibanda's wife at that time (1999) was not a member of the church;[27] many in the church lamented his distance from church fellowship and this may have been a source of tension at the time of my interview with MaNsimango, leading her not to want to mention him by name. And in terms of safety, the ZANU-PF government was in power when we had the interview (and remains so at the time of writing). The Zimbabwe government's official view of the war valorizes the role of the ZANLA guerrillas in the liberation of the country from white rule.[28] Any overt criticism of ZANLA remains risky. Those not supporting this view have since 1980 remained subject to sellout accusations.

The BICC taught that good Christians must obey earthly authorities and refrain from involvement in party politics and shun involvement in worldly governments. As such, church members faced a significant question: what do you do when you are an African member of such a church and the earthly authorities—the Rhodesian government—are a settler state facing a violent anticolonial struggle? This challenge was not uncommon throughout southern Africa as its settler colonies went through liberation struggles. One of the more famous Christian leaders balancing his craving for a more just regime with a commitment to nonviolence was Desmond Tutu. Tutu, as Anglican bishop of Cape Town during the worst years of antiapartheid violence in South Africa, found himself defending, at his own peril, the rights of people accused of being sellouts. For doing so he was himself accused of being a collaborationist.[29]

While MaNsimango's testimony reveals no explicit political stance, a position in favor of the liberation struggle's aims is discernable in the typical way performed by many in the pietistic BICC during this time: by implication, by action. In the context of this kind of interview, with a junior, foreign, white woman, MaNsimango was unlikely to talk politics with me. And yet, her stance is given by implication. When the white soldiers converged around Tshalimbe, she and the villagers seem not to have pondered for long to which side they were loyal. As she described it, they became aware of the white soldiers, and without a pause in the sentence, stated, "we ran away to those beyond the river." In telling me about the time that both white soldiers and guerrillas came near her home, she did not call the guerrillas terrorists; she called them "those beyond the river." Her very choice of these words suggests support for the liberation cause. That this was chiefly a choice disciplined by the nationalist pieties in place at the time is possible.

There are also dynamics of generation, gender, and class folded subtly into MaNsimango's account of her confrontation with the guerrillas. In terms of the discussion at the beginning of the chapter about the kinship dynamics of the interactions between guerrillas and villagers, MaNsimango figures in the story as one of the grannies in relation to the "boys," who were the ZANLA guerrillas moving through her area. Her ability to speak to them with some element of the right to scold is not solely about her sense of herself as a Christian—it is rooted also in her generational stature as someone old enough to be their grandparent, and as a woman past childbearing age: a Gogo, or granny.[30] Kinship is understood to be a gendered phenomenon. Female gender within kinship networks is, from one plane of perception, much about female subordination, but it is also about female associational strength. Also, certain women within the family have authority. For example the senior paternal aunt, or *babakazi*—especially when she was postmenopausal—had the authority to chastise junior males in her family. This could also be a mode in which MaNsimango was acting when she chastised these young men for wielding their guns and power to discipline sellouts in a way she felt was indiscriminate.

There is a social-class element as well. As a well-educated schoolteacher, former wife of the pastor, now pastor herself, and sister-in-law to a prominent, prosperous ordained BICC minister and overseer whose home was also at Tshalimbe, MaNsimango counted among the elites of this area. As Werbner, Kriger, and Staunton's discussions of the factors involved in naming and acting against sellouts point out, prosperous individuals were often named—and thereby accused.[31] At times these accusations were based chiefly on envy of that person's wealth and not on any actual cooperation with the Smith regime. Africans of some means, who had enjoyed a higher level of education, better access to colonial markets, or positions of influence, may not have cooperated with Rhodesian soldiers, but their class position made them likely to be named sellouts on a more symbolic level, having prospered under the colonial regime. As MaNsimango's daughter Musa Chidziva stated, "they [the nationalist guerrillas] hate those people especially, those that are prospering."[32] Such class-based animosity is mentioned also in Meggi Zingani's testimony in *Mothers of the Revolution,* and in Norma Kriger's analysis of peasant support for the liberation struggle.[33]

MaNsimango's late sister's husband also had a home in Tshalimbe during the war. Rev. Mangisi Sibanda had been married to Hannah, the younger sister to MaNsimango. He held a prominent position in the church as regional overseer of Matopo District, although his own homestead was in Tshalimbe.[34] His wife, Hannah, had just died a few years earlier. During the war, Sibanda faced an accusation of being a sellout. "There were people telling lies about me."[35] The guerrillas told him he was unsympathetic to the nationalist cause owing to his prosperous trade in tomatoes delivered to market in Bulawayo each week, his tin roof, and his ownership of a truck.[36] The guerrillas said he had been robbing the people. It is not evident what the guerrillas meant by saying that; were they applying Marxist theory or simply expressing envy of his truck and tin roof? Sibanda's answer to them was, "I have not done anything, and I will not even do it. I know that, what I am telling you, I am speaking the truth before the Lord. I know that I have not even cheated anybody." The Rev. Sibanda ended up saving his life by agreeing to regularly supply this group of guerrillas with trousers and shoes. His own understanding was that God had helped him: "I'm sure God did help me, because I was supposed to be killed, because there were people telling lies about me, what they say, 'Well, he has done this,' and yet I had not done anything like that. Yes."[37]

Thus, MaNsimango had very close and personal reasons to be concerned about the dangers of being accused as a sellout. In her testimony, cited above, she said, "I talked to them as a Christian, trying to lead them out of what they were to what I saw was right for them to do." In her interview with me, she framed her decision to confront the ZANLA guerrillas in terms of her desire, as a Christian, to show the guerrillas a more correct, and just, path. MaNsimango said, "They really accepted, they did not do it again," thus crediting the abeyance of accusations against sellouts in her area to the fact that she had acted in this godly capacity.[38]

What other factor accounted for MaNsimango's courage to speak out to those who were holding the guns? One reason she herself offered was that she had developed some spiritual resilience when her grandchild was ill with epilepsy, and at the time of her husband's death.[39] She referred to "struggles." MaNsimango did not want me to state explicitly the nature of these struggles. In the case of the grandchild's illness, some relatives believed ancestral spirits inhabited the child, while MaNsimango insisted on praying Christian prayers for healing even while she was being treated by the *inyanga* (traditional healer). Regarding her husband's death, it is not uncommon for widows to face trouble with the deceased husband's family, whether over inheritance matters, conflicting ideas on how to interpret the cause of death, or differences over how much consultation with the ancestors one might wish to do, a practice that devout Christians such as MaNsimango would want to avoid. In this case, MaNsimango's daughter indicated that people in the family perceived MaNsimango's courage to go on, her ability to continue leading the church after her husband's death, as a sign that she was being inhabited by ancestral spirits. Her daughter understood the struggle that ensued as a spiritual battle between her mother's faith in the Christian God and her relatives' faith in the ancestral spirits. MaNsimango said her prayers kept her safe. Her daughter understood that MaNsimango "had won the battle: she was a heroine, really" and the in-laws finally came around and made peace with her.[40]

More than one scholar has noted the discursive and behavioral parallels between accusations of practicing witchcraft and of being a sellout.[41] Werbner and other scholars have compared sellout accusations in the rural areas during the war with the dynamics of witchcraft accusations. This is true of sellout dynamics throughout southern Africa's various liberation struggles, especially seen in the literature on Zimbabwe and South Africa. Diana Jeater has crucially pointed out that ZANU's party politics has drawn on the language of contamination and the "enemy within"—a kind of moral structure that parallels the moral violations seen as being committed by witches within their communities.[42] Joyce Chadya's study of women in Mtoko and Mrewa Districts, to the northeast of Tshalimbe, also noted a convergence of witchcraft and sellout accusations during the war: "Women were often accused of different forms of female wickedness ranging from accusations of witchcraft, prostitution, and being 'enemy' collaborators."[43] MaNsimango herself did state that some family members did not understand the Christian way of mourning.[44] Whatever the exact nature of the "struggles" were at the time of her husband's death (and she preferred to remain vague on purpose), MaNsimango credited her faith, her persistence in staying loyal to "my Lord," and the effectiveness of her prayers not only for having survived that time following her husband's death, but also for giving her the courage to speak out to the guerrillas during the war.

Terence Ranger's book on nationalism in Matabeleland, *Voices from the Rocks: Nature, Culture and History in the Matopos Hills of Zimbabwe,* shows how the BICC seemed to be a colonialist mission church: that true nationalists regarded it, at best, as irrelevant and, at worst, as a church for sellouts. Ranger emphasizes that, although "Christian modernizers . . . had pioneered nationalism" during the 1940 and early 1950s, by the late 1950s and 1960s peasants in the rural heartland of Matabeleland, including BICC territory, developed a counteroffensive based on loyalty to the rain shrines in the caves of the Matopo Hills.[45] Even though many men in ZAPU from this area had a BICC background, presumably by the time they became serious about the liberation struggle, they were no longer active church members because to be openly involved in nationalist politics meant to give up one's good standing as a member of the church. To illustrate this, Ranger highlights the testimony of Makhobo Ndlovu, a student at the BICC-run Matopo Secondary School: "By 1977 [Smith's] soldiers were coming to the school and treating us badly. The guerrillas were sneaking in during the night and preaching to me about socialism and communism. I felt very good about nationalist soldiers. I took it upon myself to rebel against the school authorities and the soldiers who were at the school."[46] The testimony that Ranger quotes here points to a crucial factor. Note that the informant, Ndlovu, said, "I took it upon myself to rebel against the *school authorities*" and that therefore he was rebelling against the school as a mission institution, not necessarily against elements of his own understanding of Christian faith.[47]

Contrasting the "official" and the "unofficial" church is of great value in assessing the larger institutional response of the BICC to the war. In accordance with the church's peace position and the accompanying stance that Christians should remain separate from "worldly" politics, the African church leaders such as the bishop and his wife, the ordained clergy and their wives, paid evangelists, and the mission school administrators and teachers were obliged not to join any political organizations nor to speak in support of any of the parties engaged in the war. These people were expected to live up to, and enforce, the church's teachings and policies, and in this case, a peace church's stance of neutrality. As Doris Dube wrote of prominent churchwomen, "They had to be spiritual leaders in their communities. . . . Their lives were to be open books for all to read."[48] The ordained church leaders (all male) remained officially neutral and did not join ZAPU.[49] As one lay leader put it in a 1992 interview, "The church understood what was happening, but distinguished between spiritual and political. They saw that their duty was to help people in their relationship with God. Even today this is our position as a church."[50]

Thus it is at the *official* level that the BICC, in its neutrality, looks like a sellout church. And yet families affiliated with the BICC had people in them who were also active with ZAPU and ZIPRA. As ZAPU historian Eliakim Sibanda noted of BICC-affiliated families during the 1970s, "hardly was there a home without one or two people in the armed struggle."[51] What the church's official policy stated did not in all cases correspond with the opinions and actions of its own members and leaders. In significant cases African BICC leaders belied the church's official stance of neutrality by taking implicit actions that were in solidarity with the guerrillas.

Acts of spiritualized solidarity with the guerrillas' cause included evangelism targeted to war-traumatized displaced people in town, and coded political messages hidden in the prayers and Bible studies. The overseer for the BICC district in Matabeleland North, the Rev. Jonathan Dlodlo opened the doors of Phumula Mission Hospital to treat wounded ZIPRA guerrillas, an action for which he was jailed. Significantly, this is not mentioned in the BICC's official publication celebrating the Zimbabwe church's centennial anniversary. This story came to me in an oral interview—a more "unofficial" source—with Dlodlo's sister-in-law, and even in this respect, she emphasized not the political overtones of his action but rather his spiritual courage in using his jail time as an opportunity to evangelize. As she put it, "He told how he held services with the people in prison with him. They sang and sang, it was wonderful." His sister-in-law also recalled that he said of his time in prison, "I think the Lord sent me there to minister there. It's not like I was in jail but rather in a ministry."[52]

I interpret this avoidance of mentioning politics on the part of the church's African membership itself as a means of exercising a form of dissent against the mandated climate of politicization. Even while sympathizing with the aims of liberation, many of the most committed church members engaged with their environment via nonpolitical means and had nonpolitical aspirations. Thus, while the official institutions of the church were tied to the Rhodesian state and its economic system, and church policy remained strictly against its members being involved in politics of any kind, many individuals at every level of the church organization used their *religious work* to reach out to those most affected by the war, and used their *religious and spiritual resources* to cope with the dangers at hand.

Another dynamic at play among church members during the height of the nationalist struggle could be seen among those African men in the church who decided to become active in ZAPU and in many cases even join its army, ZIPRA. These men were deemed "wayward" or "backslidden" according to official church teachings on nonresistance. By acting on their nationalist aspirations and enacting nationalist piety, they sacrificed a claim to the church's Christian piety. Earlier chapters of this book have highlighted the tensions that African men under the colonial period felt between the imperatives of their masculine identity and political aspirations and those of the mission church's definitions of piety. As we have seen in chapter 4, only male church leaders who were both committed to the church and whose monogamous unions were fertile were able to balance their masculinity and upward mobility aspirations while remaining in good standing in the church. Into the 1970s laymen and the nonordained village male pastors found themselves balancing forbidden politics and other affiliations and activities in ways that meant their church standing was compromised or on hold for many years in the prime of their lives. One response to this tension was the Ibandla leZintandane, or Church of the Orphans. The Church of the Orphans was a subgroup of men, some of them male pastors from the rural churches, who wished to combine their nationalist sensibilities, including leadership posts within local ZAPU chapters, with their church affiliation did so by injecting liberation theology into the normally very pietistic, even quietist, BICC stance. They were resisting an either-or condition; they were both for nationalist liberation and their faith; in fact, to them it was their faith that in part motivated their actions for nationalism. The Church of the Orphans is entirely invisible in the official record and still only reluctantly acknowledged by today's church elders; it was a particularly dissident, but real, phenomenon.[53]

Women in the Rural Guerrilla War

Women bore the heaviest burden as civilians in the midst of rural guerrilla warfare. People in the rural areas of Rhodesia (colonial Zimbabwe) had to find their own way through the mortal danger they faced during the height of the guerrilla war. Africans living in areas where there were troop movements, whether of the guerrillas of the two liberation movements or of Smith's soldiers, had to come to terms with the demands put on them by the combatants. Younger men were largely gone: they had been conscripted into the security forces or fled the country to study overseas, avoid the war, or join ZANLA or ZIPRA. Many people—men, women, and children—had fled to urban Bulawayo by the end of the 1970s.

Rural pastors had to decide whether to continue gathering their congregations on Sundays. At this time, it became increasingly dangerous to meet in groups larger than two or three, lest they be suspected of having political content. Church attendance dropped in most rural locations not only because the government suspected any kind of gathering of having a political purpose but also because the guerrillas did not want people to worship.[54] Those who continued to conduct worship did so in the knowledge that they risked violent recriminations either from soldiers of the

Rhodesian Front or the liberation forces. Of those who remained in their rural homes throughout the war, many women did not attend worship because of the fear of intimidation and rape by soldiers.[55] Because certain rural male pastors in fact doubled as ZAPU functionaries, Rhodesian soldiers killed some of them. In this emergency the church established a new licensing for rural unpaid pastors, for both women and men serving as the appointed pastor for a given church. This license was an official paper certifying that their movements around the region were in the interest of church work and thereby some protection from harassment from the security forces.[56]

The sex imbalance in church attendance was partially explained by church insiders as a growing demographic imbalance due to existing patterns of labor migration and with war conscriptions falling more heavily on men than women. In the 1970s patterns of waning male membership set in motion in earlier decades accelerated to the point that rural congregations in both Matabeleland South and North were made up almost entirely of women and children.[57] There were many women-headed households. Thus there are two reasons for women bearing a disproportionately heavy burden of being civilians in the midst of rural guerrilla warfare: they were the demographic majority in most rural villages, and because it was the woman's role to cook food, it was women who were called upon to feed and provision the guerrillas. Young girls and boys also were expected to advance the guerrillas' cause as messengers and as leaders of the all-night sessions known as *pungwes* (lit., vigils).[58] As Joyce Chadya summarizes for Mtoko and Mrewa Districts, where the ZANLA (ZANU-affiliated) guerrillas operated: "The mobilization of women in their gender-ascribed roles as cooks, launderers and porters, and the mobilization of women as people who gathered intelligence for ZANLA guerrillas made them particularly vulnerable as both sides of the combatant forces accused them of fraternizing with the enemy."[59] The guerrilla forces counted on people in rural areas to provide for them: women were required to cook food and provide blankets, while men and women of means were required to supply the guerrilla armies' needs for shoes and clothing.

Rural guerrilla war fostered an intense focus on loyalty and its opposite, selling out. Smith's soldiers demanded that Africans in rural areas reveal troop movements of the guerrilla forces, and they killed or beat people deemed uncooperative or deliberately misleading. The guerrilla forces would kill villagers who refused to cook for them and beat or execute those deemed sellouts.[60] Alleged sellouts could be killed for providing information about the movements of guerrillas to the Smith army.[61] Sellouts also were killed or beaten if it was believed they were witches, or if a woman cooked food that resulted in the illness or death of a guerrilla.[62] As BICC member Batana Khumalo of Sizeze said, when asked whether she had suffered during the war, "Yes, we suffered during the war. [ZIPRA] Guerrillas were all over at our homes looking for their rivals, ZANLA and the police. Some were beaten; people were beaten."[63] It is not surprising that many thousands of people, especially women, fled to urban areas during the war.[64] Irene Staunton's interviews with Zimbabwean women who survived the guerrilla war in the rural areas indicate that support for the guerrillas might be based on nationalist sentiments or reflect compliance based on fear.[65] In many respects, the experience of BICC women, both pastors and laywomen in rural areas during the war, therefore reflect those of women throughout Rhodesia at this time. As Margaret Viki, interviewed in *Mothers of the Revolution,* put it, "We were afraid of both sides, afraid of the soldiers who would kill us if they found out [that we had cooked for the guerrillas], and afraid of the freedom fighters because if we refused to feed them that would also mean we would die."[66] Nellie Mlotshwa's memory of that time also emphasizes that people felt caught between the opposing forces: "Sometimes we were overpowered by fear of death and killing. . . . Cooking for guerrillas, no choice. If soldiers discovered you, you were in the soup. We didn't know who to please."[67]

What follows is a consideration of the experiences and tales told of other women BICC pastors in rural areas during the war. This discussion shows that what distinguishes the constructed understanding of these women is not in the nature of the challenges they faced but the way they have come to be valorized by the church leadership for their courage—an apolitical courage. The women's survival of encounters with combatants is invariably attributed to their immense faith. Consider, for example, the following account by Bishop Stephen N. Ndlovu of a woman who stood up when challenged by guerrillas to confess her Christian faith.

> I forget the woman in Filabusi, who stood—it's an old woman—when the, the terrorist, or the freedom fighters . . . gathered people and asked, "Who are Christians here?" There were pastors, there were many pastors, there were other people there, but nobody stood up. And an old woman stood up, and said, "I am a Christian." And these guys said, "Ahh! So this is a true Christian. The rest of you are fake Christians. Why didn't you stand up? So you go to these churches, preaching and saying, telling people that you are pastors when you are not pastors. This is a true Christian, she's brave. She's prepared to face anything." And that we heard, we heard that story. I was bishop at that time. It was a fascinating kind of story on the woman. The women during the war braved it. I'm not saying that some men didn't.[68]

The woman here is not named. Ndlovu is telling of an event that appears to have come to him via hearsay. The existence of such a narrative, retained in the oral memory of the church leadership over twenty years, is significant. A story such as this one, regardless of it being unspecific as to person and place, helps nourish the church's image of itself as apolitical and courageous in the faith even under the supreme pressures suffered by its members during the war, a faith upheld by the "least of these," exemplified here as an "old woman." The story is significant in that it points to how the church's definition of piety allowed an anonymous lay-woman's story to be told to her advantage, implicitly as a rebuke against more prominent men of the church who did not have the same courage as this woman.

NakaGininda (Nkanyezi Ndlovu), BICC lay pastor at Mpisini in Matabeleland North during the war, encountered immense pressure from Smith's soldiers and endured a brutal beating from them in which she was left for dead. Among other things, her experience indicates that being a woman of faith did not earn her immunity from real and potential violence. Two of the BICC churches near NakaGininda's closed down during the war.[69] She also was ordered by the guerrillas to close down her church. According to BICC chronicler Doris Dube, after guerrillas threatened to burn down the Mpisini church building, NakaGininda and her largely female congregation "agreed to quietly worship in NakaGininda's kitchen instead."[70] Doris Dube's account states that when Smith's soldiers found out that guerrillas had enjoyed a beer drink with his friends at the home of NakaGininda's son (termed "wayward") they arrived at her home while she and members of her congregation had gathered for the Sunday worship: "They were still looking for NakaGininda's son and now they were irritated by these clandestine Christians." NakaGininda then endured a brutal, near-fatal beating by the soldiers.[71]

Many BICC leaders read Dube's book, which was published in 1992. In my 1999 interview with former BICC bishop S. N. Ndlovu, he offered a very similar version of NakaGininda's encounter with Smith's soldiers. He likely had read Dube's book, but his account here distinctively also highlights that NakaGininda fed the guerrillas; her son is not mentioned.

> I remember the day she told about, she told us about her
> experience, when she was beaten up by the Smith army, or
> the what, the so-called legitimate army from the (south),
> because it was said she was harbouring the terrorists,
> therefore she needed to be beaten. Why is it that they came
> to her home, and they didn't burn up or disturb her or

interfere with her property? And why was she giving them food? And she said, "Just you, if you ask [for] food, I give it to you, because I know you are hungry. And if they come asking for food, I give it to them, because I know they are hungry. But I pray for either side." And then one of the soldiers started assaulting her; she was hit down, she fell down, and she was beaten. She got up. And then she looked at that soldier, and said, "Son, God has allowed you to do this. But I think . . . God would not continue to allow you to beat me the way you are doing." He hit her again, and she said, "You have done it again, but I don't think God will allow you to do it again." So it stopped. She was that kind of bold woman that took a stand whenever she meant to. Ja. That was NakaGininda as an example [for] other women.[72]

In spite of the discrepancies in their accounts, both Dube and Bishop Ndlovu emphasized that she survived the soldiers' blows due to God's intervention and that she was fearless in that encounter, plainly stating that God's power was on her side. Dube's account suggests that indeed NakaGininda and her congregation, by making an agreement with the guerrillas to worship at home instead of in the church, had received some special allowances, a fact the soldiers observed when they challenged her, asking why it was that their church and homes were not disturbed. The fact that the Rhodesian soldiers then beat NakaGininda and, according to Dube, burned her son's home and granaries, shows how NakaGininda's family was believed to be sympathetic to ZAPU. Eliakim Sibanda pointed out that NakaGininda's sons were in fact members of the Ibandla leZintandane, while Doris Dube's account in *Silent Labourers* makes no connection between the sons and ZAPU, instead mentioning only that they were "wayward" due to their consumption of beer and their nonattendance at their mother's worship services.[73] All this together suggests that Dube was writing for the strictly faith-based audience of church-sponsored literature and that her writing had to steer clear of all suggestions of connection between church leaders and politics, as per church teaching. It also reinforces the seeming agreement among the church membership—on a de facto level, not as an articulated policy—in this pattern of division of labor, with men, particularly younger men, attending to politics and women, especially older women, attending to worship. The episode also illustrates how mortally dangerous it could be to attempt to navigate the incompatible demands of guerrillas and soldiers.[74]

MaNsimango's Deeper Life History: "My Navel Is Buried at Matopo."

MaNsimango strongly self-identified as a Christian: for herself, in her marriage, and based on her family of origin. The land on which Matopo Mission was built, in 1898, is an important starting point for MaNsimango's story and her sense of her own history in a multigenerational African Christian family. As seen in chapter 1, just eighteen months after the 1896 war of colonial conquest, four American BICC missionaries arrived in the Matopo Hills to set up a mission station. H. Frances Davidson established at Matopo the first BICC school in Rhodesia; among her first pupils was Matshuba Ndlovu. Matshuba's sister Ntombiyaphansi was in the second group to be baptized a few years later; she went on to marry another early convert, Mnofa Nsimango, in 1913.[75] As was generally practiced, the young wife returned to her parents' homestead, located at Matopo Mission, when it came time for her first child to be born, in 1914. It was the custom to bury the umbilical cord nearby. Sithembile, the firstborn of Ntombiyaphansi and niece to Matshuba, with her cord buried under the gum trees at the mission, and who grew up to become Pastor MaNsimango, emphasized: "My navel is buried at Matopo." Unlike other informants born around the same time—such as Maria Tshuma, who reported that she was born "before the German war," because her parents were early converts and therefore also early adopters of literacy—MaNsimango had precise knowledge of the year of her birth.

MaNsimango and her eleven siblings came from a family that had already broken the pattern of intramarriage within the precolonial kingdom's status groups, when her mother, an Ndlovu of the lower Kalanga group, married Mnofa Nsimango, of the royal abezansi.[76] Theirs had been a Christian marriage and was self-consciously not motivated by status reinforcement. Their parents set the example later followed by both daughters, MaNsimango and her sister Hannah, because their father "didn't follow the [abe]zansi way [endogamous marriage]. It was a different view of Christians."[77] Both the Nsimango sisters married across the social strata: MaNsimango married Philemon Nkala, of the Sotho-derived or abenhla group, in 1939, and sister Hannah's husband, Mangisi Sibanda, was from the abantu bakaMambo; but their marriages were the exception. Most people, including Christians in the BICC, continued to marry within their own social stratum well into the mid-twentieth century.[78] The Nsimango family were, however, considered to be an exceptionally "progressive and unusually industrious family."[79]

Another example of the Nsimango-Ndlovu family following a different, Christian way is seen in the living arrangements of Ntombiyaphansi's mother. For the patrilocal Ndebele speakers, it was unusual for a woman's mother to live at her marital home, where normally only the husband's mother lived, and reigned, as the highest ranking female. However, both Mnofa and Ntombi-yaphansi's mothers lived at their home in Tshalimbe. Figure 5.2 shows Mnofa Nsimango and Ntombiyaphansi Ndlovu at their homestead around 1938 with both their mothers standing by, as well as two of their children, including the firstborn, Sithembile Nsimango (about age twenty-four).

As a small child MaNsimango started her education at the BICC village school near her parents' homestead at Silobini, which she attended each morning. In the afternoons she walked to Matopo Mission for additional instruction. When she was a little older, she lived at Mayezane with her grandmother, the mother of Matshuba Ndlovu, from 1926 to 1928. MaNsimango remembers that her mother's brother, her uncle Matshuba, at that time worked as a builder for a white farmer known to the local people as Mgqomo, and that he only came home to Mayezane on

Figure 5.2. The Nsimango family at Tshalimbe, ca. 1938. *Front row (l–r),* unidentified child of Mnofa and Ntombiyaphansi, Sithembile Nsimango; *back row (l–r),* mother of Mnofa Nsimango, Mnofa Nsimango, Ntombiyaphansi Ndlovu, NakaMatshuba (mother of Matshuba and Ntombiyaphansi). *Photo credit: Sally Kreider*

the weekends.[80] MaNsimango's parents moved to Tshalimbe in 1928, where her father became the teacher. She was fourteen years old, and the children in Tshalimbe School were far behind her level of education. Her own schooling stagnated for two years at Tshalimbe while she helped her father teach the primer classes and waited until she was able to attend the Mtshabezi Girls' Primary Boarding School. During her first year at the boarding school, 1930, MaNsimango remembered that there was a cohort of aunties who looked after the schoolgirls and saw to their spiritual development, including Sitshokupi Sibanda and NakaSeyemephi Ngwenya. In this year, at age sixteen, MaNsimango responded to the evangelist's preaching at school and stepped forward when the altar call was issued. The aunties listened to their testimonies carefully: "One was to make sure it was from the bottom of the heart. No pretense was tolerated. Screening was strict."[81] Naka-Seyemephi and the other women vouched for and continued to give spiritual counsel to all thirty-six of the girls who stood up that day, and they were baptized later that year.[82]

MaNsimango continued her education at the Matopo teacher-training program from 1934 to 1937. She married Philemon Nkala in 1938. Nkala succeeded her as father as pastor at Tshalimbe and served for several decades as the pastor there. Both Nkala and MaNsimango were teachers at the BICC Tshalimbe primary school. Philemon Nkala enrolled at the BICC's Bible school in the 1960s after many years as pastor in order to improve his qualifications for church service, but he died in 1969 while still a student.[83]

Having found it difficult to find a replacement for Nkala after he died, the members of the Tshalimbe church decided that, as MaNsimango put it, "it is better that his wife take responsibility." Members of the Nkala family who were not closely affiliated with the church were unhappy with MaNsimango's decision to carry on her husband's work as pastor. The BICC encouraged its members not to adhere to the customary practice of the widow, in which she would be in drab clothing and subdued demeanor for a full year until the *umbuyiso* ceremony, which marked the "coming home" of the deceased's spirit.[84] As her daughter expressed it, "they did not understand the Christian way of mourning," which discouraged outward shows of grief.[85] Instead, one was to carry one's life forward, rejoicing that the loved one had gone to "be with the Lord." MaNsimango found her duties as pastor, when combined with her existing work as a teacher, to be quite heavy. Nonetheless, "because of the love for God's work," she agreed to take on the new role.[86] When asked why she did not adhere to customary mourning practice, MaNsimango stated, "Because I like my Lord better. My husband also did not believe in [customary mourning practices]."[87] Surviving the disapproval of her husband's relatives was a struggle that she surmounted with the power of prayers that she and her daughters offered.[88] Anchoring her origins—the burial of her "navel"—at Matopo was not only factually, geographically true, it was also metaphorically powerfully connected to the Christian heritage of her family: Matopo as site of the BICC's origins in Zimbabwe, and the origins of a family that lived in, and creatively responded to, the tensions of a simultaneously African and Christian identity.

———

In the 1970s, MaNsimango confronted ZANLA guerrillas who were beating people named as sellouts. She was by then the village pastor and justified her confrontation through her identity "as a Christian." She came from a family with a certain willingness not to practice selected local customs, based on and encouraged by their understanding of Christian teachings. This was in evidence first in the fact that they married across the endogamous groups that most Ndebele people continued to respect as boundaries for intramarriage only. The fact that the mother of Matshuba and Ntombiyaphansi, MaNdlovu, lived at her daughter's home, was another example of custom-defying choices, in addition to her refusal to mourn in the customary fashion when her husband died. Thus when she lived through the guerrilla war for Zimbabwe's independence, she had developed a habit of filtering the expectations of her community with those of her faith.

MaNsimango's insistence on more just treatment for alleged sellouts can be understood as an attempt to protect people such as herself or her brother-in-law. And yet her way of framing the events at Tshalimbe between her and the guerrillas omits mention of her brother-in-law by name; it omits specific description of any possible parallel ordeals she may have experienced in the wake of her husband's death. The narrative she offered, unencumbered by specifics of place, names of groups, or background social contexts allowed her to emphasize those elements of the story that mattered to her most. Faith, courage, and leadership as an elder woman, as a Christian pastor to younger men—the guerrillas—who were violating the community: these are the ways she wanted me to understand the events. In line with the model of men tending to sequence their piety over the course of their lives while women tended to stay in good standing in the church for long stretches, as pastor at Tshalimbe, MaNsimango kept her church open throughout the war and in fact remained in church fellowship to the end of her life. Unlike the male pastors in Matabeleland North who were also active members of ZAPU and found their churches closed for the duration of the war, she did not have to choose between the two or find that her church was closed down by the Smith soldiers.

Unlike Irene Staunton's *Mothers of the Revolution,* a collection of testimonies gathered to help foster a nascent Zimbabwean identity for women in the newly established ZANU-PF-led nation, MaNsimango did not fashion her story to establish her nationalist credibility. BICC understandings of piety, as seen in Doris Dube's and Stephen Ndlovu's accounts of other women who "braved it" during the war, gave much space for female heroes of the faith. MaNsimango's piety and courage were not based on utter loyalty to the state, not even to the anticolonial nationalist state; they were based on utter loyalty to her understanding of her Christian walk, which adhered neither to the "abezansi way" of the

Ndebele elites nor to the customs of her husband's family. Such a rich and mixed heritage empowered her resistance to the pressure she faced to politicize her understanding of herself.[89] As a result, MaNsimango's experience during the war cannot be understood merely in terms of self preservation and safety but rather as that of a woman carefully negotiating her community's traditions and Christian commitments with creativity and agency.

SIX || Stephen N. Ndlovu
Gendered Piety, the New Zimbabwe, and the Gukurahundi, 1980–89

> Drastic change[s are] taking place in Rhodesia today. As part of this scene, the Brethren in Christ Church needs to build for the future . . . it will mean evaluating, changing, stretching, replacing, and creating. There is a real need to come into manhood quickly as a church.
>
> —*Philemon M. Khumalo, 1978*

A HIGH-CEILINGED ROOM EQUIPPED with an aging large wooden desk and metal file cabinets served as the office for former bishop Stephen N. Ndlovu during his years in the 1990s as a professor at the Theological College of Zimbabwe. Speaking in a strained, almost rasping voice, in worn penny loafers and large brown horn-rimmed glasses, Ndlovu had been fighting cancer. He was very tall, thinner than his former very imposing self, and exuded both immense dignity and caring. Our interview was interrupted several times by various people at the college needing to speak with him.

The 1990s were quieter years at the end of Ndlovu's rather tumultuous succession of careers as an athletics coordinator, teacher, ordained minister, and finally bishop of the BICC of Zimbabwe. He lived at a spacious, working homestead not far outside the city of Bulawayo, where he raised chickens and eggs for sale. Ndlovu drove to town in a battered station wagon carrying his poultry wares; more than once I bought a frozen chicken or eggs from him, and he was always glad to receive spare egg cartons. Various tellings of Ndlovu's career path all emphasized his wife's intervention at a crucial moment. She and he understood the first twenty-five years of his adult life to have been a series of evasions of a calling to full-time church work. When another summons to church service came, in 1969, his wife, MaNkala (NakaOrlean), likened his situation to that of the biblical character Jonah. Jonah ended up in the belly of a great fish in his desperate efforts to run away from God's command that he serve as prophet to the ancient city of Nineveh. Making a parallel, MaNkala said to her husband, "I don't know what belly you are going to lie in now."[1] Ndlovu credited this pungent goading from his wife as the last and crucial tipping point. He accepted the invitation to be ordained a minister in 1969; ten years later he found himself bishop of the BICC, at the beginning of Zimbabwe's postcolonial age.

When Zimbabwe emerged from guerrilla war, in 1980, as a new, majority-rule African nation, the early 1980s were years full of great hope for a brighter future. Colonial—or settler—rule had ended. The 1980 elections permitted first-ever universal suffrage for both blacks and whites and led to a black-led government ruled by ZANU, one of the two nationalist liberation parties. Racial discrimination as a state policy was over, and the talented blacks of the new Zimbabwe could look forward to taking on the leadership of the nation in the fields of education, religion, politics, and the economy.

In 1980 and after, the African leaders of the BICC also faced a momentous turning point in the church's history. Stephen Ndlovu was only the second black bishop, and now the first to serve in an independent Zimbabwe. Ndlovu had great hopes for the BICC in this new chapter of its history. Those surges of post-1980 optimism within short order—by 1982—were deeply challenged by a new form of political violence. The BICC's headquarters were in

Bulawayo, and its membership was almost solely drawn from Matabeleland, the same region from which the ZAPU political party drew much of its support. Thus Ndlovu headed a church whose regional base in great measure overlapped with that of ZAPU. The new Zimbabwe's ruling party, ZANU, under the leadership of Robert Mugabe, launched a campaign intended to permanently weaken or eliminate their ZAPU rivals; the worst of the violence that ensued was very much in the heart of the BICC's people and territory. For a pietistic church embracing the peace teaching, this situation was excruciating. If politics killed your people, how do you talk about politics and deal with those deaths, and still remain piously apolitical, especially if one is the head of such a church? Rev. Stephen N. Ndlovu's actions as bishop in the perilous decade of the 1980s were rooted in a kind of masculine piety that drew both on what he understood to be kinship-based values as well as the Brethren in Christ's teaching on nonresistance. Both these influences guided his response in the 1980s to the killings known as the Gukurahundi. This chapter's analysis of Ndlovu's gendered piety as a crucial element of his leadership of the church works from Dorothy Hodgson's insight that masculinities are "multiple, historical, relational, and contradictory."[2]

Insights about the masculinities associated with the men of the BICC in the Rhodesian period were developed in chapters 2 and 5. To revisit some of those elements: the BICC was derived from a North American church influenced by Mennonite teachings on nonviolence and pacifism. These teachings resonated differently whether one was in North America before or after the Second World War, or in Rhodesia or in Zimbabwe, but the BICC's peace position was based on the idea of practicing *peace:* that Christians should not take up arms, and on *nonresistance:* they should remain separate from government and from party politics.[3] The BICC's nonresistance teaching, along with the church's urgings to remain unworldly, worked a contradictory dynamic for the men of the BICC, as seen in the ways some men resolved the tension between the church's mandated forms of piety and those of Ndebele culture. For many, this tension resulted in a masculinity imperative that rendered church affiliation in good standing simply impossible for the better part of their adult lives. Various political moments exacerbated this pressure more than others, leading in some generations to whole ranks of church-reared young men necessarily becoming backsliders. And yet men who held prominent, official leadership roles could more readily combine their maleness with piety, and leaders such as Bishop S. N. Ndlovu exemplified this. Unlike some men in the Zimbabwean church, Ndlovu was a strong supporter of the peace teachings.

The defining political elements in this era are important factors in understanding how Ndlovu responded to the political conflict of the 1980s. The violence of the Gukurahundi offered a uniquely challenging opportunity for Ndlovu to apply the church's teachings on peace and nonresistance. Assessing Ndlovu's actions and his stated reasons for action in light of his family and marital history shows that that Ndlovu expressed his own blend of kinship-based notions of masculinity and pacifist Christian teachings.

In elections held in February 1980, ZANU won the majority of the votes and became the new Zimbabwe's ruling party, under the leadership of Robert Mugabe. The rival nationalist party, ZAPU, headed by Joshua Nkomo, was now a minority party. While ZAPU's origins, in 1961, were based on an all-Rhodesia base of support, after ZANU split away and over the course of the guerrilla war, the membership for each party increasingly came to have a regional and thereby also ethnic character. Thus it is that ZANU won more than 80 percent of the votes cast in Mashonaland, while more than 80 percent of the votes cast in Matabeleland went to ZAPU.[4] Historians James Muzondidya and Sabelo Gatsheni-Ndlovu remark that "Zimbabwe was born with a very bad ethnic birthmark."[5]

One of the first aims of the new government was to create a single Zimbabwean National Army (ZNA) out of the three military forces that had fought the guerrilla war. This effort proved difficult and indeed served as the catalyst for the deadly conflicts of the 1980s, due to rivalry between the combatants of ZANLA and

ZIPRA. Combatants were to report to assembly points, where they would either be demobilized or incorporated into the new ZNA. One assembly point was in the Bulawayo township of Entumbane. ZANU leader Enos Nkala made a speech in Bulawayo late in 1980 in which he urged his listeners to strike out against ZAPU. This proved to be incendiary, leading to a two-day pitched battle between ZIPRA and ZANLA forces in Entumbane. Attempts by ZIPRA members to enter Bulawayo from neighboring assembly points in Esigodini and Gwaai in support of their compatriots in Bulawayo were repelled by the air force. In 1981 there was continued fighting at some of the ZNA assembly points. ZIPRA members felt disadvantaged and discriminated against in the ZNA for a variety of reasons. For example, former ZIPRA members felt disadvantaged in the selection process for who would be chosen for further training abroad in places like Yugoslavia, a process that seemed to favor former ZANLA members in greater numbers than former ZIPRA. Also, in the wake of the clashes at various assembly points, increasing numbers of former ZIPRA were being purged and demobilized.[6] By February 1982 tensions reached a peak when the government revealed that ZAPU-owned properties contained concealed arms, which the government interpreted to mean that Nkomo and the former ZIPRA were intending to stage a coup and, if necessary, a civil war. Parties sympathetic to ZAPU understood the arms cache crisis to have been an exaggerated response by the government aimed at discrediting ZAPU and Nkomo, since it was allegedly well known since before 1982 that both ZIPRA and ZANLA had been caching arms after demobilization in both Matabeleland and Mashonaland. Former ZAPU head and founder Joshua Nkomo argued that the government chose to highlight the caches in Matabeleland for political purposes.[7]

In order to punish the people of Matabeleland for supporting the now-named "dissident" intentions of ZAPU and its armed wing, the Fifth Brigade was deployed first into Matabeleland North in January 1983, then into Matabeleland South. The Fifth

Brigade's commander, Perence Shiri, had carried a flag at the December 1982 parade heralding the brigade's formation; this flag bore the word Gukurahundi.[8] Gukurahundi is a term from the Shona language referring to the early rains that wash away the chaff. The chaff in this case was Matabeleland's ZAPU supporters. This chapter in Zimbabwe's history is little known outside the circle of people who directly experienced it.[9]

Areas most affected by the Fifth Brigade's activities included the rural districts of the BICC in both Matabeleland North and South. Matabeleland North was hit hardest, and first. This was reflected in its impact on the church's activities there as well. The BICC mission station in Matabeleland North, Phumula, near Gwaai, was located where some of the most severe acts of violence and intimidation occurred. In 1983 a baptism service to be held at Phumula was canceled "because the situation in the area is not safe." Phumula was the center of operation for the church's Gwaai District; the Gwaai overseer in 1983 was unable to visit the village churches under his jurisdiction due to the dangerous conditions.[10] Gwaai District's assistant overseer at that time was Rev. Raphael Mthombeni. He received word that the Fifth Brigade had targeted him. "I distributed blankets [and other supplies] and they assumed these were from ZAPU. People warned me to look out; I was in danger. They heard them saying how they doubted my so-called church link was anything other than a cover for ZAPU." Their warnings were legitimate: Mthombeni had a nearly fatal encounter. A group of instructors from the church's Bible institute had come to Gwaai District; Mthombeni had invited them to help lead a pastor's workshop.

> One day they stopped my truck. They had me get out, took away my shoes, my ID. They stripped me. Had me step some distance away from the truck and kneel down and put my head down to the ground, told me it was my last day. They searched my truck for evidence. I prayed and asked God that if today was my day, to please receive my soul. But I said if you want me okay, but remember I

am not here for myself, I am here to help these poor souls. They took their time killing me. I used that time to pray. They found an account book that I recorded offerings in, like [Pastor] NakaGininda $25. They said this is not church offering book; it is a ZAPU membership book. They flung it away. They gave me back my shoes, my ID, my clothes, and told me to drive. I drove. But God saved us. I believe this is where I think the white missionary [Curtis Book] played a role to save us. I believe they were afraid to kill us all with him. Because they debated a lot and some were saying let's kill them and some kept on pointing at Rev. Book speaking in their language, Shona.[11]

According to Mthombeni, many of the ZAPU local treasurers were in fact also the local BICC pastors. As Mthombeni put it, "Such a one was often the only man who didn't smoke, didn't drink, had only one wife. He was a leader in the community." Mthombeni remembered that "almost all" of the male BICC pastors who were also ZAPU officers were killed during the Gukurahundi. Jake Shenk, a missionary serving there at that time, remembered at least one BICC male pastor in Gwaai District being killed.[12] ZAPU and Ndebele identity were collapsed, or combined, during the Gukurahundi. As Alexander, McGregor, and Ranger put it, "an attack on the Ndebele was an attack on Zapu, an attack on Zapu was an attack on the Ndebele; and attacks on Zapu as Ndebele made even those Zapu members who were not Ndebele come to see themselves as such."[13] This dynamic, in which ZAPU became synonymous with Ndebele ethnic identity was true for Mthombeni, for whom his captors' use of Shona was key; he summarized the whole initiative as a "typical ethnic cleansing."

Mthombeni's story glares with an oxymoron: ZAPU officers who were also BICC pastors? This insistence on the part of many men of the BICC-Zimbabwe that they could combine their Christian and their "worldly" political identities was developed in chapter 5's discussion of the liberation war, especially with the emergence of the Church of the Orphans. Nonetheless, for the top leadership—the ordained ministers (abaFundisi) and bishops—party membership was impossible. For some BICC men, the injunction to remain aloof from party politics was to them a good teaching, and they abided by it.[14] And the church's official publications remained utterly apolitical. Throughout the entire Gukurahundi period, the Bulawayo-published and African-run church paper *Good Words/Amazwi Amahle,* never once mentioned the killings except in the most oblique of terms. There was the above-mentioned article that a scheduled baptism in Matabeleland North could not occur because it was "not safe." In addition, at the opening of 1985, Bishop Ndlovu noted that the prior year had been one of sadness and fear. A 1986 sketch of the life of a woman pastor, NakaRoja Ndlovu, stated, "Catastrophe struck in 1984 When on December 7, she lost her husband who had been her pillar of strength."[15] It does not indicate how he died; that he might have died at the hands of the Fifth Brigade, which is possible given the date of his death, is not mentioned. The vast majority of the paper's articles throughout the 1980s were dedicated to celebrating, promoting, and goading church growth and evangelism, as well as spiritual development for youth and new members.

Before discussion of how the BICC leadership, especially its bishop, Stephen N. Ndlovu, coped with the horrifying developments in the national political scene that culminated in the work of the Fifth Brigade, I go back in time, to explain how Ndlovu found himself in this position as head of the denomination. Analysis of his upbringing in a BICC Christian family, his decades-long evasion of what he came later to recognize as a calling to full-time church work as a minister, and his eventual turn to accept this call in the service of the BICC, with an important nudge from his wife, MaNkala, help place his actions during the Gukurahundi in a deeper historical, religious, and gendered context.

"I Don't Know What Belly You Are Going to Lie In": Ndlovu's Call

In his 1999 interview with me, Stephen Ndlovu found it significant to emphasize that he was raised in a Christian home. He depicted his mother, Deredza Dube, as a leader of Christians. He emphasized that his father, Ndabambi Ndlovu, was an early convert who became a trained teacher and pastor. His father "got the preaching" from BICC bishop Steigerwald when the latter began to evangelize in the Filabusi area, in the 1910s. He viewed his parents' relationship as a mutually chosen one of shared Christian service and leadership. This is how Ndlovu told of his parents, their courtship, and their work for the church:

> My mother was converted, too, as a young girl under one of the early teachers like my father, who was Sithole, and she was a good Sunday school teacher. So she used to walk eight miles, from her home to near my grandfather's home, where she was assembling people, teaching them Sunday school. There was no service; she started that. It was Sunday school, and then later on became a service, and the first pastor was my father, when they got married. What happened was, when my father went home to his home— that's my grandfather's home—found this girl preaching under a *mkhuna* tree. And he was a Christian, here she was a Christian, then they fell in love and decided they wanted a Christian marriage. . . . Then my father became the teacher at that school after his training—teacher training—and the two of them worked side by side, she still helped my father with the Sunday school work; my father was both a schoolteacher as well as a pastor.[16]

Ndlovu's account of his parents' courtship was established as a set narrative long before I interviewed him in 1999. In a 1987 interview with historian Scotch Ndlovu (not a close relative), Stephen Ndlovu repeated that core phrase about his father finding a girl "preaching under a *mkhuna* tree": "My mother happened to be a Sunday school teacher when my father was Bishop Steigerwald's cook at Wanezi as a single man, and when he went home he found a girl preaching under a *mkhuna* tree."[17] Ndlovu believed that his parents' wedding in 1930 was "the first unique

Christian marriage in that area." This is corroborated by the testimony of Ethel Sibanda, whose mother attended the wedding.[18] The church that they ran "side by side" was called Mazhabazha. The phrasing choices made in Ndlovu's narration of family origins point to his pride in his father's educational level and to the dynamics between gender and institutionalization in the church. Consider the manner in which he describes his mother, Deredza Dube, and her manner of involvement in the work of the church.[19] Ndlovu states that his mother was "preaching" and also was the "head" of the Sunday school. She conducted this leadership role "under a mkhuna tree." Women leading worship groups under the *natural* shelter of the tree (instead of a built church), is a theme of female—and feminine modes of—leadership.[20]

Thus, Ndlovu's mother was a leader of Christians, someone who "assembled people"—and then taught them their Bible and taught them how to be Christians. But she was not the pastor, and the group gathered around her was not a church. Once she married Ndabambi, who became "pastor of the church at Mazhabazha," she continued as a leader, preacher, and teacher, continuing to teach Sunday school. But the arrival of the church building and school came once she married someone who could be the pastor. Ndlovu's father's education at the teacher-training school at Matopo Mission is emphasized in the account above. Ndlovu stated it twice. The very first thing indicated about his father, mentioned before this excerpt, was the fact that his father was a trained teacher, an educated man.

Ndlovu's use of the phrase *side by side* in reference to the way both his parents worked for the Mazhabazha church suggests a partnership: a companionate marriage. This notion is reinforced when he said they fell in love and got married: it was not an arranged marriage. A vivid contrast to this is the story that Ndlovu's wife, Otiliya (MaNkala), told of her own parents' marriage. Her father, Nkala, was a wealthy-in-cattle polygynist, while her mother was the third wife, taken to him against her will. She said, "You know, people were not proposed, you love someone [You were not proposed to; you did not marry for love]. You were just dragged to go and marry to any man the parents liked."[21] Thus, by contrast, Ndlovu's choice of phrasing, "they fell in love and got married" carries with it the distinct imprint of his own parents' union not being arranged; it was, by contrast, a "Christian" marriage, marked by the generationally disruptive practice of having the bride and groom choose each other. A Christian wedding ceremony, known as a white wedding, celebrated in the rural areas served as one of the many ways that converts such as the Ndlovu couple marked out a Christian identity and was thereby instructional to those around them. Christian wedding ceremonies made a powerful impact on the imaginations and aspirations of the young people who attended them, inspiring girls, for example, to "set [their] standard for [a Christian wedding ceremony]."[22]

Stephen Ndlovu was the firstborn child to this aspirant Christian couple; four girls, then eight more boys followed him: all together there were thirteen children. His mother died in 1964; shortly thereafter Ndabambi remarried and with his second wife had eight more children. As Ndabambi's firstborn son, it fell to Stephen Ndlovu to look to the education of all these children. As Ndlovu put it, "all those children became my responsibility as the eldest son. That's how hard it is in our culture."[23] Taking on this responsibility is a crucial element of what I call Ndlovu's kinship-based masculinity. As Ndlovu understood it, the senior male in the family was expected to take on the care and upbringing of his father's children.[24] In the colonial period, in which education was the way to ensure access to higher-paid employment and greater levels of respectability, this meant seeing to their education. In this regard, Christian and family-based concepts of how a man should behave were in harmony with one another, particularly since the education in question was provided by the Brethren in Christ and other mission churches. Ndlovu himself did a course in primary-school teacher training at Matopo Mission from 1947 to 1948. He acquired the junior certificate by correspondence study in 1964.[25]

In another regard, his kinship-based masculine imperatives and his Christian beliefs served continuously, throughout his adult life, to pose serious challenges and even crises within the family. Not all his father's children became such devoted members of the church, nor did all their children. As the head of the family, Ndlovu was urgently required to be present for ceremonies intended to appease the ancestors or to drink beer dedicated to the honoring of the ancestors. "Because of [his] commitment to Christ," Ndlovu refused to participate. "Being the firstborn in the family, it happens all the time."[26]

The Backslidden Years

Ndlovu spent some years in his youth when he experimented with a variety of practices and professions that were seen as un-Christian, including consumption of alcohol and cigarette smoking. "I did go into drinking, I did go into all sorts of stupid things, because I wanted to find out, what's going on here?"[27] During this time, he left his first job, as a village church schoolteacher, and had a short-lived career working for the Bulawayo city council as an athletics coordinator in the early 1950s.[28] He organized boxing league matches at Stanley Square, presided over bicycle races, and worked to provide sporting venues generally.[29] At £16 per week, Ndlovu's wages were much higher working for the Bulawayo city council than the £5 per week he earned as a rural-mission schoolteacher. As seen in more detail in chapter 4, BICC's missionaries and African leadership strongly advised its membership not to go to "town," in other words the city of Bulawayo. By simply living in town in the early 1950s, the church saw Ndlovu as backslidden.

A sketch of his life appeared in the BICC-Zimbabwe's 1998 centennial volume. That account, crafted by Doris Dube, characterized Ndlovu's work in Bulawayo as a time when "Ndlovu had turned his back on all that was Christian." Dube writes that "many Christian people . . . just kept on coming after him to return to the straight path."[30] To me, Ndlovu simply remarked, "the Lord helped me to realize this was not the thing for me." In spite of the significantly higher earnings, Ndlovu left his position with the Bulawayo city council, and returned to teaching in mission schools. Ndlovu consistently attributed this change in career to the end of his backslidden period.

Ndlovu left his athletics work in Bulawayo to serve as a BICC village schoolteacher in his area of origin, Filabusi. The Rhodesian government was forcing people to leave their homes in Filabusi District and sending them to live in Matabeleland North (see chapter 3). Among those forcibly removed were close neighbors and relatives of the Ndlovu family. Doris Dube suggests that these removals motivated Ndlovu to want to move north, to live and serve among the resettled people.[31] Since his relatives were taken to an area under the influence of the Presbyterian Free Church, Ndlovu took a position for five years with that denomination at a rural mission station north of Bulawayo, at Nkayi.[32] Recently married to MaNkala, the two of them felt increasingly restricted by the Free Presbyterians' exceptionally limiting rules.[33]

In 1960 the Ndlovus left the Presbyterian mission, and Ndlovu went back to teaching for the BICC, at Mtshabezi Mission's teacher-training program. In 1969, Ndlovu found himself facing a challenge. He had an offer to become headmaster at a government school; while considering this opportunity, he attended the BICC General Conference, where the then bishop, P. M. Khumalo, came to him and asked if he would accept a call to serve as the BICC's regional overseer for Mtshabezi District. Accepting the position of overseer would require giving up the prestigious secular educational career track, taking a significant pay cut, and remaining at rural Mtshabezi Mission, near Gwanda in Matabeleland South. The drama he invested in the telling of this difficult choice indicates that he continued, three decades later, to regard it one of the most important decisions of his life.

> I was called to be an overseer by election of the church
> executive board. It wasn't easy to yield to it. I remember
> when I was approached, my wife and I weeping because I
> was doing so well in secular education, that teachers were

coming from all over, even including Bulawayo, sent by the Ministry of Education to come and see the methods I was implementing at Mtshabezi. I deliberately chose to start a class from grade 1 and go up with it, because I thought I had known enough—and this was grade 5—to see these little children turning up into something, and so Ministry of Education said, "Well, send teachers to go and see this." But then amidst all that, Ministry of Education said, "Now you [claps twice], do some more studies. We want to take you to Bulawayo to head one of the schools." So I was doing my studies and preparing to write my exams at the end of 1969, when the bishop approached me at conference. I used to translate for missionaries at the conferences, and he took me to his temporary office at Mtshabezi—usually when there is a conference they designate one room as [the] bishop's office—he put his hand up across my shoulder, and then he said, "Brother Ndlovu, the church is calling you into full time church work." I said, "What??" He said, "The church is calling you to be a full time church worker as an overseer for Mtshabezi District." That was hard. I remember that evening; I just left my food. I had not completed eating when I was called out that the bishop wanted to see me; I could not eat it. Took my wife, told her what was said to me, we both wept; but she, knowing what had transpired when I was teaching for Free Presbyterian Church of Scotland and other things. I was running away from a call that kept pressing me, and I thought maybe going to teach for another denomination would ease the problem. But here was a confrontation, very difficult. And while in the course of our weeping, my wife said, "I know that Jonah lay in the belly of a fish, but I don't know what belly you are going to lie in. If I were you, I would say, 'the will of the Lord be done' at this point." I would say of all the people, she is the one that convinced me to accept it. I went to [the bishop] the following morning and I said,

"Bishop, I don't want this thing [claps three times]. But the will of the Lord be done."

In this account, the details of Ndlovu's mode of telling the story reveal much about how significant this moment was as a turning point in his life. He has rendered his sensory memories vividly; it calls forth the sense that time slowed down for him. The bishop interrupted a meal; afterward, Ndlovu could not even finish his food: "I could not eat it." By indicating that he translated for the missionaries, Ndlovu is letting me know he carried a high honor—one that acknowledged his learning and his fluency not only at translating words but also at moving back and forth between the African church and the American missionaries. The bond of Christian brotherhood among senior males in the BICC is evident in the intimate encounter between Bishop P. M. Khumalo and Ndlovu. Khumalo puts his arm around Ndlovu's shoulders, and calls him brother. The clapping at the end communicated Ndlovu's sense of finality and portent.

Significantly, both Ndlovu and his wife, in separate interviews, described the event very similarly, both noting the weeping, remembering the reference to Jonah and the belly of the fish, and giving credit to MaNkala for being the decisive influence on Ndlovu to accept the call. Ndlovu credits his wife with perceiving that he had been running away from a call to full-time church work. Ndlovu had met his wife, Otiliya (MaNkala), when they were both in teacher training at Matopo, in 1947. After a long courtship, in which Ndlovu had to wait until MaNkala felt satisfied that she had done right by her brothers' educational needs, paying their fees from her earnings as a primary-school teacher.[34] She had seen him train as a teacher with the BICC, go "astray" for a while in Bulawayo, teach at the Presbyterian mission, then go into secular education. Here is her version of the same moment:

And I said to him—ai, he even shed tears. "No, but I don't want that. I want to go and teach. My call is in teaching" [he said]. I said, "Ja, teaching the Word of God." He said, "Oh, it is just not a matter of what. If you have a call, you have the right call." And I said to him, "If you run away, you will be like Jonah, you will be swallowed by a fish. And again, we don't know what kind of fish is going to swallow you. You better listen to what God tells you." And that really hurt him. . . . He doesn't regret that God called him for that. He really says, "Oh, yes, you kept encouraging." I encouraged him. I encouraged him to take that position.[35]

The themes and phrases appear in Ndlovu's 1987 interview with Scotch Ndlovu as well: the anguish, and MaNkala's goad to accept the call by citing the story of Jonah hiding from God in the belly of a great fish. In his 1987 telling, Bishop Ndlovu also credits MaNkala for convincing him.[36] The role of MaNkala in this story conforms to a well-understood pattern in Ndebele culture's understanding of the role of women in leadership within families. The official role of the male as head of family—and chief decision maker—is fed by consultations with his own senior sisters and his chief wife.[37] Ndlovu was quick to credit both his mother and his wife for his spiritual and therefore also his vocational journey. He acknowledged that their female piety was something he could access as a complement to his own male identity—in part supported by the role of leader in a large organization such as the church and in part undermined by a professional choice that led to less income with which to perform his kinship-based masculine role as head of family.

These repeated tropes suggest that to accept the call was simultaneously the end of a long period of evasion of what some part of Ndlovu felt was what God wanted him to do, as well as a sacrifice requiring voluntary acceptance of suffering. In this instance, the suffering was loss of prestige and material prosperity due to giving up the more well paid and higher-profile career opportunity to work for the Rhodesian department of education in Bulawayo. Given the large number of children, both his own and those of his father, for whom he was responsible, voluntarily giving up income was not easy to do. Ndlovu accepted the call

Figure 6.1. Rev. Stephen N. Ndlovu, at the BICC Africa General Conference in Choma, Zambia, 1972. *Photo credit: George Bundy*

to serve as overseer for Mtshabezi District. His term of service extended from 1970 to 1979.

Up until Ndlovu's ordination, the expectation for wives of ministers, or abaFundisi, was that they give up their paid work, if they had any (usually as teachers), so as to devote themselves full-time to support their husbands' ministries. Indeed, wives stood with their husbands at the ordination ceremony, to demonstrate this expectation. However, no separately designated income for the wife came with this arrangement. Elder, respected church-women communicated some of these expectations informally. Na-kaGininda, pastor of the Mpisini church in the Gwaai (see chapter 4), was a mentor to the first African bishops' wives, Joyce Khum-alo and Otiliya Ndlovu: "Those women were good teachers to us. We were young, bishops' wives who were young, we used to listen to them when they instructed us that 'A leader's wife must behave like this, like this, like this.'"[38] An indication of the expectations for wives of churchmen is evident in the way Mrs. P. M. Khumalo referred to the time when "we were bishop."[39] The bishops' and overseers' wives had many duties linked to the husband's work. First, the wife of a bishop automatically became the head of the all-Rhodesia BICC's women's group called the Omama Bosizo (Women who help). Overseers' wives automatically became heads for the district-based divisions of the Omama. The ordained man's wife also was busy with baking communion bread, being sure tubs and towels were clean and ready for foot-washing ceremonies, accompanying her husband when possible on his journeys to visit and supervise outlying churches, and hosting the many visitors and petitioners who came to the churchman's residence.

During the years when her husband, Alvin Book, was bishop (1965–69), Thata Book devoted herself full-time to the work of being a bishop's wife, in addition to raising their four children. Khumalo was elected bishop the same year that Ndlovu was called to full-time church work. Mrs. Khumalo quit her posi-tion at the Matopo Book Centre when her husband was elected bishop, as she was told her duties as bishop's wife were too many to accommodate any other work. MaNkala and Ndlovu both felt the pinch of the continued reduced salary at the mission church. She shocked many when, in contrast to Mrs. Khumalo, she refused to give up her work as a teacher when her husband was called to full-time church work. "They sent some people to come and talk to me" to say that they expected her to quit so she could help her husband.

> And I don't know how we can manage, helping these [family members] when I am seated doing nothing, waiting for my husband to say, "Let us visit such a place." God blessed me with five children—with my five children plus these other children, how can I manage the home? Foodwise, we just forget about clothes. . . . Where is the food going to come [from]? I said to that man who was sent by the church, "You just forgive me. Let me teach, I'll do my teaching from Monday to Friday. Friday afternoon I'm away from teaching. Help my husband Friday evening, Saturday morning and evening, Sunday morning and evening."[40]

Ndlovu supported his wife's decision to keep her job while she accepted the additional work that came with being the uMfundisi's wife. Their marriage was a partnership: they worked together to support the many children for whom they were responsible. She encouraged him to accept the call to full-time church work, fully realizing that such a decision would negatively affect the family income as well increase as her own work load, quite significantly. All this, together with the manner in which he repeatedly credited her for leading him to agree to full-time church work, indicates the degree to which they were an interdependent team, each drawing on the other's insights and distinctly gendered forms of piety to make it all work.

Ndlovu's reliance on his wife for mutual support, and his crediting her with influence on his decisions is not inconsistent with the role of wives of powerful men in the larger cultural setting.

Figure 6.2. Rev. Stephen N. Ndlovu and Otiliya Ndlovu (MaNkala), at the BICC Regional Conference in Rhodesia, Wanezi Mission, 1972. *Photo credit: George Bundy*

Pathisa Nyathi articulates the place of a wife of a male leader in what Nyathi calls "traditional Ndebele culture": "When a woman got married to a man she, in terms of how she was addressed, assumed the address of the husband. My brother's wife is my 'brother,' as if she is male. My uncle's wife is 'uncle,' as if she were male. This gives her some of the powers and status within the family of her husband."[41] Nyathi goes on to emphasize this when Ndebele men became kings or chiefs; their wives shared that status. This carried into the roles taken on by the women married to BICC ordained ministers (abaFundisi) or bishops. Wives were (and are) ordained together with their husbands. Thus the influence of MaNkala is a function of her role as the wife, and cosharer, of the leader's role with her husband, is a formative, feminine side of Ndlovu's "kinship-based masculinity."

During the 1970s, Rev. Stephen Ndlovu was overseer for Mtshabezi District; in this position he was in charge of all the district's affiliated rural village churches, numbering about forty.[42] Mission stations all over Zimbabwe were threatened by the war, and thus presiding over this rural mission station and its network of remote village churches during the war meant being at the center of any encounters with guerrillas or Rhodesian forces. Ndlovu's insights on the guerrillas were mostly limited to his perspective on its effect on rural woman pastors (a theme developed in chapter 5]. He only briefly mentioned how it was for him as head of Mtshabezi. According to other informants, he spent one night at gunpoint under pressure from ZIPRA guerrillas.[43] The guerrillas wanted to know what Mtshabezi had been doing to support the cause of liberation. Not long after this, in 1978, the mission was closed and did not reopen until after independence, in 1980. Why it closed and under whose orders is a contested matter. According to Ndlovu himself, ZIPRA ordered him to close the mission.[44] Ndlovu was in a very tight spot. The constituencies to which he had to answer were in many ways utterly at odds: the African membership of the church, the guerrillas, and the missionaries. Some missionaries were sympathetic to the cause of liberation, as unhappy with the practice of war as they were.[45] Other missionaries were understood to be very much in sympathy with the Rhodesian government.[46] Sam King, a missionary based at Mtshabezi during the war who went home at the end of 1978, recalled, "some of the African people begged us to leave."[47] The church headquarters in the United States ordered the immediate furloughing of all the missionaries, due to fears for their safety, and it seems that Ndlovu concurred and ordered the missionaries to go home.[48] Many of the missionaries were due for furlough in 1977 anyway, because the executive board for missions ordered missionaries out of the rural areas, especially after the murder of a Catholic medical missionary in Matabeleland North in 1977. There are at least three varying strands of how the war is remembered in the church today: one group wishes to see that the church stood silently but significantly with the cause of liberation, a second group continue to see only the Rhodesian-sympathizing church, and a third group firmly adhere to the ideal of the church as apolitical both now and during the nationalist period.

The fact that Mtshabezi's educational institutions relocated to Bulawayo after 1977 reflects the wartime trend of rural Africans fleeing the violence of the rural guerrilla war and moving to Bulawayo for safety. Except for his brief stint working for the Bulawayo city council organizing boxing matches, Ndlovu had spent most of his career working at rural mission stations. The pain of accepting the call to full-time mission work had much to do with sacrificing an opportunity to move to "town" (Bulawayo) back in 1969, the place where ambitious, modernizing, educated African men and their families were trying to move. The war's dangers notwithstanding, making an exodus to Bulawayo during the war did bring Ndlovu back to town, only this time in his capacity as an ordained minister and top official of the mission church. He became very involved with the urban congregation in Mpopoma Township, establishing a youth center there in 1979. Not long after that, in the same year, he was elected as bishop.

Christian Peacemaking in the New Zimbabwe: Ndlovu and the Unity Accord

Rev. Ndlovu took on the position of bishop in 1979, just in time to go "through the pains of the birth of a new nation," and the dangers only increased.[49] This time in the early years of nation building in Zimbabwe was marked by "violence against PF-ZAPU [Patriotic Front–Zimbabwe African People's Union], demonization of Joshua Nkomo and attempts at writing ZIPRA out of the liberation struggle."[50] The pains alluded to by Ndlovu included presiding over the church during the Gukurahundi. His own cousin narrowly escaped death at the hands of the Fifth Brigade at his home in the village of Sipopo, in Matabeleland North.[51] "So many people lost their lives and we decided we were not going to sit down and watch. We had to find a way to approach the leaders."[52] Ndlovu decided to participate in a faith-based, ecumenical engagement with the ZANU-PF–controlled government in 1987 in an effort to stop the Gukurahundi.

By choosing to participate in the delegation to confront the ruling ZANU-PF government, Ndlovu was taking a more politically charged, activist approach to the idea of peace making than he had in the years before 1980. There are at least two reasons for this. The timing and political circumstances are important. First, church leaders throughout Zimbabwe, Ndlovu included, were focused on the aim of nation building. Shaming the prime minister was counterproductive.

Second, the postcolonial period meant a change in the balance of power between the church in North America and the Zimbabwean church. Ndlovu saw that his church needed help to rebuild. He sought to recruit a selection of skilled missionaries from the states to come and help, for rebuilding and restaffing the mission hospitals and schools.[53] However, as part of the postcolonial Zeitgiest, missionaries were to be welcomed back in the new dispensation only if, as Ndlovu articulated in a 1981 interview, they "come to serve as a servant." He went on to say that those with "paternalistic attitudes" would "be in trouble."[54] Missionaries did return after 1980, but only in a relative trickle. In 1973–74 there were fifty-five North American BICC missionaries serving the church in Rhodesia. In 1981 the BICC-Zimbabwe had four missionaries from North America.[55] Ndlovu wanted to see the church's hospitals and schools reach ever more of the people in their areas of service. He had a strong vision and commitment to reach out to, and tap the talent of, Zimbabwe's youth. An exuberance about the possibilities for a brighter future for all was tangible on the national political scene; it beamed out of the pages of the BICC's Bulawayo-based newspaper, *Good Words/Amazwi Amahle;* it burned in the hearts of young Zimbabweans who had left the country during the war and were now returned, newly qualified from their respective training programs in the United States or the UK, and ready to serve their new nation.[56] Those missionaries who came to serve the BICC in the new Zimbabwe came under different terms—terms of less power than they had had before 1978.

The government in charge was now African-elected and no longer was a white settler state. If the missionaries felt that it was inappropriate for a church leader to take any public stance on a political issue, it could not stop Ndlovu. As an ordained leader under the Rhodesians, Ndlovu risked losing his position had he attempted to go to Ian Smith to protest the injustices of colonial rule. But this new environment opened the possibility of him going to Harare to ask for an audience with Mugabe, even as it offered new dangers. As a Ndebele-speaking churchman from Bulawayo, Ndlovu came to Harare with every marking of coming from a ZAPU-loyal area.

> There were tribal tensions. I remember myself saying to the chairman of the Heads of Denominations who had come from Harare to meet with the Heads of Denominations in Bulawayo, "My brother you have traveled all the way from Harare to come to talk to us. The only trouble we are experiencing in Matabeleland comes from Harare, from your men. You are free to speak for us. There is nothing I can say. We are both Christians. Heads of denominations there and down here. What are you doing? Are you just going to sit and watch us die? We have no voice. We can't say anything. But you have the voice." I told him what had happened to my cousin. We all broke into tears and cried. We spent time praying. It was then, that in our Heads of Denominations, we purposed to find ways to communicate with the authorities that be.[57]

Ndlovu set great store on the Christian fellowship-cum-kinship he had with the other heads of denomination in effecting a series of individual conversations between the church leaders and President Canaan Banana, PF-ZAPU head Joshua Nkomo, and Prime Minister Robert Mugabe. Ndlovu seems truly to have believed their actions hastened the successful enacting of the Unity Accord of 1987. That Ndlovu's own close family members were members of PF-ZAPU was a reason why he was able to make such a good connection with Nkomo when he had an audience with him in early 1988. By making this kind of connection, Ndlovu was making a bridge between his Christian male kinship with the mixed-ethnicity heads of denomination and his Ndebele masculine identity links to PF-ZAPU, to urge an end to the killing.[58]

Missionary Jake Shenk recalled the heads-of-denomination initiative to call Mugabe to cease the killings. At the time of the Gukurahundi, Shenk was living in Zimbabwe and serving the BICC there as the Zimbabwe church's treasurer. Shenk asserted that after the meeting with Prime Minister Mugabe, they saw fewer killings and more beatings, and stores were closed. Overt threats were made to the staff at Mtshabezi that they would be allowed to starve: "You can eat your grain, cattle, chickens, grass, each other if necessary."[59]

A 1987 interview between BICC-Zimbabwean and historian Scotch Ndlovu and Stephen Ndlovu concluded with a question on the controversy over the venue of the BICC's 1987 all-church General Conference being held at Stanley Square in Bulawayo.[60] That was the first time in the church's ninety-year history (up to that point) in Zimbabwe that the General Conference was not held at one of the cardinal rural-mission stations. While Ndlovu said that he did not like the idea, initially, he said that he "succumbed" to the wishes of the urban church representatives, who wanted conference held there. He then recalled that this was the place where he used to set up boxing matches and, according to Scotch Ndlovu's notes, Ndlovu smiled, saying, "I can preach there instead of making people fight. In that sense I am saying, 'Mn! We're turning that awkward place to good use.'"[61] There is some kind of harmonization of Ndlovu's disparate masculinities when he says with such satisfaction that long ago at Stanley Square he organized fighting and now he is preaching at that same spot. Added significance to the idea of harmonized identities is the fact that Stanley Square was also a site for big political rallies and so there is a kind of cleansing, or sacralizing, going on in Ndlovu's mind especially when we consider that 1987 was the year of the Unity Accord.[62]

Ndlovu's own articulation of the church's peace teaching and his support for it in 1999 was stated in the context of his years *after* serving as bishop, spent teaching at the Theological College of Zimbabwe, an ecumenical Protestant school for training clergy and church workers. "It's in our doctrine, and we teach it. Even here at the college we have Peace and Justice; it's one of the courses that I teach. We get divided, because we have many denominations now. Ja. But, yes, from the Bible, I agree with peace. Because Jesus could have brought armies to fight for Him. He didn't. He chose to suffer. And therefore it's one of those doctrines I teach and allow people's consciences [to grapple with] . . . ja."[63]

Peace Making, Gender, and the 1980 Divide

Ndlovu's parents' Christian identity; their companionate marriage and partnership as church leaders were an important element in Ndlovu's own spiritual formation. And yet, Ndlovu was not always a pliant and ready son of the church. He got into some trouble for his willingness to tussle with the missionaries when he was at Matopo Teacher Training. He wanted to introduce guitar music and when he argued against the missionaries' refusal to allow it by citing David's playing of the lyre as a biblical justification, he was made to apologize to the community for his disrespect. He lived for a while in Bulawayo in direct violation of church teaching; he also chose not to go into full-time church work for at least twenty of his adult years before agreeing to accept the call. His marriage to a firmly committed churchwoman was a crucial element in his own path as a church leader.[64] He consistently credited MaNkala for his decision to take the daunting step into full-time church work. In contrast to the fertility challenges experienced by Sandey Vundhla and their role in his exit from church leadership, Ndlovu and MaNkala's capacity to bring forth many children was an important element in the longevity of their partnership in work for the church. In a 1992 interview with Daryl Climenhaga, Ndlovu assessed another churchman's career—it was one in which the other man ended up leaving the church and becoming involved with ancestral-spirit veneration. Ndlovu attributed this change to the fact that this man's first wife, a "good wife," who "helped keep him straight," had died.[65]

Ndlovu's acknowledgment of the importance of his mother, his own wife, and this unnamed churchman's wife in setting the tone of piety, and the life-path career choices in these respective families is his acknowledgment of women's capacities as leaders. He opposed outward signs of women's subservience to men, most vividly evident in the BICC with the women's head covering rules. He stated in 1992 that he viewed one Bulawayo church's insistence that women wear head coverings as "oppression."[66] When the church's African elders informed his wife, MaNkala, that she would be expected to resign her teaching position once Ndlovu became bishop so she could be his helpmeet as bishop's wife full time (for no pay), MaNkala refused, with Ndlovu's support.[67] Beyond that, in his 1999 interview with me he strongly endorsed the idea of women being ordained. He also credited the women pastors of the church as the ones who showed exceptional courage during the guerrilla war.[68] As of 2011 women in the BICC-Zimbabwe are still not ordained, indicating how far from the mainstream, among male leaders, Ndlovu's views on women and their capacity for leadership were.

Within the context of a colonial mission church that insisted on an apolitical stance for all its members, and most especially its leaders, Ndlovu had to negotiate the extremely dangerously conflicting constituencies to whom he was answerable during the liberation war. With close family members and many personal associates involved with ZAPU and some of them fighting in ZIPRA, Ndlovu was well aware of the political and military landscape. In all this, he never challenged the Rhodesian government; as an ordained minister for a mission church, he was part of the system of power in place. As one BICC male leader astutely put it, the people understood that African clergy in the mission church could not be active in nationalist politics or in the war. They did, however, expect "the Ministers to exploit that opportunity of belonging to the inner circle to try & get valuable info that would help their side. So they were torn in between. If they failed to do this, they were regarded as traitors who betray their own people and could be killed at that time without any second thought."[69] Although in theory by the 1970s Africans led the church in Rhodesia, there were still many missionaries and they were still accustomed to being in charge; they still came with much funding that benefited the African church schools and other institutions. Ndlovu looked to the missionaries' safety when he insisted they evacuate the rural mission station at Mtshabezi, in 1978. He needed to do this in a way that did not seem to the guerrillas to convey sympathy for the Rhodesian cause and in a way that did not seem to the Rhodesians to be due to adherence to ZAPU's cause. When Ndlovu willingly took on suffering for the sake of accepting the call to church work, in 1969, he likely had not anticipated to what degree his role at Mtshabezi would put his own life and that of others into danger.

As an Ndebele man of high stature from a politically engaged family and known seedbed of ZAPU heavyweights such as Dumiso Dabengwa, Ndlovu could have been expected to be an active member of ZAPU. Because of his position as a BICC minister and overseer, in the 1970s, and then a bishop, in the 1980s, he never did join ZAPU or any other political party. This politically neutral official stance helped him during the liberation war. It became crucial for him in the 1980s during the Gukurahundi. As bishop, he was the leader of the whole BICC of Zimbabwe, making him eligible to join the all-Zimbabwe heads-of-denomination group, drawn from all the churches all over Zimbabwe. As a single church leader from a church almost exclusively drawn from Ndebele speakers in Matabeleland, he was on weak ground if he was going to try to speak to the ZANU government under Mugabe's leadership about the atrocities being committed by the Fifth Brigade.[70] And yet, by appealing to the Christian brotherhood or kinship of the other heads of denomination, including Shona-speaking churches based in Harare, urging them to make common cause, Ndlovu was able to be part of this group's approach to Nkomo and the ZANU heads of state.

Ndlovu's life history in relation to his affiliation to the church shows a man who was raised in a Christian family, trained to teach at the church's educational institutions, then spent a period of his young adult life living in town and working at "worldly" pursuits, such as when he arranged boxing matches at Stanley Square for the Bulawayo city council. His marriage to BICC member Otiliya Nkala was long and fruitful. Her unwavering support for his calling to church work influenced his eventual agreement to be called into full-time ministry for the church. This positioned him to be the bishop at the time that Rhodesia became Zimbabwe and during the years of violence in Matabeleland known as the Gukurahundi. He remained a leader after his time as bishop ended, in 1989, serving as a senior helping uMfundisi at Bulawayo Central Church and professor at the Theological College of Zimbabwe until his death from cancer, in August 2000. He, like so many other men of the BICC, sequenced his piety in such a way that some of the work of manhood led him into a backslidden condition. Unlike many, however, the period of waywardness was relatively short. He built a career as a prominent leader inside the church and remained so from the prime of his career through to the end. Ndlovu's Christian fictive-kin "brotherhood" with the Shona-speaking Harare-area clergymen during the 1980s gave him access to the conversation about trying to stop the Gukurahundi; his actual kinship-clan links with ZAPU people from Matabeleland bridged him back into that world where the deaths were occurring, and navigating both sets of kinships simultaneously is how he managed to get an audience with Mugabe. Then there is the kinship he had with his mother and wife, and the relational gendered dynamics between him and his wife especially—whose influences in my mind undoubtedly were key to why he was a cler-gyman at all and trying to live according to this apolitical-pacifist ideal in the midst of a politically charged time.

Conclusion

Gendered Lives of Piety

TRACKING INDIVIDUALS THROUGH THEIR entire lives within the context of their families yields insights about the place of the church in African history. There is fruitfulness in considering the whole-life trajectory. In this study, I selected six members of the BICC-Zimbabwe for attention; their lives span the church's inception, in the late 1890s, through to the postcolonial period, at the end of the twentieth century. Although each chapter features an individual, the web of family relationships around them is considered as fully as the evidence permits. All the stories have more power and subtlety because each life history does not consider the person as an individual but rather as one in context with a wider family network. Other family members' actions are shaped at least in part by their positions as persons of one sex or another, by their degree of blood relatedness, and by their generation. All these elements of familial identity in turn interplayed with dynamics of piety. This summary thus recaps the ways each person was embedded in a family network through which they lived their gendered lives of piety.

Matshuba Ndlovu's story permits consideration of the phenomenon of boys and young men who came to mission stations shortly after conquest, and their early interactions with missionaries. Matshuba's father, Mjobhiza Ndlovu—close to the disappeared and defeated King Lobengula—urged him to go to the mission at Matopo to learn the ways of the newly arrived colonial rulers. Matshuba's first decade with the BICC is marked by conversion, increasing faith, and the missionaries' acknowledgment of his talent and the passing on of increasing responsibilities in the work of the church. To follow his story into full adult male maturity, we see complex dynamics at work as we witness Matshuba struggle with the church's adaptation to institutionalized segregation as the settler state firmed up its control over land, legislation, and educational policy. Matshuba's hard-won stature as an educated, progressive, Christian man—by the 1920s he was the head of household and senior African member of the mission church at Mayezane—was incompatible with the mission's expectation of a continued type of deference that suited him well enough as a boy and a youth but was no longer reflective of his place in his community and his family. It is within this context that the AMEC's appeal to Matshuba and members of his cohort becomes comprehensible.

A whole-life assessment of Maria Tshuma yields insights unattainable without consideration of her later years. A study of girls who tried to avoid arranged marriages by going to mission stations might produce a history about gendered generational conflict and family rupture, with girls defying fathers and their would-be, much-older husbands. Although the moments of conflict are compelling, and unpacking them yields important insights, we must follow stories such as Maria Tshuma's through the full arc of their lives. Maria Tshuma eventually reconciled with her family, even though many of them did not stay in or even join the church, including a sister who served out her life at the Mwali shrine and brothers who were active in ZAPU. Maria herself spent her postmenopausal years as a tireless evangelist and church planter. Following her story through to the eventual reconciliation with her father, who had flung her to the missionaries, declaring "she is no longer my child," offers a far more textured and nuanced—and perhaps less conflicted—story, albeit dramatic in a different way.

NakaSeyemephi's story offers another view into the tensions that emerged within families that practiced arranged marriages once the mission stations were established. The BICC mission offered both a new morality of conjugality and a physical zone in which it was promoted and protected. The choices NakaSeyemephi made indicate a woman aware of opportunities to make a new and different kind of life. As a young, junior wife in a polygynous household in Filabusi District, she was drawn to the newly established BICC congregation nearby. When NakaSeyemephi was widowed, she opted to leave her husband's family to live at Mtshabezi Mission, far away from the levirate marriage that awaited her among her husband's people, and in the midst of the schooling she so keenly wanted for her daughters. Like Maria Tshuma, though, her choice to leave her husband's family did not indicate a permanent rupture. Some fifteen years after her original departure in the early 1920s, when a son from one of her cowives implored her to come back home, she did. From there they were eventually removed to Lupane, joining the thousands that the Rhodesian state forcibly evicted into remote areas of Matabeleland North in the 1950s. In this belated enforcement of the Land Apportionment Act of 1930, almost half the affected families were from the BICC areas of Wanezi and Matopo. NakaSeyemephi's story is also a vivid exemplar of why it is fruitful to consider the broader family context when offering a life history. If this book were only a history of people who entered and remained in good standing with the church, NakaSeyemephi's tale would be of a family of women: herself and her two daughters. Her husband and her cowife's son were not members of the church; and yet their actions and desires had a significant impact on her life path and how she lived out her Christian faith.

Sandey Vundhla's life ran concurrently with Zimbabwe's post-WWII modernization trends. A broad program to promote economic development and modernization accompanied the Rhodesian state's enforcement of the Land Act after the Second World War. Encouraging the growth of an African middle class was part of this plan. Secondary schools proliferated in the 1950s, and the BICC's schools joined the trend, opening the Matopo, the Wanezi, and eventually the Mtshabezi secondary schools. The cities of Bulawayo and Salisbury also grew, as did African organizations devoted to labor reform and political rights. Protest movements opposing enforced agricultural practices designed to encourage the prevention of soil erosion also flowered in the 1950s. All these elements had their part in the creation of African nationalist political parties whose aim was majority rule—the parties themselves being expressions of modernity, albeit not the sort envisioned by the Rhodesian leadership.

Vundhla himself had earned a certificate endorsing his mastery of modern techniques of farming. While Vundhla was helping encourage the flourishing of new church communities in Gwaai District of Matabeleland North, disgruntled African cultivators in that region were protesting against the agricultural demonstrators' insistence on contour rows. His ordination as uMfundisi along with two other Africans, in 1959, doubled the number of abaFundisi in the BICC from three to six. The feeling in the air was that promising African leaders must be groomed for leadership, a trend occurring in the wider Rhodesian setting as well as in the church. Vundhla's rise in the church reflected the merit-based society envisioned by a policy of modernization. Vundhla came from an unchurched family that did not descend from the elite, abezansi layer of the Ndebele-speaking people. Vundhla's ordination and advancement to a leadership position coordinating church growth in Bulawayo indicate the tremendous confidence placed in him, and his career trajectory reflects the hope—and ultimate frustration—of energetic, progressive African men in the 1960s. His precipitous exit from church leadership and church membership, after breathtaking successes as a church planter in the African suburbs of Bulawayo, paralleled the initial energy and hope of the nationalist parties until the Unilateral Declaration of Independence closed down options so far that armed struggle against the Rhodesian state became the next step. Vundhla's career trajectory paralleled that of the nationalist movement.

As with Maria Tshuma's defiance of her father's plan for her arranged marriage, and Seyemephi Ngwenya's decision to walk away from the levirate union expected of a young widow in her husband's family, Vundhla's dramatic break with the church, if treated out of context of the whole of his life, would paint a picture of conflict and rupture. The fact that much later, in the 1990s, he came back to church, made a public repentance to the people at his former church community in Mpopoma, and occasionally thereafter attended worship in the final years of his life, is significant. Vundhla's actions in his later years demonstrate this book's point that men typically sequenced their piety: growing up in the church or converting early in life, but falling away from good standing in the church due to the work of masculinity, returning to the church in the later years of life. Vundhla, like many BICC men, circled back to the church in his old age, just as women circled back to their families and their male family heads in *their* maturity.

The guerrilla war of the 1970s was of monumental importance to the history—and demise—of Rhodesia; it led to the Lancaster House Agreement, which created the new state of Zimbabwe, in 1980. How was a church—entwined materially and institutionally, from the ground up, with the settler state, and embracing an intentionally pacifist and nonresistant stance toward politics—going to cope with a brutal civil war that swept across the rural areas? Sithembile Nkala's story as one of the first female pastors of Matabeleland South is developed within the context of her extended family and, more broadly, the liberation war. Her family's varied experiences of the war lend subtlety to our understanding of the guerrilla war's impact on rural Christians. Her understanding of herself as a generational senior; as a grandmother, or Gogo; as a pastor and protector of her congregation; and as a Christian shaped her dramatic encounter with ZANLA guerrillas. Sithembile Nkala confronted the guerrillas as their generational elder and Gogo and as a woman of spiritual authority in her role as pastor to the small community in which she lived, to challenge their use of sellout accusations, some of which were leveled against her own relatives.

The life Stephen N. Ndlovu reaches from 1930 until well into the postcolonial era. His secondary education at Matopo High School after the Second World War launched him into adulthood as the new African middle class was embracing the professions and moving to urban townships newly constructed for this group. Running away from his rural, BICC upbringing to embrace the forbidden opportunities in Bulawayo, in spite of being the son of first-generation Christians, Ndlovu became a sports organizer, a pugilist, and eventually a teacher in the Rhodesian school system. At midlife, Ndlovu's age-mate and fellow Matopo Secondary School alumnus Rev. Philemon M. Khumalo issued the call: return to the BICC, become an ordained minister. His wife, MaNkala, reflecting her influence in their strong, companionate marriage, facilitated Ndlovu's positive response to the church's call with her stinging reference to Jonah and the whale, asking Ndlovu into which belly he was going to run this time. Ndlovu's eventual ordination as uMfundisi culminated in him becoming the second black bishop of the church, in 1980, just as Zimbabwe became a newly born nation. Ndlovu presided over the first days of the Zimbabwean nation's euphoria and hope—the guerrilla war was over and the settler state removed from power—and into the years of intense, postcolonial suffering when Matabeleland, and the reaches of the BICC, endured the Gukurahundi killings of the mid-1980s. Drawing on networks of fictive Christian kinship both within the mostly Ndebele-speaking church as well as across ethnic and denominational lines, Ndlovu attempted to navigate roles as comforter to the bereaved and advocate for ending the killing on behalf of his flock to the ZANU-PF government.

All three of the women featured in *The Gender of Piety* had foundational experiences at the Mtshabezi Girls' Primary Boarding School in the 1920s and 1930s. Each born in the first years of the twentieth century, Maria Tshuma and Sinini Ngwenya experienced the first generation of Christian mission schooling for girls and its attendant disruptions on relations with their male kin. Meanwhile, Sithembile Nkala's parents were in the very first cohort of baptized African BICC members and supported Sithembile's schooling, which meant that she had far more education—and professional qualifications—than Tshuma or Ngwenya, thus illustrating the difference a generation of mission education could make. Two taught primary school; two went on to become pioneering congregational pastors, while Maria Tshuma became an itinerant evangelist and church planter of exceptional proportions both in remote Matabeleland North and the urban centers of Salisbury (Harare), Gwanda, and Bulawayo. Two of the three—Maria Tshuma and Sithembile Nkala—experienced the anticolonial guerrilla war of the 1970s and continued to exercise church-related leadership roles after 1980. Sithembile Nkala lived through the liberation war at her rural home while serving as pastor and teacher; by the 1990s she was living in Bulawayo. By the 1990s both MaNsimango and MaTshuma remained active members of the Omama Bosizo.

The BICC-Zimbabwe since 2000

The history of the BICC as told in this volume may help better our understanding of the place of churches such as the BICC that appear relatively quiescent in Zimbabwe's current crisis. The BICC leadership continues to wrestle with a mandate to stand separate from politics and to determine what it is to be a "peace church" in the postcolonial period. President Robert Mugabe was a guest at the Bulawayo Central Church in 2000. On that occasion he apologized for the pain inflicted by the Fifth Brigade during the Gukurahundi and acknowledged the need for compensation for the atrocities committed; Mugabe urged people to report their injuries and material losses to the district administrators' offices. The authors of a history of the BICC published under the auspices of the Mennonite World Conference highlight Mugabe's 2000 apology. The authors indicated that no compensation is yet forthcoming, and yet they valorized individuals who had embraced a position of forgiveness and nonbitterness vis-à-vis the Gukurahundi era as exemplifying the ideals informed by the BICC's peace teaching.[1]

The ZANU-PF government was under multiple pressures during the 1990s. Zimbabwe, along with many other former colonies, took on Economic Structural Adjustment Programs, mandated by the World Bank, resulting in economic hardship for many, as income inequality deepened with rising commodity prices. The pressure for restoration of the land grew; liberation war veterans became increasingly insistent that the land for which they had fought be redistributed.[2] At the same time, anger mounted over diamond-mining interests held by the government. The late 1990s' emergence of the Movement for Democratic Change (MDC) gave ZANU-PF its first substantial political challenge since PF-ZAPU joined ZANU in the Unity Accord of 1987.

In the aftermath of the 1999 death of former PF-ZAPU head Joshua Nkomo, President Robert Mugabe delivered a speech indicating that the government was ready to promote the repossession and redistribution of much of the farmland owned by the large-scale commercial farmers of Zimbabwe. In due course, the Zimbabwe government promoted the Third Chimurenga. The aim was to complete the process of liberation from colonial rule started in the Second Chimurenga (liberation war) of the 1970s, which had failed to deliver the promised large-scale transfer of land back to blacks. The subsequent repossession of farms in the early 2000s led to some turmoil in the economy and food supply. In addition, members of the ZANU-PF youth brigades were revivifying the pungwes of the 1970s, which at times became violently intimidating for those subjected to them.[3]

In the midst of these crises, the BICC has maintained its focus on evangelism and piety, encouraging church growth and offering programming to support spiritual growth. At the same time, there has been a marked increase in efforts to advocate for church members suffering from preventable government policies or actions. Bishop Steven Ndlovu attempted to gain an audience with the head of state at the time of the Gukurahundi, in the 1980s, for the purpose of asking that the killing be stopped. Bishop Danisa Ndlovu, head of the BICC-Zimbabwe from 2000 to 2014, has presided over the church in times of extreme duress and has taken his cue from the example set by Bishop Steven Ndlovu. He writes a monthly column for the church newspaper, *Good Words/Amazwi Amahle*. Bishop Danisa Ndlovu's remarks published in August 2002, around the time of the launching of the Third Chimurenga, are worth reproducing here:

> Zimbabwe, the beautiful country that saw us rejoice and sing hysterically at independence in 1980, is groaning with pains of hopelessness. It is sick with a horrifying disease—an ailment that seems to have affected its brains, and therefore, its capacity and ability to reason and help itself. Our nation has become like a madman walking up and down crowded streets and yet oblivious of one's surroundings and talking to oneself. The nation has become a danger to itself and its very existence. As a result our nation can hardly stop and listen to the many voices expressing concern.
>
> Our nation is badly and sadly divided on political, tribal, racial, and regional lines. Lives have been lost as a result. Some have lost their jobs. Others are reported failing to access food provisions due to political affiliation. It would seem like nobody cares about what is going on. The prevailing attitude of most of our people seems to be, "It's none of my business." Could this be your attitude?
>
> . . . It is disturbing to realize that as a nation we have become our own greatest enemy. We have used every imaginative weapon to destroy each other's lives. We have made Satan, the greatest enemy of humanity, really happy. If at all as a nation we could see the truth of Jesus' words when he said, "Any country that divides itself into groups which fight each other will not last very long. And any town or family that divides itself into groups which fight each other will fall apart . . ." (Matt. 12:25—Today's English Version). . . ."

As a young herdboy, it was the discipline of stopping in the midst of the anxiety of losing one's cattle, studying the hoof prints, and listening to the mooing of the cows and bell sounds that resulted in my finding the strayed beasts and having restored joy. When we stop and listen, we are likely to find our lost nation, lost aspirations, lost saltiness, lost justice, lost hope, lost life, and maybe the living God we have forsaken.[4]

In Bishop Danisa Ndlovu's essay, we see a keen awareness of the crisis around him, and he names it a national one—he names Zimbabwe, "the beautiful country," and refers to "our nation." In his assertion that "our nation has become like a madman," one might read into that a substitution of "our nation" for "the government." I suggest this because of the sentences that follow—"the nation has become a danger to itself" and "[it] can hardly stop and listen to the many voices expressing concern." He notes that food relief has become politicized. He states that people have "reported failing to access food provisions due to political affiliation." This way of putting it is one step removed from owning the accusation himself. However, the president and his ruling party are not named directly; Ndlovu holds back from overt criticism of the government. His BICC is a church that continues to officially keep at a remove from politics. Rather than really challenging the nation, Ndlovu addresses himself to the BICC membership, urging them not to detach from the surrounding problems. Bishop Danisa's piece, though it mentions politics obliquely, returns in the consistent tradition of the church's history to focus on the piety of his flock. He frames the problems they face as being due to some successes on the part of Satan and urges the people of the church to stop, listen, find ways to stop divisions along any category, and see if by doing so they might recover not only the nation but nearness to "the living God."

The launching of the Third Chimurenga with accompanying land redistribution also saw the passage of the Public Order and Security Act (POSA). People seen as political enemies of the state were identified and arrested, at times beaten or tortured. True to the Catholic Church's track record in Zimbabwe of public chastising of the government on behalf of human rights, the Bulawayo-based Catholic archbishop, Pius Ncube, in November 2002 allowed a special prayer service offered as healing for victims of political violence to be held at St. Mary's Cathedral in Bulawayo. Although Danisa Ndlovu did not sign the letter of support for Roman Catholic Archbishop Pius Ncube's November 2002 speech openly criticizing the government along with the other seven heads of denominations,[5] Ndlovu was a founding member of the Bulawayo-based group Christians Together for Justice and Peace, established "to stand together as concerned Christians of whatever denomination, making a Christian witness to the Kingdom values of truth, justice, and peace in Zimbabwe, including . . . solidarity with the victims of injustice."[6] By participating as a signatory member of Christians Together for Justice and Peace, and by writing, if only obliquely, about the nation's crisis in the church's paper, Bishop Danisa Ndlovu was proceeding similarly to Bishop Steven Ndlovu's actions in the 1980s: taking more steps than had been taken in the colonial period within the constraints of maintaining an overtly apolitical stance and a focus on personal piety.

By 2005, Zimbabweans were living with 80 percent unemployment and 144 percent inflation. That same year, Operation Murambatsvina extended the program of the Third Chimurenga with a major slum-clearing initiative. Murambatsvina means "clean out the filth" in Shona. The police and army demolished informal market stands and garden plots, and evicted shack dwellers in Zimbabwe's cities on a national scale; the operation took place in the winter months of May through August 2005.[7] A group of pastors of Bulawayo churches held a special prayer service at the BICC's Bulawayo Central Church in late June 2005, with the aim of addressing the needs of the people displaced by the operation.[8] The pastor of the BICC's Lobengula Church in Bulawayo, Rev. Albert Ndlovu, contacted the United Nations, the Red Cross, and government agencies, to alert them to the suffering of the people in Bulawayo displaced by government initiative to rid the urban areas of informal businesses, squatters, and other marginal entities.[9]

In 2006, after Operation Murambatsvina—along with devastating inflation, rolling power cuts, and other markers of crisis—had bitten yet deeper into the fabric of daily survival, Bishop Danisa Ndlovu's Easter message did not shy away from enumerating the sufferings of the people. He mentioned unemployment, hunger, the shortage of basic commodities such as maize meal and gasoline, and the unaffordability of rent and school fees. He took his message straight back to the condition of the believer's heart: "Hearts are aching, groaning and screaming with pain but not even the owners hear them! Those who care to listen have their own hearts shredded and squashed by the piercing pain and the burden of desperation that seems to daily stalk our people." From there the bishop reminded his readers that the church is the "bearer of good news in hopeless situations" and exhorted them to remain steadfast in their faith that "God who raised Jesus from the dead will in His timing bring a change to our situation."[10] These injunctions seem to simply reinforce notions of the BICC as a politically quietist institution. And yet, also in 2006, the bishop supported the issuance of a discussion document titled "The Zimbabwe We Want," signed by the three major umbrella Christian groups in Zimbabwe (the Zimbabwe Council of Churches, the Zimbabwe Catholic Bishops' Conference, and the Evangelical Fellowship of Zimbabwe), which was presented to President Mugabe.[11] The BICC is a church whose membership is chiefly based in a region that endured the Gukurahundi of the 1980s—and Bishop Danisa Ndlovu is simply one among a significant percentage of the church membership who lost family members during those years. Oblique references to the political origins of their economic sufferings are strategically wise. Such an approach helps ensure that their other work can continue: the business of evangelism, church growth, and changing people's hearts; keeping the civic and infrastructural doors open so they can continue ministries in the fields of HIV/AIDS outreach, care for orphans, operation of medical clinics, and education.

Some leading women in the church have engaged with the crisis of the early 2000s in ways that do not fit a narrow conception of party politics but do exemplify the embrace of pietistic Christian practice that is the hallmark of the BICC. For example, Nellie Mlotshwa's ministry, teaching peaceful conflict mediation, is apolitical but remains rooted in a desire to respond to the conflicts rending Matabeleland both politically and within families. She attended the Summer Peacebuilding Institute held at Virginia's Eastern Mennonite University in May and June 2002. Mlotshwa noted that the political conflicts of the time of the liberation war of the 1970s continued to affect individual lives in Zimbabwe. She felt compelled to respond to this with a mediation and peace-building ministry of her own, to be targeted at the family level: "my contribution will be a drop in the bucket, but I hope to start from grass roots" by helping families learn to resolve conflicts.[12] Ten years later, she was still active in this work, which she initiated on her own and conducted for little if any pay, and reported to the BICC-Zimbabwe's General Conference in 2012 that her own family of origin had been holding a family meeting regularly each month in the interest promoting unity and keeping conflicts to a minimum. She urged all families in the church to do something similar. Her remarks at the General Conference typified the church's approach to the larger political context: since the era of the nationalist struggle, the church's official communications have acknowledged the existence of war or political strife but have routinely refocused members' responses to be at the level of the individual person: "At church and at homes peace usually disappears even when there is no gun fire."[13] Her mention of gunfire was shorthand and code for the ongoing political conflict and the history of war in the region. The solution: start by building peace in your own heart, within your own family, and in your own church community.

An approach such as Nellie Mlotshwa's is not only consistent with the historical pattern of the church, it is also prudent, given that the political environment remains unsafe for open expressions of dissent. Focusing on church growth and evangelism both in Zimbabwe and regionally in southern Africa remains a major effort of the BICC-Zimbabwe. BICC churches have been established in Botswana, Mozambique, Malawi, and South Africa over the past fifteen years. These churches are both targeted at the people who were already living in those places and also intended to minister to the Zimbabweans of BICC origin who were moving there in response to the crises of the 2000s. Since the year 2000, an estimated 1.5 million to 3 million Zimbabweans, including members of the BICC-Zimbabwe, have entered a new kind of global diaspora.[14] Instead of the dislocations of regional labor migration that occurred under colonial rule and still continue into the present, Zimbabweans have responded to economic desperation and political oppression by flight on both a regional and a global scale: not only to South Africa, but also the UK, Namibia, Canada, and the United States.

The BICC-Zimbabwe's diaspora continues to find ways to remain connected to their homeland and their home church. One prime example of this is the North America's Great Grace Camp, a yearly gathering of Zimbabwean BICC members held at a rotating location. Their 2013 meeting was held in Texas and brought together some 130 people who had grown up in the BICC-Zimbabwe in Matabeleland. Although some members of the BICC-Zimbabwe's far-flung membership are active in a movement to revive Ndebele nationalist aspirations,[15] others remain committed to an apolitical kind of activism. For example, Hlengiwe Lindani Sibanda (MaMlotshwa), who left Zimbabwe at the height of the 1970s liberation war by escaping to a ZAPU camp in Botswana, went on to make her life in California as an oncology nurse. In the past eight years she has spearheaded the creation of an NGO, Hope for Mtshhabezi, whose primary aim is to bring medical supplies and emergency medical services to her home region surrounding

Mtshabezi Mission.[16] Mlotshwa has successfully mobilized BICC members inside Zimbabwe and many fellows of the North American Zimbabwe diaspora to contribute to the success of this organization.[17] Ronald L. Moyo, a son of the BICC who lost family members during the Gukurahundi, left Zimbabwe in 2006. After some time working in Atlanta with his family in Bulawayo, they joined him and are now living in Kansas; he is training to become a Mennonite ordained minister. He wishes to publish a book of poems, in both Ndebele and English, to address and perhaps heal the spiritual wounds of those who remain. Holding to an Anabaptist stance of unworldliness, Moyo insists the book would address this highly politicized regional trauma in a way that goes beyond party politics. His dream is healing for all involved, to allow Zimbabweans and Zimbabwe to move forward.[18] In terms of extension of the work begun here, a life history approach to studying the Zimbabwean diasporic phenomenon among members of a variety of religious affiliations might offer very fruitful updated understandings of intermingled dynamics of family, gender, and piety in the Zimbabwe BICC's postcolonial and diasporic period.

The approach of *The Gender of Piety*, which places individuals back into a broader historical context, allows the reader to analyze twentieth-century African Christianity at the grass roots and through the lives of indigenous believers. It weaves together engaging personal stories with the unfolding chronological development of tensions and conflicts in the wider society, as the church spread from its heartland in the Matopos to both Bulawayo and northern Matabeleland. There are six life stories, three each from men and women equally, spanning the century and illustrating the advances and challenges to the new faith within a racially oppressive society. Few "gendered" studies really keep both men and women in their analytical gaze throughout, yet the balance offered here makes possible my central argument about the gendering and sequencing of piety by male and female believers. It also brings a fresh look at colonial encounters by foregrounding the household and family as a site for investigating the tensions resulting from the impact of Christian missions, colonial land alienation and migrant labor, and the corresponding changes in the understanding of gender roles.

Ndlovu and Nsimango family tree

Created by Katherine Urban-Mead

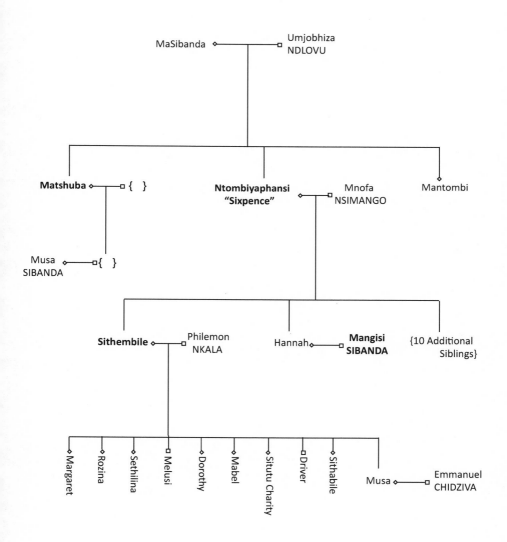

Notes

Introduction: The Gender of Piety in Matabeleland

1. "Woza moni odangele" is hymn number 207 from the Zulu hymnal, *Amagama okuhlabalela,* used in the Brethren in Christ Church throughout the twentieth century and up to the time of writing (1850; repr., Overport, SA: Mission Press, 1996).

2. Material on the Msimanga family and homestead appearing in the following three pages is drawn from Huggins Msimanga, interviews by telephone, 18 January 2001, 17 December 2008.

3. MaNdimande means that she is a female member of the Ndimande family—Ndimande was the family name of her father. She was also named after her firstborn child, Sibonani—"mother of Sibonani" or, in Ndebele, "NakaSibonani."

4. Recollections of NakaSibonani and the Msimanga family by Nancy Kreider Hoke, former BICC missionary to Rhodesia, shared with Huggins Msimanga, 17 December 2009.

5. Huggins Msimanga, who became a chemistry professor, feels certain that his father's constant exposure to the DDT used to treat cattle had been a contributing cause of the cancer that took his father's life.

6. For an account of the group Sofasihamba, which was active in the part of Matabeleland South near where the Msimanga family lived, see Terence Ranger, *Voices from the Rocks: Nature, Culture and History in the Matopos Hills of Zimbabwe* (London: James Currey, 1999).

7. http://www.bic-church.org/wm/explore/zimbabwe.asp.

8. http://www.merriam-webster.com/dictionary/pietism.

9. Led by Philip Otterbein and Martin Boehm. See Stephen L. Longenecker, *Piety and Tolerance: Pennsylvania German Religion, 1700–1850* (Metuchen, NJ: Scarecrow Press, 1994); Carlton O. Wittlinger, *Quest for*

Piety and Obedience: The Story of the Brethren in Christ (Nappanee, IN: Evangel Press, 1978), 10–11. The BICC were originally known as the River Brethren.

10. The term *trine-immersion,* meaning a baptism in which the person is immersed three times, is specific to the BICC. Wittlinger, *Quest for Piety,* 60–68.

11. Ibid., 41. See also C. Stoner, "Points of Difference," *Evangelical Visitor,* 1 August 1892, 230.

12. The BICC mixed with so-called German Baptists and Wesleyan Methodists and took in English speakers. After twenty years of debate, the BICC accepted Wesleyan holiness teachings on sanctification in 1915. See Wittlinger, *Quest for Piety,* 234–53.

13. Luke L. Keefer, Jr., "The Three Streams in Our Heritage: Separate or Parts of the Whole?"; E. Morris Sider, "The Anabaptist Vision and the Brethren in Christ Church," both in *Reflections on a Heritage: Defining the Brethren in Christ,* ed. E. Morris Sider (Grantham, PA: Brethren in Christ Historical Society, 1999), 31–70.

14. Wittlinger, *Quest for Piety,* 227.

15. E. Morris Sider, pers. comm. with the author. See also Owen Alderfer, "Acceptance of the Holiness Doctrine by the Brethren in Christ Church, 1910–1937," *Brethren in Christ History and Life* 15, no. 3 (1992): 397–421.

16. Wittlinger, *Quest for Piety,* 248.

17. Ibid., 208–9.

18. *Origin, Confession of Faith and Church Government . . . of the Brethren in Christ, . . . 1871–1901 Inclusive* (Abilene, KS: News Book and Job Print, 1901), 89, quoted in Wittlinger, *Quest for Piety,* 69.

19. Keefer has argued that the means by which the BICC worked out its response to holiness teachings was in fact reflective of the communitarian (Anabaptist) element of the church's decision-making process. The question of whether one must experience a second work of grace was taken to General Conference and voted on by church members. Keefer, "Three Streams."

20. Wendy Urban-Mead, "An 'Unwomanly' Woman and Her Sons in Christ: Faith, Empire, and Gender in Colonial Rhodesia, 1899–1906," in *Competing Kingdoms: Women, Mission, Nation, and the American Protestant Empire, 1812–1960,* ed. Barbara Reeves-Ellington, Kathryn Kish Sklar, and Connie Shemo (Durham, NC: Duke University Press, 2010), 94–116.

21. *Evangelical Visitor,* 4 November 1912, 14.

22. *Evangelical Visitor,* 3 December 1917, 15.

23. For a discussion of "finding victory," see chapter 1.

24. John Wesley, the founder of Methodism, is known for this articulation of his own crisis conversion experience: "I felt my heart strangely warmed." Cited in Frederick Dryer, "Faith and Experience in the Thought of John Wesley," *American Historical Review* 88, no. 1 (1983): 15.

25. See R. Devee Boyd, M.D.'s, "Heartbeats," series appearing in several issues of *Good Words/Amazwi Amahle* in 1986. Boyd stated, "And what is more certain from the Bible that all mankind has a lethal congenital cardiac problem—a problem with which we were born—that being a heart not right with God?" *Good Words/Amazwi Amahle*, no. 15 (March 1986).

26. Jean Comaroff and John Comaroff, *Of Revelation and Revolution*, vol. 1, *Christianity, Colonialism and Consciousness in South Africa;* vol. 2, *The Dialectics of Modernity on a South African Frontier* (Chicago: University of Chicago Press, 1991, 1997). See also Norman Etherington, ed., *Missions and Empire* (Oxford: Oxford University Press, 2005).

27. Isabel Hofmeyr, *The Portable Bunyan: A Transnational History of* The Pilgrim's Progress (Princeton: Princeton University Press, 2003); Paul Landau, *The Realm of the Word: Language, Gender and Christianity in a Southern African Kingdom* (Portsmouth, NH: Heinemann, 1995); Terence Ranger, *Are We Not Also Men? The Samkange Family and African Politics in Zimbabwe, 1920–1964* (Portsmouth, NH: Heinemann, 1995). Stephen Volz has skillfully shown how Batswana Christians did the work of translation of the Bible into Tswana in the nineteenth century even as their missionary collaborators, such as Robert Moffat, rendered this African contribution invisible. Volz, "Written on Our Hearts: Tswana Christians and the 'Word of God' in the Mid-Nineteenth Century," *Journal of Religion in Africa* 38, no. 2 (2008): 112–40. See also Derek R. Peterson, *Creative Writing: Translation, Bookkeeping, and the Work of Imagination in Colonial Kenya* (Portsmouth, NH: Heinemann, 2004).

28. Jon Sensbach, *Rebecca's Revival: Creating Black Christianity in the Atlantic World* (Cambridge, MA: Harvard University Press, 2005); Deborah Valenze, *Prophetic Sons and Daughters: Female Preaching and Popular Religion in Industrial England* (Princeton: Princeton University Press, 1985); Beverly Mayne Kienzle and Pamela J. Walker, eds., *Women Preachers and Prophets through Two Millennia of Christianity* (Berkeley: University of California Press, 1998).

29. John Lonsdale, "Agency in Tight Corners: Narrative and Initiative in African History," *Journal of African Cultural Studies* 13, no. 1 (2000): 9.

30. Shula Marks, *Not Either an Experimental Doll: The Separate Worlds of Three South African Women* (Bloomington: Indiana University Press, 1987). See also Marks's reflections on this study for the postapartheid era: "Changing History, Changing Histories: Separations and Connections in the Lives of South African Women," *Journal of African Cultural Studies* 13, no. 1 (2000): 94–106.

31. Studies giving welcome space to analysis of religious experience are David Maxwell, *African Gifts of the Spirit: Pentecostalism and the Rise of a Zimbabwean Transnational Religious Movement* (Athens: Ohio University Press, 2006); Bengt Sundkler, *Bantu Prophets in South Africa* (New

York: Oxford University Press, for the International African Institute, 1961); Marthinus Daneel, *Old and New in Southern Shona Independent Churches* (The Hague: Mouton, 1971).

32. Julian Cobbing, "The Ndebele State," in *Before and after Shaka: Papers in Nguni History*, ed. Jeff Peires (Grahamstown: Institute of Social and Economic Research, Rhodes University, 1981), 165, 173. See also Terence Ranger, *Revolt in Southern Rhodesia, 1896–97: A Study in African Resistance* (London: Heinemann, 1967), 26–30.

33. See Jocelyn Alexander, JoAnn McGregor, and Terence Ranger, *Violence and Memory: One Hundred Years in the "Dark Forests" of Matabeleland* (Oxford: James Currey, 2000). See also Julian R. D. Cobbing, "The Ndebele under the Khumalos, 1820–1896" (PhD diss., University of Lancaster, 1976).

34. See Cobbing, "Ndebele under the Khumalos," chap. 4, "The Incorporative and Tributary State," 139.

35. Paul S. Landau, *Popular Politics in the History of South Africa, 1400–1948* (Cambridge: Cambridge University Press, 2010), 11.

36. See Cobbing, "Ndebele under the Khumalos"; Pathisa Nyathi, *Traditional Ceremonies of AmaNdebele* (Gweru: Mambo Press, 2001).

37. Richard Werbner, ed., *Regional Cults* (London: Academic Press, 1977); David Beach, *The Shona and Zimbabwe, 900–1850: An Outline of Shona History* (New York: Holmes and Meier, 1980); Ranger, *Voices from the Rocks*.

38. Marthinus Daneel refers to Mwali as "he/she." Daneel, *African Earthkeepers: Wholistic Interfaith Mission* (Maryknoll, NY: Orbis, 2001), 20. Lynette Nyathi discusses the gendered elements of Mwali. Nyathi, "The Matobo Hills Shrines: A Comparative Study" (BA honours thesis, University of Zimbabwe, 2003). Some BICC missionaries from the early twentieth century routinely referred to Mwali as a "he." See H. Frances Davidson, "Progress of the Work in Mapane Land," *Evangelical Visitor*, 15 December 1905, 15; Harvey J. Frey, "Africa, Chapter VI: Native Religions," *Evangelical Visitor*, 19 May 1913, 264.

39. See Wendy Urban-Mead, "Religion, Women, and Gender in the Brethren in Christ Church, Matabeleland, Zimbabwe, 1898–1978" (PhD diss., Columbia University, 2004), 51.

40. D. G. H. Flood, "The Contribution of the London Missionary Society to African Education in Ndebeleland, 1859–1959," in *Christianity South of the Zambezi*, ed. A. J. Dachs (Gwelo: Mambo Press, 1973); Ngwabi Bhebe, *Christianity and Traditional Religion in Western Zimbabwe, 1859–1923* (London: Longman, 1979).

41. The BSAC ceded a total of 325,730 acres to different Christian mission societies. From the Rep[ort] of the Comm[ission] Appointed to Enquire into Matters of Native Education in All Its Bearings in the Colony of South.

Rhodesia (Chairman: F. L. Hadfield) Sess[ional] Pap[er]s, CSR 1925, no. 20. As quoted in Eliakim Sibanda, "The Brethren in Christ in Southern Rhodesia, 1898–1980: A Historical Study of Its Contributions towards the Promotion of Human Rights" (PhD diss., Iliff School of Theology and University of Denver, 1998), 212.

42. Ngwabi Bhebe notes that the SDA tended not to respect the territorial designations, incurring the displeasure of other groups. Bhebe, *Christianity and Traditional Religion*, 132–33.

43. Neville Jones to Hope Fountain Supporters, 10 June 1929, London Missionary Society, South Africa Reports, box 7, 1927–31, envelope 1929, Center for World Mission, School of Oriental and African Studies.

44. A crisis in membership numbers in the North American church in the 1940s led church leaders to begin to question the "multiple, self-supporting ministry" model. See Carlton O. Wittlinger, "Who Are the Brethren in Christ?" in Sider, *Reflections on a Heritage*, 25.

45. See Wendy Urban-Mead "Sitshokupi Sibanda: 'Bible Woman' or Evangelist? Ways of Naming and Remembering Female Leadership in a Mission Church of Colonial Zimbabwe," special issue, "Transnational Bible Women." Guest editors: Deborah Gaitskell and Wendy Urban-Mead. *Women's History Review* 17, no. 4 (2008): 653–70.

46. "Relative to the political aspirations of the Natives. It was dlely [duly] decided upon motion that we discourage our members from having any part in politics given scriptural reasons for the same." "Article Six 1925" (Native Conference), Records of the Brethren in Christ Church of Zimbabwe, Bulawayo, Zimbabwe (hereafter, BICC-BYO).

47. Michael O. West, "Ndabaningi Sithole, Garfield Todd and the Dadaya School Strike of 1947," *Journal of Southern African Studies* 18, no. 2 (1992): 313.

48. "Some missionaries were supporters of the government. You find that there is no difference." Anon., interview by telephone, 21 March 2002.

49. Catholic Commission for Justice and Peace in Zimbabwe / Legal Resources Foundation, *Gukurahundi in Zimbabwe: A Report on the Disturbances in Matabeleland and Midlands, 1980–1988*, introduction by Elinor Sisulu, foreword by Archbishop Pius Ncube (New York: Columbia University Press, 2008).

50. Generational sensitivity is an approach well developed by Meredith McKittrick in *To Dwell Secure: Generation, Christianity, and Colonialism in Ovamboland* (Portsmouth, NH: Heinemann, 2002). My work owes much to McKittrick's attention to generational conflicts, shifts, and distinctions in Ovambo society over the course of colonial rule in Namibia.

51. Marja Hinfelaar's study of churchwomen in Harare, also weaving together oral testimonies with study of the archival record, makes visible of the difference between versions of the Methodist and Catholic churches

histories in Zimbabwe between archival/male/official versions, and those generated by oral evidence/female/unofficial versions. For example, officially the Catholic uniformed women's group, Chita chaMaria, was founded by a priest; however, the oral evidence Hinfelaar gathered by interviewing aged women members of the group indicates that women were behind the group's founding. See *Respectable and Responsible Women: Methodist and Roman Catholic Women's Organisations in Harare, Zimbabwe, 1919–1985* (Utrecht: Boekencentrum, 2003).

52. One exception is Charles Van Onselen's portrait of a male sharecropper in South Africa, one of the best known of the history-from-below life histories based on oral sources. Van Onselen, *The Seed Is Mine: The Life of Kas Maine, a South African Sharecropper, 1894–1985* (New York: Hill and Wang, 1996).

53. Jean Davison, *Voices from Mutira: Change in the Lives of Rural Gikuyu Women, 1910–1995* (Boulder: Lynne Rienner, 1996); Irene Staunton, *Mothers of the Revolution* (Harare: Baobab, 1990); Belinda Bozzoli, *Women of Phokeng: Consciousness, Life Strategy, and Migrancy in South Africa, 1900–1983*, with Mmantho Nkotsoe (Portsmouth, NH: Heinemann, 1991).

54. Teresa A. Barnes and Everjoyce Win, *To Live a Better Life: An Oral History of Women in the City of Harare, 1930–70* (Harare: Baobab Books, 1992).

55. Teresa A. Barnes, *"We Women Worked So Hard": Gender, Urbanization and Social Reproduction in Colonial Harare, Zimbabwe, 1930–1956* (Portsmouth, NH: Heinemann, 1999).

56. Deborah Gaitskell, "'Wailing for Purity': Prayer Unions, African Mothers and Adolescent Daughters, 1912–1940," in *Industrialisation and Social Change in South Africa: African Class Formation, Culture and Consciousness, 1870–1930*, ed. Shula Marks and Richard Rathbone (New York: Longman, 1982), 338–57.

57. Luise White, *The Comforts of Home: Prostitution in Colonial Nairobi* (Chicago: University of Chicago Press, 1990); Margaret Strobel, *Three Swahili Women: Life Histories from Mombasa Kenya* (Bloomington: Indiana University Press, 1989); Susan Geiger, *TANU Women: Gender and Culture in the Making of Tanganyikan Nationalism, 1955–1965* (Portsmouth, NH: Heinemann, 1997); Marcia Wright, *Strategies of Slaves and Women: Life-Stories from East/Central Africa* (New York: Lilian Barber, 1993).

58. Luise White, Stephan F. Miescher, and David William Cohen, eds., *African Words, African Voices: Critical Practices in Oral History* (Bloomington: Indiana University Press, 2001), 19.

59. Stephan Miescher, *Making Men in Ghana* (Bloomington: Indiana University Press, 2005). See also Gregory Mann, *Native Sons: West African Veterans and France in the Twentieth Century* (Durham, NC: Duke University Press, 2006): while not a masculinity study per se, *Native Sons*

is a history of several generations of Malian military men based on a series of "long-running conversations" (11). See also Lisa A. Lindsay and Stephan F. Miescher, eds., *Men and Masculinities in Modern Africa* (Portsmouth, NH: Heinemann, 2003).

60. Teresa Cruz e Silva's study on the impact of the Swiss mission on social consciousness in Mozambique includes a substantial final chapter featuring life histories of both men and women whose different life paths all included an education by Swiss missionaries. Silva's is one of the few other works collecting life histories in which stories of both men and women are included in the same study, for the express purpose of exploring "the specific ways in which gender affected their lives and the development of their consciousness." Silva, *Protestant Churches and the Formation of Political Consciousness in Southern Mozambique (1930–1974)* (Basel: Schlettwein, 2001), 158.

61. Achim Van Oppen and Silke Strickrodt, "Introduction: Religious Biography: Transcending Boundaries," *Journal of Southern African Studies* 38, no. 3 (2012): 429–32.

62. Derek R. Peterson, "Casting Characters: Autobiography and Political Imagination in Central Kenya," *Researching African Literatures* 37, no. 3 (2006): 176–92.

63. Barbara Nkala, ed., *Celebrating the Vision: A Century of Sowing and Reaping* (Bulawayo: Brethren in Christ Church, 1998.)

64. Proverbs 31, selected verses, Revised Standard Version.

65. Luise White, "True Stories: Narrative, Event, History, and Blood in the Lake Victoria Basin," in *African Words, African Voices: Critical Practices in Oral History,* ed. Luise White, Stefan F. Miescher, and David William Cohen (Bloomington: Indiana University Press, 2001), 281–304, esp. 291.

66. Elias Moyo, interview, London, 11 November 2007.

67. Eleanor O'Gorman, *The Front Line Runs through Every Woman: Women and Local Resistance in the Zimbabwean Liberation War* (Harare: Weaver Press, 2011), 67.

68. Ibid., 12.

69. For example, Thomas Kirsch explains why he used pseudonyms for the places and people in his anthropological study of a spirit church in Zambia. Kirsch, *Spirits and Letters: Reading, Writing and Charisma in African Christianity* (New York: Berghahn Books, 2008).

70. A reference to White, *Comforts of Home.*

71. Terence Ranger, "Protestant Missions in Africa: The Dialectic of Conversion in the American Methodist Episcopal Church in Eastern Zimbabwe, 1900–1950," in *Religion in Africa: Experience and Expression,* ed. Thomas D. Blakely, Walter E. A. van Beek, and Dennis L. Thompson (London: James Currey, 1994), 275–313.

72. M. Louise Pirouet, *Black Evangelists: The Spread of Christianity in Uganda, 1891–1914* (London: Rex Collings, 1978).

73. Adrian Hastings, *The Church in Africa, 1450–1950. Oxford History of the Christian Church,* ed. Henry Chadwick and Owen Chadwick (Oxford: Clarendon Press, 1996); Bengt Sundkler and Christopher Steed, *A History of the Church in Africa* (Cambridge: Cambridge University Press, 2000); Norman Etherington, "Recent Trends in the Historiography of Christianity in Southern Africa," *Journal of Southern African Studies* 22, no. 2 (1996): 201–19; Richard Elphick, "Writing Religion into History: The Case of South African Christianity," in *Missions and Christianity in South African History,* ed. Henry Bredekamp and Robert Ross (Johannesburg: University of the Witwatersrand Press, 1995), 1–26.

74. Barbara M. Cooper, *Evangelical Christians in the Muslim Sahel* (Bloomington: Indiana University Press, 2006).

75. Ibid., 28–29.

76. Dorothy Hodgson, "Modernity and the Production of Maasai Masculinities," in Lindsay and Miescher, ed. *Men and Masculinities in Modern Africa,* 211–13; also, Dorothy Hodgson, *The Church of Women: Gendered Encounters between Maasai and Missionaries* (Bloomington: Indiana University Press, 2005).

77. Carol Summers, *Colonial Lessons: Africans' Education in Southern Rhodesia, 1918–1940* (Portsmouth, NH: Heinemann, 2002).

78. Ranger, *Are We Not Also Men?;* Ranger, *Voices from the Rocks.*

Chapter 1: Matshuba Ndlovu

1. H. Frances Davidson, "Mission Boys' Letters," *Evangelical Visitor,* 1 August 1904, 13.

2. Wendy Urban-Mead, "An 'Unwomanly' Woman and Her Sons in Christ: Faith, Empire, and Gender in Colonial Rhodesia, 1899–1906," in *Competing Kingdoms: Women, Mission, Nation, and the American Protestant Empire, 1812–1960,* ed. Barbara Reeves-Ellington, Kathryn Kish Sklar, and Connie Shemo (Durham, NC: Duke University Press, 2010): 94–116.

3. For a lengthier treatment of Davidson's relationship with Matshuba and another young convert, Ndhlalambi Moyo, see Urban-Mead, "'Unwomanly' Woman."

4. H. Frances Davidson, *South and South Central Africa: A Record of Fifteen Years' Missionary Labors among Primitive Peoples* (Elgin, IL: Brethren Publishing House, 1915), 139.

5. Overheard by Davidson in 1904: "What shall I do? My many sins are weighing me down. Woe Matshuba." Hannah Frances Davidson (hereafter, HFD) diary transcripts, 15 February 1904, 112, Papers of H. Frances Davidson, Manuscript Group (MG) 40, Brethren in Christ Historical Library and Archives, Mechanicsburg, PA (hereafter, BICC-PA).

6. Luise White, "True Stories: Narrative, Event, History, and Blood in the Lake Victoria Basin," in *African Words, African Voices: Critical*

Practices in Oral History, ed. Luise White, Stephan F. Miescher, and David William Cohen (Bloomington: Indiana University Press, 2001), 282.

7. Stephan F. Miescher, "Becoming an *Opanyin*: Elders, Gender, and Masculinities in Ghana since the Nineteenth Century," in *Africa after Gender?*, ed. Catherine M. Cole, Takyiwaa Manuh, and Miescher (Bloomington: Indiana University Press, 2007), 255.

8. Pathisa Nyathi, *Traditional Ceremonies of AmaNdebele* (Gweru: Mambo Press, 2001), 39.

9. For a fuller description of the religious and gendered world of the nineteenth-century Ndebele Kingdom, see Wendy Urban-Mead, "Religion, Women, and Gender in the Brethren in Christ Church, Matabeleland, Zimbabwe, 1898–1978" (PhD diss., Columbia University, 2004).

10. Julian Cobbing, "The Ndebele under the Khumalos, 1820–1896" (PhD diss., University of Lancaster, 1976), 345.

11. Mqhele Dlodlo, e-mail message to author, 17 March 2003.

12. Mbangwa Mdamba Khumalo, as recited to Pathisa Nyathi in 1994. "Transparent ears" refers to the fact that the fair skin of Europeans allowed sunlight to pass through the ears. Translation by Nyathi. P. Nyathi, *Traditional Ceremonies,* 41.

13. Nhluganisa Mlandu, and Mapita Ndiweni. Mlandu was the induna in the immediate area assigned to the Brethren in Christ. Ndiweni was a near neighbor.

14. Mjobhiza Nldovu's title was *isangoma* (pl., *izangoma*), or diviner; *isangoma* has been translated as "medicine man" in Ngwabi Bhebe, *Christianity and Traditional Religion in Western Zimbabwe, 1859–1923* (London: Longman, 1979), 6; or as "witchdoctor" in *A Practical Ndebele Dictionary,* 2nd ed. (Harare: Longman Zimbabwe, 1996). For Ndlovu's role as "witchdoctor" see also Anna Engle, John A. Climenhaga, and Leoda A. Buckwalter, *There Is No Difference: God Works in Africa and India* (Nappanee, IN: E. V. Publishing House, 1950), 194. His grandniece recalled, "[Mjobhiza] would be called by the king, would ask for predictions on the outcome of an *impi* [war party]. He must have passed away when the missionaries were there. His grave is near the gum trees near the mission." Sithembile Nkala, interview, Musa Chidziva interpreting, Bulawayo, 15 August 2000.

15. Bhebe, *Christianity and Traditional Religion,* 115–17, 120; Bhebe also highlights instances of chiefs discouraging and dreading the impact of Christianity, 121–22. This is echoed in testimony from Melwa Ntini: "So [our people] decided to follow our conventional wisdom of learning the witch/wizard's ways in order to survive his/her threat. So we went to school and churches to learn their tools, tricks and ways of survival so that armed with that knowledge we could at least learn how to live with them, and hopefully defeat them and take back our land." Melwa Ntini, interview by Eliakim Sibanda, 27 December 1980, quoted in Sibanda, "The Brethren in

Christ in Southern Rhodesia, 1898–1980: A Historical Study of Its Contributions towards the Promotion of Human Rights" (PhD diss., Iliff School of Theology and University of Denver, 1998), 214–15.

16. E. Morris Sider, "Hannah Frances Davidson," in *Nine Portraits: Brethren in Christ Biographical Sketches* (Nappanee, IN: Evangel Press, 1978), 159–212.

17. See Margaret Strobel and Michael Adas, *Gender, Sex, and Empire, Essays on Global and Comparative History* (Washington, DC: American Historical Association, 1993); T. J. Boisseau, "'They Called Me Bebe Bwana': A Critical Study of an Imperial Feminist," *Signs* 21, no. 1 (1995): 116–46.

18. Davidson, *South and South Central Africa*, 80.

19. J. B. Brady, Government Inspector's Report, 27 August 1909, quoted in J. N. Hostetter, "Mission Education in a Changing Society: Brethren in Christ Mission Education in Southern Rhodesia, Africa, 1899–1959" (DEd diss., SUNY Buffalo, 1967), 43. Also see J. M. Foggin, Government Inspector's Report, quoted in Hostetter diss., 41.

20. Dwight Thomas, "A Sketch of the Life of David (Ndhlalambi) Moyo," *Brethren in Christ History and Life* 33, no. 3 (2010): 594–656.

21. Davidson, *South and South Central Africa*, 139.

22. The next three paragraphs are drawn from Urban-Mead, "'Unwomanly' Woman," 99–104.

23. Sara Cress, "Letter from Sister Cress," 22 August 1899, *Evangelical Visitor*, 1 November, 1899, 419–20.

24. Amy Kaplan discusses W. E. B. DuBois's observation that American racism should be seen as part of an "international network of imperial relations." Kaplan, *The Anarchy of Empire in the Making of U.S. Culture* (Cambridge, MA: Harvard University Press, 2002), 179.

25. Davidson, *South and South Central Africa*, 109. This is cross-referenced in another letter from Emma Long Doner, who wrote, "On Christmas eve several of our boys became burdened about their souls, likewise our girls. Going to Sister Davidson's hut they commenced to confess out their sins." Doner, "Sister Doner Tells of the African Children," *Evangelical Visitor*, 1 April 1902, 133.

26. Davidson, *South and South Central Africa*, 109.

27. Ibid., 81.

28. HFD diary transcript, 28 June 1899, vol. 1, 63, 1899, Papers of H. Frances Davidson, MG 40, BICC-PA.

29. Davidson, *South and South Central Africa*, 81.

30. Ibid.

31. Engle, Climenhaga, and Buckwalter, *There Is No Difference*, 195.

32. Sithembile Nkala (MaNsimango), interview, Musa Chidziva translating, Bulawayo, 15 August 2000. Around 1912, Davidson described Matshuba's mother: "This old woman, also neatly dressed, is Matshuba's

mother, long a slave to her old religion, her superstitious ideas, her beer and her tobacco. Now she has accepted Christ as her Savior and He has cleansed her and she is in the church." Davidson, *South and South Central Africa*, 225.

33. Emma [Long Doner], "Matoppa Mission," *Evangelical Visitor*, 14 November 1903, 15.

34. Terence Ranger, *Revolt in Southern Rhodesia, 1896–97: A Study in African Resistance* (London: Heinemann, 1967), 318, 340. For more on the impact of the wars of conquest on Matabeleland, see also Ranger, *The African Voice in Southern Rhodesia, 1898–1930* (Evanston, IL: Northwestern University Press, 1970).

35. Terence Ranger, *Voices from the Rocks: Nature, Culture and History in the Matopos Hills of Zimbabwe* (Bloomington: Indiana University Press, 1999), 72–76.

36. The short-lived Mapane Mission, started in 1904 by Levi Doner, was superseded by the Mtshabezi Mission, fifteen miles away, in 1904, which endures to this day. Scotch M. Ndlovu, *Brethren in Christ Church among the Ndebele, 1890–1977* (Baltimore: PublishAmerica, 2006), 181.

37. Sithembile Nkala, interview, Musa Chidziva translating, Nketa, Bulawayo, 15 August 2000.

38. Joyce Khumalo (MaMlotshwa), interview, Bulawayo, 27 August 1997. She was the wife of the first black bishop of the BICC (1970–79), Philemon M. Khumalo. See chapters 4, 6.

39. The brother and sister in question are Mawogelana and Lomapholisa Khumalo. Zama Ncube (MaKhumalo), interviews, Bulawayo, 24, 27 May 1999.

40. Bhebe, *Christianity and Traditional Religion*, 165.

41. H. Frances Davidson, "Dwellers in Darkness," *Evangelical Visitor*, 1 September 1900, 339.

42. H. J. Frey, "Africa, Chapter VII: Native Religions (Continued): Magic," *Evangelical Visitor*, 2 June 1913, 7.

43. Sibanda, "Brethren in Christ and Human Rights," 261–62.

44. Frey, "Africa, Chapter VII," 7.

45. Davidson, *South and South Central Africa*, 107, 110.

46. One young adult male convert, Bhunu Ncube, struggled with whether to stay on with his work as a builder and teacher at Mtshabezi Mission or to find a higher-paying job elsewhere, so as to earn enough money to pay for the *lobola* (bridewealth) cattle that his future father-in-law had requested. H. J. Frey to C. N. Hostetter Sr., 3 February 1911, Papers of Christian N. Hostetter, Sr., MG 1, BICC-PA.

47. Misty L. Bastian's study of mission work and conversion among the youth in Onitsha, Nigeria, offers a fruitful case of comparison and contrast. Bastian notes that the first converts to the Church Missionary Society's Anglican church were the lowest-status young people: twins (which were

considered an abomination) and their reviled mothers, and young people working in European-owned mercantile establishments. Bastian, "Young Converts: Christian Missions, Gender and Youth in Onitsha, Nigeria 1880–1929," *Anthropological Quarterly* 73, no. 3 (2000): 145–58.

48. Ndhlalambi's isibongo (praise-name), or surname—Moyo—was the designation for the royal "heart" clan of the Mambo people.

49. H. Frances Davidson, "One More Day's Work for Jesus," *Evangelical Visitor,* 15 November 1905, 14.

50. Meredith McKittrick emphasizes the importance of age-set, or generations, in understanding the impact of Christianity. McKittrick, *To Dwell Secure: Generation, Christianity, and Colonialism in Ovamboland* (Portsmouth, NH: Heinemann, 2002).

51. Davidson, *South and South Central Africa,* 223–24, photo, 217.

52. Sithembile Nkala, interview, Musa Chidziva translating, Nketa, Bulawayo, 15 August 2000.

53. H. H. Brubaker to the Foreign Mission Board, 1 August 1929, papers of H. H. Brubaker, MG 36–1-1.8, BICC-PA.

54. Minutes from the General Conference of 1913, file Executive Board and Conference, 1907–1946, Records of the Brethren in Christ Church of Zimbabwe, Bulawayo (hereafter, BICC-BYO).

55. For treatment of the segregationist policies and their impact on education in Southern Rhodesia, see Carol Summers, *From Civilization to Segregation: Social Ideals and Social Control in Southern Rhodesia, 1890–1934* (Athens: Ohio University Press, 1994).

56. Sadie Book, "Faith, Hope, and Charity," *Evangelical Visitor,* 3 March 1924, 7.

57. H. J. Frey to C. N. Hostetter, Sr., 28 April 1922, Papers of Christian N. Hostetter, Sr., MG 1, BICC-PA.

58. Sithembile Nkala, interview, Musa Chidziva translating, Nketa, Bulawayo, 15 August 2000; Samuel Mlotshwa, interview, Mayezane, 22 May 1999; Jonah Mlotshwa, interview by Hlengiwe Sibanda (MaMlotshwa), Mayezane, June 2006.

59. James Campbell, *Songs of Zion: The African Methodist Episcopal Church in the United States and South Africa* (New York: Oxford University Press, 1995).

60. Michael O. West, "The Seeds Are Sown: The Impact of Garveyism in Zimbabwe in the Interwar Years," *International Journal of African Historical Studies* 35, nos. 2–3 (2002)," 343.

61. Ranger, *African Voice,* 43.

62. Ibid., 41–43.

63. They wanted something arable and well watered, not the waterless Gwaai District they had been offered. Ranger, *African Voice,* 68–87.

64. West, "Seeds Are Sown," 335–62, 341.

65. For more on the "New African Man" in the BICC at this time, see Urban-Mead, "Negotiating 'Plainness' and Gender: Dancing and Apparel at Christian Weddings in Matabeleland, Zimbabwe, 1913–1944," *Journal of Religion in Africa* 38, no. 3 (2008): 209–46.

66. Ranger discusses the developing identities and aspirations of the men of the Wenlock District, which includes Mayezane, in the early decades of the twentieth century. Ranger, *Voices from the Rocks,* 99–121.

67. According to Brubaker, "a missionary should reside there for a short time in order to help quieten things." H. H. Brubaker, "Early Experiences on the Mission Field," n.d., papers of H. H. Brubaker, MG 36–1-1.8, BICC-PA; my emphasis.

68. H. H. Brubaker, "Four Week End Services," written for the *Evangelical Visitor,* 1936, papers of H. H. Brubaker, MG. 36–1-1.8, BICC-PA.

69. Sadie Book, "What Hath God Wrought!" *Evangelical Visitor,* 8 November 1926, 11–12.

70. Samuel Mlotshwa, interview, Mayezane, 22 May 1999; emphasis in original.

71. See Urban-Mead, "Religion, Women," chap. 2.

72. Walter O. Winger wrote, "we praise God he [Matshuba] is still going on and standing true to the Lord." Winger to the Lancaster, Manor and Peque Sunday Schools, 3 February 1927, Papers of Christian N. Hostetter, Sr., MG-1, BICC-PA.

73. H. H. Brubaker to Foreign Mission Board, 1 August 1929, upon the occasion of Brubaker being chosen as new general superintendent, to succeed Steigerwald. Papers of H. H. Brubaker, MG 36-1-1.8, BICC-PA.

74. "Our hearts yearn for him and the two sisters in the church who are implicated in his fall, and who with him have been hiding their sin for over a year." "The Workers" to the Foreign Mission Board, 20 January 1911; H. J. Frey to Brother Sheets, 3 February 1911, Papers of Christian N. Hostetter, Sr., MG 1, BICC-PA. See also Levi Doner, letter from Matopo Mission, 22 March 1911, *Evangelical Visitor,* 1 May 1911, 15.

75. H. H. Brubaker to Foreign Mission Board, 1 August 1929, Papers of H. H. Brubaker, MG 36-1-1.8, BICC-PA.

76. H. J. Frey to Brother Sheets, 3 February 1911, Papers of Christian N. Hostetter, Sr., MG 1, BICC-PA.

77. Musa Sibanda entered the Mtshabezi Mission School on 19 August 1930, from Buntuli at grade 1 level and left in June 1932 at the level of grade 3. In the "remarks" column: "Married to Matshuba's son in 1935 (Ethiopian)," "Mtshabezi Central Primary," attendance records, BICC-BYO. The materials in Bulawayo are not catalogued.

78. H. H. Brubaker, "Mnofa's Promise," written for the *Evangelical Visitor,* 6 September 1939, Papers of H. H. Brubaker, MG 36–1-1.8, BICC-PA.

79. The account continues: "She pled with her son to come back to God, saying she could not die with him away from the Lord." Engle, Climenhaga, and Buckwalter, *There Is No Difference,* 195.

80. Memories of Abbie Bert Winger, in Papers of Walter O. Winger, MG 29, BICC-PA.

81. Nellie Maduma Mlotshwa, pers. comm. to Barbara Clara Nkala, August 2013.

82. Samuel Mlotshwa, interview, Mayezane, 22 May 1999; Nellie Mlotshwa (Maduma), interview, Wanezi Mission, 23 August 1997; Jonah Mlotshwa, interview by Lindani Sibanda (MaMlotshwa), Mayezane, June 2006.

83. Miescher, "Becoming an *Opanyin*," 264.

84. The "comforts of home" as seen in Luise White, *The Comforts of Home: Prostitution in Colonial Nairobi* (Chicago: University of Chicago Press, 1995).

85. Terence Ranger, *Bulawayo Burning: The Social History of a Southern African City, 1893–1960* (Harare: Weaver Press, 2010).

86. "The Workers" to the Foreign Mission Board, 20 January 1911, Papers of Christian N. Hostetter, Sr., MG 1, BICC-PA.

Chapter 2: Maria Tshuma

1. Information in the first two paragraphs is drawn from Maria Tshuma, interview, Nellie Mlotshwa interpreting, Mbaulo, 8 August 1999; MaTshuma, interview by Nellie Mlotshwa, Mbaulo, June 2003. In the 1999 interview, MaTshuma said her father had fifteen wives; in a 2003 interview she said he had sixteen wives. The year 1931 is given as the year she refused to marry Mguni—the date is a guess based on circumstantial evidence. Maria Tshuma said she was born not long before the "German war" (First World War), putting her birth year at perhaps 1913. MaTshuma left her home with missionaries H. J. Frey and his wife, and they did not come to the Wanezi District until 1931. See Barbara Nkala, ed., *Celebrating the Vision: A Century of Sowing and Reaping* (Bulawayo: Brethren in Christ Church, 1998), 29.

2. Ann Laura Stoler unpacks many meanings of "intimate" for the colonial world. In this instance, a senior African man claiming sexual rights to a girl promised to him in marriage, the resonance of "intimate" is somewhat different from Stoler's discussion of the inherent and complex layers of violence in domestic encounters between European men and "native" women. Stoler, *Carnal Knowledge and Imperial Power: Race and the Intimate in Colonial Rule* (Berkeley: University of California Press, 2002).

3. Up to now I have referred to her as Maria to distinguish her from her sister Sifile. Hereafter she will appear by her praise-name: MaTshuma.

4. Sean Redding discusses African girls who defied their families and went to mission schools in South Africa, and she points to the extensive

literature there. Redding, "Women as Diviners and as Christian Converts in Rural South Africa" (unpublished paper, 2012). For discussion of this phenomenon in Zimbabwe (Rhodesia), see Wendy Urban-Mead, "Girls of the Gate: Questions of Purity and Piety at Mtshabezi Girls' Primary Boarding School," *Le fait missionnaire* 11 (2001): 75–99 (also published in *Brethren in Christ History and Life* 25, no.1 [2002]: 3–32); Carol Summers, "'If You Can Educate the Native Woman . . . ': Debates over the Schooling and Education of Girls and Women in Southern Rhodesia, 1900–1934," *History of Education Quarterly* 36, no. 4 (1996): 449–71; Diana Jeater, *Marriage, Perversion, and Power: The Construction of Moral Discourse in Southern Rhodesia, 1894–1930* (Oxford: Clarendon Press, 1993), 201–5.

5. Mable E. Hall, "Mtshabezi Mission," *Evangelical Visitor*, 17 February 1936, 60.

6. Maria Tshuma, interview by Nellie Mlotshwa, Mbaulo, June 2003.

7. Ibid.

8. Others have grappled with the questions inherent in the gleaning, representation, and use of other informants' stories. See Susan Geiger, "Women's Life Histories: Method and Content," *Signs* 11, no. 2 (1986): 332–51; Kirk Hoppe, "'Whose Life Is It Anyway?': Issues of Representation in Life Narrative Texts of African Women," *Journal of African Historical Studies* 26, no. 3 (1994): 623–36; Heidi Gengenbach, "Truth-Telling and the Politics of Women's Life History Research in Africa: A Reply to Kirk Hoppe," *JAHS* 27, no. 3 (1994): 619–27; Christine Hardung, "Everyday Life of Slaves in Northern Dahomey: The Process of Remembering," *Journal of African Cultural Studies* 15, no. 1 (2002): 35–44.

9. For more on the Big Man, see Jane I. Guyer, "Wealth in People, Wealth in Things: Introduction," *Journal of African History* 36, no. 1 (1995): 83–90.

10. Sithabile Tshuma (Maria Tshuma's daughter), interview by Nellie Mlotshwa, July 2003; Nellie Mlotshwa, e-mail message to author, 8 July 2003. The shrine was at Dolo Mountain. For more on the role of Mwali in Matabeleland, see Terence Ranger, *Voices from the Rocks: Nature, Culture and History in the Matopos Hills of Zimbabwe* (Bloomington: Indiana University Press, 1999); Richard Werbner, ed., *Regional Cults* (London: Academic Press, 1977).

11. Maria Tshuma, interview, Musa Chidziva interpreting, Wanezi Mission, 22 August 1997.

12. Jeater, *Marriage, Perversion,* 201–5. Or similarly, men whose wives became Christian found they no longer had the same authority once their wives had another source of power—the mission—to whom they could appeal. Isaac N. Mpofu, "Strange Religion Comes to the Ndebele: A Centennial Play," *Brethren in Christ History and Life* 21, no. 3 (1998): 361–95.

13. Maria Tshuma, interview, Mbaulo, 8 August 1999.

14. Maria Tshuma, interview, Wanezi Mission, 22 August 1997.

15. Maria Tshuma, interviews, Wanezi Mission, 22 August 1997; Mbaulo, 8 August 1999; interview by Nellie Mlotshwa, Mbaulo, June 2003.

16. See Jocelyn Alexander, "The State, Agrarian Policy and Rural Politics in Zimbabwe: Case Studies of Insiza and Chimanimani Districts" (PhD diss., Oxford University, 1993), 14, 15. See also chapter 3 of this book for a lengthier discussion of the impact of land removals.

17. Maria Tshuma, interview, Mbaulo, 8 August 1999.

18. See Wendy Urban-Mead, "Religion, Women, and Gender in the Brethren in Christ Church, Matabeleland, Zimbabwe, 1898–1978" (PhD diss., Columbia University, 2004).

19. Nkala, *Celebrating the Vision,* 29.

20. Maria Tshuma, interview, Mbaulo, 8 August 1999.

21. P. Nyathi, *Traditional Ceremonies of AmaNdebele.* Gweru: Mambo Press, 2001.

22. Elizabeth Schmidt, *Peasants Traders and Wives: Shona Women in the History of Zimbabwe, 1870–1939* (Portsmouth, NH: Heinemann, 1992), 22–23.

23. Maria Tshuma, interview, Mbaulo, 8 August 1999.

24. From Urban-Mead, "Girls of the Gate." For more on the development of a new moral discourse in colonial Rhodesia, see Jeater, *Marriage, Perversion.*

25. The text from here to the next section ("Piety, Purity, and Repentance") is taken from Urban-Mead, "Girls of the Gate."

26. "Mtshabezi Central Primary," attendance records, BICC-BYO.

27. I prefer to use the informal *intombi egedini* rather than the more grammatically correct form used by Doris Dube, *izintombi zegetini,* since the former was the version I most commonly heard in interviews. Dube, "Naka Caleb: Faithful to the End," in *Silent Labourers* (Bulawayo, Zimbabwe: Matopo Book Centre, 1992), 23.

28. Ibid.

29. See Dube's account of her mother's life, *Golide: Gogo Khokho—Lived, Loved and Left a Legacy,* with Barbara Nkala (Harare: Radiant Publishing Company, 2011).

30. The most explicit expression of this view, though echoed by many BICC elder women. Mangisi Sibanda (MaNdlovu), interview, Bulawayo, 12 March 1999: Nellie Mlotshwa, interview, Wanezi Mission, 23 August 1997. Marieke Faber Clarke holds a sharply contrasting view of precolonial standards of sexual behavior for women in the Ndebele state: "Young Ndebele women had some freedom of movement and a chance to choose lovers. Lobengula apparently believed that, before marriage, a girl's body belonged to herself." Clarke, *Lozikeyi Dlodlo: Queen of the Ndebele: A Very Dangerous and Intriguing Woman,* with Pathisa Nyathi (Bulawayo: AmaGugu Publishers, 2011).

31. Sadie Book, "Concerning the Girls' School," *Evangelical Visitor*, 12 November 1911, 13.

32. See Ngwabi Bhebe, *Christianity and Traditional Religion in Western Zimbabwe, 1859–1923* (London: Longman, 1979); Jeater, *Marriage, Perversion;* Summers, "'If You Can Educate.'"

33. Sadie Book, "Concerning the Girls' School," *Evangelical Visitor*, 13 November 1911, 13; Book, "Mission Notes," *Evangelical Visitor*, 10 November 1924, 14.

34. There was also a smaller-scale night school for boys; they lived at the mission and worked chiefly as laborers, performing the heaviest farm and building work. In addition, many children living in the surrounding homesteads attended a day school on the main mission campus for their lower primary work in the lowest standards. In 1925 there were eighty co-education day scholars at the "morning school." Letter from Sadie Book, *Evangelical Visitor*, 7 December 1925, 14.

35. For photos of the mission station buildings, see Isaac N. Mpofu and Jacob R. Shenk, *Izithelo* (Bulawayo: Brethren in Christ Church, 1975); Brethren in Christ Church, *Sowing and Reaping: The Story of a Work of God in Rhodesia, 1898–1948* (Bulawayo: Rhodesian Printing and Publishing, 1948); see also cover photos on the title pages of the following issues of the *Handbook of Missions Home and Foreign of the Brethren in Christ Church:* 1921, 1923, 1925.

36. Letter from Sadie Book, *Evangelical Visitor*, 7 December 1925, 14.

37. Martha Kauffman Eshelman diary, Papers of Martha Kauffman Eshelman, MG 80-1.1, BICC-PA.

38. Alice Ndlovu (MaNkala), interview, Bulawayo, 27 August 1997.

39. Missionary nurse Martha Kauffman noted in her diary in 1935 that she was expected to know whether girls were pregnant or not, and when a particular girl turned up pregnant, Kauffman got into trouble with her missionary-in-charge for having failed to keep an adequate watch on the pupils. Martha Kauffman Eshelman Diary, Papers of Martha Kauffman Eshelman, MG 80-1.1, BICC-PA. Compare with Lynette Jackson's study, which includes discussion of women who came to towns or mining compounds to work during the colonial period and had to submit to "inspections" proving they were free of venereal disease: Jackson, *Surfacing Up: Psychiatry and Social Order in Colonial Zimbabwe, 1908–1968,* Cornell Studies in the History of Psychiatry (Ithaca: Cornell University Press, 2005).

40. Mangisi Sibanda (MaNdlovu), interview, Nondulo Vundhla translating, Magwegwe West, Bulawayo, 12 March 1999. For a study of mission schoolgirl letter writing and pregnancies for a slightly later period, in East Africa, see Lynn M. Thomas, "Schoolgirl Pregnancies, Letter-Writing, and 'Modern' Persons in Late Colonial East Africa," in *Africa's Hidden*

Histories: Everyday Literacy and Making the Self, ed. Karin Barber (Bloomington: Indiana University Press, 2006), 180–208.

41. For more on the interactive dynamics of western commodities and colonialism in Zimbabwe, see Timothy Burke, *Lifebuoy Men, Lux Women: Commodification, Consumption, and Cleanliness in Modern Zimbabwe* (Durham, NC: Duke University Press, 1996).

42. For more on BICC clothing, fashions, and weddings from the 1920s to the 1940s, see Wendy Urban-Mead, "Negotiating 'Plainness' and Gender: Dancing and Apparel at Christian Weddings in Matabeleland, Zimbabwe, 1913–1944," *Journal of Religion in Africa* 38, no. 3 (2008): 209–46.

43. Pathisa Nyathi, e-mail message to author, 2 April 2012.

44. Sithembile Nkala (MaNsimango), interview, Musa Chidziva interpreting, Wanezi Mission, 22 August 1997.

45. Lessie Moyo (MaSibanda), interview, Nondulo Vundhla interpreting, Matopo, 13 March 1999.

46. "Mtshabezi Central Primary," attendance records, BICC-BYO. This volume contains the names, home villages, and educational attainments of all the girls enrolled at Mtshabezi Boarding Primary School from 1920 through the 1950s. There is a remarks column where the recording missionary wrote comments relevant to the girls' careers after they left school, noting events such as marriage, matriculation in teacher training or nursing programs, or stating that they had "fallen," as indicated above.

47. "Requests for Prayer," *Evangelical Visitor*, 21 May 1934, 172.

48. Statistics compiled from "Mtshabezi Central Primary," attendance records, BICC-BYO.

49. Lessie Moyo (MaSibanda), interview, Nondulo Vundhla translating, 13 March 1999; Martha Kauffman Eshelman Diary, entry for 9 September 1935, Papers of Martha Kauffman Eshelman, MG-80–1.2, BICC-PA.

50. Martha Kauffmann Eshelman Diary, 25 November 1935, Papers of Martha Kauffman Eshelman, MG-80–1.2, BICC-PA.

51. *Evangelical Visitor*, 22 July 1929, 14.

52. Doris Dube, "Maria Tshuma," in Nkala, *Celebrating the Vision*, 179.

53. Donald Zook, interview by telephone, 1 June 2001.

54. Ibid.

55. Teresa A. Barnes, "*We Women Worked So Hard*": *Gender, Urbanization and Social Reproduction in Colonial Harare, Zimbabwe, 1930–1956* (Portsmouth, NH: Heinemann, 1999), 33. For discussion of the history of the Omama Bosizo, see Urban-Mead, "Religion, Women."

56. This is the time given by Doris Dube in "Maria Tshuma," 179.

57. Maria Tshuma, interview, Mbaulo, 8 August 1999. Compare this to the version of this calling as depicted in D. Dube, "Maria Tshuma," 179.

58. "The possibility of having two full-time women workers was also discussed. The following names were suggested: Mrs. S. Nkala, Naka

Ganinda [*sic*], Mrs. Ida Moyo, Maria Tshuma, Mrs. Abbie Dube, and Naka Ivy." "We recommend that Naka Gininda and Maria Tshuma be contacted immediately to see if they can give two months of service in the Gwaai until the end of the year. Their wage would be £6–0–0 per month and transport would be by bus fares paid." Minutes of Church Executive Committee, Rhodesia, at the Bishop's Residence 28th to 29th November 1969, file "Church Executive Committee 1956–73," BICC-BYO. Tshuma said that her children were in primary school at the time. Maria Tshuma, interview, Mbaulo, 8 August 1999.

59. D. Dube, "Maria Tshuma," 175–81.

60. Ibid., 179.

61. Grace Holland, interview by telephone, 9 June 2001.

62. Grace Holland, interview, Grantham, PA, 7 December 1999.

63. Ibid.

64. Rev. Bruce Khumalo, e-mail message to author, 28 May 2001.

65. Marcia Wright, "Bwanikwa," in *Strategies of Slaves and Women: Life-Stories from East/Central Africa* (London: Lilian Barber, 1992), 156.

66. Michael O. West, *The Rise of an African Middle Class: Colonial Zimbabwe, 1898–1965* (Bloomington: Indiana University Press, 2002).

67. "Elite Asante women went through gendered stages: first as girls, then into young womanhood with puberty and nobility rites, then as childbearing women devoted to household and family, and finally as postmenopausal women. Women at this stage no longer posed a spiritual danger. They had become 'ritual men' who, in special circumstances, occupied male stools, or chiefly offices. . . . These women embodied a form of 'female masculinity,' attaining social positions reserved for men." Stephan F. Miescher, "Becoming an *Opanyin*: Elders, Gender, and Masculinities in Ghana since the Nineteenth Century," in *Africa after Gender?* ed. Catherine M. Cole, Takyiwaa Manuh, and Miescher (Bloomington: Indiana University Press, 2007), 254.

68. Ibid., 256, quoting Arhim Brempong, "The Role of Nana Yaa Asantewaa in the 1900 Asante War of Resistance," *Le Griot* 8 (2000).

Chapter 3: NakaSeyemephi Ngwenya

1. "Mrs. Moyo" is a pseudonym used at the interviewee's request. Mrs. Moyo to Walter O. Winger, 4 February 1963, papers of Walter O. Winger, MG 29, BICC-PA.

2. Rev. Raphael Mthombeni, interview, Bulawayo, 13 May 1999.

3. Ibid.

4. Pastor John Dube, interview, Rev. Rabson Zikhali translating, Tsholotsho, 11 June 1999.

5. Mrs. Moyo, interview, Bulawayo, 9 April 1999.

6. Rev. Elias Moyo, interview, London, 17 November 2007.

7. Maria Tshuma, interview, Nellie Mlotshwa interpreting, Mbaulo, 8 August 1999.

8. Ngwabi Bhebe, *Benjamin Burombo: African Politics in Zimbabwe, 1947–1958* (Harare: College Press, 1989), 73.

9. These Crown Lands were areas still available for distribution at the discretion of the government and mainly occupied by Africans who had been there since before the beginning of colonial rule.

10. Stephen N. Ndlovu was born in Gwatemba in 1930 to a family under chief Msindaze. Msindaze's chieftaincy was removed to the Gwaai in the 1950s. The land next to Ndlovu's father's farm was given to a white serviceman who "had come from the world war." Ndlovu's family's land, when the Land Act was enforced, was designated as part of the Native Purchase Area. Stephen N. Ndlovu, interviews, Bulawayo, 24 February, 16 June 1999.

11. Another BICC area affected by forced removals was a section of Crown Lands in Gwanda District, where the Africans living there were removed further south to extremely arid lands in Tuli. Bhebe, *Benjamin Burombo,* 75.

12. Statistics compiled from BICC, *Handbook of Missions* (Brethren in Christ Church, 1952).

13. John Dube, interview, Tsholotsho, 11 June 1999. See also Scotch Ndlovu, *Brethren in Christ Church among the Ndebele, 1890–1977.* Baltimore: PublishAmerica, 2006.

14. Arthur M. Climenhaga interview by Eliakim Sibanda, as quoted in Sibanda, "The Brethren in Christ in Southern Rhodesia, 1898–1980: A Historical Study of Its Contributions towards the Promotion of Human Rights" (PhD diss., Iliff School of Theology and University of Denver, 1998)," 457, 467.

15. BICC, *Handbook of Missions* (Brethren in Christ Church, 1955), 13.

16. *Evangelical Visitor,* 28 March 1955, 8.

17. "A Visit to the First Church-School in the Gwaai Reserve," *Evangelical Visitor,* 31 January 1955, 8.

18. Jocelyn Alexander, JoAnn McGregor, and Terence Ranger, *Violence and Memory: One Hundred Years in the "Dark Forests" of Matabeleland* (Oxford: James Currey, 2000).

19. By contrast, for other denominations getting established in the wake of their people being forced to move to Matabeleland North, "the continuity and growth of churches depended more upon individual Christian settlers than upon evangelists." Ibid., 53.

20. MaTshuma later, in the 1980s, brought her message into areas along the Zambezi not even settled by BICC'ers from the south.

21. BICC, *Handbook of Missions* (Brethren in Christ Church, 1955), 13. Vundhla's name appears in the documentary record with various spellings, most commonly "Sandy," "Sandey," and "Sandi" and "Vundla" or

"Vundhla." I have chosen to use "Sandey Vundhla" throughout, while retaining the original spelling offered when citing original sources.

22. Alvin Book and Thata Book, "A Visit to the First Church-School in the Gwaai Reserve," *Evangelical Visitor*, 31 January 1955, 8.

23. For more on the strong bond between Climenhaga and Vundhla, see chapter 4.

24. BICC missionary Virginia Kauffman, MD, went to live at Phumula in 1960 to head the new clinic. Virginia Kauffman, interview by telephone, 8 January 2001.

25. J. H. Stern, "Matopo Mission," 1968 Annual Report, file "Annual Reports 1964," BICC-BYO. Evangelist Jim Sibanda and his wife made a six-month evangelistic tour in Maguswini in 1968. BICC, *Handbook of Missions* (Brethren in Christ Church, 1969), 16.

26. "Whereas there seems to be *a serious lack* in our various congregations *as regards giving* to the Lord's work, due largely perhaps to the lack of system, Resolved, that more definite teaching be given on this line, and that we give every member a contribution card, the same to be in connection with the Membership cards mentioned in Art. 1." Miscellaneous on Rules of the Church, Article 7, 1913, file District Councils 1933–1944/1964-[?], BICC-BYO.

27. See also Lynette Jackson, "'Stray Women' and 'Girls on the Move': Gender, Space and Disease in Colonial Zimbabwe," in *Sacred Spaces and Public Quarrels: African Cultural and Economic Landscapes*, ed. Paul Zeleza and Ezekai Kalipeni (Trenton: Africa World Press, 1999), 147–70.

28. Alexander, McGregor, and Ranger, *Violence and Memory*, 52.

29. Save as wife to an ordained minister, a position reserved for very few, or as the extremely exceptional person such as Sitshokupi Sibanda, whose career as the BICC's sole celibate, itinerant Bible Woman was hardly reproducible for many. See Wendy Urban-Mead, "Sitshokupi Sibanda: 'Bible Woman' or Evangelist? Ways of Naming and Remembering Female Leadership in a Mission Church of Colonial Zimbabwe," *Women's History Review* 17, no. 4 (2008): 653–70.

30. "NakaSeyemephi Ngwenya" was listed as the pastor at "Guka" for 1966 through 1973, file "Pastoral Appointments for Rhodesia," BICC-BYO.

31. Walter Winger, the superintendent at Mtshabezi Mission when NakaSeyemephi came to live there, many years later wrote about her arrival there with her daughters, in a 1966 letter to Dr. Martin Luther King, Jr., Papers of Walter O. Winger, MG 29–1.1, BICC-PA.

32. These are some of the things the two women discussed together at the beginning of the interview. Seyemephi Gwebu, interview, Nellie Mlotshwa interpreting, Gwakwe, 21 May 1999.

33. As per my request, she transcribed all the Ndebele as she heard it on the tape as well as put down an after-the-fact translation for each passage of

Ndebele. She wrote in an A4 school exercise book in blue ink. I then typed her handwritten transcript.

34. The Mafu chieftainship was called Godhlwayo; those who hailed from that area said that they came *koGodhlwayo* (from Godhlwayo). Pathisa Nyathi, *Zimbabwe's Cultural Heritage* (Bulawayo: 'amaBooks, 2005), 45.

35. Those added to the kingdom were called the abenhla. Later, the Ndebele moved yet further north, into what is now Zimbabwe. They conquered and incorporated a third group, called the abantu bakaMambo, who formed the third and lowest group in the kingdom from the 1830s on.

36. Mrs. Moyo, interview, Bulawayo, 9 April 1999. Mrs. Moyo herself was married to someone from the abantu bakaMambo, and counted it a progressive change such that, as she put it, "Now it's perfectly smooth, anybody is your equal."

37. The three wives: Mahlangu, Mabhena, and Ngwenya.

38. Maria Tshuma's family also was from the Mafu chieftaincy; see chapter 2.

39. Mrs. Moyo, interview, Bulawayo, 9 April 1999.

40. Pathisa Nyathi, *Traditional Ceremonies of AmaNdebele* (Gweru: Mambo Press, 2001), 116.

41. Sithembile Nkala (MaNsimango), interview, Musa Chidziva interpreting, Wanezi Mission, 22 August 1997.

42. Samuel Mlotshwa, interview by Hlengiwe Sibanda (MaMlotshwa), Bulawayo, 4 June 2006.

43. The full Ndebele term is *unina ka Seyemephi* (the mother of Seyemephi), which was abbreviated in daily speech to NakaSeyemephi.

44. Seyemephi Gwebu (MaMguni), interview, Nellie Mlotshwa interpreting, Gwakwe, 21 May 1999.

45. Isaac N. Mpofu, "Strange Religion Comes to the Ndebele: A Centennial Play," *Brethren in Christ History and Life* 21, no. 3 (1998): 343–60.

46. See Wendy Urban-Mead, "Religion, Women, and Gender in the Brethren in Christ Church, Matabeleland, Zimbabwe, 1898–1978" (PhD diss., Columbia University, 2004).

47. Mrs. Moyo, interview, Bulawayo, 9 April 1999.

48. Papers of H. H. Brubaker, MG 3.6–1.4, BICC-PA.

49. Nyathi, *Traditional Ceremonies*, 116.

50. Mrs. Moyo, interview, Bulawayo, 9 April 1999.

51. Seyemephi Gwebu (MaMguni), interview, Nellie Mlotshwa translating, Gwakwe, 21 May 1999.

52. Ibid.

53. Mrs. Moyo, Bulawayo, interview, 9 April 1999.

54. As indicated above, Mrs. Moyo did not want her real name used. Her real biblical name, by which she subsequently has been widely known,

is quite unusual. I have not encountered anyone else with that name, so I decided not to use it here.

55. Mrs. Moyo, interview, Bulawayo, 9 April 1999.

56. Ibid.

57. Seyemephi Gwebu (MaMguni), interview, Nellie Mlotshwa translating, Gwakwe, 21 May 1999.

58. Orlean Dlodlo (MaGwebu), interview, West Somerton, Bulawayo, 19 March, 1999.

59. Mrs. Moyo, interview, Bulawayo, 9 April 1999.

60. Ethel Sibanda, interview, Bulawayo, 16 April 1999.

61. Jocelyn Alexander and Terence Ranger, "Competition and Integration in the Religious History of North-Western Zimbabwe," *Journal of Religion in Africa* 28, no. 1 (1998): 3–31; Jocelyn Alexander and JoAnn McGregor, "Modernity and Ethnicity: Understanding Difference in Northwestern Zimbabwe," *Journal of Southern African Studies* 23, no. 2 (1997): 187–201; Alexander, McGregor, and Ranger, *Violence and Memory.*

62. Violet Ndlovu and Kezia Mhlanga, interview, Rev. Rabson Zikhali interpreting, Tsholotsho 11 June 11 1999; Rev. Elliot Ziduli, interview, Bulawayo, 28 July 1999; Mrs. Ethel Sibanda, interview, Bulawayo, 16 April 1999.

63. Seyemephi Gwebu (MaMguni), interview, Nellie Mlotshwa translating, Gwakwe, 21 May 1999.

64. Seyemephi said, "Bephonga thathwa beyebekwa emgwaqweni ukuthi ilory zi zibathwale zibahambise lapha abachithelwa khona." Seyemephi Gwebu (MaMguni), interview, Nellie Mlotshwa translating, Gwakwe, 21 May 1999.

65. Orlean Dlodlo (MaGwebu), interview, West Somerton, Bulawayo, 19 March 1999.

66. See Alexander, McGregor, and Ranger, *Violence and Memory,* 72–73.

67. Alexander and Ranger, "Competition and Integration," 7.

68. Rev. Jacob Shenk (bishop of the BICC-Zimbabwe, 1992–2000), interview, Bulawayo, 5 February 1999.

69. "Bafanya Mlilo sponsored the idea of 'Every Man Win Another' as part of a drive to address specific spiritual problems and needs within the church." Minutes of the Church Executive Committee, 11–12 May 1965, file "Church Executive Committee 1956–1973," BICC-BYO.

70. It is ironic that, in this case, Bafanya Mlilo, who only two years before had been ordained and elevated to overseer for the Gwaai, was expelled from the church for a "moral" lapse. "Umhlangano Wekomiti Yebandla—3rd October, 1969," file Executive Board Minutes 1964/71, BICC- BYO.

71. Alexander, McGregor, and Ranger, *Violence and Memory,* 87.

72. Rev. Raphael Mthombeni, interview, Mpopoma, Bulawayo, 13 May 1999.

73. John Dube, interview, Tsholotsho, 11 June 1999.

74. Seyemephi Gwebu (MaMguni), interview, Nellie Mlotshwa interpreting, Gwakwe, 21 May 1999.

75. Mrs. Moyo, interview, Bulawayo, 9 April 1999.

76. Seyemephi Gwebu (MaMguni), interview, Nellie Mlotshwa interpreting, Gwakwe, 21 May 1999.

77. "The Brethren in Christ Church in Rhodesia: How Far . . . Self-Propagating? Self-Supporting? Self-Governing?" *Evangelical Visitor*, mission supplement, 5 June 1955.

78. Rev. Elliot Ziduli, interview, Bulawayo, 28 July 1999.

79. BICC, *Handbook of Missions* (Brethren in Christ Church, 1959), 12.

80. BICC school buildings served a dual function: as worship sites on Sundays and as school buildings during the week. This connection ended when, after 1971, the Rhodesian government nationalized all the mission-run primary schools. After that, worship groups had to find another place to meet on Sundays.

81. Doris Dube, "NakaGininda-Nkanyezi Ndlovu: The Pastor who Prays under a Tree," *Silent Labourers*. Dube's account of NakaGininda's life was reprised in the BICC-Zimbabwe's 1998 centennial history: Barbara Nkala, ed., *Celebrating the Vision: A Century of Sowing and Reaping* (Bulawayo: Brethren in Christ Church, 1998), 167–71.

82. Nkala, *Celebrating the Vision*, 169. See also "Annual Written Reports 1971," file "Annual Reports 1964," BICC-BYO. Also, NakaGininda's assistant was a woman; all the people helping build were women: "I hardly remember any adult men in the congregation." Grace Holland, interview by telephone, 9 June 2001.

83. Jacob Shenk, "God Is My Manure," *Every Tongue Shall Confess. 1973 Yearbook Brethren in Christ Missions*, 47.

84. Interview, Thata Book, Bulawayo, [from memory, recorded days later in field notebook], 1999.

85. Seyemephi Gwebu (MaMguni), interview, Nellie Mlotshwa interpreting, Gwakwe, 21 May 1999.

86. Mrs. Moyo, interview, Bulawayo, 9 April 1999

87. He became the BICC's first African bishop in 1969.

88. "Annual Report Matopo District 1967," P. M. Khumalo, file "Annual Reports 1964," BICC-BYO.

89. Doris Dube, "Naka Gininda—Nkanyezi Ndlovu," in Nkala, *Celebrating the Vision*, 169. In the New Testament, Timothy served as assistant to the apostle Paul.

90. See Nyathi, *Traditional Ceremonies;* Barbara Mahamba, e-mail message to author, 28 February 2001. See also Barbara Mahamba, "Women in the History of the Ndebele State" (MA thesis, University of Zimbabwe, 1996).

91. See discussion of MaNdimande in the introduction to this book.

92. Terence Ranger, "Protestant Missions in Africa: The Dialectic of Conversion in the American Methodist Episcopal Church in Eastern Zimbabwe, 1900–1950," in *Religion in Africa: Experience and Expression,* ed. Thomas D. Blakely, Walter E. A. van Beek, and Dennis L. Thompson (London: James Currey, 1994), 275–313.

93. See Urban-Mead, "Religion, Women." Sunday school in this setting was not for children, as it is often understood in North America. Rather, Sunday school was a weekly session of Bible study led by a member of the congregation; attendees were the other adult members of the church.

94. Orlean Dlodlo (MaGwebu), interview, West Somerton, Bulawayo, 19 March 1999.

95. Maria Tshuma's evangelism in Matabeleland North was later on the timeline, starting in the 1960s.

96. Susan Juster, *Disorderly Women: Sexual Politics and Evangelicalism in Revolutionary New England* (Ithaca: Cornell University Press, 1994), 3. Juster used these phrases in reference to the women leaders of splinter Baptist groups in colonial America.

97. Within the BICC of Zimbabwe itself, two of their female forebears were Lomapholisa Khumalo and Sitshokupi Sibanda, whose evangelistic tour to Zambia and substantive participation in Levi Doner's short-lived mission to Mashonaland in the 1910s has been even more hidden from institutional memory than the accomplishments of the women pastors and evangelists of Matabeleland North in the 1950s.

98. See chapter 1.

Chapter 4: Sandey Vundhla

1. Donald Zook, interview by telephone, 1 June 2001.

2. Ibid. Zook came to Southern Rhodesia in 1955 as a conscientious objector on a two-year Voluntary Service (VS) program, which was a substitute for U.S. military service.

3. Grace Holland, interview by telephone, 9 June 2001.

4. Over the course of the twentieth century there was change regarding nationalist leaders and their attitudes toward mission Christianity. The position against elite Christians hardened as the movement became more militant, into the early 1960s. See Terence Ranger, *Are We Not Also Men? The Samkange Family and African Politics in Zimbabwe, 1920–1964* (Portsmouth, NH: Heinemann, 1995); Ranger, *Voices from the Rocks: Nature, Culture and History in the Matopos Hills of Zimbabwe* (London: James Currey, 1999). Also, Timothy Scarnecchia's *The Urban Roots of Democracy and Political Violence in Zimbabwe: Harare and Highfield* (Rochester: Rochester University Press, 2008) takes the reader through a very subtly tracked set of transitions in the radicalizing of the nationalist movement in the 1950s and 1960s. By the time of the ZAPU-ZANU split, in 1963, the

Africanist focus of the parties was such that little, if any, space remained in the nationalist discourse for mission Christianity. For purposes of this chapter, which is chiefly about the later 1950s through to 1970, the dichotomized versions of the nationalists' and mission Christians' competing narratives were at play.

5. See Scarnecchia, *Urban Roots*, chs. 5, 6.

6. Zama Ncube, interview, Bulawayo, 27 May 1999.

7. BICC, *Handbook of Missions: Forty-Fifth Annual Edition* (Brethren in Christ Church, 1962), 62.

8. See Enocent Msindo, "Language and Ethnicity in Matabeleland: Ndebele-Kalanga Relations in Southern Zimbabwe, 1930–1960," *International Journal of African Historical Studies*, 38, no. 1 (2005): 79–103; Terence Ranger, *Bulawayo Burning: The Social History of a Southern African City, 1893–1960* (Harare: Weaver Press, 2010).

9. Other groups well established in town by the late 1950s were the Methodists, Presbyterians, London Missionary Society, Salvation Army, Seventh-Day Adventists, and the Church of Christ. "Female Elder," interview by Daryl Climenhaga, Bulawayo, 12 February 1992, in Daryl Ray Climenhaga Interview Transcripts (hereafter, DRC transcripts). Climenhaga's research protocol entailed anonymizing by categories such as "male elder," "female elder," or "clergy." DRC transcripts are held at BICC-PA

10. See Terence Ranger, "Pugilism and Pathology: African Boxing and the Black Urban Experience in Southern Rhodesia," in *Sport in Africa: Essays in Social History*, ed. William J. Baker and James A. Mangan (New York: African Publishing, 1987), 196–213.

11. Donald Zook, interview by telephone, 1 June 2001.

12. MaNkala objected to being required to censor the mail sent and received by the pupils. Alice Ndlovu (MaNkala), interview, Bulawayo, 27 August 1997.

13. Ibid.

14. Ibid.

15. Leslie Dlodlo, interview, Bulawayo, 4 August 1999.

16. Preben Kaarsholm, "*Si ye pambili*—Which Way Forward? Urban Development, Culture and Politics in Bulawayo," in *Sites of Struggle: Essays in Zimbabwe's Urban History*, ed. Brian Raftopoulos and Tsuneo Yoshikuni (Harare: Weaver Press, 1999), 233–39.

17. "Report of the NC, Bulawayo for year ended 31st December, 1959," file S2827/2/2/7, National Archives of Zimbabwe (hereafter NAZ).

18. Harry F. Wolcott, *The African Beer Gardens of Bulawayo: Integrated Drinking in a Segregated Society* (New Brunswick, NJ: Rutgers Center of Alcohol Studies, 1974), 24.

19. Isaac N. Mpofu, interview, Bulawayo, 12 May 1999.

20. 1920 African Conference, Matopo Mission, August 1920, file "Executive Board and Conference, 1907–1946," BICC-BYO.

21. Anna K. H. Weinrich, *African Marriage in Zimbabwe and the Impact of Christianity* (Gweru: Mambo Press, 1982), 15.

22. DRC transcripts, passim.

23. DRC transcripts, 62; Zama Ncube, interviews, Bulawayo, 24, 27 May 1999.

24. Nicholas M. Creary on the Catholic Church bears this out: *Domesticating a Religious Import: The Jesuits and the Inculturation of the Catholic Church in Zimbabwe, 1879–1980* (New York: Fordham University Press, 2011); as does Ngwabi Bhebe's history of the Swedish Lutherans: *The ZAPU and ZANU Guerrilla Warfare and the Evangelical Lutheran Church in Zimbabwe* (Gweru: Mambo Press, 1999); while Terence Ranger's work on the Methodists shows that the Methodists were ahead of many of the other denominations: "Protestant Missions in Africa: The Dialectic of Conversion in the American Methodist Episcopal Church in Eastern Zimbabwe, 1900–1950," in *Religion in Africa: Experience and Expression,* edited by Thomas D. Blakely, Walter E. A. van Beek, and Dennis L. Thompson, 275–313 (London: James Currey, 1994).

25. Urban-Mead, "Religion, Women."

26. Barbara Nkala, ed., *Celebrating the Vision: A Century of Sowing and Reaping* (Bulawayo: Brethren in Christ, 1998), 86. Rev. Donald Zook, who was in charge of the Matopo Book Centre, noted that MBC sold around 60 percent of all Zulu and Ndebele scriptures (twenty-three thousand Bibles, testaments, Gospels) in addition to its role as chief distributor of tens of thousands of free religious tracts and Sunday school papers. BICC, *Handbook of Missions* (Brethren in Christ Church, 1968), 13.

27. Eleanor Ginder, "We Will Now Squeeze This Matter Today . . . ," in *Every Tongue Shall Confess: 1972 Yearbook, Brethren in Christ Missions* (Elizabethtown, PA, 1972), 22–23. A sample of one of these proverbs expresses the key BICC teaching that "God is no respecter of persons"—rendered in English as "Among kings there are some people who are in the eyes, but to God we are all of the same size."

28. Rev. Jake Shenk, in consultation with Isaac N. Mpofu, A. V. Masiye, and K. Nldovu, also wrote *A New Ndebele Grammar* (Bulawayo: Matopo Book Centre, Brethren in Christ Church, n.d.).

29. *Ibhayibhili elingcwele: Elilezingwalo zeDuterokhanonika,* 1st ed. (Harare: Bible Society of Zimbabwe, 1978). Isaac N. Mpofu has been involved with Bible translation into Ndebele since the early 1960s. Isaac N. Mpofu, interview, Bulawayo, 12 May 1999.

30. According to Terence Ranger, "[Nkomo] believed in the possibility, indeed the desirability, of everyone possessing such a hierarchy of identities, each deep and valid and each enriching the other." Ranger, *Voices from the Rocks,* 210–12.

31. For discussion of the persistence of intracaste marriage patterns well into the twentieth century, see Wendy Urban-Mead, "Gender and the Limits of 'Ndebeleness,' 1910–1960s: Abezansi Churchwomen's Domestic and Associational Alliances," in *Gendering Ethnicity in African Women's Lives*, ed. Jan Bender Shetler (Madison: University of Wisconsin Press, 2015), 153–77.

32. Eliakim Sibanda, "The Brethren in Christ in Southern Rhodesia, 1898–1980: A Historical Study of Its Contributions towards the Promotion of Human Rights" (PhD diss., Iliff School of Theology and University of Denver, 1998).

33. Nkala, *Celebrating the Vision*, 131–37.

34. Ibid., 132.

35. According to Nkala, Vundhla was born in 1909, while in the 1941 marriage certificate he gave his age as thirty-four. Nkala, *Celebrating the Vision*, 132. So there is a small discrepancy. The marriage certificate states that he married "Dazzie Moyo," age twenty-nine, on 6 September 1941. The ceremony was at the Matopo Mission church. Their respective professions were listed as "farmer" and "housemaid," and their residence was given as "Matopo Mission, Matobo District." Marriage register, BICC-BYO.

36. Barbara Nkala, e-mail message to author, 8 January 2010.

37. Timothy N. B. Ndlovu was born about 1918 and attended school at Matopo Mission in the early 1930s, then the London Missionary Society secondary school, Tiger Kloof, in the northern part of the Cape of Good Hope Province of South Africa, in the mid-1930s. He returned to teach at Matopo Mission for three years in the later 1930s, before going on to teach at Waddilove High School in the 1940s. This would likely place the years of Vundhla's informal instruction from Ndlovu at about 1937 to 1940. Eliakim Sibanda, pers. comm. to author, 30 December 2009.

38. According to Dube, a historian of the church in Zimbabwe, Vundhla went to BICC pastor Timothy Ndlovu's home for the instruction. Bekithemba Dube, interview by telephone, 16 July 2001.

39. Dazzie Vundhla (MaMoyo), interview, Nondulo Vundhla interpreting, Matopo, 13 March 1999.

40. For additional discussion of rural Christian courtship in the 1930s and 1940s, see Wendy Urban-Mead, "Negotiating 'Plainness' and Gender: Dancing and Apparel at Christian Weddings in Matabeleland, Zimbabwe, 1913–1944," *Journal of Religion in Africa* 38, no. 3 (2008): 209–46.

41. The appearance of this room remained the same for over forty years, based on a comparison of my observations when I was there in 1999 and on Nancy Kreider Hoke's memories. Nancy Kreider Hoke, interview, Grantham, PA, 5 June 2001.

42. This certificate stated that the program was based in Swaziland and run by the Scandinavian Alliance Mission of North America, 1948.

43. The text of the certificate stated, "Sandi Vundhla, R.C. No. 5758 Matobo, having abandoned Native methods of tillage on all his lands and having

put his lands under a systematic Crop-Rotation Scheme using proper methods of tillage is awarded the Certificate and Badge of a Master of Tillage."

44. Nkala, *Celebrating the Vision*, 132.

45. Being solely a pastor (as opposed to a pastor-teacher) was not a paid position. Evangelists, on the other hand, received a small amount of pay from the mission church for their seasonal, itinerant work during the Rhodesian winter.

46. Nkala, *Celebrating the Vision*, 132.

47. Ibid., 132–33.

48. For more on Vundhla in Matabeleland North, see chapter 3.

49. Arthur Climenhaga, *Evangelical Visitor*, special supplement on missions, June 1955, 1–2.

50. For more on the church's move to town, see Nkala, *Celebrating the Vision*, 48–58.; see also Daryl Ray Climenhaga, "Adapting to a Revolution: A Study of the Brethren in Christ in the Changing Context of Bulawayo, Zimbabwe" (DMiss diss., Asbury Theological Seminary, Wilmore, KY, 1993).

51. The two other Africans were Mangisi Sibanda and Naison Moyo. Donald Zook, interview, by telephone, 1 June 2001. See also *Evangelical Visitor*, 27 January 1958.

52. See Urban-Mead, "Religion, Women."

53. Dazzie Vundhla (MaMoyo), interview, Nondulo Vundhla interpreting, Matopo, 13 March 1999. See also "Evangelism: Urban and Rural/Urban Evangelism: Bulawayo Church Activities," *Handbook of Missions* (Brethren in Christ Church, 1958), 89.

54. Nguboyenja was the next church to be established in town. BICC, *Handbook of Missions* (Brethren in Christ Church, 1964), 57; Climenhaga, "Adapting," 54. Congregations at Luveve and Tshabalala began as preaching points nurtured by Vundhla in 1962. DRC transcripts, 135. Tshabalala began in the house of a railroad worker from Zambia; Vundhla appointed Simon Dlodlo to be the first pastor. Also in Nkala, *Celebrating the Vision*, 136.

55. "Urban Evangelism: Bulawayo Church Work," *Handbook of Missions* (Brethren in Christ Church, 1959), 25.

56. Carol Summers, "Mission Boys, Civilized Men, and Marriage: Educated African Men in the Missions, 1920–1945," in *Colonial Lessons: Africans' Education in Southern Rhodesia, 1918–1940* (Portsmouth, NH: Heinemann, 2002), 176–96.

57. Dazzie Vundhla (MaMoyo), interview, Nondulo Vundhla interpreting, Matopo, 13 March 1999.

58. The Swedish Lutherans, another very influential rural-based Protestant mission society in Matabeleland, moved to town even later than the BICC. Bhebe, *ZAPU and ZANU*, 135.

59. The Roman Catholic Church in Mbare Township—formerly Harari Township in Salisbury—established a uniformed women's prayer association

in the 1940s. Marja Hinfelaar, "Well-Known Catholic Women: The Public and Political Role of the Chita chaMaria Movement in Mbare Township, Zimbabwe, 1945–65," *Le fait missionnaire/Social Sciences and Missions* 14 (July 2004): 47–73.

60. Dazzie Vundhla (MaMoyo), interview, Nondulo Vundhla interpreting, Matopo, 13 March 1999.

61. "Bulawayo Churches," *Handbook of Missions* (Brethren in Christ Church, 1964), 57.

62. "Evangelism: Urban and Rural: Urban Evangelism: Bulawayo Church Work," *Handbook of Missions* (Brethren in Christ Church, 1959), 25.

63. For a more detailed discussion of the rural roots of women's work in the BICC, see Urban-Mead, "Women, Religion."

64. Nkala, *Celebrating the Vision*, 201.

65. Ranger, *Are We Not Also Men?*, 42.

66. Mia Brandel-Syrier, *Black Woman in Search of God* (London: Lutterworth Press, 1962); Deborah Gaitskell, "'Wailing for Purity': Prayer Unions, African Mothers and Adolescent Daughters, 1912–1940," in *Industrialisation and Social Change in South Africa: African Class Formation, Culture and Consciousness, 1870–1930*, ed. Shula Marks and Richard Rathbone (New York: Longman, 1982), 338–57.

67. Barbara A. Moss, "'And the Bones Come Together': Women's Religious Expectations in Southern Africa, c. 1900–1945," *Journal of Religious History*, 23, no. 1 (1999): 108–27.

68. Stephen Thornton, "The Struggle for Profit and Participation by an Emerging Petty-Bourgeoisie in Bulawayo, 1893–1933," in Raftopoulos and Yoshikuni, *Sites of Struggle*, 37.

69. Sita Ranchod-Nilsson, "'Educating Eve': The Women's Club Movement and Political Consciousness among Rural African Women in Southern Rhodesia, 1950–1980," in *African Encounters with Domesticity*, ed. Karen Tranberg Hansen (New Brunswick, NJ: Rutgers University Press, 1992), 195–97.

70. Dazzie Vundhla (MaMoyo), interview, Nondulo Vundhla interpreting, Matopo, 13 March 1999. Year of death confirmed by Doris Dube, e-mail message to author, 8 February 2010.

71. A look at the *Bantu Mirror* helps underscore how far out of the circle of interdenominational cooperation the BICC generally was. The *Bantu Mirror* was Bulawayo's one major newspaper aimed at the literate, newspaper-buying African population. This population was largely urban, with the exception of the educated elite living at rural mission stations. Reflecting the BICC's purely rural, and thus relatively isolated, condition vis-à-vis other denominations, the *Bantu Mirror* makes virtually no mention of the BICC, either in articles or letters to the editor, all the way through the 1930s, 1940s, and 1950s. This contrasts sharply with denominations with a strong urban presence through much

of the twentieth century, such as the London Missionary Society or Church of Christ, whose members frequently contributed to the paper and whose social and church doings were featured in the main articles. *Bantu Mirror,* on file at NAZ (Harare) and the Historical Reference Library, Bulawayo.

72. Grace Holland, interview by telephone, 9 June 2001.

73. "Evangelism: Urban and Rural: Urban Evangelism: Bulawayo Church Work," *Handbook of Missions* (Brethren in Christ Church, 1959), 25.

74. "Bulawayo Churches," *Handbook of Missions* (Brethren in Christ Church, 1964), 57.

75. Climenhaga, "Adapting," 50.

76. Dazzie Vundhla (MaMoyo), interview, Nondulo Vundhla interpreting, Matopo, 13 March 1999.

77. "Senior African Minister," interview by Daryl Climenhaga, DRC transcripts, 129. Daryl Climenhaga's interviews with many others echo these themes of Vundhla's popular appeal, courage, and effectiveness. See DRC transcripts, 144, 153, 155–56.

78. "Male Elder," interview by Daryl Climenhaga, DRC transcripts, 75; Don Zook interview; BICC, *Handbook of Missions* (Brethren in Christ Church, 1964), 57.

79. In 1959, a year after the Mpopoma church building was finished, there were 124,000 resident Africans in Bulawayo; 59,000 were men, 21,000 women, and 44,500 children.

80. Kaarsholm, "*Si ye Pambili,*" 231.

81. DRC transcripts, 33.

82. *Evangelical Visitor,* 19 July 1965, 7.

83. Zama Ncube, interview, Bulawayo, 27 May 1999.

84. "Report of the NC, Bulawayo, for year ended 31st December, 1959," file S2827/2/2/7, NAZ.

85. Michael O. West, "African Middle-Class Formation in Colonial Zimbabwe, 1890–1965" (PhD diss., Harvard University, 1990), 173. West's dissertation contains material that does not appear in his book *The Rise of an African Middle Class: Colonial Zimbabwe, 1898–1965* (Bloomington: Indiana University Press, 2002).

86. Northern Rhodesia gained its independence, as Zambia, in 1962.

87. As Ranger has shown, independent Zimbabwe was born of both rural and urban nationalist initiatives. See Ranger, *Voices from the Rocks.*

88. Note that sources from the 1950s and 1960s spell his name Vundla (without the "h"). "Bulawayo Churches," *Handbook of Missions* (Brethren in Christ Church, 1962), 56.

89. DRC transcripts, 75, 144.

90. Ibid.; Daryl Climenhaga, interview by telephone, 4 June 2001. For background on zhii, see West, *Rise of an African Middle Class,* 223; Scarnecchia, *Urban Roots,* 95.

91. Timothy Ndlovu, interview by Eliakim Sibanda, 17 January 1996, quoted in Sibanda, "Brethren in Christ," 468–69.

92. Climenhaga, "Adapting," 54.

93. Doris Dube, e-mail message to author, 10 February 2012.

94. Climenhaga, "Adapting," 115; P. M. Khumalo, "Matopo District (including Bulawayo Churches)," *Handbook of Missions* (Brethren in Christ Church, 1969), 14.

95. See file Matopo District Council Minutes, BICC-BYO; Climenhaga, "Adapting," 26.

96. Nkala, "Bishop Philemon Mtsholi Kumalo," in *Celebrating the Vision*, 139.

97. "African Minister," interview by Daryl Climenhaga, DRC transcripts, 130.

98. "Male Elder," interview by Daryl Climenhaga, DRC transcripts, 155.

99. Matopo District Council Meeting, 8–10 March 1968, file "Council Minutes, Matopo," BICC-BYO.

100. P. M. Khumalo, "Matopo District (including Bulawayo Churches)," *Handbook of Missions* (Brethren in Christ Church, 1969), 14.

101. Matopo District Council Meeting, 4–6 July 1969, file "Council Minutes, Matopo," BICC-BYO.

102. Climenhaga, "Adapting," 115–16.

103. Matopo District Council Meeting, 23–25 July 1971, file "Council Minutes, Matopo," BICC-BYO.

104. Climenhaga, "Adapting."

105. The urban district, until very recently, consisted of all BICC urban church congregations from Bulawayo, Gwanda, Gweru, and Harare.

106. DRC transcripts, 169.

107. Dazzie Vundhla (MaMoyo), interview, Nondulo Vundhla interpreting, Matopo, 13 March 1999.

108. Mangisi Ottilia Dube, pers. comm. to author, 21 July 1999. Another Christian widow depicted wearing her dress inside out, with a blanket over her head, is in Eleanor Ginder, "Ndlovu Is Absent," *Every Tongue Shall Confess: BICC Missions Yearbook* (Elizabethtown, PA), 1973, 14.

109. Doris Dube, "Sandi Vundhla," in Nkala, *Celebrating the Vision*, 132.

110. West, "African Middle-Class Formation," 81.

111. Anonymous (source requested anonymity), interview.

112. Heather Hughes, *The First President: A Life of John L. Dube, Founding President of the ANC* (Auckland Park, South Africa: Jacana Media, 2011).

113. Adrian Hastings points to the challenge of monogamy for African male members of Christian churches throughout Africa. Hastings, *The Church in Africa, 1450–1950* (Oxford: Clarendon Press, 1996), 588.

114. "Arthur Climenhaga was in touch with Ndebele in a way that most missionaries never were. He would have spoken to Vundhla effectively." Daryl Climenhaga, interview by telephone, 8 March 2001.

115. Wendy Urban-Mead, "Pious Wives, Backslidden Husbands: Gender and Christianity in the Era of Mass Nationalism, Colonial Zimbabwe, 1950–1970," paper presented at the annual meeting of the African Studies Association, Washington, DC, 5 December 2002.

116. Rev. Jacob Shenk, e-mail message to author, 1 January 2010. See also Doris Dube's account in Nkala, *Celebrating the Vision*, 131–37.

117. Rev. Raphael Mthombeni referred to an ordained leader who was mentored by Vundhla as "the son of Vundhla by spiritual leadership." Mthombeni, e-mail message to author, 3 November 2009.

Chapter 5: MaNsimango (Sithembile Nkala)

1. MaNsimango is a form of address based on her birth family's name, Nsimango. Her full name was Sithembile Nsimango, married to Philemon Nkala. In the western style of address, she could be called Mrs. Nkala. But in her home area she is known as MaNsimango.

2. MaNsimango (Sithembile Nkala), Musa Chidziva interpreting, 27 August 1997.

3. Barbara M. Cooper, "Oral Sources and the Challenge of African History," in *Writing African History*, ed. John Edward Philips (Rochester: Rochester University Press, 2005), 202–4.

4. Musa was MaNsimango's youngest daughter. Both are now deceased.

5. This move is commonly referred to as the UDI, or Unilateral Declaration of Independence.

6. Ian Linden, *The Catholic Church and the Struggle for Zimbabwe* (London: Longman, 1980); Janice McLaughlin, *On the Frontline: Catholic Missions in Zimbabwe's Liberation War* (Harare: Baobab, 1996); Ngwabi Bhebe, *The ZAPU and ZANU Guerrilla Warfare and the Evangelical Lutheran Church in Zimbabwe* (Gweru: Mambo Press, 1999).

7. David Lan, *Guns and Rain: Guerrillas and Spirit Mediums in Zimbabwe* (London: James Currey, 1985); Terence Ranger and Mark Ncube, "Religion in the Guerrilla War: The Case of Southern Matabeleland," in *Society in Zimbabwe's Liberation War*, ed. Ngwabi Bhebe and Ranger (Portsmouth, NH: Heinemann; 1996); Ranger, *Voices from the Rocks: Nature, Culture and History in the Matopos Hills of Zimbabwe*. London: James Currey, 1999.

8. Linden, *Catholic Church*, 164, 171, 228.

9. Bhebe, *ZAPU and ZANU*, 124–25.

10. Ibid., 125.

11. Ibid., 307

12. Ibid., 135.

13. Norma J. Kriger, *Zimbabwe's Guerrilla War: Peasant Voices* (Cambridge: Cambridge University Press, 1992).

14. For another discussion of informers, see Eleanor O'Gorman, *The Front Line Runs through Every Woman: Women and Local Resistance in the Zimbabwean Liberation War* (Harare: Weaver Press, 2011), 119–20.

15. The Organization of African Unity did not deal with him; the Frontline States, working for the liberation of the settler regimes of southern Africa, declared him reactionary. The Frontline States were Angola, Botswana, Lesotho, Mozambique, Tanzania, Zambia, and Zimbabwe.

16. K. Nyamayaro Mufuka, "Rhodesia's Internal Settlement: A Tragedy," *African Affairs* 78, no. 313 (October 1979): 441.

17. Timothy Scarnecchia, *The Urban Roots of Democracy and Political Violence in Zimbabwe: Harare and Highfield* (Rochester: Rochester University Press, 2008), 94.

18. Ibid., 100–113.

19. Ibid., 127.

20. Ibid., 129–30.

21. Rev. Mangisi Sibanda, interview, Tshalimbe, 26 May 1999.

22. Richard Werbner, "Human Rights and Moral Knowledge: Arguments of Accountability in Zimbabwe," in *Shifting Contexts: Transformations in Anthropological Knowledge,* ed. Marilyn Strathern (London: Routledge, 1995), 107.

23. "Setbacks, Yes . . . But the Work Goes On," Editorial, *Good Words/ Amazwi Amahle,* no. 95 (August 1980).

24. Sithembile Nkala (MaNsimango), interview, Musa Chidziva translating and interpreting, Nketa, Bulawayo, 3 April 1999.

25. Situtu Charity (Nkala) Mbambo, letter to author, 14 June 2012.

26. Ibid.

27. Rev. Jake Shenk, pers. comm. to author, 8 April 2001.

28. Werbner, "Human Rights," 111.

29. John Allen, *Desmond Tutu: Rabble-Rouser for Peace: The Authorized Biography* (Chicago: Lawrence Hill Books, 2008), 224–26.

30. "Gogo" is Ndebele for grandmother.

31. Richard Werbner, *Tears of the Dead: The Social Biography of an African Family* (Edinburgh: Edinburgh University Press, 1991); Kriger, *Zimbabwe's Guerrilla War;* Irene Staunton, ed., *Mothers of the Revolution* (Harare: Baobab Books, 1990).

32. Sithembile Nkala (MaNsimango), interview, Musa Chidziva translating, Bulawayo, 3 April 1999; Nellie Mlotshwa (Maduma), interview by telephone, 15 July 2002.

33. Staunton, *Mothers of the Revolution,* 127; Kriger, *Zimbabwe's Liberation War,* 187, 241.

34. Sibanda was overseer for Wanezi District from 1951 to 1970 and then was transferred to be overseer for Matopo District in 1970. Rev. Mangisi Sibanda, interview, Tshalimbe, 26 May 1999.

35. Rev. Mangisi Sibanda, interview, Tshalimbe, 26 May 1999.

36. Ibid.

37. Ibid.

38. This accounting for the relatively low number of sellout deaths contrasts with that of another woman, also from the same area near Esigodini, highlighted in *Mothers of the Revolution,* who explained that few died as sellouts in their area because "we worked together. People were dying and we knew that if we sold out on one another we would only cause more death." Thema Khumalo, quoted in Staunton, *Mothers of the Revolution,* 76.

39. Sithembile Nkala (MaNsimango), interview, Musa Chidziva interpreting, Wanezi Mission, 22 August 1997.

40. Situtu Charity (Nkala) Mbambo to author, 14 June 2012.

41. For a discussion of colonial-era patterns of sellout and witchcraft accusations and setting them into a discussion of citizenship in post-2000 Zimbabwe, see Diana Jeater, "Citizen, Witch or Non-person? Contested Concepts of Personhood in Political Violence and Reconciliation in Zimbabwe 1978–2008," paper presented at the 4th European Conference on African Studies (Uppsala, 15–18 June 2011). Among others see also Peter Delius, *A Lion amongst the Cattle: Reconstruction and Resistance in the Northern Transvaal* (Portsmouth, NH: Heinemann, 1997); Werbner, *Tears of the Dead.* For a study showing deep roots of the intermixing of witchcraft, concepts of evil, and political power going back centuries in South African polities, see Clifton Crais, *The Politics of Evil: Magic, State Power and the Political Imagination in South Africa* (Cambridge: Cambridge University Press, 2002).

42. Jeater, "Citizen, Witch?," 4.

43. Joyce Chadya, "The Untold Story: War, Flight, and the Internal Displacement of Women to Harare during the Zimbabwean Liberation Struggle, 1974–1980" (PhD diss., University of Minnesota, 2005), 25.

44. Sithembile Nkala (MaNsimango), interview, Musa Chidziva interpreting, Wanezi Mission, 22 August 1997.

45. Ranger, *Voices from the Rocks,* 209. Ranger highlights the role of Mwali in recent decades. From the 1950s and into the present, Mwali's voice at Njelele especially has been an important part of the religious and political landscape in Matabeleland. One could term the coexistence of the BICC and Mwali today to be a competitive situation.

46. Makhobo Ndlovu, interview by Nicholas Nkomo, 30 September 1995, as quoted in Ranger, *Voices from the Rocks,* 234.

47. Emphasis mine.

48. Doris Dube, *Silent Labourers* (Bulawayo, Zimbabwe: Matopo Book Centre, 1992), 15.

49. The area served by the BICC is almost entirely within the regions represented by ZAPU.

50. DRC transcripts, 247.

51. Eliakim Sibanda, e-mail message to author, 15 June 2003.

52. Barbara Nkala, ed., *Celebrating the Vision: A Century of Sowing and Reaping.* Bulawayo: Brethren in Christ Church, 1998; Nellie Mlotshwa (Maduma), interview by telephone, 15 July 2002. One of Dlodlo's own daughters had joined the struggle and was a member of ZAPU. Eliakim Sibanda, e-mail message to author, 15 June 2003.

53. Eliakim Sibanda, "The Brethren in Christ in Southern Rhodesia, 1898–1980: A Historical Study of Its Contributions towards the Promotion of Human Rights" (PhD diss., Iliff School of Theology and University of Denver, 1998), 476.

54. Nellie Mlotshwa, interview by telephone, 15 July 2002.

55. Dazzie Vundhla (MaMoyo), interview, Nondulo Vundhla interpreting, Matopo, 13 March 1999. See also Nkala, *Celebrating the Vision,* 171.

56. Elliot Ziduli, interview, Bulawayo, 28 July 1999. "Report of the Sub-Committee of the Ministerial and Examining Committee, 1970, I. Re: Licensed Ministers; Minutes of Church Executive Committee Rhodesia at Mtshabezi Mission," 27 August 1968, file "Church Executive Committee 1956–73," BICC-BYO.

57. Matopo District Council Meeting; Silobi School, 17–19 July 1970; Minutes of the Business Session—18 July, file Council Minutes Matopo, BICC-BYO.

58. See Kriger, *Zimbabwe's Guerrilla War;* O'Gorman, *Front Line.*

59. Chadya, "Untold Story," 3.

60. Margaret Viki and Josephine Ndiweni, interview by Irene Staunton, quoted in Staunton, *Mothers of the Revolution,* 150–51, 211. Nellie Mlotshwa, interview by telephone, 15 July 2002.

61. See also the case of a Catholic priest, Rev. Ignatius Mhonda, in which he argued that he faced a death sentence no matter what he did. Janice McLaughlin, "Avila Mission: A Turning Point in Church Relations with the State and with the Liberation Forces," in *Society in Zimbabwe's Liberation War,* ed. Ngwabi Bhebe and Terence Ranger (Portsmouth, NH: Heinemann, 1996), 96.

62. Werbner, *Tears of the Dead,* 151.

63. Batana Khumalo, interview, Nondulo Vundhla interpreting, Bulawayo, 1 April 1999.

64. See Chadya, "Untold Story."

65. Staunton, *Mothers of the Revolution.*

66. Ibid., 150.

67. Nellie Mlotshwa, interview by telephone, 15 July 2002.

68. Bishop Stephen N. Ndlovu, interview, Bulawayo, 24 February 1999.

69. Rev. Jake Shenk, interview, Bulawayo, 21 June 1999.

70. Doris Dube, "Naka Gininda–Nkanyezi Ndlovu: The Pastor Who Prays under a Tree," in Dube, *Silent Labourers,* 31. The closure of the Mpisini church was ordered "for the safety of the members against the Smith soldiers who had begun to pose as guerrillas and kill civilians and then the government would blame it on the guerrillas." Eliakim Sibanda, e-mail message to author, 15 June 2003.

71. Dube, "Naka Gininda," 31–32.

72. Bishop Stephen N. Ndlovu, interview, Bulawayo, 24 February 1999.

73. E-mail message to author, 15 June 2003.

74. Dube, "Naka Gininda," 31–32.

75. The missionaries called her Sixpence.

76. Mnofa was descended from the original members of Lobengula's queen Xhwalile's *umthimba,* or marriage procession, from Gaza. Sithembile Nkala, interview, Musa Chidziva interpreting, Nketa, Bulawayo, 15 August 2000.

77. Ibid.

78. See Urban-Mead, "Religion, Women."

79. Mary Kreider to her sister Anna, 15 June 1936, Papers of Mary Kreider, MG 88–1.3, BICC-PA.

80. Sithembile Nkala (MaNsimango), interview, Musa Chidziva interpreting, Bulawayo, 15 August 2000.

81. Sithembile Nkala (MaNsimango), interview, Musa Chidziva interpreting, Wanezi Mission, 22 August 1997.

82. Sithembile Nkala (MaNsimango), interview, Musa Chidziva interpreting, Bulawayo, 3 April 1999.

83. BICC, *Handbook of Missions* (Brethren in Christ Church, 1970), 13.

84. A ceremony that "calls home" the spirit of the departed individual, so as to prevent it from wandering forever, causing disruptions in the lives of the living.

85. Sithembile Nkala (MaNsimango), interview, Musa Chidziva interpreting, Bulawayo, 15 August 2000.

86. Sithembile Nkala (MaNsimango), interview, Musa Chidziva interpreting, Bulawayo, 3 April 1999.

87. Sithembile Nkala (MaNsimango), interview, Musa Chidziva interpreting, Wanezi Mission, 22–23 August 1997.

88. Sithembile Nkala (MaNsimango), interviews. Wanezi Mission, 22 August 1997; Bulawayo, 3 April 1999; Bulawayo, 15 August 2000.

89. For another discussion of a different group of African Christians' apolitical approaches, see David Maxwell, *African Gifts of the Spirit: Pentecostalism and the Rise of a Zimbabwean Transnational Religious Movement* (Athens: Ohio University Press, 2006).

Chapter 6: Stephen N. Ndlovu

1. Otiliya Ndlovu (MaNkala), interview, Bulawayo, 3 March 1999.

2. Dorothy Hodgson, "Modernity and the Production of Maasai Masculinities," in *Men and Masculinities in Modern Africa*, ed. Lisa A. Lindsay and Stephan F. Miescher (Portsmouth, NH: Heinemann, 2003), 211–12.

3. Carlton O. Wittlinger, *Quest for Piety and Obedience: The Story of the Brethren in Christ* (Nappanee, IN: Evangel Press, 1978).

4. For more on the early history of ZAPU and ZANU, see Terence Ranger, *Voices from the Rocks: Nature, Culture and History in the Matopos Hills of Zimbabwe*. London: James Currey, 1999; Timothy Scarnecchia, *The Urban Roots of Democracy and Political Violence in Zimbabwe: Harare and Highfield*. Rochester: Rochester University Press, 2008. My understanding of ZAPU as an all-Rhodesia party, with Nkomo as a leader who drew support from many corners of the African population, follows Ranger. Scarnecchia shows vividly the character of ZANU's inception and its early tactics for garnering support.

5. James Muzondidya and Sabelo Ndlovu-Gatsheni, "'Echoing Silences': Ethnicity in Post-colonial Zimbabwe, 1980–2007," *African Journal of Conflict Resolution* 27, no. 2 (2007): 282.

6. Eliakim Sibanda, *The Zimbabwe African People's Union, 1961–87: A Political History of Insurgency in Southern Rhodesia* (Trenton, NJ: Africa World Press, 2005), 244. See also, Jocelyn Alexander, "Dissident Perspectives on Zimbabwe's Post-independence War," *Africa: Journal of the International Africa Institute* 68, no. 2 (1998): 152–56.

7. Joshua Nkomo, *The Story of My Life* (London: Methuen, 1984), 224–26; Sibanda, *Zimbabwe African People's Union*, 250.

8. Alexander, "Dissident Perspectives," 159.

9. Catholic Commission for Justice and Peace in Zimbabwe; Legal Resources Foundation, *Breaking the Silence Building a True Peace: A Report on the Disturbances in Matabeleland and the Midlands 1980 to 1988* (Harare: Catholic Commission; Legal Resources Foundation, 1997), xii.

10. "From the Bishop's Desk," *Good Words/Amazwi Amahle*, no. 128 (May 1983), 6.

11. Rev. Raphael Mthombeni, interview, Atlanta, GA, 6 October 2007. Rev. Raphael Mthombeni, e-mail message to author, 15 December 2007.

12. Rev. Jacob Shenk stated that David Moyo of the Gwaai District church at Phelandaba was killed during the Gukurahundi by the Fifth Brigade. Rev. Jacob Shenk, interview, Bulawayo, 21 June 1999.

13. Jocelyn Alexander, JoAnn McGregor, and Terence Ranger, *Violence and Memory: One Hundred Years in the "Dark Forests" of Matabeleland* (Oxford: James Currey, 2000), 223.

14. Leslie Dlodlo, interview, West Somerton, Bulawayo, 4 August 1999; Rev. Elliot Ziduli, interview, Bulawayo, 28 July 1999.

15. "The Life History of Naka Roja Ndlovu," submitted by Rev. K. Q. Moyo, *Good Words/Amazwi Amahle*, no. 163 (June 1986), 10–11.

16. Stephen N. Ndlovu, interview, Bulawayo, 24 February 1999.

17. Stephen N. Ndlovu, interview by Scotch Ndlovu, 24 August 1987, as quoted in Scotch Malinga Ndlovu, "The Brethren in Christ Church among the Ndebele, 1898–1977" (PhD draft diss., Indiana University, 1992), 300.

18. Ethel Sibanda, interview, Bulawayo, 16 April 1999.

19. For his mother's name, see Doris Dube, "Bishop Stephen Ndabambi Ndlovu," in Nkala, *Celebrating the Vision,* 140–45.

20. For additional development of this theme, see Isabel Mukonyora, *Wandering a Gendered Wilderness: Suffering and Healing in an African Initiated Church* (New York: Peter Lang, 2007).

21. Otiliya Ndlovu (MaNkala), interview, Bulawayo, 3 March 1999.

22. Michael O. West notes that the term *white wedding*—complete with bridal gowns, wedding rings, and church ceremonies—denoted, for middle-class Africans at mid-century, something not only for "white people" but "for all educated and civilised people." West, "African Middle-Class Formation in Colonial Zimbabwe, 1890–1965" (PhD diss., Harvard University, 1990), 122. Ethel Sibanda described the thrilling impact of Alice Ndlovu (MaNkala)'s wedding, sealing her desire to have a white wedding herself. Ethel Sibanda, interview, Bulawayo, 16 April 1999. A key difference for the BICC's nonworldly emphasis meant that bridal gowns, veils, and rings were not part of the BICC wedding practice until after 1957. See Wendy Urban-Mead, "Negotiating 'Plainness' and Gender: Dancing and Apparel at Christian Weddings in Matabeleland, Zimbabwe, 1913–1944," *Journal of Religion in Africa* 38, no. 3 (2008): 209–46; Urban-Mead, "Religion, Women, and Gender in the Brethren in Christ Church, Matabeleland, Zimbabwe, 1898–1978 (PhD diss., Columbia University, 2004).

23. Stephen N. Ndlovu, interview, Bulawayo, 24 February 1999.

24. "[The primary son had] responsibilities and that went together with some privileges. When it came to inheritance, he got more than the younger brothers because he had the added responsibility of paying *lobola* [bride-wealth] for all the younger brothers. . . . He became the 'father' to all the younger siblings. He had to provide for the family." Pathisa Nyathi, pers. comm. with author, 2 April 2012.

25. "Stephen Ndanbambi [*sic*] Ndlovu, The Rev.," *Prominent African Personalities of Rhodesia* (Salisbury, Rhodesia: Cover Publicity Services, n.d.), 153.

26. Stephen N. Ndlovu, interview, Bulawayo, 24 February 1999.

27. Stephen N. Ndlovu, interview, Bulawayo, 16 June 1999.

28. His official title at that time was "Secretary and sports organisor [*sic*]," as given in *Prominent African Personalities of Rhodesia,* 153.

29. Barbara Nkala, ed., *Celebrating the Vision: A Century of Sowing and Reaping* (Bulawayo: Brethren in Christ Church, 1998), 141.

30. "Bishop Stephen Ndabambi Ndlovu," in Nkala, *Celebrating the Vision,* 141–42.

31. Ibid., 142.

32. Otiliya Ndlovu (MaNkala), interview, Bulawayo, 3 March 1999. For discussion of the Free Presbyterian mission at Nkayi See also Alexander, McGregor, and Ranger, *Violence and Memory.*

33. Otiliya Ndlovu (MaNkala), interview, Bulawayo, 3 March 1999. In keeping with the consistent nature of Ndlovu's and MaNkala's narratives about themselves, this discomfort with the Free Presbyterians' strictness is also reflected in *Celebrating the Vision,* 143.

34. Otiliya Ndlovu (MaNkala), interview, Bulawayo, 3 March 1999.

35. Ibid.

36. Stephen N. Ndlovu, interview by Scotch Ndlovu, August 1987, as quoted in Scotch Ndlovu, "Brethren in Christ," 301.

37. See Daryl R. Climenhaga, "Adapting to a Revolution: A Study of the Brethren in Christ in the Changing Context of Bulawayo, Zimbabwe" (DMiss diss., Asbury Theological Seminary, Wilmore, KY, 1993).

38. Otiliya Ndlovu (MaNkala), interview, Bulawayo, 3 March 1999.

39. Joyce Khumalo (MaMlotshwa), interview, Bulawayo, 27 August 1997.

40. Otiliya Ndlovu (MaNkala), interview, Bulawayo, 3 March 1999. Other overseers' wives during the 1970s also refused to give up their teaching positions for the same reasons articulated by Mrs. Ndlovu.

41. E-mail from Pathisa Nyathi to the author, 2 April 2012.

42. For two of those ten years (1975–76) Ndlovu also served as the acting bishop. Bishop Khumalo was in the United States at the time, studying at Fuller Theological Seminary.

43. Donald Vundhla, interview by telephone, 21 March 2002.

44. Stephen N. Ndlovu, interview, Bulawayo, 13 August 1999.

45. Nancy Kreider Hoke, interview, Grantham, PA, 28 May 1997.

46. Donald Vundhla, who was a teacher at the Ekuphileni Bible Institute (EBI) on the grounds of Mtshabezi Mission during the war, believes it was Ndlovu who made the decision to close the mission and its schools. He stated, "ZIPRAs [ZIPRA guerrillas] did not say 'close.' We closed them ourselves from fear. S. N. Ndlovu said close it, that's why we [EBI] went to town." Donald Vundhla, interview by telephone, 21 March 2002.

47. Sam King, interview by telephone, April 2001.

48. Donald Vundhla, interview by telephone, 21 March 2002.

49. Stephen N. Ndlovu, interview by Scotch Ndlovu, August 1987, as quoted in Scotch Ndlovu, "Brethren in Christ," 303–4.

50. Sabelo Ndlovu-Gatsheni, "Fatherhood and Nationhood: Joshua Nkomo and the Re-imagination of the Zimbabwe Nation," in *Manning the Nation: Father Figures in Zimbabwean Literature and Society,* ed. Kichito Z. Muchemwa and Robert Muponde (Harare: Weaver Press, 2007), 74.

The Patriotic Front–Zimbabwe African People's Union (PF-ZAPU) was so named as part of the 1987 Unity Accord made with ZANU-PF.

51. Nomsa Moyo (Stephen N. Ndlovu's niece), interview by telephone, 7 October 2011.

52. Stephen Ndlovu, "Church Mediation of the ZAPU/ZANU Conflict in Zimbabwe," in *African Churches and Peace,* Mennonite Central Committee (MCC) Occasional Paper no. 15 (April 1992), 31.

53. Stephen N. Ndlovu, interviews, Bulawayo, 24 February, 16 June 1999.

54. Stephen Ndlovu, "Really Becoming a Church: Interview with Stephen Ndlovu," *Evangelical Visitor,* 25 September 1981, 8–9.

55. *Discipling Believers in Today's World* (Elizabethtown, PA: Yearbook Brethren in Christ Missions, 1975), 60; *therefore* (BICC missions) 9, no. 1 (January–February 1981); no. 5 (September–October 1981).

56. In 1983, BICC members Mqhele and Flora Dlodlo returned to Zimbabwe from the United States, and the church also welcomed the arrival of physician Devee Boyd from Pennsylvania. *Good Words/Amazwi Amahle,* no. 130 (July 1983); no. 132 (September 1983).

57. Stephen Ndlovu, "Church Mediation," 30.

58. Ibid.

59. Rev. Jacob Shenk, interview, Bulawayo, 21 June 1999.

60. Stephen N. Ndlovu, interview by Scotch Ndlovu, Bulawayo, 24 August 1987. Stanley Square has since been designated a monument under the care of the National Museums and Monuments of Zimbabwe. The declaration followed research conducted by Pathisa Nyathi. It had been commissioned by the NMMZ. The declaration was on the basis of its political, cultural, and social roles as a venue. Nyathi, e-mail message to author, 2 April 2012.

61. Quoting from Scotch Ndlovu, "Brethren in Christ," 304.

62. For more on Stanley Square's place in the social and political history of Bulawayo, see Terence Ranger, *Bulawayo Burning: The Social History of a Southern African City, 1893–1960* (Harare: Weaver Press, 2010).

63. Stephen N. Ndlovu, interview, Bulawayo, 16 June 1999.

64. Carol Summers, *Colonial Lessons: Africans' Education in Southern Rhodesia, 1918–1940* (Portsmouth, NH: Heinemann, 2002).

65. Stephen N. Ndlovu, interview by Daryl Climenhaga, 3 April 1992, in DRC transcripts, 130.

66. Ibid., 133.

67. Otiliya Ndlovu (MaNkala), interview, Bulawayo, 3 March 1999.

68. For more on women pastors in rural congregations in Matabeleland during the 1970s liberation war, see chapter 4.

69. Ronald Lizwe Moyo, e-mail message to author, 19 September 2011.

70. For more on the ethnic dynamics in the politics of ZAPU and ZANU,

particularly after 1980, see Alexander, "Dissident Perspectives"; Muzon-didya and Ndlovu-Gatsheni, "'Echoing Silences.'"

Conclusion: Gendered Lives of Piety

1. Doris Dube, Bekithemba Dube, and Barbara Nkala, "The Church in Southern Africa," in *A Global Mennonite History*, vol. 1, *Africa*, ed. John A. Lapp and C. Arnold Snyder (Kitchener, ON: Pandora Press, 2003), 165.

2. Norma Kriger, *Guerrilla Veterans in Post-War Zimbabwe: Symbolic and Violent Politics, 1980–1987* (Cambridge: Cambridge University Press, 2003).

3. Sabelo J. Ndlovu-Gatsheni, "Reaping the Bitter Fruits of Stalinist Tendencies in Zimbabwe," Association of Concerned African Scholars Bulletin, no. 79 (Winter 2008).

4. Bishop Danisa Ndlovu, "From the Bishop's Desk: A Call to Stop and Listen," *Good Words/Amazwi Amahle*, August 2002, 2. "Saltiness" refers to a passage in the Bible in which Jesus urges his followers to be the salt of the earth: Matthew 5:13.

5. "Subsequently new laws have been passed to intimidate and control civil society; the Public order and Security Act is even more draconian than its predecessor which was brought in by a colonial government and makes it almost impossible to hold any kind of political meeting or demonstration of any kind that does not favour government. . . . All this is being done to destroy the opposition and to cling onto power, the arrests, the arson, torture and selective distribution of food all serve to keep the population under control." Archbishop Pius Ncube, "The Archbishop Denis Hurley Lecture November 2002," http://archive.kubatana.net/html/archive/relig/021111hurleypn.asp?sector=relig&year=2002&range_start=1; "Archbishop Ncube Slams Mugabe," *Zimbabwe Independent*, 17 November 2002, http://www.zimbabwesituation.com/nov16b_2002.html#link3. The specific acts of violence during the Gukurahundi were exposed by the Catholic Commission for Justice and Peace when it released *Breaking the Silence, Building True Peace: Report on the Disturbances in Matabeleland and the Midlands* in March 1997, http://archive.org/stream/BreakingTheSilenceBuildingTruePeace/MatabelelandReport_djvu.txt.

6. http://www.archive.kubatana.net/html/sectors/chr010.asp?orgcode=CHR010&year=2004&range_start=1.

7. For more on Operation Murambatsvina, see Busani Mpofu, "Operation 'Live Well' or 'Cry Well'? An Analysis of the 'Rebuilding' Programme in Bulawayo, Zimbabwe," *Journal of Southern African Studies* 37, 1 (March 2011): 177–92; Joost Fontein, "Anticipating the Tsunami: Rumours, Planning, and the Arbitrary State in Zimbabwe," *Africa* 79, no. 3 (2009): 369–98; Anna Kajumulo Tibaijuka, "Report of the Fact-Finding Mission to Zimbabwe to Assess the Scope and Impact of Operation Murambatsvina," UN

Special Envoy on Human Settlements Issues in Zimbabwe, 18 July 2005, http://www.un.org/News/dh/infocus/zimbabwe/zimbabwe_rpt.pdf.

8. Eliakim Sibanda, e-mail to author, 24 June 2005. See also Doris Dube and Jethro Dube, report to the Mennonite World Conference on the situation in Bulawayo in the aftermath of Operation Murambatsvina, 13 June 2005, in possession of author.

9. Savious Kwinika, "Churches Aid the Displaced," *Zimbabwe Standard,* 11 July 2005.

10. Bishop Danisa Ndlovu, "From the Bishop's Desk: No Situation Is Hopeless to God," *Good Words/Amazwi Amahle* (May 2006), 2–3.

11. "The Zimbabwe We Want: 'Towards a National Vision for Zimbabwe,'" www.africamission-mafr.org/zimbabwe.doc. See also http://www.bic-church.org/news/churchwide/zimbabwe/zimbishopplea.asp.

12. Nellie Mlotshwa (Maduma), interview by telephone, 22 May, 2002; Chris Edwards, "World Peacebuilders Gather at EMU," *Eastern Mennonite University News,* May 2002, http://www.emu.edu/marketing/news/spi0502a.html.

13. Minutes of the Zimbabwe Brethren in Christ Church 37th Annual General Conference, Mtshabezi Mission, 22–26 August 2012, section 6.1, "Peace and Social Justice," 4–5.

14. Amanda Hammar, JoAnn McGregor, and Loren Landau, "Introduction: Displacing Zimbabwe: Crisis and Construction in Southern Africa," *Journal of Southern African Studies* 36, no. 2 (2010): 263.

15. See the manifesto available on the following website. Some—but far from all—BICC Zimbabwe members both at home and in the diaspora sympathize with this movement for a separate Ndebele state. http://www.africafederation.net/Matabeleland.htm.

16. http://www.hopeformtshabezi.org/.

17. Wendy Urban-Mead, "Protestant Women Activists in Matabeleland: Historical Perspectives on 'Apolitical,' Faith-Based Action in Response to the Health Care Crisis of 2000–2010," paper presented the Britain-Zimbabwe Society Research Days, St. Antony's College, Oxford, 19–20 June 2010.

18. Ronald L. Moyo, e-mail to the author, 9 November 2013.

Glossary

A term's language of origin appears in parentheses.

abaFundisi   See *uMfundisi.*

abantu   Lit., "people of the Mambo." Mambo was the title of the
bakaMambo   king of the Rozvi polity, which ruled much of present-day
Zimbabwe from the seventeenth century until the mid-
nineteenth century. Referring to the peoples who were
already occupying the land when the Ndebele Kingdom
arrived, *abantu bakaMambo* is a way of connoting
the peoples who were incorporated into the Ndebele
Kingdom when the Ndebele came to Zimbabwe after
1840. They constituted the lowest of the three social strata
in the kingdom. (Ndebele)

abenhla   Lit., "those from the north; those from upstream"; refers
to the people who were incorporated into the Ndebele
Kingdom from among the Sotho and Tswana speakers.
Abenhla constituted the second of the three social strata
of the kingdom. (Ndebele)

abezansi   Lit., "people from the south" or "people from
downstream"; the term connotes the people who made
up the elite stratum of the Ndebele Kingdom, those of
Nguni background whose families originated in today's
KwaZulu-Natal, in South Africa. (Ndebele)

amajaha   See *ijaha.*

chiShona   The Shona language.

eMaguswini   Lit., "in the forest." A place-name for Matabeleland
North, particularly the forested areas around Lupane and
Nkayi Districts. From *igusu,* forest. (Ndebele)

Gukurahundi	Lit., "the early rain which washes away the chaff before the spring rains"; it connotes the time from 1982 to 1987 when perceived "dissidents"—who mainly lived in Matabeleland and Midlands Provinces and were seen as supporters of the ZAPU political party—were suppressed in actions taken by the Fifth Brigade, a special unit of the military directly answerable to the prime minister's office. (Shona)
ijaha	Young man who is not yet married; during the time of the Ndebele Kingdom, young warrior [pl., *amajaha*]. (Ndebele)
induna	A chief (pl: *izinduna*). (Ndebele)
intombi	A young woman who is not yet married but considered of marriageable age; one who has reached puberty and has experienced menstruation (*ukuthomba*), hence *intombi* (pl: *izintombi*). (Ndebele)
intombi egedini	Lit., "girls of the gate"; the girls who attended the Mtshabezi Primary School in the early decades of the twentieth century. The girls were kept inside the demarcated area and were not to go beyond the gate. (Ndebele)
iqhiye	A woman's head covering. In the first half of the twentieth century, a BICC woman's *iqhiye* ideally was a stiffly starched, very tightly fitting cloth wrapped around the head concealing every hair. In Afrikaans it is called a *doek*. (Ndebele)
isangoma	A diviner. Isangoma uses divination by becoming a medium through which the spirits of the ancestors communicate with the living and thus bring healing or protection. (Ndebele)
isiNdebele	The Ndebele language.
izinduna	See *induna*.
izintombi	See *intombi*.
lobola	Bridewealth. When used in English, it is a noun—*lobola*—referring to the bridewealth. In Ndebele, it is either a noun, *amalobolo*, or a verb, *ukulobola*, an instruction

to formalize the new relationship between the clans by giving the cattle or other goods for the bride to the bride's guardian. (Ndebele)

manyano   Uniformed, women's prayer and service association. Refers specifically to Methodist groups in southern Africa, particularly South Africa and Zimbabwe.

Ndebele   See *isiNdebele*.

Nguni   The group of closely related languages spoken in southern Africa, including *isiXhosa, isiZulu, siSwati,* and *isiNdebele*.

pungwe   A struggle session (politicization) or all-night meeting held in rural villages (usually outside the village, where there was better security) during the Zimbabwean liberation war of the 1970s, especially in areas that came under the control of ZANLA. The purpose was to raise the revolutionary consciousness of the people, identify sellouts, and recruit helpers who would assist the guerrilla fighters. The meetings included the singing of revolutionary songs. (Shona)

rinderpest   An infectious viral disease of cattle that affected up to 80 percent of cattle in southern Africa in the 1890s epizootic. The Ndebele called the disease *indalimane*.

uMfundisi   A teacher or minister of religion. In the context of the BICC, it particularly refers to one who has had formal training in theology and has been ordained to the ministry; usually the *uMfundisi* has a supervisory role over congregational pastors. *uMfundisi* is also a title ("Reverend") (pl: *abaFundisi*). (Ndebele)

umkhuna   A tree of southern Africa (*Parinari curatellifloria*) that bears an edible fruit [pl., *imikhuna*]. (Ndebele)

umthimba   The procession of a bride from her parents' home to that of her new husband, accompanied by women of her father's family, who ply her with advice on how to be a wife: how to get along with her mother-in-law; how to please her husband. A few men were part of *umthimba* to provide security. (Ndebele)

veld   A savanna.

Bibliography

Archives

Brethren in Christ Historical Library and Archives, Mechanicsburg, PA (BICC-PA)
Center for World Mission, School of Oriental and African Studies, London
Historical Reference Collection, Bulawayo Public Library
National Archives of Zimbabwe (NAZ), Harare and Bulawayo
Records of the Brethren in Christ Church, Bulawayo, Zimbabwe (BICC-BYO)
Rhodes House, Oxford

Newspapers

Bantu Mirror (Bulawayo)
Chronicle (Bulawayo)
Evangelical Visitor
Good Words/Amazwi Amahle (Bulawayo)
Sunday News (Bulawayo)
Zimbabwe Independent (Harare)
Zimbabwe Standard (Harare)

Interviews

All interviews were conducted in English, by the author, unless otherwise indicated. Some interviews were conducted in Ndebele and included the work of a *translator:* someone who translated the words of the interviewee as closely and directly as possible, or an *interpreter:* someone who, in addition to translation, offered her own interpretations of the interviewee's meaning. Some interviews were recorded with a cassette or digital recorder and transcribed; others were captured by hand, with pen and paper. In the case of several interviewees, an initial in-person interview was followed up with one or more telephone conversations or e-mails, not all of which are indicated in this list. Women are listed alphabetically by their married surname; their family names (izibongo) are given in parentheses.

Book, Thata.
    Bulawayo, 5 March 1999.
    Grantham, PA, 8 December 1999.
Climenhaga, Rev. Dr. Arthur A.
    Mechanicsburg, PA, 8 December 1999.
Climenhaga, Rev. Dr. Daryl R.
    By telephone, 8 March 2001.
    By telephone, 13 October 2011.
Climenhaga, Rev. David.
    By telephone, 22 March 2001.
Dlodlo, Leslie.
    Bulawayo, 4 August 1999.
Dlodlo, Orlean (MaGwebu).
    Bulawayo, 19 March 1999.
Dube, Bekithemba.
    Bulawayo, August 2000.
    By telephone, 16 July 2001.
Dube, John.
    Rev. Rabson Zikhali, translator, Tsholotsho, 11 June 1999.
Gwebu, Seyemephi (MaMguni).
    Nellie Mlotshwa and Mangisi Ottilia Dube, translators, Gwakwe, 21 May 1999.
Hoke, Nancy Kreider.
    Mechanicsburg, PA, 28 May 1997.
    Mechanicsburg, PA, 5 June 2001.
    Mechanicsburg, PA, 13 January 2012.
Holland, Grace.
    Grantham, PA, 7 December 1999.
    By telephone, 9 June 2001.
Kauffman, Dr. Virginia.
    By telephone, 8 January, 2001.
Khabi, Alma (MaKhumalo).
    Bulawayo, 2 July 1999.
Khumalo, Batana (MaMlandu).
    Nondulo Vundhla (MaKhumalo), translator, Bulawayo, 1 April 1999.
Khumalo, Rev. Bruce.
    Written testimony submitted via e-mail, 28 May 2001.
Khumalo, Joyce (MaMlotshwa).
    Bulawayo, 27 August 1997.
King, Sam.
    By telephone, April 2001.
Mhlanga, Kezia (NakaOrpah/ MaMkwananzi).
    Rev. Rabson Zikhale, interpreter, Tsholotsho, 11 June 1999.

Mlotshwa, Nellie (Maduma).
   Wanezi Mission, 23 August 1997.
   Bulawayo, 22 May 1999.
   Bulawayo, 3 June 1999.
   Bulawayo, 27 June 1999.
   Bulawayo, August, 1999.
   By telephone, 22 May 2002.
   By telephone, 15 July 2002.
   By telephone, 15 July 2010.
Mlotshwa, Samuel.
   Mayezane, 22 May 1999.
   Interviewed by Hlengiwe Sibanda (MaMlotshwa), Bulawayo, 4 June 2006.
Mnkandla, Sipilisiwe (MaSibanda).
   Bulawayo, June 1999.
Moyo, Rev. Elias.
   London, 11 November 2007.
"Moyo, Mrs." [anonymity requested].
   Bulawayo, 9 April 1999.
Moyo, (Mrs. Thomas), MaSibanda.
   Nondulo Vundhla (MaKhumlao), translator, near Matopo Mission, 13
      March 1999.
Moyo, Nomsa.
   By telephone, 5 October 2011.
Mpofu, Isaac M.
   Bulawayo, 12 May 1999.
   Bulawayo, 13 August, 2000.
Msimanga, Huggins.
   By telephone, 18 January 2001.
   By telephone, 17 December 2008.
Mthombeni, Rev. Raphael.
   Bulawayo, 13 May 1999.
   Atlanta, 7 October 2007.
Ncube, Ngcathu.
   Jackson Ndlovu and R. Lizwe Moyo, translators, Njelele shrine, 1999.
Ncube, Zama (MaKhumalo).
   Bulawayo, 24 May 1999.
   Bulawayo, 27 May 1999.
Ndlovu, Alice (MaNkala).
   Bulawayo, 27 August 1997.
Ndlovu, Edgar.
   Bulawayo, 16 August 2000.
Ndlovu, Jackson.
   Bulawayo, 14 August 2000.

Ndlovu, Otiliya (MaNkala).
    Bulawayo, 3 March 1999.
Ndlovu, Sibusisiwe (MaSibanda).
    Bulawayo, 20 July 1999.
Ndlovu, Rev. Stephen Ndabambi.
    Interviewed by Scotch M. Ndlovu, Bulawayo, 1987.
    Interviewed by Daryl Ray Climenhaga, Bulawayo, 1992.
    Bulawayo, 24 February 1999.
    Bulawayo, 16 June 1999.
    Bulawayo, 13 August 1999.
Ndlovu, Violet.
    Rev. Rabson Zikhali, interpreter, Tsholotsho, 11 June 1999.
Newcomer, Steven.
    By telephone, 9 April 2002.
Nkala, Ivy.
    By telephone, 17 November 2007.
Nkala, Sithembile (MaNsimango).
    Musa Chidziva, interpreter, Wanezi Mission, 22 August 1997.
    Musa Chidziva, interpreter, Bulawayo, 3 April 1999.
    Musa Chidziva, interpreter, Bulawayo, 15 August 2000.
Nyathi, Pathisa.
    Bulawayo, 8 April 1999.
    Bulawayo, 14 August 2000.
Shenk, Rev. Jacob.
    Bulawayo, 5 February 1999.
    Bulawayo, 16 February 1999.
Sibanda, Eliakim.
    By telephone, 4 June 2001.
    By telephone, 30 December 2009.
    By telephone, 26 April 2012.
Sibanda, Ethel (MaSibanda).
    Bulawayo, 16 April 1999.
Sibanda, Hlengiwe Lindani (MaMlotshwa).
    By telephone, 24 September 2008.
    By telephone, 15 October 2008.
    By telephone, 16 November 2009.
    By telephone, 2 December 2009.
Sibanda, Mangisi (MaNdlovu).
    Nondulo Vundhla (MaKhumalo), translator, Bulawayo, 12 March 1999.
Sibanda, Rev. Mangisi.
    Tshalimbe, 26 May 1999.

Tshuma, Maria.
    Musa Chidziva, interpreter, Wanezi Mission, August 1997.
    Nellie Mlotshwa, interpreter, Mbaulo, 8 August 1999.
    Interviewed by Nellie Mlotshwa, Mbaulo, June 2003.
Tshuma, Sithabile.
    Interviewed by Nellie Mlotshwa, by telephone, 8 July 2003.
Vundhla, Dazzie (MaMoyo).
    Nondulo Vundhla (MaKhumalo), translator, near Matopo Mission, 13 March 1999.
Vundhla, Donald.
    By telephone, 8 March 2002.
Ziduli, Rev. Elliot.
    Bulawayo, 28 July 1999.
Zook, Donald
    By telephone, 1 June 2001.

Books and Articles

Alderfer, Owen. "Acceptance of the Holiness Doctrine by the Brethren in Christ Church, 1910–1937." *Brethren in Christ History and Life* 15, no. 3 (1992): 397–421.

Alexander, Jocelyn. "Dissident Perspectives on Zimbabwe's Post-independence War." *Africa: Journal of the International Africa Institute* 68, no. 2 (1998): 151–82.

———. "The State, Agrarian Policy and Rural Politics in Zimbabwe: Case Studies of Insiza and Chimanimani Districts." PhD diss., Oxford University, 1993.

Alexander, Jocelyn, and JoAnn McGregor. "Modernity and Ethnicity: Understanding Difference in Northwestern Zimbabwe." *Journal of Southern African Studies* 23, no. 2 (1997): 187–201.

Alexander, Jocelyn, JoAnn McGregor, and Terence Ranger. *Violence and Memory: One Hundred Years in the "Dark Forests" of Matabeleland.* Oxford: James Currey, 2000.

Alexander, Jocelyn, and Terence Ranger. "Competition and Integration in the Religious History of North-Western Zimbabwe." *Journal of Religion in Africa* 28, no. 1 (1998): 3–31.

Allen, John. *Desmond Tutu: Rabble-Rouser for Peace The Authorized Biography.* Chicago: Lawrence Hill Books, 2008.

Amadiume, Ifi. *Male Daughters, Female Husbands: Gender and Sex in an African Society.* London: Zed Books, 1987.

American Zulu Mission. *Amagama okuhlabelela.* 1850. Reprint, Overport, SA: Mission Press, 1996.

Barnes, Teresa A. *"We Women Worked So Hard": Gender, Urbanization and Social Reproduction in Colonial Harare, Zimbabwe, 1930–1956*. Portsmouth, NH: Heinemann, 1999.

Barnes, Teresa A., and Everjoyce Win. *To Live a Better Life: An Oral History of Women in the City of Harare, 1930–70*. Harare: Baobab Books, 1992.

Bastian, Misty L. "Young Converts: Christian Missions, Gender and Youth in Onitsha, Nigeria 1880–1929." *Anthropological Quarterly* 73, no. 3 (2000): 145–58.

Beach, David. *The Shona and Zimbabwe, 900–1850: An Outline of Shona History*. New York: Holmes and Meier, 1980.

Berger, Iris. "'Beasts of Burden' Revisited: Interpretations of Women and Gender in Southern African Societies." In *Paths toward the Past: African Historical Essays in Honor of Jan Vansina*, edited by Robert W. Harms, Joseph C. Miller, David S. Newbury, and Michele D. Wagner, 123–41. Atlanta: African Studies Association Press, 1994.

Bhebe, Ngwabi. *Benjamin Burombo: African Politics in Zimbabwe, 1947–1958*. Harare: College Press, 1989.

———. *Christianity and Traditional Religion in Western Zimbabwe, 1859–1923*. London: Longman, 1979.

———. "Some Aspects of Ndebele Relations with the Shona in the Nineteenth Century." *Rhodesian History* 4 (1978): 31–38.

———. *The ZAPU and ZANU Guerrilla Warfare and the Evangelical Lutheran Church in Zimbabwe*. Gweru: Mambo Press, 1999.

Bhebe, Ngwabi, and Terence Ranger, eds. *Society in Zimbabwe's Liberation War*. Portsmouth, NH: Heinemann, 1996.

———. *Soldiers in Zimbabwe's Liberation War*. Portsmouth, NH: Heinemann, 1991.

Bowie, Fiona, Deborah Kirkwood, and Shirley Ardener, eds. *Women and Missions: Past and Present: Anthropological and Historical Perceptions*. Providence, RI: Berg, 1993.

Bozongwana, Rev. W. *Ndebele Religion and Customs*. Gweru: Mambo Press, 1983.

Bozzoli, Belinda. *Women of Phokeng: Consciousness, Life Strategy, and Migrancy in South Africa, 1900–1983*. With Mmantho Nkotsoe. Portsmouth, NH: Heinemann, 1991.

Bradford, Helen. "Women, Gender and Colonialism: Rethinking the History of the British Cape Colony and Its Frontier Zones." *Journal of African History*, 37, no. 3 (1996): 351–70.

Brandel-Syrier, Mia. *Black Woman in Search of God*. London: Lutterworth Press, 1962.

Brethren in Christ Church. *Sowing and Reaping: The Story of a Work of God in Rhodesia, 1898–1948*. Bulawayo: Rhodesian Printing and Publishing, 1948.

Brickhill, Jeremy. "Daring to Storm the Heavens: The Military Strategy of ZAPU 1976 to 1979." In *Soldiers in Zimbabwe's Liberation War*, edited by Ngwabi Bhebe and Terence Ranger, 48–72. London: James Currey, 1995.

Burke, Timothy. *Lifebuoy Men, Lux Women: Commodification, Consumption, and Cleanliness in Modern Zimbabwe*. Durham, NC: Duke University Press, 1996.

Campbell, James. *Songs of Zion: The African Methodist Episcopal Church in the United States and South Africa*. New York: Oxford University Press, 1995.

Catholic Commission for Justice and Peace in Zimbabwe/Legal Resources Foundation. *Gukurahundi in Zimbabwe: A Report on the Disturbances in Matabeleland and Midlands, 1980–1988*. With an introduction by Elinor Sisulu and foreword by Archbishop Pius Ncube. New York: Columbia University Press, 2008.

Chadya, Joyce. "The Untold Story: War, Flight, and the Internal Displacement of Women to Harare during the Zimbabwean Liberation Struggle, 1974–1980." PhD diss., University of Minnesota, 2005.

Clarke, Marieke Faber. *Lozikeyi Dlodlo: Queen of the Ndebele: A Very Dangerous and Intriguing Woman*. With Pathisa Nyathi. Bulawayo: AmaGugu Publishers, 2011.

Climenhaga, Daryl R. "Adapting to a Revolution: A Study of the Brethren in Christ in the Changing Context of Bulawayo, Zimbabwe." DMiss diss., Asbury Theological Seminary (Wilmore, Kentucky), 1993.

———. "Through African Eyes: Reflections on Anniversary Plays." *Brethren in Christ History and Life* 21, no. 3 (1998): 343–60.

Clinton, Iris. *Hope Fountain Story: A Tale of One Hundred Years*. Gwelo: Mambo Press, 1969.

Cobbing, Julian. "The Ndebele State." In *Before and after Shaka: Papers in Nguni History*, edited by Jeff Peires. Grahamstown: Institute of Social and Economic Research, Rhodes University, 1981.

———. "The Ndebele under the Khumalos, 1820–1896." PhD diss., University of Lancaster, 1976.

Comaroff, Jean, and John Comaroff. *Of Revelation and Revolution*. Vol. 1, *Christianity, Colonialism and Consciousness in South Africa*. Vol. 2, *The Dialectics of Modernity on a South African Frontier*. Chicago: University of Chicago Press, 1991, 1997.

Cooper, Barbara M. *Evangelical Christians in the Muslim Sahel*. Bloomington: Indiana University Press, 2006.

———. "Oral Sources and the Challenge of African History." In *Writing African History*, edited by John Edward Philips, 191–215. Rochester: Rochester University Press, 2005.

Crais, Clifton. *The Politics of Evil: Magic, State Power and the Political Imagination in South Africa*. Cambridge: Cambridge University Press, 2002.

Creary, Nicholas M. *Domesticating a Religious Import: The Jesuits and the Inculturation of the Catholic Church in Zimbabwe, 1879–1980*. New York: Fordham University Press, 2011.

Dabengwa, Dumiso. "ZIPRA in the Zimbabwe War of National Liberation." In Bhebe and Ranger, *Soldiers*, 24–35.

Daneel, Marthinus. *African Earthkeepers: Wholistic Interfaith Mission*. Maryknoll, NY: Orbis, 2001.

———. *Old and New in Southern Shona Independent Churches*. The Hague: Mouton, 1971.

Davidson, H. Frances. *South and South Central Africa: A Record of Fifteen Years' Missionary Labors among Primitive Peoples*. Elgin, IL: Brethren Publishing House, 1915.

Davis, Natalie Zemon. *The Return of Martin Guerre*. Cambridge, MA: Harvard University Press, 1983.

Davison, Jean. *Voices from Mutira: Change in the Lives of Rural Gikuyu Women, 1910–1995*. Boulder: Lynne Rienner, 1996.

Delius, Peter. *A Lion amongst the Cattle: Reconstruction and Resistance in the Northern Transvaal*. Portsmouth, NH: Heinemann, 1997.

Dube, Doris. *Golide: Gogo Khokho—Lived, Loved and Left a Legacy*. With Barbara Nkala. Harare: Radiant Publishing, 2011.

———. "Maria Tshuma." In Nkala, *Celebrating the Vision*, 175–81.

———. "Naka Gininda–Nkanyezi Ndlovu: The Pastor Who Prays under a Tree," In *Silent Labourers*, 28–33.

———. *Silent Labourers*. Bulawayo, Zimbabwe: Matopo Book Centre, 1992.

Dube, Doris, Bekithemba Dube, and Barbara Nkala. "The Church in Southern Africa." In *A Global Mennonite History*. Vol. 1, *Africa,* edited by John A. Lapp and C. Arnold Snyder, 119–220. Kitchener, ON: Pandora Press, 2003.

Elphick, Richard. "Writing Religion into History: The Case of South African Christianity." In *Missions and Christianity in South African History,* edited by Henry Bredekamp and Robert Ross, 1–26. Johannesburg: University of the Witwatersrand Press, 1995.

Engle, Anna, John A. Climenhaga, and Leoda A. Buckwalter. *There Is No Difference: God Works in Africa and India*. Nappanee, IN: E. V. Publishing House, 1950.

Eshelman, C. F. "Trends in the Education of Teachers for Southern Rhodesia." MA thesis, School of Education, Cornell University, 1938.

Etherington, Norman, ed. *Missions and Empire*. Oxford: Oxford University Press, 2005.

———. "Recent Trends in the Historiography of Christianity in Southern Africa." *Journal of Southern African Studies* 22, no. 2 (1996): 201–19;

Flood, D. G. H. "The Contribution of the London Missionary Society to African Education in Ndebeleland, 1859–1959." In *Christianity South of the Zambezi,* edited by A. J. Dachs, 41–52. Gwelo: Mambo Press, 1973.

Fontein, Joost. "Anticipating the Tsunami: Rumours, Planning, and the Arbitrary State in Zimbabwe." *Africa* 79, no. 3 (2009): 369–98.

Gaitskell, Deborah. "'Christian Compounds for Girls': Church Hostels for African Women in Johannesburg, 1907–1970." *Journal of Southern African Studies* 6, no. 1 (1979): 44–69.

———. "'Wailing for Purity': Prayer Unions, African Mothers and Adolescent Daughters, 1912–1940." In *Industrialisation and Social Change in South Africa: African Class Formation, Culture and Consciousness, 1870–1930.* Edited by Shula Marks and Richard Rathbone, 338–57. New York: Longman, 1982.

Geiger, Susan. *TANU Women: Gender and Culture in the Making of Tanganyikan Nationalism, 1955–1965.* Portsmouth, NH: Heinemann, 1997.

———. "Women's Life Histories: Method and Content." *Signs* 11, no. 2 (Winter 1986): 332–51.

Gelfand, Michael, ed. *Gubulawayo and Beyond: Letters and Journals of the Early Jesuit Missionaries to Zambesia (1879–1887).* New York: Barnes and Noble, 1968.

Gengenbach, Heidi. "Truth-Telling and the Politics of Women's Life History Research in Africa: A Reply to Kirk Hoppe." *Journal of African Historical Studies* 27, no. 3 (1994): 619–27.

Gluck, Sherna Berger, and Daphne Patai. *Women's Words: The Feminist Practice of Oral History.* New York: Routledge, 1991.

Guyer, Jane I. "Wealth in People, Wealth in Things: Introduction." *Journal of African History* 36, no. 1 (1995): 83–90.

Hallencreutz, Carl, and Ambrose Moyo, Eds. *Church and State in Zimbabwe.* Gweru: Mambo Press, 1988.

Hamilton, Carolyn, ed. *The Mfecane Aftermath: Reconstructive Debates in Southern African History.* Johannesburg: Witwatersrand University Press, 1995.

———. *Terrific Majesty: The Powers of Shaka Zulu and the Limits of Historical Invention.* Cambridge, MA: Harvard University Press, 1998.

Hammar, Amanda, JoAnn McGregor, and Loren Landau. "Introduction: Displacing Zimbabwe: Crisis and Construction in Southern Africa." *Journal of Southern African Studies* 36, no. 2 (2010): 263–83.

Hardung, Christine. "Everyday Life of Slaves in Northern Dahomey: The Process of Remembering." *Journal of African Cultural Studies* 15, no. 1 (2002): 35–44.

Hastings, Adrian. *The Church in Africa, 1450–1950.* Oxford History of the Christian Church. Edited by Henry Chadwick and Owen Chadwick. Oxford: Clarendon Press, 1996.

Hinfelaar, Marja. *Respectable and Responsible Women: Methodist and Roman Catholic Women's Organisations in Harare, Zimbabwe, 1919–1985.* Utrecht: Boekencentrum, 2003.

Hodgson, Dorothy. *The Church of Women: Gendered Encounters between Maasai and Missionaries.* Bloomington: Indiana University Press, 2005.

———. "Modernity and the Production of Maasai Masculinities." In Lindsay and Miescher, *Men and Masculinities*, 211–29.

Hodgson, Janet. *Princess Emma*. Craighall, South Africa: Ad. Donker, 1987.

Hofmeyr, Isabel. *The Portable Bunyan: A Transnational History of* The Pilgrim's Progress. Princeton: Princeton University Press, 2003.

Hoppe, Kirk. "'Whose Life Is It Anyway?' Issues of Representation in Life Narrative Texts of African Women." *Journal of African Historical Studies* 26, no. 3 (1994): 623–36.

Hostetter, J. N. "Mission Education in a Changing Society: Brethren in Christ Mission Education in Southern Rhodesia, Africa, 1899–1959." DEd diss., SUNY Buffalo, 1967.

Hughes, Heather. *The First President: A Life of John L. Dube, Founding President of the ANC*. Auckland Park, South Africa: Jacana Media, 2011.

———. "'A Lighthouse for African Womanhood': Inanda Seminary, 1869–1945." In *Women and Gender in Southern Africa,* edited by Cherryl Walker, 197–220. Cape Town: David Philip, 1990.

Hunter, Jane. *The Gospel of Domesticity: American Women Missionaries in Turn-of-the-Century China*. New Haven: Yale University Press, 1984.

Jackson, Lynette. "'Stray Women' and 'Girls on the Move': Gender, Space and Disease in Colonial Zimbabwe." In *Sacred Spaces and Public Quarrels: African Cultural and Economic Landscapes,* edited by Paul Zeleza and Ezekai Kalipeni, 147–70. Trenton: Africa World Press, 1999.

———. *Surfacing Up: Psychiatry and Social Order in Colonial Zimbabwe, 1908–1968*. Cornell Studies in the History of Psychiatry. Ithaca: Cornell University Press, 2005.

Jeater, Diana. "Citizen, Witch or Non-person? Contested Concepts of Personhood in Political Violence and Reconciliation in Zimbabwe, 1978–2008." Paper presented at the 4th European Conference on African Studies, Uppsala, 15–18 June 2011.

———. *Marriage, Perversion, and Power: The Construction of Moral Discourse in Southern Rhodesia, 1894–1930*. Oxford: Clarendon Press, 1993.

———. "Speaking like a Native: Vernacular Languages and the State in Southern Rhodesia, 1890–1935." *Journal of African History* 42, no. 3 (2001): 449–68.

Juster, Susan. *Disorderly Women: Sexual Politics and Evangelicalism in Revolutionary New England*. Ithaca: Cornell University Press, 1994.

Kaarsholm, Preben. "*Si ye pambili*—Which Way Forward? Urban Development, Culture and Politics in Bulawayo." In Raftopoulos and Yoshikuni, *Sites of Struggle*, 233–39.

Kaplan, Amy. *The Anarchy of Empire in the Making of U.S. Culture*. Cambridge, MA: Harvard University Press, 2002.

Keefer, Luke L., Jr. "Holiness: A Brethren in Christ Historical Case Study." *Brethren in Christ History and Life* 22, no. 1 (1999): 63–89.

————. "The Three Streams in Our Heritage: Separate or Parts of the Whole?" In Sider, *Reflections on a Heritage*, 31–60.

Kennedy, Dane. *Islands of White: Settler Society and Culture in Kenya and Southern Rhodesia, 1890–1939*. Durham, NC: Duke University Press, 1987.

Kienzle, Beverly Mayne, and Pamela J. Walker, eds. *Women Preachers and Prophets through Two Millennia of Christianity*. Berkeley: University of California Press, 1998.

Kimambo, Isaria N. and Terence Ranger, eds. *The Historical Study of African Religion*. Berkeley: University of California Press, 1972.

King, Paul S., comp. *Missions in Southern Rhodesia*. Inyati, Zimbabwe: Inyati Centenary Trust, 1956.

Kirsch, Thomas. *Spirits and Letters: Reading, Writing and Charisma in African Christianity*. New York: Berghahn Books, 2008.

Kriger, Norma J. *Guerrilla Veterans in Post-war Zimbabwe: Symbolic and Violent Politics, 1980–1987*. Cambridge: Cambridge University Press, 2003.

————. *Zimbabwe's Guerrilla War: Peasant Voices*. Cambridge: Cambridge University Press, 1992.

Lan, David. *Guns and Rain: Guerrillas and Spirit Mediums in Zimbabwe*. London: James Currey, 1985.

Landau, Paul S. *Popular Politics in the History of South Africa, 1400–1948*. Cambridge: Cambridge University Press, 2010.

————. *The Realm of the Word: Language, Gender and Christianity in a Southern African Kingdom*. Portsmouth, NH: Heinemann, 1995.

————. "'Religion' and Christian Conversion in African History: A New Model." *Journal of Religious History* 23, no. 1 (1999): 8–30.

Larson, Pier M. "'Capacities and Modes of Thinking': Intellectual Engagements and Subaltern Hegemony in the Early History of Malagasy Christianity." *American Historical Review* 102, no. 4 (1997): 969–1002.

Linden, Ian. *The Catholic Church and the Struggle for Zimbabwe*. London: Longman, 1980.

Lindsay, Lisa A., and Stephan F. Miescher, eds. *Men and Masculinities in Modern Africa*. Portsmouth, NH: Heinemann, 2003.

Longenecker, Stephen L. *Piety and Tolerance: Pennsylvania German Religion, 1700–1850*. Metuchen, NJ: Scarecrow Press, 1994.

Lonsdale, John. "Agency in Tight Corners: Narrative and Initiative in African History." *Journal of African Cultural Studies* 13, no. 1 (2000): 5–16.

Lovemore, Jessie. *"Thy Beginning": Being the Recollections of Mrs. Jessie Lovemore, Daughter of the Rev. and Mrs. Charles Helm, of Life in Matabeleland from 1875 until Her Marriage in 1900*. Edited by J. A. Hughes. Bulawayo: Rhodesian Pioneers and Early Settlers Society, 1956.

Mahamba, Barbara. "Women in the History of the Ndebele State." MA thesis, University of Zimbabwe, 1996.

Mann, Gregory. *Native Sons: West African Veterans and France in the Twentieth Century*. Durham, NC: Duke University Press, 2006.

Marks, Shula. "Changing History, Changing Histories: Separations and Connections in the Lives of South African Women." *Journal of African Cultural Studies* 13, no. 1 (2000): 94–106.

———. *Not Either an Experimental Doll: The Separate Worlds of Three South African Women*. Bloomington: Indiana University Press, 1987.

Maxwell, David. *African Gifts of the Spirit: Pentecostalism and the Rise of a Zimbabwean Transnational Religious Movement*. Athens: Ohio University Press, 2006.

———. *Christians and Chiefs in Zimbabwe: A Social History of the Hwesa People*. Westport, CT: Praeger, 1999.

———. "Decolonisation." In *Missions and Empire,* edited by Norman Etherington. Oxford Histories of the British Empire Companion Series. Oxford: Oxford University Press, 2005.

McCord, Margaret. *The Calling of Katie Makanya*. Cape Town: David Philip, 1995.

McKittrick, Meredith. "Faithful Daughter, Murdering Mother: Transgression and Social Control in Colonial Namibia." *Journal of African History,* 40, no. 2 (1999): 265–83.

———. "Forsaking Their Fathers? Colonialism, Christianity, and Coming of Age in Ovamboland, Northern Namibia." In Lindsay and Miescher, *Men and Masculinities,* 33–51.

———. *To Dwell Secure: Generation, Christianity, and Colonialism in Ovamboland*. Portsmouth, NH: Heinemann, 2002.

McLaughlin, Janice. *On the Frontline: Catholic Missions in Zimbabwe's Liberation War*. Harare: Baobab, 1996.

Mhlagazanhlansi [Neville Jones]. *My Friend Kumalo.* 1944. Bulawayo: Books of Rhodesia, 1972.

Miescher, Stephan F. "Becoming an *Opanyin:* Elders, Gender, and Masculinities in Ghana since the Nineteenth Century." In *Africa after Gender?* edited by Catherine M. Cole, Takyiwaa Manuh, and Miescher, 253–69. Bloomington: Indiana University Press, 2007.

———. "Life Histories of Boakye Yiadom (Akasease Kofi of Abetifi, Kwawu): Exploring the Subjectivity and 'Voices' of a Teacher-Catechist in Colonial Ghana." In White, Miescher, and Cohen, *African Words,* 162–93.

———. *Making Men in Ghana*. Bloomington: Indiana University Press, 2005.

Moffat, Robert. *The Matabele Journals of Robert Moffat, 1829–1860.* Edited by John P. R. Wallis. 2 vols. Salisbury: National Archives of Rhodesia, 1976.

Moodie, T. Dunbar. *Going for Gold: Men, Mines, and Migration*. With Vivienne Ndatshe. Berkeley: University of California Press, 1994.

Moss, Barbara A. "'And the Bones Come Together': Women's Religious Expectations in Southern Africa, c. 1900–1945." *Journal of Religious History* 23, no. 1 (1999): 108–27.

Mpofu, Busani. "Operation 'Live Well' or 'Cry Well'? An Analysis of the 'Rebuilding' Programme in Bulawayo, Zimbabwe." *Journal of Southern African Studies* 37, no. 1 (2011): 177–92.

Mpofu, Isaac N. "Strange Religion Comes to the Ndebele: A Centennial Play." *Brethren in Christ History and Life* 21, no. 3 (1998): 343–60.

Mpofu, Isaac N., and Jacob R. Shenk. *Izithelo*. Bulawayo: Brethren in Christ Church, 1975.

Msindo, Enocent. "Language and Ethnicity in Matabeleland: Ndebele-Kalanga Relations in Southern Zimbabwe, 1930–1960." *International Journal of African Historical Studies* 38, no. 1 (2005): 79–103.

———. *Ethnicity in Zimbabwe: Transformations in Kalanga and Ndebele Societies, 1860–1990*. Rochester: University of Rochester Press, 2012.

Mufuka, K. Nyamayara. "Rhodesia's Internal Settlement: A Tragedy." *African Affairs* 78, no. 313 (1979): 439–50.

Mukonyora, Isabel. *Wandering a Gendered Wilderness: Suffering and Healing in an African Initiated Church*. New York: Peter Lang, 2007.

Muzondidya, James, and Sabelo Ndlovu-Gatsheni. "'Echoing Silences': Ethnicity in Post-colonial Zimbabwe, 1980–2007." *African Journal of Conflict Resolution* 27, no. 2 (2007): 275–97.

Ndlovu, Scotch M. *Brethren in Christ Church among the Ndebele, 1890–1977*. Baltimore: PublishAmerica, 2006.

———. "The Brethren in Christ Church among the Ndebele, 1898–1977." PhD draft diss., Indiana University, 1992.

Ndlovu, Stephen. "Church Mediation of the ZAPU/ZANU Conflict in Zimbabwe." In *African Churches and Peace*, 28–35. MCC Consultation on African Churches and Peace. Akron, PA: Mennonite Central Committee and MCC U.S., 1992.

Ndlovu-Gatsheni, Sabelo J. "Fatherhood and Nationhood: Joshua Nkomo and the Re-imagination of the Zimbabwe Nation." In *Manning the Nation: Father Figures in Zimbabwean Literature and Society*, edited by Kichito Z. Muchemwa and Robert Muponde, 73–87. Harare: Weaver Press, 2007.

———. "Reaping the Bitter Fruits of Stalinist Tendencies in Zimbabwe." Association of Concerned African Scholars Bulletin, no. 79, special issue on the Zimbabwe Crisis, 2008.

Nkala, Barbara, ed. *Celebrating the Vision: A Century of Sowing and Reaping*. Bulawayo: Brethren in Christ Church, 1998.

Nkomo, Joshua. *The Story of My Life*. London: Methuen, 1984.

Nyathi, Lynette. "The Matobo Hills Shrines: A Comparative Study of the Dula, Njelele and the Zhame Shrines and Their Influence on the Surrounding Communities." BA (Honours) thesis, University of Zimbabwe, 2003.

Nyathi, Pathisa. *Alvord Mabhena: The Man and His Roots. A Biography*. Harare: Priority Projects Publishing, 2000.

————. *Masotsha Ndlovu: In Search of Freedom*. Harare: Longman Zimbabwe, 1998.

————. *Traditional Ceremonies of AmaNdebele*. Gweru: Mambo Press, 2001.

————. *Zimbabwe's Cultural Heritage*. Bulawayo: 'amaBooks, 2005.

Oates, C. G. *Matabele Land and the Victoria Falls: A Naturalist's Wanderings in the Interior of South Africa: From the Letters and Journals of Frank Oates, FRGS*. London: Kegan Paul, 1889.

O'Gorman, Eleanor. *The Front Line Runs through Every Woman: Women and Local Resistance in the Zimbabwean Liberation War*. Harare: Weaver Press, 2011.

Pederson, Jane Marie. "'She May Be Amish Now, but She Won't Be Amish Long': Anabaptist Women and Antimodernism." In *Strangers at Home: Amish and Mennonite Women in History*, edited by Kimberly D. Schmidt, Diane Zimmerman Umble, and Steven D. Reschly, 339–64. Baltimore: Johns Hopkins University Press, 2002.

Pelling, J. N. *Ndebele Proverbs and Other Sayings*. Gweru: Mambo Press, 1977.

————, comp. *A Practical Ndebele Dictionary*. 2nd ed. Harare: Longman Zimbabwe, 1996.

Personal Narratives Group, ed. *Interpreting Women's Lives: Feminist Theory and Personal Narratives*. Bloomington: Indiana University Press, 1989.

Peterson, Derek R. "Casting Characters: Autobiography and Political Imagination in Central Kenya." *Researching African Literatures* 37, no. 3 (2006): 176–92.

————. *Creative Writing: Translation, Bookkeeping, and the Work of Imagination in Colonial Kenya*. Portsmouth, NH: Heinemann, 2004.

Phimister, Ian. *An Economic and Social History of Zimbabwe, 1890–1948: Capital Accumulation and Class Struggle*. London: Longman, 1988.

Pirouet, M. Louise. *Black Evangelists: The Spread of Christianity in Uganda, 1891–1914*. London: Rex Collings, 1978.

Raftopoulos, Brian, and Tsuneo Yoshikuni, eds. *Sites of Struggle: Essays in Zimbabwe's Urban History*. Harare: Weaver Press, 1999

Ranchod-Nilsson, Sita. "'Educating Eve': The Women's Club Movement and Political Consciousness among Rural African Women in Southern Rhodesia, 1950–1980." In *African Encounters with Domesticity*, edited by Karen Tranberg Hansen, 195–218. New Brunswick, NJ: Rutgers University Press, 1992.

Ranger, Terence. *The African Voice in Southern Rhodesia, 1898–1930*. Evanston, IL: Northwestern University Press, 1970.

————. *Are We Not Also Men? The Samkange Family and African Politics in Zimbabwe, 1920–1964*. Portsmouth, NH: Heinemann, 1995.

————. *Bulawayo Burning: The Social History of a Southern African City, 1893–1960*. Harare: Weaver Press, 2010.

————. *Invention of Tribalism in Zimbabwe*. Mambo Occasional Papers. Socio-Economic Series, no. 19. Gweru: Mambo Press, 1985.

———. "Missionaries, Migrants, and the Manyika: The Invention of Ethnicity in Zimbabwe." In *The Creation of Tribalism in Southern Africa,* edited by Leroy Vail, 118–50. Berkeley: University of California Press, 1991.

———. "Protestant Missions in Africa: The Dialectic of Conversion in the American Methodist Episcopal Church in Eastern Zimbabwe, 1900–1950." In *Religion in Africa: Experience and Expression,* edited by Thomas D. Blakely, Walter E. A. van Beek, and Dennis L. Thompson, 275–313. London: James Currey, 1994.

———. "Pugilism and Pathology: African Boxing and the Black Urban Experience in Southern Rhodesia." In *Sport in Africa: Essays in Social History,* edited by William J. Baker and James A. Mangan, 196–213. New York: African Publishing, 1987.

———. *Revolt in Southern Rhodesia, 1896–97: A Study in African Resistance.* London: Heinemann, 1967.

———. "Taking Hold of the Land: Holy Places and Pilgrimages in Twentieth-Century Zimbabwe." *Past and Present* 117, no. 1 (1987): 158–94.

———. *Voices from the Rocks: Nature, Culture and History in the Matopos Hills of Zimbabwe.* Bloomington: Indiana University Press, 1999.

Ranger, Terence, and Mark Ncube. "Religion in the Guerrilla War: The Case of Southern Matabeleland." In *Society in Zimbabwe's Liberation War,* edited by Ngwabi Bhebe and Terence Ranger, 35–57. Portsmouth, NH: Heinemann, 1996.

Rasmussen, R. Kent. *Migrant Kingdom: Mzilikazi's Ndebele in South Africa.* London: Rex Collings, 1978.

Scarnecchia, Timothy. *The Urban Roots of Democracy and Political Violence in Zimbabwe: Harare and Highfield.* Rochester: Rochester University Press, 2008.

Schmidt, Elizabeth. *Peasants Traders and Wives: Shona Women in the History of Zimbabwe, 1870–1939.* Portsmouth, NH: Heinemann, 1992.

Sensbach, Jon. *Rebecca's Revival: Creating Black Christianity in the Atlantic World.* Cambridge, MA: Harvard University Press, 2005.

Shenk, Rev. Jacob. *A New Ndebele Grammar.* With Isaac N. Mpofu, Agrippa V. Masiye, and K. Ndlovu. Bulawayo: Matopo Book Centre, Brethren in Christ Church, n.d.

Sibanda, Eliakim. "The Brethren in Christ in Southern Rhodesia, 1898–1980: A Historical Study of Its Contributions towards the Promotion of Human Rights." PhD diss., Iliff School of Theology and University of Denver, 1998.

———. *The Zimbabwe African People's Union, 1961–87: A Political History of Insurgency in Southern Rhodesia.* Trenton, NJ: Africa World Press, 2005.

Sider, E. Morris. "Hannah Frances Davidson." In *Nine Portraits: Brethren in Christ Biographical Sketches,* 159–212. Nappanee, IN: Evangel Press, 1978.

———, ed. *Reflections on a Heritage: Defining the Brethren in Christ.* Grantham, PA: Brethren in Christ Historical Society, 1999.

Silva, Teresa Cruz e. *Protestant Churches and the Formation of Political Consciousness in Southern Mozambique (1930–1974)*. Basel: Schlettwein, 2001.

Staunton, Irene. *Mothers of the Revolution*. Harare: Baobab, 1990.

Stoler, Ann Laura. *Carnal Knowledge and Imperial Power: Race and the Intimate in Colonial Rule*. Berkeley: University of California Press, 2002.

Strobel, Margaret. *Three Swahili Women: Life Histories from Mombasa Kenya*. Bloomington: Indiana University Press, 1989.

Strobel, Margaret, and Michael Adas. *Gender, Sex, and Empire*. Essays on Global and Comparative History. Washington, DC: American Historical Association, 1993.

Summers, Carol. *Colonial Lessons: Africans' Education in Southern Rhodesia, 1918–1940*. Portsmouth, NH: Heinemann, 2002.

———. *From Civilization to Segregation: Social Ideals and Social Control in Southern Rhodesia, 1890–1934*. Athens: Ohio University Press, 1994.

———. "'If You Can Educate the Native Woman . . . ': Debates over the Schooling and Education of Girls and Women in Southern Rhodesia, 1900–1934." *History of Education Quarterly* 36, no. 4 (1996): 449–71.

Sundkler, Bengt. *Bantu Prophets in South Africa*. New York: Oxford University Press, for the International African Institute, 1961.

Sundkler, Bengt, and Christopher Steed. *A History of the Church in Africa*. Cambridge: Cambridge University Press, 2000.

Thomas, Dwight. "A Sketch of the Life of David (Ndhlalambi) Moyo." *Brethren in Christ History and Life* 33, no. 3 (2010): 594–656.

Thomas, Lynn M. "Schoolgirl Pregnancies, Letter-Writing, and 'Modern' Persons in Late Colonial East Africa." In *Africa's Hidden Histories: Everyday Literacy and Making the Self,* edited by Karin Barber, 180–208. Bloomington: Indiana University Press, 2006.

Thomas, Thomas Morgan. *Eleven Years in Central South Africa*. London: John Snow and Co., 1872.

Thornton, Stephen. "The Struggle for Profit and Participation by an Emerging Petty-Bourgeoisie in Bulawayo, 1893–1933." In Raftopoulos and Yoshikuni, *Sites of Struggle,* 19–52.

Tibaijuka, Anna Kajumulo. "Report of the Fact-Finding Mission to Zimbabwe to Assess the Scope and Impact of Operation Murambatsvina." UN Special Envoy on Human Settlements Issues in Zimbabwe, 18 July 2005.

Urban-Mead, Wendy. "Gender and the Limits of 'Ndebeleness,' 1910–1960s: Abezansi Churchwomen's Domestic and Associational Alliances." In *Gendering Ethnicity in African Women's Lives,* edited by Jan Bender Shetler, 153–77. Madison, WI: Wisconsin University Press, 2015.

———."Girls of the Gate: Questions of Purity and Piety at Mtshabezi Girls' Primary Boarding School." *Le fait missionnaire* 11 (2001): 75–99 [also published in *Brethren in Christ History and Life* 25, no.1 (2002): 3–32.]

————. "Negotiating 'Plainness' and Gender: Dancing and Apparel at Christian Weddings in Matabeleland, Zimbabwe, 1913–1944." *Journal of Religion in Africa* 38, no. 3 (2008): 209–46.

————. "Protestant Women Activists in Matabeleland: Historical Perspectives on 'Apolitical,' Faith-Based Action in Response to the Health Care Crisis of 2000–2010." Paper presented at the Britain-Zimbabwe Society Research Days, St. Antony's College. Oxford, UK, 19–20 June 2010.

————. "Religion, Women, and Gender in the Brethren in Christ Church, Matabeleland, Zimbabwe, 1898–1978." PhD diss., Columbia University, 2004.

————. "Sitshokupi Sibanda: 'Bible Woman' or Evangelist? Ways of Naming and Remembering Female Leadership in a Mission Church of Colonial Zimbabwe." Special issue, "Transnational Bible Women." Guest editors: Deborah Gaitskell and Wendy Urban-Mead. *Women's History Review* 17, no. 4 (2008): 653–70.

————. "An 'Unwomanly' Woman and Her Sons in Christ: Faith, Empire, and Gender in Colonial Rhodesia, 1899–1906." In *Competing Kingdoms: Women, Mission, Nation, and the American Protestant Empire, 1812–1960*, edited by Barbara Reeves-Ellington, Kathryn Kish Sklar, and Connie Shemo, 94–116. Durham, NC: Duke University Press, 2010.

Vail, Leroy, ed. *The Creation of Tribalism in Southern Africa*. Berkeley: University of California Press, 1991.

Vail, Leroy, and Landeg White. "The Development of Forms. Ndebele Royal Praises." In *Power and the Praise Poem: Southern African Voices in History*, 84–111. Charlottesville: University Press of Virginia, 1991.

————, eds. *Power and the Praise Poem: Southern African Voices in History*. Charlottesville: University Press of Virginia, 1991.

Valenze, Deborah. *Prophetic Sons and Daughters: Female Preaching and Popular Religion in Industrial England*. Princeton: Princeton University Press, 1985.

Van Onselen, Charles. *Chibaro. African Mine Labour in Southern Rhodesia, 1900–1933*. London: Pluto Press, 1976.

————. *The Seed Is Mine: The Life of Kas Maine, a South African Sharecropper, 1894–1985*. New York: Hill and Wang, 1996.

Van Oppen, Achim, and Silke Strickrodt. "Introduction: Religious Biography: Transcending Boundaries." *Journal of Southern African Studies* 38, no. 3 (2012): 429–32.

Volz, Stephen. "Written on Our Hearts: Tswana Christians and the 'Word of God' in the Mid-Nineteenth Century." *Journal of Religion in Africa* 38, no. 2 (2008): 112–40.

Weinrich, Anna K. H. *African Marriage in Zimbabwe and the Impact of Christianity*. Gweru: Mambo Press, 1982.

Werbner, Richard. "Human Rights and Moral Knowledge: Arguments of Accountability in Zimbabwe." In *Shifting Contexts: Transformations in*

Anthropological Knowledge, edited by Marilyn Strathern, 99–116. London: Routledge, 1995.

———, ed. *Regional Cults.* London: Academic Press, 1977.

———. *Tears of the Dead: The Social Biography of an African Family.* Edinburgh: Edinburgh University Press, 1991.

West, Michael O. "African Middle-Class Formation in Colonial Zimbabwe, 1890–1965." PhD diss., Harvard University, 1990.

———. "Ndabaningi Sithole, Garfield Todd and the Dadaya School Strike of 1947." *Journal of Southern African Studies* 18, no. 2 (1992): 297–316.

———. *The Rise of an African Middle Class: Colonial Zimbabwe, 1898–1965.* Bloomington: Indiana University Press, 2002.

———. "The Seeds Are Sown: The Impact of Garveyism in Zimbabwe in the Interwar Years." *International Journal of African Historical Studies* 35, nos. 2–3 (2002): 335–62.

White, Luise. *The Comforts of Home: Prostitution in Colonial Nairobi.* Chicago: University of Chicago Press, 1990.

White, Luise, Stephan F. Miescher, and David William Cohen, eds. *African Words, African Voices: Critical Practices in Oral History.* Bloomington: Indiana University Press, 2001.

Wittlinger, Carlton O. *Quest for Piety and Obedience: The Story of the Brethren in Christ.* Nappanee, IN: Evangel Press, 1978.

———. "Who Are the Brethren in Christ?" In Sider, *Reflections on a Heritage.*

Wolcott, Harry F. *The African Beer Gardens of Bulawayo: Integrated Drinking in a Segregated Society.* New Brunswick, NJ: Rutgers Center of Alcohol Studies, 1974.

Wright, Marcia. *Strategies of Slaves and Women: Life-Stories from East/Central Africa.* London: Lilian Barber, 1992.

Index

Page references in italics denote illustrations on those pages.

race, 48, 50, 57, 61–62, 64, 68, 101
Ranger, Terence, 32, 36, 59, 119, 142, 174, 187, 263n66, 277n24, 288n4
repentance, 32, 35, 49, 63, 64, 68, 77, 82, 85–87, 128, 168, 237. See also piety
Responsible Government, 57
Rhodes, Cecil John, 15, 44, 52
Rhodesia, 16, 18–19, 21, 46, 57, 59, 62, 66–68, 107, 178
Rhodesian army, 176
Rhodesian Front, 173, 191
rinderpest, 40, 44, 297

Salisbury, 18, 88, 91, 96, 157, 236
Scarnecchia, Tim, 177
segregation, 16, 41, 57, 62, 141, 234
sellout politics, 123, 135, 173, 176–78, 180–87, 192, 201, 223, 237, 285n38
settler, 11, 17, 39, 58, 80
Shamba School, 74, 76, 83
Shangani Reserve, 98. See also Matabeleland North
Shenk, Jacob. See Shenk, Rev. Jake
Shenk, Rev. Jake, 121–22, 141, 209, 227, 288n12
Shiri, Perence, 208
Shona, 18, 77, 120, 175–76, 180–81, 208–9, 231, 243
Sibanda, Eliakim, 102, 142, 159, 188, 195
Sibanda, Ethel, 118, 212
Sibanda, Hannah (MaNsimango), 87, 88, 94, 150, 197
Sibanda, Hlengiwe Lindani (MaMlotshwa), 246
Sibanda, Rev. Mangisi, 88, 155, 178, 181–85, 197, 279n51
Sibanda, Sitshokupi, 18, 148, 199, 271n29, 275n97
Sibanda, Sofi, 84
sin, 31, 32, 48–50, 54, 64, 68, 77, 83, 85; falling into, 79
Sithole, Rev. Ndabaningi, 173, 178
Sixpence. See Nsimango, Ntombiyaphansi
Smith, Ian, 173, 226
soldiers, 54, 173, 177, 179, 180, 183, 184, 187, 190–92, 194–96
Sotho language, 112, 142, 176, 197
South Africa, 12, 65, 182, 246; antiapartheid struggle, 182
Southern Rhodesia, 1, 3, 15, 16, 21, 58, 59, 101, 137, 141, 149

Southern Rhodesian African National Congress (SRANC), 157
Stanley Square, 227, 228, 291n60
Staunton, Irene, 22, 192, 201
Steigerwald, Rev. H. P., 50–51, 56, 60, 62
Summers, Carol, 34, 150
Swedish Lutheran Mission, 15, 174, 175

Tanzania, 34, 284n15
Theological College of Zimbabwe (TCZ), 203, 228, 231
Tshalimbe, 179–84, 186, 197, 199, 201
Tshuma, Maria, 69, 70, 74, 76, 92, 196, 238, 239; attending Shamba Church, 77; baptism denied, 77, 78, 83, 93; bond with MaNzima, 77–78, 95; calling, 73; church planting in Salisbury, Gwanda, Hwange, Binga, 91; discovers fetus in Mtshabezi River bed, 84; evangelism, 71, 75, 87, 88, 90, 95, 100; evangelism in Matabeleland North, 89, 91, 100, 105, 122; family, 70, 73, 75, 76, 89, 234; homestead, 87; interviews, 71–73; interview with Doris Dube, 90; kinship, 90; leadership (unofficial), 95; life history, 70, 71, 93, 94; Mtshabezi Mission school, 78; official record, 71; piety, 71, 88, 90, 93, 95; polygyny, 70; pregnancy, 87, 88, 93, 94; as subleader, 87; teaching career, 86, 87, 93, 94
Tshuma, Masalantombi. See Tshuma, Maria
Tshuma, Ntali, 69, 70, 73–76, 79
Tshuma, Sifile, 69
Tutu, Rt. Rev. Desmond, 182

uMfundisi, 17, 18, 136, 146, 149–51, 156, 159–61, 221, 231, 236, 238, 297
Unilateral Declaration of Independence (UDI), 157, 236
United African National Congress (UANC), 175
United Kingdom, 173, 246
United States, 38, 47, 109, 134, 147, 161, 173, 223, 225, 246, 290n42, 291n56
Unity Accord 1987, 227, 228, 240, 291n50
utshwala, 7. See also drinking (alcohol)

Vundhla, Dazzie (MaMoyo), *147;*
bereavement, 164; in Bulawayo, 150,
151; childlessness, 164, 166, 169,
170; church leadership, 154, 170;
conversion, 151; education, 151;
homestead, 146, 147, 154; interview,
142, 145–47; marriage, 143, 145;
origins, 150, 151; as wife of minister
(uMfundisi), 150
Vundhla, Nondulo (MaKhumalo), 146
Vundhla, Rev. Sandey, *155,* 228, 235;
childlessness, 165–70; chosen
for leadership, 156, 167, 169;
conflict with P. M. Khumalo,
160–63; dismissal, 167, 236, 237;
documentary record, 143; education,
145; evangelism, 236; evangelism
in Bulawayo, 134, 136, 155, 159,
168, 170, 236; evangelism in
Matabeleland North, 104–6, 148,
156; evangelism to men, 136, 155,
157; interview with Doris Dube, 143;
leadership, 155; marriage, 143, 145,
163–66, 168; masculinity, 166, 168;
modernizer, 236; ordination, 149;
origins, 137, 143; piety, 145, 167, 168,
237; political sensibility, 159, 169;
potential breakaway, 160, 163; as
uMfundisi, 159

Wanezi Bible School, 148
Wanezi Mission, 71, 74–76, 89, 99, 171
war 1893, 15, 44, 52
war 1896, 15, 44, 46, 52, 61, 80, 145, 196
Werbner, Richard, 178
Wesleyan Methodist, 15, 153, 252n12
Wesleyan perfectionism, 7, 8
West, Michael O., 59, 165, 289n22
White, Luise, 23, 28
widowhood, 115, 133, 142, 147, 156, 164,
179, 185, 199–200, 237
Winger, Rev. Walter O., 63, 77, 85, 96
witchcraft accusations, 185, 186, 192,
285n41
Wittlinger, Carlton O., 5, 6
women, 22, 24, 27–33, 85; Christian
matrons, 88; church leaders, 97, 98,
107, 108; clubs, homecraft, 153, 154;
pastors, 97, 98, 100, 120, 121

World Council of Churches, 175
worldliness, 4–9, 12, 19, 22, 29, 35, 39,
41, 66–67, 81–82, 99, 101, 120, 123,
135, 138–39, 158–59, 162, 180, 182,
187–89, 205, 209, 231, 289n22
World War I, 58, 72, 196, 264n1
World War II, 99, 101, 135, 139, 149, 153,
205, 235, 238
Wright, Marcia, 23–24, 93

Zambezi River, 12, 13
ZANLA. *See* Zimbabwe African National
Liberation Army
ZANU. *See* Zimbabwe African National
Union
ZANU-PF. *See* Zimbabwe African
National Union
ZAPU. *See* Zimbabwe African People's
Union
zhii, 159
Zimbabwe, 177; postindependence, 182,
201, 204–6, 225–26, 233, 237–47
Zimbabwe African National Liberation
Army (ZANLA), 173, 174, 176,
177, 179–82, 183, 185, 190–92, 200,
207, 237
Zimbabwe African National Union
(ZANU), 11, 19, 93, 123, 157, 173,
175–77, 182, 186, 191, 201, 204–7,
230, 231, 238, 240, 275n4, 291n50;
postindependence, 225
Zimbabwe African People's Union
(ZAPU), 19, 25, 100, 122–23, 157,
159, 169, 173, 175, 177–79, 187–91,
195, 201, 205–9, 224, 229–31, 234,
240, 246, 275n4, 286n49, 291n50;
postindependence, 226–27
Zimbabwean National Army (ZNA),
206–7
Zimbabwe Council of Churches, 244
Zimbabwe People's Revolutionary Army
(ZIPRA), 173–74, 176–77, 179,
181, 188–90, 192, 207, 223–24, 229,
290n46
ZIPRA. *See* Zimbabwe People's
Revolutionary Army
ZNA. *See* Zimbabwean National Army
Zook, Rev. Donald, 134, 149
Zulu language, 17, 42, 47, 48, 141